*The American College
in the Nineteenth Century*

The
American College in the Nineteenth Century

Edited by Roger Geiger

VANDERBILT UNIVERSITY PRESS
Nashville

04 03 02 01 00   5 4 3 2 1

Library of Congress Cataloging-in-Publication Data

The American college in the nineteenth century / [edited by] Roger Geiger.— 1st ed.
p. cm. — (Vanderbilt issues in higher education)
Includes bibliographical references and index.
ISBN 0-8265-1336-0 (cloth : alk. paper)
ISBN 0-8265-1364-6 (pbk. : alk. paper)
1. Education, Higher—United States—History—19th century. 2.
Universities and colleges—United States—History—19th century. I.
Geiger, Roger L., 1943- II. Series.
LA227.1 .A64 2000
378.73—dc21   00-008025

Published by Vanderbilt University Press
Printed in the United States of America

"Curriculum and Enrollment," reprinted by permission from the *History of Higher Education Annual* 1 (1981): 88–109. "The Rights of Man and the Rites of Youth," reprinted by permission from the *History of Higher Education Annual* 15 (1995): 5–49. "College As It Was in the Mid–Nineteenth Century," reprinted by permission from the *History of Higher Education Annual* 16 (1996): 105–115. "'We Desire Our Future Rulers to Be Educated Men,'" reprinted by permission from the *History of Higher Education Annual* 14 (1994): 39–71. "Agency, Denominations, and the Western Colleges, 1830–1860," reprinted by permission from *Church History* 50 (March 1981): 64–80. "The Era of Multipurpose Colleges in American Higher Education, 1850–1890," reprinted by permission from the *History of Higher Education Annual* 15 (1995): 51–92. "The Rise and Fall of Useful Knowledge," reprinted by permission from the *History of Higher Education Annual* 18 (1998): 47–65. "A Salutary Rivalry," reprinted with permission from the *History of Higher Education Annual* 16 (1996): 21–38. "Noah Porter Writ Large?" reprinted with permission from the *History of Higher Education Annual* 16 (1996): 39–70. "The German Model and the Graduate School," reprinted with permission from the *History of Higher Education Annual* 13 (1993): 69–98. "A 'Curious Working of Cross Purposes' in the Founding of the University of Chicago," reprinted with permission from the *History of Higher Education Annual* 15 (1995): 93–126.

Contents

Preface

This volume arose from a sense of frustration with the historiography of American higher education. On the one hand, this field has seen an abundance of new and exciting scholarship. On the other hand, new interpretations have been lacking to link these new findings together. This has particularly been the case for the era preceding the emergence of our twentieth-century system of mass higher education. New scholarship has shown that the familiar stereotypes of the nineteenth-century college are seriously deficient, but has done little to suggest broad concepts that might replace them.

In some ways this situation mirrors that of American history as a whole. There, thoughtful commentators have decried the fragmentation of the discipline, even while recognizing the necessity and the achievements of an implacable specialization.[1] But for all its fragmentation American history rests upon a rich foundation of interpretation that has been continuously scrutinized and debated. For the history of American colleges and universities the same kind of fragmentation is evident, but the process of challenging established accounts has grown rather stale. This state of affairs is specifically addressed in the first part of my introduction.

The intention to link scholarship and interpretation has determined the form of this book. More than simply a collection of exemplary studies, this volume proposes several new themes that might inform the historiography of the American college. These themes are set forth in the introduction, and much of the supporting scholarship is contained in the following chapters. The first theme is the profound transformation of student life, from submission and regimentation at the outset of the century to an extracurriculum entirely under student control at the end. The second theme highlights the stark regional distinctions that developed between the Northeast, the South, and the Midwest. Apparent by 1830, these distinctive traits persisted for most of the rest of the century. The third theme suggests that the decades bracketing the Civil War, roughly 1850 to 1875, define a transitional period with its own character. To recognize this, and to abandon the conventional view that the Civil War was the turning point toward modernity, permits the innovations of those years to be understood in their own historical context. Such understanding is particularly important for interpreting the origins of higher education for women and the antecedents of the land-grant colleges. The final theme relates the emergence of the American university to its collegiate roots and the inescapable challenge it posed for the colleges.

The overall picture is one of movement rather than the conventional image of stasis or abrupt, discontinuous change. This picture obviously needs to be filled out.[2] A good deal of material already exists, but even as this work is knitted together new questions will arise and need to be addressed. This volume is intended to stimulate this process. More important, perhaps, it seeks to fulfill an immediate need for a history of the nineteenth-century college that reflects the achievements of recent scholarship.

All but one of the previously published articles in this collection appeared in the *History of Higher Education Annual.* Although the *Annual* is by no means the sole outlet for scholarship in this field, it has for nearly twenty years provided a focus for advancing the history of colleges and universities. The chapter by David Potts dates from the journal's first volume, and it reflects the concerns of the community of scholars who were then committed to reforming the field. The other articles were published after I assumed the editorship of the *Annual* in 1993. On the surface this fact might seem a coincidence: the articles were chosen for their merit, intrinsic interest, and contribution to the above-mentioned themes. On a deeper level my preoccupation with comprehending the nineteenth-century college no doubt played a role in encouraging at least some of these submissions to the *Annual.* Nevertheless I can honestly say that a reciprocal relationship existed between the interpretations developed in the introduction and the selections chosen for inclusion. As a result I believe that the whole of this volume is greater than the sum of its parts.

The present chapters may differ in small ways from the original articles as a result of a double process of editing. To eliminate duplication or undue length, some passages were deleted from most selections. The prose was then edited for consistency as well. This manuscript, like those of all the volumes of the *History of Higher Education Annuals* that I have edited, has been significantly improved by the assiduous preparatory work of Trudi Haupt.

My thinking on the nineteenth-century college has been advanced in a number of ways. Being editor of the *Annual*—and interacting with contributors and members of the editorial board—has been an invaluable privilege. I am grateful to the Spencer Foundation for providing the support that launched my investigations of nineteenth-century higher education. The notion of the multipurpose college was subjected to perceptive critiques at a symposium at the 1995 Annual

Meeting of the History of Education Society. Particular thanks are owed to Brad Burke, Hugh Hawkins, Bruce Leslie, and David Potts for their comments on the introduction to this volume. Finally nothing has done more to develop my interpretation of American higher education than the process of explaining and defending my ideas to successive cohorts of history students in the Penn State Higher Education Program.

The American College
in the Nineteenth Century

Introduction

New Themes in the History of Nineteenth-Century Colleges

≈

ROGER L. GEIGER

Historians and the Colleges

*A*merican higher education has existed for only three full centuries. Harvard College stood alone for the better part of the seventeenth century, being joined by Yale College and the College of William and Mary only as the eighteenth century commenced. At the time of the Revolution, 9 colleges enrolled perhaps 750 students. By the end of the century the number of functioning colleges had risen to 18, but only 400 more students attended them, and fewer than 1 in 200 young white males earned a college degree. By the dawn of the next century higher education had altered dramatically. More than 450 colleges and universities existed, and just classifying them requires a lengthy explanation.[1] (See "The Era of Multipurpose Colleges in American Higher Education.") Collegiate enrollments had increased a hundredfold. The proportion of males graduating tripled during the century, but women attended as well. Most significant the institutional structure was in place for the transition to mass higher education in the twentieth century. The incredible dynamism of the twentieth century raises multiple issues for historical investigation; but much like that of the eighteenth century, the fundamental structure of the higher education system is not problematic. On precisely this point the nineteenth century is different.

The nineteenth century witnessed the transformation from the rudimentary college to the basic framework of the modern American university;[2] from institutions that conveyed only textbook knowledge to mostly adolescent boys to a panoply of institutions that included advanced and professional studies for young men and women. Despite these far-reaching changes, the college remained the central institution of American higher education until the end of the century. For historians, coming to terms with the college has been the foremost challenge for explaining higher education in this era.

In most early histories of this period the college loomed as the obstacle to the organization of a modern system of higher education.[3] The college was portrayed as the virtual antithesis of what the twentieth-century American university came to be: small, parochial, and inherently religious in outlook; locked into a fixed curriculum and dominated by the rote learning of Latin and Greek; hence, incapable of incorporating truly advanced study of any subject, or of offering practical instruction in work-related skills; and finally undemocratic in its narrow appeal to a largely upper-class clientele.

This viewpoint, which saw the college chiefly as a problem to be overcome, was largely incorporated into the principal narrative histories that have provided the only general treatments of nineteenth-century higher education for more than a generation. In these accounts the "antebellum college" is described as a seemingly unchanging entity. Its perverse persistence is explained by invoking such factors as the autonomy of private colleges guaranteed by the Dartmouth College case (1819), the dominance of the classical curriculum as propounded in the 1828 Yale Report, and "denominationalism"—the promiscuous creation by the Protestant churches of too many competing colleges. A dramatic motif is supplied by the prescient visions of critics and would-be reformers—George Ticknor and James Marsh in the 1820s, Francis Wayland and Henry Tappan in the 1850s—who recognized the iniquities of the antebellum college and struggled vainly to rectify them. (See "Curriculum and Enrollment.") After the Civil War, by and large, the supposedly superannuated college was quickly forgotten as the land-grant colleges brought utilitarian instruction, Johns Hopkins pioneered graduate education, and Harvard president Charles W. Eliot introduced the elective system. The issue that begged explanation for historians was, in Walter Metzger's words, "the college's failure to answer the needs of society."[4]

These narrative histories may still be read with profit, but even more so if their predilections are recognized. Richard Hofstadter is perhaps the most analytic of these authors, and for that reason the most vulnerable to attack where his analysis went awry.[5] Frederick Rudolph is more anecdotal and most adept at conveying the seeming absurdity of quaint college custom. John Brubacher and Willis Rudy are the most determinedly presentist in portraying the implacable march to modernity.[6]

In the 1970s a new generation of historians began to produce studies that challenged the traditional view. They approached the American college, for the most part, as social historians, thus mirroring a major trend within the profession. Their general thrust, in contradistinction to Walter Metzger, was that the colleges *did* reflect American society and to a considerable degree provided what it actually demanded and could afford. Making common cause under the banner of "revisionists," they soon attacked with some vehemence the negative portrait of the colleges found in the traditional narratives. The exact membership of this school was uncertain because it embraced a wide swath of new scholarship, whether or not it consciously repudiated the traditional view. A core group nevertheless led the crusade, and the focus was chiefly the nineteenth-century college.[7]

One of its number, James McLachlan, ably summarized the revisionist critique as an endeavor to overturn four broad assumptions. Examining each of these permits an overview of the arguments marshaled by some revisionists as well as some of the limitations.[8]

First, "American colleges and their alumni were somehow irrelevant to the 'mainstream' of American social and cultural development, and . . . the colleges perpetuated a narrow social elite." Ignoring for the moment the contradiction between irrelevance and elites, the relative presence of college graduates at the commanding heights of American society and culture can be argued both ways. College graduates accounted for no more than 1 percent of the male workforce before the Civil War. Even given the ambiguity of the notion of career in this era, they were concentrated in the clergy, education, government, medicine, and the law. Before the Civil War the percentage of college graduates among those entering all of these professions was nevertheless in decline. As for the small number of American scientists, they were more likely to be employed outside colleges than as professors.[9] On the other hand, McLachlan points out, John Adams and Thomas Jefferson chose college graduates for the majority of their civil servants, and—more surprisingly—so did Andrew Jackson. Peter Dobkin Hall has argued a larger point—that the graduates of New England colleges were instrumental in bearing that culture, with its values of education and service, to the developing communities of the American West.[10] Furthermore, insofar as colleges catered to elites they were scarcely irrelevant. Ronald Story has depicted how Harvard fit into a network of institutions that defined and perpetuated the mercantile and cultural "aristocracy" of eastern Massachusetts.[11] In this volume Michael Sugrue analyzes the key role played by South Carolina College in shaping the political class of the Old South (see "We Desire Our Future Rulers to Be Educated Men").

Harvard and South Carolina are among the few colleges—perhaps Columbia and the University of Virginia fit here as well—whose students were drawn heavily from social elites. Elsewhere the colleges found their students among the humble and the well-to-do alike. Professionals were clearly more likely to send their sons to college, but large numbers of students came from the families of more-or-less prosperous farmers. Evangelical Protestantism bore considerable responsibility for this latter pattern.

David Allmendinger has documented how the relatively poor, landless sons of Massachusetts farmers found their way to the newer New England colleges as aspirants to the ministry, often starting college in their early twenties.[12] In a much more comprehensive study Colin Burke synthesized new and existing data on the origins and careers of students. He found considerable variations—by region, by institution, and over time—but in general the colleges offered the prospect of upward social mobility for large numbers of young men from middling circumstances.[13] Overall the 1 to 2 percent of youth that reached college before the Civil War were selected as much by individual traits of social ambition and intellectual curiosity as by privileged socioeconomic status.

The second assumption identified by McLachlan holds that, "because of their 'irrelevance' . . . and the 'unpopular' nature of their curricula and daily regimes, the colleges 'declined' numerically until after the Civil War." David Potts specifically examines the link between curriculum and enrollment in this volume's next chapter (see "Curriculum and Enrollment"). Student life in the colleges is a subject on which revisionists had comparatively little to say, but which merits attention (see "The Rights of Man and the Rites of Youth" and "College As It Was in the Mid–Nineteenth Century").

The general derision with which traditionalists treat the classical curriculum has not elicited a commensurate defense by revisionists. Their discussions of curriculum invariably cite the study by Stanley M. Guralnick, *Science in the Ante-bellum American College,* which shows that eastern colleges were generally eager to add scientific subjects to their course of study. Even so this endeavor made little headway before 1820, and by the 1840s it was choked by the finite dimensions of the fixed course. Thus this same work might also be invoked to show that the fixed curriculum prevented even the colleges that could afford professors of science from teaching those subjects beyond the introductory level.[14]

Traditional disparagement of the classical curriculum draws freely from the reminiscences of old grads, written in a later era. (See "College As It Was in the Mid–Nineteenth Century.") Historians have attributed much of its inexplicable strength to the power of the report that the Yale president and faculty wrote in 1828 to justify their course of study to the Yale trustees. The Yale Report has been almost universally misinterpreted as a conservative document, seeking to turn the clock back or to perpetuate something like the colonial course of study. In fact the classical curriculum had to be reinvented in the nineteenth century, and Yale was proud to be in the forefront of this endeavor.[15] The study of Greek was rehabilitated and broadened beyond the New Testament to Greek literature; and both

Latin and Greek literature were extended into the junior and senior years. Yale felt compelled to rationalize this course of study for the new function that a college education had assumed: preparation for later professional study rather than the formation of an eighteenth-century minister and/or gentleman.[16]

David Potts addresses not the content of the curriculum per se, but its alleged effect of discouraging young people from attending college. His chapter, "Curriculum and Enrollment," while amply conveying the exasperation with which revisionist scholars regarded the uncritical denigration of the colleges, establishes the important point that departures from the classical curriculum cannot be shown to have increased popularity by attracting a new type of student. Yale, after all, was the most popular American college for most of the antebellum period. Its supposed antithesis was Union College under its colorful president Eliphalet Nott (1804–1866), who began offering students curricular choice the same year that Yale published its famous report. Union too had robust enrollments. Its class records show that upperclassmen largely avoided classes in advanced Greek. But most unpopular of all, at Union and elsewhere, was advanced mathematics. (See "College As It Was in the Mid–Nineteenth Century.") Whatever the source of its attraction, Union's curriculum was not a magnet for aspiring scientists.[17]

Another reformer admired by traditionalists is Brown president Francis Wayland, perhaps the most authoritative critic of the colleges. Given the opportunity in 1850 to rectify their alleged failings, he completely revamped the Brown curriculum to include practical subjects and shorter degree courses. Students could take a single two-year course for a certificate or combinations of such courses in three years for a regular degree. Potts is nevertheless correct in dismissing any notion that Wayland's reforms were a success.[18] Neither here nor elsewhere can enrollment data be invoked to demonstrate that significant numbers of antebellum students yearned for a more practical collegiate curriculum. (See "The Rise and Fall of Useful Knowledge.")

The number and nature of colleges, as well as their enrollments, are central to the third traditionalist assumption identified by McLachlan: "denominationalism," or "that the colleges were weapons in a narrow competition between Protestant denominations." Here the revisionists made their most compelling case. Colin Burke's monograph, *American Collegiate Populations,* provided a credible enumeration of colleges and students from 1800 to 1860, and presented these findings as a decisive repudiation of the traditional view.[19]

Burke's book debunked a 1932 study by Donald Tewksbury that had been a pillar of sorts for the traditional view.[20] By comparing the number of colleges chartered in a selected number of states with those still surviving in the 1920s, Tewksbury calculated a frightful mortality rate of 81 percent. Richard Hofstadter invoked this finding to buttress the notion that competing denominations had founded far too many nonviable colleges, thus weakening American higher education as a whole. This notion in itself was little more than conventional wisdom, having been repeated from the beginning to the end of the nineteenth century.[21] Tewksbury merely provided plausible numbers, and Hofstadter incorporated them into a larger indictment of denominationalism. But the flaws of Tewksbury's study were exposed. His actual counts were lost and unrecoverable, and many of the charters he enumerated were clearly for colleges that never opened or never offered a college course.[22] Burke's census of operating colleges, in contrast, produced a failure rate of merely 17 percent. Together with demographic data showing a consistent expansion of enrollment rates, the discrediting of Tewksbury seemed to undermine Hofstadter's thesis of a "great retrogression"—the bête noire of revisionism.

Hofstadter had asserted that the displacement after 1800 of the American Enlightenment by the evangelical piety of the Second Great Awakening caused a decline in the vitality of colleges—the great retrogression. The plausibility of this thesis rested on a fairly select body of evidence. Hofstadter drew upon Thomas Wertenbaker's history of Princeton, a college that clearly did decline for two decades after the disastrous student riot of 1807. He also chose examples from areas of the South (the Universities of Transylvania and Nashville) where religious fragmentation and rivalry were unusually high. Furthermore he highlighted the role of Presbyterians, probably the most fractious church. However, their *intra*denominational strife was even fiercer than their quarrels with other denominations.[23] (See "A Salutary Rivalry.") In sum the great retrogression thesis failed to capture the dominant trends within American higher education in the early nineteenth century.

Perhaps its most obvious weakness escaped the notice of revisionists: 1800 could scarcely be the fulcrum of decline since, excepting the Revolutionary years, the beginning of the century was roughly the low point in the history of the colleges in terms of relative enrollments, faculty, and curricular offerings.[24] The first decade of the nineteenth century saw progress on all these fronts in New England, paced by pious Yale as well as liberal Harvard, and the 1820s witnessed a far broader advance. Beyond this neglected issue, the crux of the revisionist argument was that the proliferation of colleges, which began in earnest in the 1820s, reflected the educational needs of a decentralized, rural society. Burke in particular stressed that the multilevel, multipurpose nature of these small enterprises, which the traditional view found so unmodern, compensated for the absence of secondary and often primary schooling.

The charge of denominationalism was further undercut by David Potts. Based on his extensive study of Baptist colleges, he depicted the contribution of local boosters as crucial to the establishment of the typical denominational college.[25] The relative roles of localities and denominations varied greatly from college to college within this general framework, but some clear trends stand out. Denominations generally appeared more concerned about taking care of their own flocks than competing against other churches. (See "Agency, Denominations, and the Western Colleges.") Furthermore tacit or explicit cooperation was so common within the evangelical mainstream that it was often referred to as the "benevolent empire." Among colleges, the American Education Society was a conspicuous manifestation of this common cause from the late 1820s to the 1840s. After midcentury, as the denominations assumed more bureaucratic organization, they attempted to assert more direct control over their affiliates.[26] There is far more to be learned about this entire process, but the dynamics of denominationalism, as described in "The Era of Multipurpose Colleges in American Higher Education," were both more defensive and more dependent upon local boosterism than those posited in the traditional view.

The final traditionalist assumption noted by McLachlan concerns the supposed dominance of the university in the period after the Civil War. Here the revisionists have faced a more formidable task. The university indubitably rose to a dominant position by the dawn of the twentieth century, and few have wished to challenge Laurence Veysey's celebrated account of the intellectual ferment that accompanied this process.[27] Concomitantly the nineteenth-century college was obliterated. Its defining features—the classical A.B., the fixed course, and the inviolable academic classes—all disappeared. However, the tenor of American higher education did not change in 1865; rather, a profound transformation occurred around 1890 and happened relatively quickly. (See "The Crisis of the Old Order.") This chronology still leaves a substantial postbellum period in which the old order of colleges was predominant while the new order was taking shape.

The colleges, of course, did not turn out to be as superannuated as some university builders thought. For some institutions the challenges of modernization were traumatic,[28] but recent writings have explored how the more successful eastern colleges navigated these waters. Bruce Leslie's comparative study of four mid-Atlantic colleges reveals that their greatest assets were social. Alumni played a crucial role in secularizing the outlook of the colleges, reinforcing the importance of collegiate life, and providing the funds with which to modernize both faculty and campus. David Potts's history of Wesleyan University adds depth and authority to this pattern.[29] Both studies document how basically nineteenth-century institutions came to assume recognizably familiar twentieth-century forms. However, considerably more investigation might be done to elucidate the unfamiliar world of higher education in the years from 1850 to 1890. The era saw the brief flourishing of several species of institution—the multipurpose college, early women's colleges, and scientific schools—that failed to survive the transition to modernity. (See "The Era of Multipurpose Colleges in American Higher Education," "The Rise and Fall of Useful Knowledge," "A Salutary Rivalry," and "The 'Superior Instruction of Women.'")

Leslie's 1992 book may be the last publication to invoke the totems of revisionism in order to frame its subject. As a rallying point, revisionism's day seems to have passed. Thus it may now be possible to assess the movement that set the tone for the history of American higher education for two decades.

There can be no question that the revisionist project led a rejuvenation of the history of American higher education. It either inspired or energized a host of monographic studies, and it gathered a community of scholars where none had existed before. Although scholarship on diverse topics was claimed by or attributed to the revisionist banner, its greatest impact was felt in the interpretation and understanding of the antebellum college. Walter Metzger, one of its ostensible targets, readily conceded that it managed "to reopen what had been regarded as settled questions."[30] Above all, the revisionists propounded a more historical view of the colleges as products of nineteenth-century society that advanced education to the extent that conditions allowed. However, the principal shortcoming of revisionism was the failure to complete this picture.

Revisionist scholars produced no synthesis of their monographic findings to displace the traditional narratives. Those older volumes may still be purchased in bookstores while revisionist scholarship must be ferreted out of the library stacks. Largely for that reason, as Bruce Leslie has complained, general works in American history still tend to perpetuate the traditional view. Colin Burke's study, in some ways the most comprehensive revisionist volume, claims merely to clear the field of error so that a new "scientific" history may be erected.[31] The ultimate effect intellectually has been that the revisionist project has remained incomplete even where it was most focused. A collection of studies, often quite admirable in themselves, it has yielded no consistent or cogent image of the nineteenth-century college.[32]

This incompleteness arises in part from the strongly partisan flavor of the most committed revisionist writings. The élan that launched and sustained the movement deprecated past scholarship to such an extent that it became difficult to incorporate the more persuasive evidence supporting the traditional view. Hence revisionists are comparatively silent on the unattractive features of the classical curriculum and the recitations by which it was taught, on the precarious and constrictive finances of the colleges, on student misbehavior, and on other inherent shortcomings—i.e., where colleges failed to attain their own expectations—that traditionalists may have overemphasized but did not wholly invent.

Ultimately the endeavor to defend the colleges seems to have led the revisionists into the same error as those they attacked: namely, positing a single, generic, antebellum college for the plurality of institutions bearing that name.

Although the central organizing features of course and class proved remarkably resilient, almost everything else about the American college evolved significantly during the nineteenth century, before the Civil War and afterward. This volume brings together a collection of recent studies explicitly to explore this dynamism and diversity of the colleges. A collection of this kind provides no substitute for a complete interpretive history, but it can illuminate themes that any future history ought to incorporate.

First, an important transformation of student life occurred during the nineteenth century. The close control of Harvard students at the beginning of the century analyzed by Leon Jackson in "The Rights of Man and the Rites of Youth" is strikingly different from the considerable autonomy that students enjoyed by midcentury (see "College As It Was in the Mid–Nineteenth Century"). This unshackling of student life was but a prelude to an explosion of activities organized by and for students in the last decades of the century. Remarkably this development constituted a 180-degree reversal of attitude—from the most resented aspect of the collegiate experience to the most valued—and accordingly had far-reaching repercussions for institutions.

Second, few discussions of antebellum higher education make sense without an appreciation of regional differences. By 1830, if not sooner, different traditions had emerged to distinguish the established colleges of the northeastern seaboard (see "College As It Was in the Mid–Nineteenth Century"), the major state universities of the South (see "We Desire Our Future Rulers to Be Educated Men"), and the denominational colleges that were multiplying from western New York across the Mississippi Valley (see "Agency, Denominations, and the Western Colleges").

Third, the traditional division of the history of American higher education at the Civil War not only encourages a misleading presentism, but also completely obscures the actual developments of the third quarter of the century. Most of the innovations associated with the postbellum years appeared in the 1850s—colleges for women, scientific schools, and practical courses in engineering and agriculture. (See "The Era of Multipurpose Colleges in American Higher Education," "The Rise and Fall of Useful Knowledge," "A Salutary Rivalry," and "The 'Superior Instruction of Women.'") These developments accelerated during the 1860s, at least outside the defeated South, and into the decade of the 1870s. The peculiar institutional forms that were appropriate to that era, however, underwent substantial changes in the following years. The years from 1850 to 1875 thus deserve particular scrutiny as an era with its own internal logic and consistency, rather than mere signposts on the road to modernity.

Fourth, the final chapters all point to the ascendancy of the university, but they reveal in different ways how that process was rooted in the colleges. (See "Noah Porter Writ Large?"; "The German Model and the Graduate School"; "A 'Curious Working of Cross Purposes'"; and "The Crisis of the Old Order.") Specifically they reveal how the Yale College alumni forced the development of Yale University; how the Germanic spirit of research triumphed at the University of Michigan even while attempts to impose Germanic educational structure floundered; how the undergraduate college proved indispensable in the elaboration of the mightiest of the new research universities—the University of Chicago; and how the fate of the college appeared to be in doubt after 1890 because of the aggrandizement of other educational institutions. The remainder of this introduction will elaborate these four themes.

The Rise of the Student Estate

No challenge facing American colleges at the dawn of the nineteenth century was more pressing than that of controlling their students. Low enrollments, inadequate resources, and a dearth of qualified teachers were serious concerns, to be sure. However, those woes were exacerbated by periodic eruptions of student misbehavior and the damaging public impressions that ensued.

Pranks and stealthy misbehavior appear to have been endemic in the colonial colleges, but the only incident that seriously affected college governance occurred when concerted student harassment drove Yale's unpopular president, Thomas Clap, from office in 1766.[33] The colonial colleges, at least outwardly, expected a rigorous standard of student discipline. Misbehavior was punished in a distinctive manner through graded punishments ranging from fines to expulsion. Serious offenses elicited admonitions—verbal reprimands—according to the principle that the more serious the transgression, the more numerous the witnesses to the disgrace. Multiple or grave offenses might cause a student to be sent away from the college, most often temporarily. This form of discipline was effective because it rested upon a powerful social consensus that was tacitly acquiescent toward youthful exuberance but severe in judging moral character.

After the Revolution, students probably behaved with greater license, and the consensus undergirding social control began to fray. At the end of the century a new phenomenon emerged: the student revolt, or full-fledged defiance of college authority by a significant portion of the student body. The first decade of the new century may have been the high tide of such revolts, but their persistence characterized the eastern colleges for the next two decades.[34] Harvard was the largest college of the early Republic, and perhaps the one most affected by the waning of clerical dominion. The student disorders it experienced near the end of the eighteenth century foreshadowed the widespread riots that followed. In "The Rights of Man and the Rites of Youth," Leon Jackson has offered a penetrating psychological profile of studenthood at Harvard that illuminates the mainspring of this behavior.

Frustrations arose out of the basic predicament of students who occupied an inherently subordinate status without protective rights. Having an indeterminate status of youth, they had no legitimate avenues for dealing with grievances, even those of their own making. Hence pretexts for confrontations arose from overly severe punishments, infringement of student customs, problems arising in the commons, or disputes over the course of studies. Living under a regime that aspired to completely control their lives, students compensated through collective resistance, surreptitious most often but becoming overt at moments of heightened confrontation.

Why the early years of the nineteenth century were plagued with student revolts is a fundamental question. The principal study of this phenomenon, by Steven Novak, leans heavily upon notions of generational conflict that were current when he wrote in the 1970s.[35] His suggestion that students felt a psychological need to emulate the revolutionary acts of their fathers is probably the least convincing aspect of this work. Jackson shows how republican rhetoric had become a cliché, by the 1790s. More likely generational tensions arose from the rapid social evolution taking place. As Gordon Wood has shown, the United States was fast becoming a markedly democratic and egalitarian society in terms of beliefs, at the same time that commercial activity was forging a social stratum of newly wealthy entrepreneurs.[36] The colleges, however, embodied the previous century's preoccupation with hierarchy and authority.

Contemporary college leaders had their own interpretation of student unrest. They condemned the fact that too much spending money drew some students into idleness and vice, and they attempted to rectify this situation by limiting student funds. They also recognized that many students matriculated at too young an age. Students during the first decade of the century were the youngest on average that colleges ever taught.[37] Minimum ages for matriculation were subsequently imposed, originally set at fourteen. Both these conditions reflected a growing constituency of students from newly wealthy families who shared little of the pious outlook of the "immediate government" of president and faculty. The latter, for their part, also believed that student disorders stemmed chiefly from want of discipline. They thus responded, often at the urging of trustees, by codifying and imposing ever more stringent college rules. As Jackson's analysis makes clear, such a response virtually guaranteed the opposite result. The wave of student revolts may have been a consequence of increasingly authoritarian colleges seeking to impose their will upon increasingly recalcitrant youth.

Although these later developments lie beyond the purview of his study, Jackson nevertheless signals a path out of this vicious circle. Phi Beta Kappa may have produced unique effects at Harvard, but the sense of loyalty and responsibility it apparently fostered among students was the key to transcending the era of violent student resistance. Contemporaneously at Yale, President Timothy Dwight (1795–1817) had begun to impose what he called a parental system of discipline that sought to instill maturity and responsibility in students. He dispensed with a multitude of petty regulations and fines, chastised students privately rather than before their peers, and sought to persuade his charges instead of humiliate them. He also did not hesitate to dismiss those who resisted his entreaties. Dwight incorporated parents into these disciplinary efforts, keeping them informed by devising the first system of numerical grades as well as report cards.[38] Yale under Dwight was spared from student riots and experienced revivals instead (although his successor was not so fortunate). But elsewhere the root causes of rebellion did not ebb until the 1820s.

The cause of the waning of student riots has yet to receive the historical attention it deserves, but there can be little doubt that it reflected a profound transformation in the nature of college life. Students obtained more freedom as the application of discipline, and sometimes the rules as well, became more tolerant; and they acquired more responsibility too as they gained greater control over their everyday lives. The disciplinary regime based on submission and control seems to have atrophied as much from its high psychological cost as from its inherent ineffectiveness. An increasingly professional faculty loathed the duties of enforcement and certainly wished to minimize them.[39] At the same time poor but growing colleges found it difficult to keep all students immured within residence halls or to sustain the commons.[40] Institutions made some concessions as well, as when Princeton in 1828 allowed its students time for recreation and exercise (see "College As It Was in the Mid–Nineteenth Century"). Yale in 1830 achieved a breakthrough by replacing the old system of punishments with one based on "marks" (demerits). Students could calculate how many times they might be late or absent or disobedient before facing serious consequences. Still, freedom without responsibility was no panacea. Harvard students exploited freedom by running wild under the kindly but ineffectual presidency of John T. Kirkland (1810–1828), ultimately fomenting the college's worst riot in 1823.[41] Responsibility grew slowly among students as they used what latitude they were permitted to shape their existence. The one device that accorded students both freedom and responsibility was the college literary society. As described by James McLachlan, the thriving societies at Princeton served some of the same functions that Jackson attributes to Phi Beta Kappa.[42] Through the libraries and debates of the societies, students on their own were able to partake of current literature and hone forensic skills. Here students sought and shaped an education that they considered relevant to their future lives.

Literary societies were obviously not sufficient in themselves to prevent student disorders—nor was Phi Beta Kappa. However, after 1830 a new tone became evident in student life, especially at the eastern colleges. At Williams College the changes occurred during the presidency of Mark Hopkins (1836–1872). Frederick Rudolph's depiction of those developments may be the single fullest exposition of a campus during this early-collegiate era. Prior to Hopkins's arrival, a senior of 1835 made a scathing commencement speech, denouncing the petty, overzealous discipline of the college and refusing his diploma. A few years later one of the first graduates to study four years under Hopkins expressed his love for "the faculty and the students and the members of our dear church," as well as the Williams campus.[43] A telling sign of the new climate was the spread of fraternities, beginning in the 1830s. College fraternities had been born, significantly enough, at Union College in the 1820s. President Eliphalet Nott began his tenure there in 1804 as a law-and-order figure, like his contemporary peers, but by the 1820s he had mollified his views to such an extent that he was considered the most lax of college leaders.[44] Fraternities were merely one means by which students enlarged their dominion over extracurricular life. In the early-collegiate era, prior to the Civil War, they possessed comparatively few formally organized student activities. Nevertheless, by 1850, college students were sufficiently enthralled with campus life to begin celebrating it in their own literary creations.

What these writings reveal about eastern colleges at midcentury is explored in "College As It Was in the Mid–Nineteenth Century." The centerpiece is a portrayal of student life at Princeton, only recently published, composed by two seniors of the class of 1853. This account provides an illuminating comparison with the most detailed student memoir of the era, *Four Years at Yale* by Lyman Bagg, class of 1869. The remarkable fact about all this literature is that it was written at all—that students found their college experiences so deeply fulfilling that they wished to convey these feelings to a wider audience.

The essential components of the early-collegiate era can be distilled from the depiction of Princeton. Outwardly little seemed to have changed since the era of submission and control: the formidable rules and the recitations in Latin and Greek were still fixtures of the college regime. But the efforts they exacted from students seemed eminently manageable, psychologically and in practice. The enforcement of rules, while preserving outward decorum, was a standing challenge to the ingenuity of students. Recitations and their preparation occupied but a fraction of available time. This largely self-contained community of late-adolescent boys had considerable time and freedom to devote to the activities that they considered most important. Some of these were sanctioned by the colleges, such as literary societies, required student orations, or a literary magazine. Others fed a rich social life, intensified by the bonds and collective experiences of each college class.

When Lyman Bagg attended Yale immediately after the Civil War, student life there was at a point of transition from the early-collegiate to the high-collegiate era. Whereas Princeton presidents John Maclean (1854–1868) and James McCosh (1868–1888) still felt a compulsion to control student behavior, Yale left students largely to their own devices. The college also conceded increasingly greater scope for them to organize on their own an expanding roster of student activities. Bagg devotes most of his seven hundred pages to describing this world that the students fashioned. At Yale it included elective societies for each class, intramural sports, multiple publications of newspapers and magazines, and special clubs for interests such as debate, drama, and singing. Just appearing were intercollegiate athletics. When they arrived, with the popularity of baseball in the 1870s and the hypertrophy of football in the 1880s, and as the other forms of student-run activities multiplied, the high-collegiate era was born.[45]

The high-collegiate era is perhaps the most celebrated in the popular history of American higher education. It stimulated an outpouring of contemporary writings, including the college novel; and it subsequently inspired such nostalgic classics as *Eight O'clock Chapel,* about the New England colleges in the 1880s, and *Alma Mater,* idealizing turn-of-the-century Yale.[46] The basic features of this era were epitomized in the eastern colleges, but they spread rapidly to colleges and universities throughout the country. Colleges were essentially transformed by the extremely sharp focus placed on traits that had been present, more or less, for some time.

Extracurricular activities provided students the deepest meaning to their college experience, overshadowing the exertions required in the classroom. This sentiment was widely aired at the time, among students, educators, and the public. The most valuable lessons of college, many felt, were learned outside the classroom. Lyman Bagg confidently asserts that character was the utmost value and, in what became a well-worn refrain, that colleges provided a completely democratic arena for the formation and judging of character (see "College As It Was in the Mid–Nineteenth Century"). In this respect the students may well have anticipated college leaders, who soon trumpeted that the ultimate mission of college was the formation of the "whole man" rather than the former mission of instilling mental discipline.[47]

Character and college democracy were linked, above all, to the intense competition that characterized high-collegiate life. Students spontaneously applied their energy to obtain positions in organizations, be elected to offices, and be selected to secret/social groups—all of which were allocated on a competitive basis by students themselves. But college democracy had a social dimension so ubiquitous as to be almost invisible to the earnest competitors. The college arena increasingly became an upper-middle-class youth culture, something it had not formerly been.[48] Lyman Bagg's strictures are telling: in order to have a successful career at Yale, students should not enter too young, or too old, or with advanced standing. They were also advised to attend the right boarding schools. Anyone could become a success at Yale through his own talents, as the humble origins of sports hero Amos Alonzo Stagg might illustrate, but the powerful Yale culture enforced conformity to a social type.[49]

One curious by-product of the high-collegiate era was a pronounced reaction against coeducation. Women apparently soured the atmosphere for competition and camaraderie. As the hallmark of collegiate prestige increasingly became associated with this culture, women became persona non grata at the few coeducational eastern schools. Wesleyan ultimately excluded its women students; and men at Cornell evinced a visible hostility toward local coeds. The same phenomenon influenced midwestern universities in more muted form.[50] For their part, the leading eastern women's schools—the Seven Sisters—elaborated an even more rarified form of high-collegiate culture.[51]

For the colleges as a whole the high-collegiate era undermined critical parts of the old collegiate structure. Literary societies, as semisponsored organizations, were superseded in part by secret fraternities but also by the sheer welter of student-run activities. More profound was the gradual replacement of the academic class as the locus of bonds of loyalty. For the Princeton authors of 1853 all college experience was mediated through the class unit, and Lyman Bagg's experience was no different. However, the rise of intercollegiate athletics, as well as other class-spanning activities, gave the whole institution greater prominence. A similar shift of allegiance occurred among alumni. They too related far more readily to the burgeoning extracurriculum than to the course of study, whether reformed or not. The high-collegiate era thus induced far greater alumni interest and involvement in the colleges. The controversy surrounding the "Young Yale" movement, portrayed in "Noah Porter Writ Large?" signaled an early stage of this portentous development.

The high-collegiate era may be seen in greater relief by contrasting it with the late-collegiate era that followed after 1900. If anything, the idealization of extracurricular activities intensified, but the foundations shifted. The institutions themselves began to exert more control. Especially in athletics, university personnel began to displace student control. The two most influential presidents of the new century, Woodrow Wilson at Princeton (1902–1910) and Abbott Lawrence Lowell at Harvard (1909–1933), strongly supported the extracurricular side of college life, but also felt it needed to be harnessed and balanced with student intellectual development. Both deplored as well the growing social segregation among students. As college became more closely identified with subsequent material success, social class intruded more blatantly in elections to the most prized student offices and societies.[52] The vaunted college democracy of the previous era receded before the trappings of social class, which came to be idealized by the Roaring Twenties.

Regional Differences, 1830–1860

Arguably regional differences existed in American higher education from its beginnings. William and Mary operated quite differently from the northern colleges in the colonial era, and the first frontier colleges after independence exhibited distinctive traits.[53] Nevertheless, during the early Republic, greater unity developed as newly founded institutions throughout the country depended heavily upon models and teachers from the older colleges. By the 1820s, however, a number of disparate developments accentuated regional distinctions as well as growing regional consciousness. The established colleges of the Northeast made the greatest strides in academic development in addition to nurturing the early-collegiate culture. The growing regional assertiveness of the slaveholding South is well known, and it seemed to place an increasingly apparent stamp upon the major colleges of the region. But the South was noteworthy as well for thriving state colleges or universities, which also shaped the character of higher education in important ways (see "We Desire Our Future Rulers to Be Educated Men"). The West—beginning somewhere in upstate New York or across the Appalachian ridges of Pennsylvania, and extending across the Mississippi basin and eventually beyond—became the land of denominational colleges (see "Agency, Denominations, and the Western Colleges").

The year that the Yale faculty defended the classical curriculum, their institution was in fact a university of more than five hundred students. Two-thirds of them were in the college, to be sure; but the rest were enrolled in the professional schools of medicine, law, and divinity, and there were five "resident graduates." The hallmark of Yale was scarcely a myopic concern for the classics, but rather its broad academic development.[54] In this respect Yale was outpaced by Harvard. President John Kirkland (1810–1828) sought above all to make Harvard a university that would support "a few men of genius in the pursuit of letters [learning]." By 1820 Harvard had ten professors, four of whom had just returned from postgraduate study in Europe. Harvard's academic development was anything but smooth. A backlash of sorts stalled these efforts until well into the 1830s, but then an even more professional faculty exerted its influence to obtain advanced elective studies for interested students. The late 1840s brought further ratcheting up with the establishment of the Lawrence Scientific School, which, like its counterpart at Yale, permitted a broader and deeper coverage of science.[55] Yale and Harvard led a process of academic development that, to varying degrees, characterized the colleges of the Northeast after the 1820s. It consisted of assembling a

larger and more specialized faculty, extending the coverage and depth of the curriculum, raising standards for admission and course work, and recognizing a distinctive form of collegiate culture. Concomitantly the colleges of the Northeast
developed explicit forms of cooperation and communication in pursuit of their
common goals.

Early in the century most colleges were fortunate if they had two professors
to supplement the instruction of president and tutors. A professor of languages
would direct the tutors in teaching Latin and Greek while offering some instruction to the upper classes in those subjects. A second professor of mathematics and
natural philosophy might have similar duties in teaching math to the lower
classes while lecturing in basic science subjects, especially to juniors. The president, who often held the old professorship of divinity, typically instructed the
seniors in moral philosophy and probably supervised the required oratorical
exercises. Each of the three positions essentially became subdivided into new professorships as the content coalesced into more clearly defined subjects. By the
1830s a respectable eastern college needed at least six professors. Science
demanded three positions—mathematics (sometimes including astronomy),
chemistry (including geology and mineralogy), and physical science and/or natural history and biology. The classics called for separate professors in Latin and
Greek. A professor of belles lettres (and/or rhetoric) was a necessity to teach literature and history, and to supervise orations. These positions were ripe for subdi-
vision too, and also beckoning for full recognition were modern languages,
political economy, and the offshoots of philosophy (logic, ethics, psychology).[56]

In 1840 eight of the eastern colleges listed eight or more professors, while
only one institution elsewhere in the country could credibly make such a claim
(University of Virginia).[57] Thus the stereotype of a static curriculum scarcely
holds for these eastern colleges. They achieved a remarkable degree of academic
development within a single generation. Furthermore the succeeding generation
registered a comparable advance through appointments in many of the subfields
named above. These later developments become too complex to easily describe,
due to the increasing use of junior faculty and to appendages such as the scientific
schools (see below).[58] However, these colleges clearly set the standard.

The Northeast had been distinguished since early colonial times for its high
general level of education. The early nineteenth century saw a gradual proliferation of private academies that taught a broad spectrum of subjects, including
those needed for college.[59] Cities, in general, tended to sprout a variety of educational alternatives. The eastern colleges thus existed in an educationally rich
environment, and the situation encouraged them to concentrate exclusively
on collegiate education. First, they consistently endeavored to raise admission
requirements so that they might elevate the level and seriousness of instruction.

The process extended throughout much of the century, but it was possible because of the increasing availability and quality of academies. Second, the eastern colleges were able to dispense with preparatory departments, which they deemed inappropriate for a college. Third, following the curricular controversies of the 1820s, the eastern colleges became quite comfortable in offering a liberal education through the classical course—largely as defined in the 1828 Yale Report. For these schools, the basic premise that collegiate education should chiefly provide intellectual preparation for subsequent professional studies reflected the aspirations of their students. With fewer than one-third of the colleges, the Northeast contained more than half of the nation's schools of medicine, law, and theology. Moreover the eastern colleges actively sought to propagate this model.

Close relations among these colleges began at an early date. In 1818 and 1819 the nation's first educational association formed. Calling itself the Collegial Convention of Colleges North of the Delaware, the members conferred chiefly about raising standards for admission and upholding discipline.[60] A more enduring form of communication emerged in the next decade out of the American Education Society. Formed in 1815 to assist in building a learned ministry, it supported the education of pious youth aspiring to such careers. The society was first based at the Andover Theological Seminary and was committed to mainstream evangelical Protestantism (thus excluding Unitarian Harvard) rather than any denomination. After reorganizing in 1826, it grew rapidly in size and influence to achieve its maximal impact in the 1830s. As it supported aspiring ministers, it also sought to shape ministerial education. It strongly endorsed a thorough four-year classical course, followed by a full three-year course in a theological seminary.[61] This Yale-Andover model was a lengthy educational path that older students and those with limited means frequently abbreviated, despite society assistance. Still, the model was closer to the norm in the East than elsewhere.

From 1827 to 1842 the society published the *Quarterly Register,* a compendium of information on religion and education, but chiefly a journal of higher education. In this forum the society buttressed its notions of a thorough collegiate education. When the Yale Report appeared, for example, it received a ringing endorsement. The society also placed most of its resources behind the eastern colleges, plus a few midwestern *epigone* that exemplified this approach. Although individuals might be supported anywhere, the largest number of society students were usually found at Dartmouth, Middlebury, Williams, Amherst, and Yale. Through these actions, the country's most influential educational organization placed its full weight behind the Yale-Andover model, giving it particular strength throughout the Northeast.[62]

The manner in which the eastern colleges fashioned a distinctive student culture has already been noted. This newfound student appreciation for the college experience became especially important as the status of these institutions was redefined. The Dartmouth College case of 1819 was the legal watershed in the evolution of several leading institutions from quasi-public to private status. Each campus possessed its own story. However, the private financial support that made this change possible came largely from alumni. In this respect the deep loyalties engendered by the collegiate culture were hugely consequential, especially for the colleges that drew support from beyond their immediate locale. By midcentury the alumni of Williams and Amherst were active in the affairs of those colleges, and although such influence was resisted at Yale, its alumni too eventually won places as trustees (see "Noah Porter Writ Large?").[63] On a more general level the autonomy achieved by the eastern colleges through private sources of support gave them a remarkable degree of independence. Unlike most other colleges, they were beholden only to themselves—or, more accurately, to their own self-defined communities. Thus it could be said that these academic leaders of American higher education were responsive to American society, but on their own terms.

Aside from William and Mary, the southern colleges of the early nineteenth century had fairly close links with the collegiate hearth in the Northeast. The University of North Carolina drew its inspiration and first teachers from Princeton. Josiah Meigs left Yale to head Georgia's first college. And South Carolina, when planning its state college, canvassed northern schools for guidance and then named as president Jonathan Maxcy, a prominent young educator who had previously led Brown and Union Colleges. Somewhat later this pattern was repeated when Horace Holley was called from Boston to Transylvania University, and Philip Lindsley left Princeton to head the University of Nashville. But if southern colleges looked northward for academic leadership, they received little recognition in return. Although South Carolina College outstripped most northern colleges early in the century, it was snubbed in its request for a Phi Beta Kappa chapter.[64] As the northeastern colleges clubbed together (note the name of their association), southern institutions were accorded scant respect.

Thomas Jefferson's radical design for the University of Virginia was, in effect, a declaration of academic independence, an attempt to transcend intellectually and institutionally the confining protocols of the American college. Increasing sectional tensions made interregional linkages less and less likely after 1830. However, the presidency of Thomas Cooper at South Carolina College (1820–1834), as described by Michael Sugrue in "We Desire Our Future Rulers to Be Educated Men," confirmed a distinctive southern tradition in antebellum higher education. Cooper's advocacy of the favorite causes of the Old South, slavery and state's rights, placed a political stamp upon a system that already possessed distinctive structural and social traits.[65]

The South was characterized, above all, by its state universities. Georgia and North Carolina included provisions for universities in their state constitutions, although neither state was able to provide regular support. South Carolina College, however, achieved the distinction of being the first institution to receive regular state appropriations. South Carolina was a wealthy state, and its leaders, as Sugrue explains, agreed upon the importance of the college in unifying its political leadership. An initial annual appropriation of $6,000 (later increased) assured it the status of a substantial institution from its opening in 1805. The University of Virginia fit this same pattern. Although its state support was at times criticized, it remained at $10,000 throughout the antebellum period. The backing of the governing elite in both states precluded the kind of erosion of legislative support that state institutions experienced elsewhere.[66]

The southern state colleges catered explicitly to the region's social and political elite. Despite their state subsidies, the institutions were among the most expensive in the country to attend. Even the University of North Carolina, in a relatively poor state, charged higher tuition than any northern school, save Harvard. The University of Virginia in 1840 listed the highest estimated cost of attendance in the country.[67] A constituency of wealthy planters may have been a political asset, but it was an academic liability. The hijinks and mayhem described by Sugrue were duplicated by planters' sons across the South. Patterns of attendance and diligence nevertheless varied considerably. Ironically Jefferson's university was most compromised by the social proclivities of its young student-gentlemen. The majority attended only for a single year, and few remained more than two. On the other hand, students at South Carolina College tended to be well prepared, usually entering as sophomores or juniors and remaining to graduate. Many of them aspired to the law, and apparently took a keen interest in studies relevant to that profession. Kemp Plumer Battle, later president and historian of the University of North Carolina, estimated that one-third of his classmates studied for a respectable class rank—a significant portion perhaps, but certainly less than at coeval Princeton (see "College As It Was in the Mid–Nineteenth Century").[68]

The public colleges of the South were remarkably secular institutions. The University of Virginia was the only college in the country without formal religious observances, and South Carolina College appointed Thomas Cooper, an outspoken anticlerical, as president. Also, with a few exceptions, they eschewed professional studies. Given their students, they were prone to violent upheavals long after such disturbances disappeared from the North. Since they served only a tiny and select portion of the population, it is scarcely surprising that other colleges appeared.

After 1830, denominational colleges were founded with increasing frequency across the South. Compared with their counterparts in the North, or even coeval foundings in the Midwest, they manifested a notably more intense piety. Southern Baptists, Methodists, and Presbyterian splinter churches were slow and ambivalent about accepting the notion of a college-trained ministry. When their regional church organizations finally did commit to sponsoring colleges, they still valued faith more highly than intellect. Revivals were regular occurrences, and it was not uncommon for a majority of students to be converted church members. In addition with the more secular and socially prominent citizens patronizing the state colleges, a marked social division existed between the two types of institution. Thus the southern church colleges tended to provide college training for evangelical Christians of middling circumstance. Most of these colleges at one time included "manual labor" schemes, designed to allow such students to support their education.[69]

The state and church systems of colleges did not coexist amicably. By the 1850s, church colleges wielded considerable influence, particularly outside the ambit of the planter aristocracy. They seem largely responsible for hounding the Universities of Transylvania and Nashville into closure during that decade. Elsewhere the state colleges predominated, in part because they came to exemplify the ideology of the ruling class. Sugrue's depiction of South Carolina College thus explains a key element in the development of a regional identity for higher education in the South.

Denominational colleges were the signature institution for higher education in the West, but the institutions had a distinctive character compared with their counterparts in the East or the South. Revisionist historians have principally sought to rehabilitate these institutions. As a type, they nevertheless remain frustratingly ambiguous.

The majority of colleges founded in the American colonies and the early Republic fit within a well-established Congregational-Presbyterian tradition. They were grounded in religion, associated with a particular church, and dedicated to an inclusive public purpose.[70] The prominence of these traits might vary. Church ties were particularly strong for Yale and Princeton; and ostensibly public institutions with few exceptions had a religious coloration. However, colleges dedicated to serving a single church foundered: the Dutch Reformed were unable to make Queen's College viable, and the Methodists failed with Cokesbury College (1794–1795). This collegiate model was exported westward through the Plan of Union (1801), by which Congregationalists and Presbyterians pledged to cooperate in Christianizing the West. But this arrangement became increasingly untenable after 1820. Not only did the Dartmouth College case create a distinction between public and private, but religious fragmentation undermined the claims to stewardship of the "Presbygationalists." It was at this point that the true denominational college appeared, first in the East.

The denominational colleges that opened in the 1820s and thereafter were essentially institutions of religious minorities. As such, they were usually sponsored by church bodies, and often the chief motivation was the training of ministers. But the education of the laity could not be neglected for long. Episcopalians in Connecticut struggled for years before breaking the Yale monopoly in that state. They opened Washington (Trinity) College in Hartford (1826), and at the same time founded Hobart and Kenyon Colleges in the West. Baptists in the 1820s were undecided about colleges and educated ministers. They originally compromised by establishing literary and theological seminaries. Those in Maine (Waterville/Colby) and the District of Columbia (Columbian/George Washington) quickly evolved into colleges, but the seminary in Hamilton (Madison/Colgate), New York, educated only ministers for two decades. Lutherans too looked first to educate ministers, but soon concluded that their seminary in Gettysburg needed a complementary college (Pennsylvania College, 1832). The Dutch Reformed appended Rutgers to the seminary that had succeeded Queen's (1824). Methodists came late to college founding. Remaining distrustful of educational requirements for their ministers, they finally accepted the laity's need for collegiate education. After Wesleyan (1831) and Randolph-Macon (1832) opened, the Methodists quickly became the most prolific sponsors of colleges. By that juncture the newer colleges of Presbyterians and Congregationalists also reflected their status as denominational minorities.

Translated to the West, the dynamics of denominations produced two patterns of growth—distinct yet juxtaposed. As explained in "The Era of Multipurpose Colleges in American Higher Education," a pattern of *expansion* brought the establishment of a few rudimentary colleges in the wake of the expanding frontier. The founders were evangelical missionaries, most often Presbyterians or Congregationalists, but driven by inner faith to seek to provide Christian ministers and teachers to civilize the new lands. These visionaries interacted with their localities in a variety of ways. The "Yale Band," from the Yale Divinity School, founded Illinois College even as Jacksonville was being built around them. Oberlin was hacked from the wilderness by its dedicated, evangelical supporters; and a similar venture scarcely a decade later founded Knox College as part of a speculative land development.[71]

The second pattern, that of *elaboration,* occurred in more settled circumstances and describes how organized churches established colleges to serve their minority interests. Initiative here originated with the denomination's state or regional body. Resolving to establish a college, they would next consider offers of support—land, buildings, and/or money—from interested communities. The most lucrative offer generally took precedence over such matters as geographical accessibility or concentrations of coreligionists. The western colleges thus had an implicit obligation to their locality as well as their denominational sponsors. The revisionists have emphasized this facet of their existence. Besides bringing money into the community (asylums for the blind or insane were avidly sought after too), a local college provided readily accessible education. Virtually all had preparatory departments offering basic education. Although they all began by offering the standard classical course, they soon evolved into multilevel, multipurpose institutions. But despite such benefits, an established college had little leverage for tapping additional resources from its locale. Rather, it depended on the denomination for indispensable revenues.

In "Agency, Denominations, and the Western Colleges," James Findlay's explication of the crucial role of college agents penetrates to the heart of this relationship. To appreciate the significance of fund-raising, one need recognize that the colleges were truly eleemosynary institutions, inherently incapable of supporting themselves. Annual tuition in the West rarely exceeded twenty dollars (1840): at that rate sixty full-paying students would barely support the president's salary. Student charges rarely covered the basic operating budget, let alone additional expenses.[72] Fund-raising was indispensable, and the arteries of support sustained by college agents defined the relationship of college and denomination.

Presbygationalists, despite their early initiatives, had relatively few denominational supporters in the West in these decades. They consequently retained a lifeline to their base in the East, not only through individual agents but also through organizations. The American Education Society assisted some of these colleges in the 1830s, and the Western College Society (SPCTEW; see "Agency, Denominations, and the Western Colleges") was created in the 1840s to assume this burden. Their eastern connections clearly affected these schools, encouraging them to emulate high academic standards and the Yale-Andover model. Baptist colleges, on the other hand, lay at the opposite end of the spectrum. Organized in conjunction with local or regional Baptist associations, they recruited students, raised funds, and were undoubtedly responsive to coreligionists within that orbit. Methodists, organized into state or regional conferences, had the coverage to transcend the Baptist model for at least some of their colleges. Findlay describes Indiana Asbury, in particular, as being championed by the state conference. Ohio Wesleyan enjoyed this same status (see "The Era of Multipurpose Colleges in American Higher Education"). Both institutions became large and vigorous, capable of incorporating multiple curricula to serve the Methodist laity. Methodist colleges left to their own devices, like McKendree College, focused on their local region not unlike their Baptist counterparts.

These denominational ties shaped the academic development of western colleges as well. Colleges that looked to the East for support inevitably felt pressure to emulate the academic standards of that region. The efforts of both the American Education Society and, more explicitly, the Western College Society were aimed at assisting western colleges to meet this challenge. Episcopalian colleges responded similarly to eastern ties. This eastern influence made this group of colleges less likely to admit women, for example, or to dilute their classical course. Just the opposite pressures influenced Baptist colleges, with their regional focus, and the same was especially true for colleges sponsored by smaller denominations. For them, serving coreligionists of the region became paramount, and they typically had no qualms about opening their doors to women or adding practical courses.[73]

This picture clarifies the collegiate dynamics of the Midwest. Localism and denominationalism were at bottom complementary forces.[74] The organization of colleges was largely associated with the defensive process of elaborating denominational networks in order to meet the needs and preserve the integrity of religious communities. But the colleges themselves were above all intended for everyone who might benefit, both because of their evangelical social mission and the importance of having locally available instruction. The shibboleth that there were too many colleges appears slightly ridiculous in light of the vastness of the western lands and their educational needs. Over time, however, the dependence upon denominations for the provision of vital resources increased rather than diminished. Hence the power of church organizations over affiliated colleges, as David Potts has pointed out, increased markedly after the Civil War.[75]

Midcentury Transformations

The conventional history of higher education divides the nineteenth century at the Civil War, with the benighted antebellum college dominating the first period and modernizing forces triumphing in the second. Completely obscured is the fact that the war bisected a dynamic period of experiment and change. However, the innovations of these years merely foreshadowed what was to come. Some of them—land-grant colleges, institutes of technology, coeducation—required subsequent modifications before becoming integral features of twentieth-century higher education. Other innovations—the multipurpose college, schools of science, the original women's colleges—in large measure proved to be evolutionary dead ends. But survival into the twentieth century is the wrong measure to employ here. The colleges from roughly 1850 to 1875 adapted to the needs and the possibilities of their own era; and in doing so they made measured but real strides in making higher education more comprehensive, more advanced, and available to more people.

The ferment in higher education was stirring already in the 1840s when the reform themes of the 1820s received new airing. Applied science and engineering could make more credible claims. Across the country as a whole the demand for education was expanding, including collegiate education. Enrollments and the founding of new colleges rose at a brisk rate throughout the 1850s. More remarkable, this process continued through the 1860s, despite the devastation of higher education in the South. By 1875 when this growth spurt finally slowed, the number of colleges was 75 percent greater than in 1860, and the number of students had roughly doubled.[76]

Higher education in this era grew chiefly by sprouting new colleges rather than expanding existing ones. The characteristic institution responsible for the bulk of the growth was the multipurpose college. As described in "The Era of Multipurpose Colleges in American Higher Education," these institutions offered the standard classical course—indeed, they would scarcely be colleges without it—but they supplemented it with precollege schooling and nonclassical courses. In addition they often admitted women, which usually entailed a separate ladies' or teachers' course. The colleges were less concerned with educating future ministers than they were with providing educational opportunities to the laity of the denomination and the ambient communities. They thrived in the "island communities" that formed the tissue of the nation. These islands were joined in trade as a result of the transportation revolution and nurtured a burgeoning middle class, but they were relatively insular in culture and social relations.[77]

The multipurpose colleges fulfilled a crucial portion of the educational needs of those communities, offering instruction beyond the common schools within a trusted cultural milieu. As late as 1888 one informed observer could write: "all collegiate institutions of learning . . . are chiefly local in their patronage." Their "attractive influence" extended up to one hundred miles, but in some cases considerably less.[78] Propinquity was clearly a major factor in attendance. In one relatively isolated locale, for example, one-half of local families with daughters sent one to Alfred Academy or University.[79] The multipurpose colleges were well suited to provide general educational services for an underserved population defined by geography and religion. But this model had inherent limitations. Its base of operations most often was too limited to provide the capital base required for offering more advanced or more specialized forms of learning.[80] A glance at Ohio corroborates this point: the only institutions to transcend this model before 1900 drew upon public or philanthropic capital (see "The Era of Multipurpose Colleges in American Higher Education"). The multipurpose colleges were also ill suited to counter competition from below, which became increasingly prevalent in the form of publicly supported normal schools and high schools. After 1900 those institutions that were able began a slow, and often painful, transition toward a specialized and delimited role as liberal arts colleges.[81]

The teaching of science and engineering was the second major area of mid-century transition. Laurence Veysey noted that the ten years after 1865 were dominated by "concessions to the utilitarian type of demand for reform."[82] However, these reforms were the culmination of events that began in the 1840s. These efforts differed from the parallel B.S. courses that sprouted in the multipurpose colleges. Those courses substituted more extensive offerings in science and modern languages as alternatives to the classical course, but did not offer advanced scientific training. Yet the opportunities for teaching useful knowledge became increasingly apparent in the 1840s, as the railroad boom created employment for engineers and as advances in organic chemistry promised applications to agriculture.[83] To train expert practitioners in these areas required an alternative to the classical college. This notion took hold in the mid-1840s at both Harvard and Yale, the former quite deliberately and the latter almost spontaneously. Both institutions soon evolved separate "scientific schools," one of the distinctive innovations of the period (see "The Rise and Fall of Useful Knowledge").

The scientific schools uneasily balanced the ambition to cultivate advanced learning with the popular demand for training applied scientific practitioners. Neither purpose could be reconciled with the classical A.B. course. The Yale school originated from two professorships created in 1846 "for the purpose of giving instruction to graduates and others *not members of the undergraduate classes.*" The following year the Department of Philosophy and the Arts was created—a self-supporting umbrella that sheltered instruction in subjects ranging from advanced Greek literature to agriculture.[84] At Harvard, Edward Everett had assumed the presidency in 1846 with a desire to create a "school of theoretical and practical science." A gift from Amos Lawrence the following year made it possible to realize this wish. The assured income it provided to the Lawrence Scientific School allowed the appointment of eminent scientists, who then applied themselves to their own investigations far more than to teaching.[85] Both schools nevertheless presented a tacit model for the separate incorporation of advanced and/or applied science in the American college.

To Daniel Coit Gilman, whose career was shaped in Yale's Sheffield Scientific School, this arrangement seemed ideal for fulfilling the terms of the 1862 Morrill Land-Grant Act. He called the projected land-grant colleges "our national schools of science," wishing to see them pursue both theoretical and applied science (see "The Rise and Fall of Useful Knowledge"). The Sheffield School was the first institution to receive land-grant designation. However, the Morrill mandate was seen differently in most statehouses, and the bulk of the new land-grant beneficiaries were fashioned primarily to convey practical education. Most were named agricultural and mechanical (A&M) or simply agricultural colleges. The supporters of this group of institutions vastly overestimated both the demand for this kind of instruction and the efficacy of the existing knowledge base. In this respect A&M colleges no less than scientific schools were artifacts of this transitional era (see "The Rise and Fall of Useful Knowledge").

After a frustrating effort to implant the Sheffield spirit at the University of California, Gilman became the founding president of the Johns Hopkins University, and a leader of the university movement. For Gilman and others the university became the sole viable model for advanced scientific training and research. In fact the opening of Johns Hopkins in 1876 signaled the obsolescence of separate schools of science. None was subsequently created, and existing scientific schools were gradually folded into their respective university structures.[86]

Perhaps the most momentous transformation of midcentury was the accommodation of women into higher education. Here too the initial institutional arrangements that suited those times by and large failed to endure. In addition, like collegiate education generally, higher education for women should be seen in regional terms. Pioneering breakthroughs occurred in the 1830s in the East, the South, and the West, but the different orientations were apparent even at that early date.

The first explicit colleges for women were started in the South. Georgia (later Wesleyan) Female College in Macon was chartered in 1836 and began instruction three years later. Imitators emerged slowly at first, but then became commonplace by the 1850s (see "The 'Superior Instruction of Women'"). On the eve of the war more than thirty degree-granting colleges for women existed in the region. The institutions seem to have been patronized by families of planters and professionals who sought for their daughters some measure of personal fulfillment, cultural refinement, and social distinction.[87] In the East the advanced education of women was raised to a new level in 1837 when Mary Lyon opened Mount Holyoke Female Seminary. Although loosely inspired by the Amherst curriculum, sans classics, Mount Holyoke chiefly sought to educate middle-class women to be teachers in a cloistered and strongly evangelical setting. Unlike women in the South, New England women would be educated for work in noncollegiate institutions. In the West, Oberlin admitted women into the collegiate course in 1837 and graduated the first female A.B.'s in 1841.[88] Other evangelical denominations generally supported the full education of women, and by the 1850s both coeducational and female collegiate institutions were widespread. The founder of Western Female Seminary (1855) considered the West to be "crowded" with such institutions (see "A Salutary Rivalry").

Oxford, Ohio—the setting described by Margaret Nash in "A Salutary Rivalry"—became crowded when three women's institutions attempted to operate there. Their differences, however, illuminate the range of possibilities for women's colleges. First, nomenclature was wholly inconsistent. An institute, a seminary, and a college all aspired to teach at approximately the same level. Second, patterns of attendance were determined by cultural and social cleavages. Although Oxford appeared to be a heavily Presbyterian enclave, Western Female Seminary catered to girls from middle-class, evangelical families, while wealthier, more conservative Presbyterians patronized the other two schools. Regional patterns seem to be scrambled here, as Western looked eastward to Mount Holyoke for a model, and Oxford Female College resembled counterparts in the South. In curriculum Nash perceives the "salutary rivalry" in Oxford as stimulating each institution to elevate its standards and offerings. The effects of competition probably affected women's colleges generally.

Despite Oberlin's audacious gambit in admitting women to the classical course, most antebellum women's colleges offered an abbreviated, nonclassical course. In this respect higher education for women was similar across the regions, including coeducational colleges. The antebellum collegiate course for women most often comprised three years of study emphasizing English and modern languages instead of classics. When a classical course was offered, it typically began with Latin grammar and rarely included Greek. Otherwise women studied the same subjects as male collegians (excepting higher mathematics), in many cases using the same textbooks. However, the instructors were not likely to be as highly trained as those in established men's colleges. The most distinctive feature was an ample offering of "feminine accomplishments"—music, art, and domestic crafts. The ornamental subjects were nevertheless controversial, and Mount Holyoke and its sisters as well as some southern colleges de-emphasized them. Women's institutions graduated a relatively small proportion of their students, and few in a classical course. Graduation was scarcely required for any future endeavor. Hence women came to study for their own edification, to prepare for teaching, or to gain refinement through ornamental subjects. Given this general picture, it should be clear why the women's collegiate course was compared unfavorably with the men's. The leaders of these institutions were nevertheless aware of this situation and labored for improvement. The women's course was consequently in constant evolution—growing from three to four years, extending its coverage of Latin, and raising standards for admission—all without transcending this somewhat invidious status.

A few women's colleges sought equality before the Civil War. Mary Sharp College in Tennessee, for example, attempted to offer a classical course equal to a men's college; Mount Holyoke began to teach Latin; and Elmira College in New York in 1855 set its sights on equivalence. This impulse emerged more powerfully after Appomattox, furthered by philanthropy. Vassar College opened in 1865 as a new departure in the higher education of women. It sought to fashion a distinctly feminine course equivalent to that offered in the best eastern men's colleges, and its benefactor provided the resources to make this possible. Smith and Wellesley Colleges, founded a decade later, had similar aspirations although different approaches. However, until well into the 1880s these schools struggled with the same difficulties that beset the earlier women's colleges—lack of suitably prepared students, large numbers of "special" students, and preoccupation with ornamental subjects (see "The 'Superior Instruction of Women'"). But as the new era dawned, these clouds dissipated. The endowed eastern women's colleges—soon known as the Seven Sisters—were admirably suited to adapt to the new academic demands. They possessed large incomes from both gifts and tuition, numerous faculty, and superb facilities; and they soon evolved unique forms of academic and social distinction.[89]

At precisely this juncture the United States Bureau of Education officially consecrated the assumed inferiority of the bulk of women's colleges. It created an elite "Division A" for the Seven Sisters and a handful of others, while the rest were consigned to "Division B" (see "The 'Superior Instruction of Women'"). As a population the "B" colleges were already in a decline that became ever more precipitous during the next two decades. Even given the conventional image of impermanence among nineteenth-century colleges, the attrition of these institutions requires explanation. Most of them failed to transcend their original multipurpose character. Their conception of women's education fit awkwardly into a contracting gap between fully equal coeducation, which had become widespread, and the advancing popularity of high schools and normal schools. The latter, for example, ultimately leeched a viable student clientele from Mary Sharp College in the 1890s, and probably many others as well.[90] The difficulties of the "B" colleges were compounded by their weakness as organizations. Many were centered on a charismatic founder and did not long survive his or her departure. They failed to develop wider sponsorship. Local worthies commonly served as trustees, but rarely contributed significant resources. Ingham University (1857–1892) in Le Roy, New York, was disowned by the Presbyterian Church and later, after the founder's death, had its property foreclosed by one of its own trustees.[91] Unlike the majority of multipurpose colleges, the original women's colleges largely failed to make the difficult transition to the modern academic system and instead went out of business.

From Colleges to Universities

The college was mother to the American university. However, the principal obstacles to university development were the filial bonds of this relationship. At the high tide of the university movement, circa 1890, the overriding question was how to foreshorten or displace the college's educational role (see "The Crisis of the Old Order"). But by century's end, if not before, it became apparent that the university could not thrive without a collegiate foundation.

A key issue, which had hovered over American higher education for most of the century, was how to incorporate advanced learning into institutions of higher education.[92] Forcing this issue were the increasingly visible achievements of German learning—ensconced, to be sure, in the German universities. Not just the United States, but France, Britain, and other nations faced an imperative need to keep abreast of the advancement of academic knowledge. Philology, the cutting-edge humanistic field, promised the key to deeper understanding of the Western heritage, including classical civilization and the origins of Christianity. Relentless advances in the physical sciences, particularly chemistry, had obvious ramifications for industry and agriculture. A parallel revolution in biology and physiology promised untold benefits for the improvement of medicine and public health. German universities emerged as far more effective institutions for advancing and transmitting the new academic knowledge than the assortment of learned societies, scientific academies, and higher schools existing in other countries.[93] Everywhere the challenge was not necessarily to imitate German universities, but to find means to incorporate advanced learning into institutions of higher education. In the United States every specific attempt to address this issue suggested measures to modify or bypass the college. In this respect the emergence of the American university followed a half century of institutional experiments with equivocal results.

Some midcentury attempts to grapple with this issue have been discussed. The theme of advancing knowledge was inextricably linked with its application during these years, and the schools of science were the most characteristic result. The most radical formulation of the issue was no doubt Henry Tappan's *University Education* (1851), which would have built the true university over a truncated, preparatory college. In practice at the University of Michigan, Tappan introduced partial improvements within the collegiate structure (see "The German Model and the Graduate School"). His protégé, Andrew Dickson White, extended this model further by seeking to provide advanced instruction for undergraduates through concentration in a major subject. For both Tappan and (initially) White the shape and structure of graduate education were not yet evident.

The Johns Hopkins University (1876) was the boldest experiment of the university movement, and its founding brought the issue of doctoral education to center stage. President Gilman, disillusioned after years of attempting to integrate research and collegiate instruction, would have dispensed with a college entirely if the Hopkins trustees had let him. Even with a three-year undergraduate course the new university was chiefly devoted to doctoral education and inherently linked with research.[94] In the next decade this model was carried even further as Clark University (1889) and Catholic University (1889) opened as entirely graduate institutions. This notion, in addition, was an important part of the mix of ideas and ambitions that produced the University of Chicago (1892). (See "A 'Curious Working of Cross Purposes.'") Little wonder that the university builders at this juncture saw the colleges as essentially preparatory for the higher learning. But this vision was not realized. Instead the four-year undergraduate college, reformed and rehabilitated to be sure, became the inescapable platform for both doctoral and professional education.

The institutions that exemplified the new American university, although similar in academic structure, were strikingly different in other respects. Most venerable were colonial foundings that by 1900 were largely beholden to their alumni for their affluence and stature. Another group was publicly supported, the flagship educational institutions of their respective states. And most revolutionary were universities created from acts of individual philanthropy. "Noah Porter Writ Large?"; "The German Model and the Graduate School"; and "A 'Curious Working of Cross Purposes'" offer insight into the manner in which three universities, representing each of these types, navigated the swirling collegiate and university currents to become academic leaders of American higher education.

The rise of the alumni to preponderant influence at Yale, the focus of Peter Dobkin Hall's reflections on modernization in "Noah Porter Writ Large?" was a protracted process. President Theodore Dwight Woolsey (1851–1871) had originally regarded alumni influence with trepidation, remarking in 1852 that it was better to "shut their mouths with long addresses" than to allow alumni gatherings to discuss the affairs of the college.[95] Not until James T. Hadley assumed the presidency (1899–1921) was the leadership of Yale in basic harmony with the alumni viewpoint. Surely the most dramatic episode in this transformation was the challenge mounted by the Young Yale movement in choosing a successor to Woolsey. Yale College at this juncture seemed to face the same alternatives that confronted Harvard two years earlier, when the election of Charles William Eliot to the presidency irrevocably committed the university to sweeping reform.[96] Eliot was above all noted for his administrative skills and was an expert as well on "the New Education" (see "The Rise and Fall of Useful Knowledge" and "Noah Porter Writ Large?"). Yale possessed a strikingly similar candidate in Daniel Coit Gilman, who had handled a variety of administrative tasks at the Sheffield Scientific School and was an authority on the land-grant colleges. The Young Yale alumni sought not only representation on the corporation, but a Gilman presidency to lead the institution into the brave new era. But there were important differences between the situations of the two institutions.

Cambridge for twenty-five years had been seething with discontent over the state of the college, its curriculum, and conditions in the associated professional schools. A series of ineffectual presidents had done little to address those sore points, and the alumni in particular demanded change. Yale, on the other hand, could justly say that it was doing many things well. Its scientific school was a model of the New Education, even to Mr. Eliot; and it had awarded the first American Ph.D.'s in 1861. Yale's scholarly prowess was no less remarkable in the humanities, where the "New Haven scholars" purveyed "a particular nineteenth-century hybrid of the conventions of German academic scholarship grafted to the stalk of Scottish philosophy."[97] And if evidence is needed for the efficacy of its powerful collegiate culture, Lyman Bagg's memoir of Yale student life appeared in 1871 (see "College As It Was in the Mid–Nineteenth Century"). Despite the ruckus raised by the Young Yale movement, there was little conviction in New Haven that the institution needed to be new modeled. The election of Noah Porter (1871–1886) to the Yale presidency was an affirmation of the waning present despite rapidly changing times. In 1872 the corporation virtually thumbed its nose at the university movement by resolving that "Yale College has . . . attained the form of a university" since it comprised "the four departments of which a university is commonly understood to consist, *viz.*, the Department of Theology, of Law, of Medicine, and of Philosophy and the Arts."[98] The corporation's definition of the university was the one that had prevailed in American higher education; however, the opening of Johns Hopkins only four years later elevated this standard.

More important for the future was the concession of alumni representation on the corporation that accompanied Porter's elevation. The Sons of Yale at first withheld their largesse, as Hall points out; but in 1890 they established an alumni fund and kept it under their own control. By the twentieth century Yale graduates, like those of progressive Harvard, were donating ever-larger sums for the greater glory of alma mater.[99] The revolution in governance and the alumni support that accompanied it were the keys to the transformation of eastern colleges and universities. Noah Porter may have been right that alumni brought no special insight into the management of educational institutions; but as his adversary William Phelps charged, neither did the Reverend Pickerings of Squashville (see "Noah Porter Writ Large?"). The decisive factor that tipped the balance in favor of alumni was the emerging student culture of the high-collegiate era that resonated so powerfully with recent graduates and convinced them that alma mater merited support. Where clerical tradition impeded that culture, as at Dartmouth, confrontations with alumni became acrimonious. Conversely in the colleges studied by Bruce Leslie, successful modernization followed closely upon the assertion of alumni influence.[100] The same could be said for emerging universities: where alumni influence predominated, the college was safe from the tampering of university builders. Harvard alumni, for example, had no sympathy with Eliot's plan for a three-year bachelor's degree. At Yale, on the other hand, the issue of foreshortening the college course was never raised.

If the high-collegiate era saw the entrenchment of alumni influence, the late-collegiate era experienced an unprecedented flow of giving. As Hall suggests, here the jeremiads of Thorstein Veblen against the stewardship of the economically successful carry some weight. At least some large donors thought it quite appropriate that the growing disparities of privilege and status on campus reflected the great disparity of wealth in American society.[101] In perhaps the most symbolic confrontation of this era, Princeton alumni repudiated President Woodrow Wilson (1902–1910) on just such an issue. By all indications Wilson was an alumni favorite—a friend of athletics and a stirring speaker at alumni gatherings. However, he wished to recapture for the Princeton campus the democratic aura of the high-collegiate era by displacing the snobbish eating clubs. The wealthy alumni, upon whom such a scheme depended, opted decisively to uphold the existing social system, and Wilson opted to pursue a different career among constituents who voted with ballots rather than dollars.[102]

The long romance of the University of Michigan with German educational models, described in "The German Model and the Graduate School," had an ironic ending: innovations of Germanic inspiration fell by the wayside, and the basic form of the American university was consecrated in the wedding of the college and the graduate school. But the German university remains indispensable to this story. As a superior ideal, it inspired the exertions of Henry Tappan and his successors. The very upgrading of the college through the introduction of electives and lectures made it impervious to the imposition of Germanic structures. The German-inspired university system at Michigan scarcely made an impression. Instead, as the authors precisely state, "Americans discarded the *educational* program of German universities [but] took the German invention of highly specialized *professorial* research" ("The German Model and the Graduate School") as the basis for the American graduate school.

This was the revolution launched by Johns Hopkins and forced by advancements in German learning. The richly nuanced depiction of the course of events at Michigan, however, suggests that continuity with collegiate education was inherent to this process. The irony of this outcome transcended the University of Michigan. Even as the university builders contemplated reconfiguring the college, circa 1890, they were organizing formal graduate schools that were predicated on the preparatory function of a four-year college course. Harvard organized its graduate school in 1890, Michigan in 1891, and Yale in 1892. At the end of the decade the principal universities engaged in graduate education joined together in the Association of American Universities (1900) to set the standards not only for the American Ph.D., but also for the colleges that prepared students for such study. This action implicitly defined a preparatory role and standard that fixed the structural position of the college in American higher education.[103] From this juncture the measure of the colleges would be the extent to which their graduates were prepared for study in university graduate programs.[104]

Still, the formula for the American university was anything but clear at the outset of the 1890s. Thus the "cross purposes" inherent in the founding of the University of Chicago involved a tug-of-war between the college and specialized faculty research (see "A 'Curious Working of Cross Purposes'"). Willard Pugh's reinterpretation of the university's origins provides the most plausible explanation yet offered of the multiplex mind of William Rainey Harper. His overriding commitment to research differed from the ivory-tower, Germanic approach represented by Johns Hopkins. Harper saw his university as the knowledge center for a far-reaching intellectual enterprise, disseminating learning through summer schools, a university press, extension and correspondence courses, and affiliated colleges. Despite his original overriding commitment to research in a "great graduate university," he remained flexible enough to accommodate and ultimately embrace the university's college.[105]

From his background he knew the situation of American colleges well. Although he had little confidence in the majority of small colleges, he was fully aware of the considerable progress that had been made by the stronger ones. In particular he emphasized that the last two years of college could be devoted to specialized studies.[106] Given this bifurcated nature of college by the end of the century, Harper conjured up possibilities of having the lower classes at a different campus or forging links with external junior colleges. But he never envisioned his graduate research university to be like Clark University—devoid of undergraduates. One of his first appointments (and not easily accomplished) was football coach Amos Alonzo Stagg, who became "Associate Professor and Director of the Department of Physical Culture and Athletics."[107] Harper's great accomplishment (beyond cajoling John D. Rockefeller out of $32 million) was his initial success in staffing the Chicago departments with proven scholars who shared his devotion to academic investigation. Their expectations for research were in many cases more exaggerated than his own.[108] Once this foundation was laid, Harper seems to have turned much attention to the "horizontal" expansion of the university professional schools as well as further tinkering with the college. However, the result of the "curious working of cross purposes" was a "multiversity" in which all units were infused with the university spirit of research.

The spectacular success of the University of Chicago and the similar accomplishments of the other leading universities have largely obscured the malaise that engulfed the bulk of American higher education. After 1890 American higher education was bifurcated into a rapidly developing sector of universities, shadowed by other institutions struggling to keep pace with their academic development, and the colleges facing the end of the old order (see "The Crisis of the Old Order"). For the colleges the 1890s brought an abrupt and traumatic transformation that extended from the routine of daily activity to the mission of a college education.

Most symbolic of the crisis of the old order was the collapse of the classical A.B. course, along with its less classical variations. Its demise was the culmination of many developments, to be sure. Even through the 1880s most colleges had preserved the fixed courses, larded by that point with a range of options for upperclassmen. The fixed course was the peg upholding an entire way of life: a daily routine centered on three recitations, morning and evening chapel, as well as the academic segregation of the four classes.[109] The appeal of such studies and the regime that delivered them were clearly on the wane. Despite the educational expansion of the 1880s, the annual number of classical A.B.'s awarded scarcely budged (see "The Crisis of the Old Order"). At the same time the pressure to teach the new knowledge being spawned by the academic disciplines continued to mount.

In contrast Eliot's elective system by 1890 presented an infinity of curricular possibilities that might be chosen from Harvard's bounteous offerings. As the colleges fitfully but ineluctably followed in this path—teaching disciplinary knowledge through an elective curriculum—the old college order irretrievably crumbled. In most respects it was a positive development. Few lamented the passing of the old daily routine or the rules with which it was upheld. The abandonment of mental discipline in favor of wider and more advanced studies may have been regretted by faculty traditionalists, but not by students. At the typical college greater personal and curricular freedom was accompanied during the 1890s by the rapid adoption of the gamut of activities of the high-collegiate era. Still, effecting such a transition was a severe challenge for the great majority of colleges.

To cope with the crisis, colleges had no alternative but to enlarge the scale and scope of their operations. Whereas a faculty of 10 was considered adequate to teach the fixed course in 1880, 25 were deemed appropriate by one estimate in order to offer an elective curriculum after 1900 (see "The Crisis of the Old Order"). Yet in 1900 the modal college enrolled only 83 students. Few colleges reached a faculty size of 25 before 1920.

Given the insuperable curricular superiority of the universities, university builders questioned the college's future role. The first two years of the fixed course were largely devoted to the rote learning of languages and math that could be (and actually was) accomplished in less elevated institutions. If the third and fourth years were to be devoted to advanced studies, universities were the proper venue for such pursuits—or so it seemed around 1890 (see "The Crisis of the Old Order"). As just discussed, a full four years of undergraduate study proved indispensable at Michigan, Chicago, and the other universities that tried to foreshorten the collegiate course (Johns Hopkins, Harvard, and Columbia). In this respect the universities provided the curricular template that the colleges could also use to fashion a credible course of study.

An analogous pattern emerged for professional education. However, here the failings of the colleges transcended the opinions of university builders and reflected student enrollments. Throughout the nineteenth century the colleges had been criticized for offering chiefly preprofessional preparation—the aim emphasized in the Yale Report of 1828. At the end of the century not only were more professional degrees being awarded than bachelor's degrees, but few of the former recipients bothered to earn the latter. The rupture of this historical relationship reflected trends in professional licensing that stretched back to the Jacksonian era, as well as the proliferation of medical and law schools at the end of the century. The fact remained that collegiate education had become increasingly irrelevant for one of its principal avowed purposes. The long reformation of education in the major professions is only sketched in "The Crisis of the Old Order." The initial efforts to elevate and reform the professional schools were undertaken by the universities, led by Eliot at Harvard. Soldering the nexus between collegiate preparation and professional studies nevertheless had to await the curricular restructuring of the colleges. Only in the twentieth century did professional schools become truly postgraduate units. But this development, even more than the emergence of academic specialization in the graduate school, consecrated an irreplaceable role for the undergraduate college.

The undergraduate college of the twentieth century developed into a vastly different entity from the colleges that populated American higher education until the last decade of the nineteenth century. Moreover this evolution was irrevocably in place by 1900—within a decade of the questioning of the college's role with which the 1890s had opened. Columbia president Seth Low was no doubt correct when he pronounced that the college no longer topped the educational system of the United States (see "the Crisis of the Old Order"). However, the four-year undergraduate college, either free-standing or within the university, would persist as the centerpiece of American higher education for the next century.

Curriculum and Enrollment
Assessing the Popularity of Antebellum Colleges

~

DAVID B. POTTS

*T*wo frequent themes in histories of early-nineteenth-century higher education have been the impracticality and unpopularity of antebellum colleges. When measured against the hopes of reformers such as George Ticknor or Francis Wayland, these colleges are found to be too limited in their curricula; when measured against what reformers and/or historians determine to be the educational needs of antebellum society, they are found to be islands of institutional elitism amidst a rising tide of democratic sentiment. It is then concluded that, as they failed to respond to these needs and rejected the pleas of reformers, antebellum colleges must have become increasingly unpopular institutions.

Evidence to support the themes of impracticality and unpopularity is typically drawn from documents written by contemporary collegiate reformers and from observations made by late-nineteenth-century university reformers such as Charles Kendall Adams and Andrew D. White. Given the problems of allowing for biases that might shape perceptions from such sources, it is encouraging to find that the most recent versions of the century-old interpretation reach out to the new area of student demography[1] for hard data to support the theme of antebellum colleges being out of touch with their times. What better way to measure popularity than at the gate?

The early results of integrating student statistics with the established general interpretation, however, are much more unsettling than might be anticipated. Careful scrutiny of the evidence from student studies suggests severe limitations to what enrollment data may tell us about the practicality and popularity of colleges during the antebellum period. Moreover, to the degree that enrollment data indicate anything about public favor or disfavor toward colleges, these statistics suggest a slow but steady increase in popularity from 1800 to 1860. We seem, then, to be at a point where there is reason not only to question the sufficiency of the evidence supporting the established interpretation, but also to see that more recently assembled data suggest the possibility of standing that interpretation on its head.[2]

One work, Frederick Rudolph's *Curriculum: A History of the Undergraduate Course of Study since 1636,* can be used to illustrate the weaknesses of the established interpretation and the hazards of accepting its more recent versions.[3] Rudolph observes that the curriculum has been "an arena" for interesting and important interactions between society and higher education. The arena analogy suggests that even in curriculum development—perhaps especially in curriculum development—there might be the elements of high drama and entertainment.

Only when the colonial period has been presented through a sound summary of recent scholarship does Rudolph's story become emotionally charged. In contrast to the theme of "gradual and subtle" improvements prior to 1800, "a reactionary mood . . . set in among college governors and others during the first decade of the nineteenth century." Chapter 3 begins with the Columbia trustees of 1830 in a state of "panic and pandering" because of declining enrollments and the competitive threat of the University of the City of New York (later New York University). The perspective quickly expands to a national context, where "egalitarian impulses challenged the essentially elitist pretensions of the colleges." For the next fifty pages or so the text is liberally salted with highly charged language. Faced with an "alarming bundle of movements and tendencies that undermined the traditional prestige of classical learning," colleges then "stumbled around in search of some secure identity" and "sometimes behaved quite as bizarrely as the trustees of Columbia College." College founders engaged in a "rash of overbuilding." Science teaching was expanded and modern languages were introduced, but "not . . . without great struggle and bitterness." Reactionary faculty "sabotaged reforms." By the 1850s "colleges geared to the needs of village elites to flaunt their Latin and Greek" are "plagued by unpopularity" and are experiencing a period of "crisis." They must "be practical or perish."[4] As in Greek tragedy a large and explicit theme of inevitability is woven through the entire drama.

Those acquainted with Rudolph's earlier work, with Richard Hofstadter's portrayal of the "great retrogression," and with other studies in the same vein will find the story familiar, although perhaps stated in its most strident rendition.[5] In showing the ways in which the narrative increasingly intersects with student enrollment statistics recently collected or scrutinized, let us look at each of the four principal players cited by Rudolph and most other historians staging this saga of early-nineteenth-century higher education. In order of appearance this cast of characters includes the Yale Report of 1828; a hardy band of thwarted reformers at Harvard, Amherst, and a few other institutions; Eliphalet Nott, president of Union College from 1804 to 1866; and Francis Wayland, president of Brown University from 1827 to 1855.

The Yale Report of 1828 occupies its accustomed role as witting or unwitting villain. For Rudolph the portrayal has always been one of an unwitting villain, but his analysis of the dramatic role has become more detailed over the years.

Rudolph finds much to praise in the report. In *The American College and University* he lauded this document as "a magnificent assertion of the humanist tradition and therefore of unquestionable importance in liberating the American college from an excessive religious orientation."[6] In *Curriculum* a lengthy and sympathetic summary of the report emphasizes that the Yale faculty had constructed not only a defense of the classics but also a "plea for quality" that was "widely read and just as widely heeded."[7] It is strongly implied that such an effort to engage human wisdom in the service of a bustling young nation was greatly needed.

Yet Rudolph's final assessment is based on inadequacies of the report that render this document "a kind of last gesture, a summoning of energy and purity and clarity of purpose appropriate to a tribe on the edge of extinction." The villainous plot unwittingly aided and abetted by the report rests on the connection, Rudolph asserts, between faculty psychology and its use by local reactionaries to justify a low-cost curriculum serving elitist purposes. Thus the Yale Report delivered to those who used authority, traditions, and institutions to hold man in "moral and intellectual . . . slavery" all they needed in the way of "a veneer of educational philosophy." For one such reactionary, a trustee at the College of California in the 1860s, the Yale reputation (enhanced by the report) "subsidized his swagger." As a document whose inadequacies produced unintended consequences, the report is therefore viewed as an impediment to progress. But Rudolph's detailed and multifaceted discussion of the report is also in part a lament. He concludes with the almost wistful comment: "It was not enough."[8]

What evidence is offered to support this somewhat reluctant criticism? Acknowledging that faculty psychology was "the conventional wisdom of its time," Rudolph moves to more advantageous ground by using the present to measure the past. If confronted with the report's model of how the mind develops and operates, "a twentieth-century psychologist would be appalled."

From this point forward, the book employs a sharp contrast between outmoded faculty psychology and "the psychology of individual differences and interests."[9] Overlooked in this contrast (and in Rudolph's footnote references) is the monograph by Walter B. Kolesnik tracing the many historical stages of thinking about transfer of training, an area in psychology that is far from definitively researched.[10] Rudolph's sweeping dismissal of faculty psychology therefore obscures complex issues of psychological understanding and historical interpretation. His sources on conservatism and elitism are mostly limited to undocumented and underdocumented observations made by historians whose primary purpose is to explain events occurring in the late nineteenth century and who have a strong interest in establishing a contrast with the preceding half century.[11] These sources, moreover, are used in lieu of the best available research on college students during the antebellum years. David Allmendinger's important monograph, for example, which supplies a great deal of evidence contradicting the thesis of elitism, is neither addressed in the text nor cited in the bibliography.[12]

The greatest weakness in the traditional interpretation of the Yale Report, however, is not the absence of data on disbelief in mental discipline among the general public in Jacksonian America or the selective use of secondary sources in asserting that colleges of this era were elitist. The main problem is confronting the fact that Yale College, as measured by enrollments for 1828 and the years beyond, was among the most popular institutions in the country. Rudolph generously acknowledges Yale's prosperity, but makes no attempt to integrate the meaning of this statistic with his subsequent observations that low enrollments at institutions with a basically classical curriculum constitute evidence for their unpopularity. If the relationship between enrollments and a classical curriculum is an indicator of a college's popularity, it is appropriate to ask whether Yale's enrollments after 1828 reflected public disfavor by declining or at least leveling off. Might this not be particularly expected in a bustling commercial and manufacturing city rather than the small town, at which Rudolph asserts that a traditional college would be able to perpetuate itself by merely serving a local elite? Unfortunately for the established view of antebellum colleges, student data show that Yale's enrollments increased by more than 60 percent between 1828 and 1860.[13]

What about Harvard? Harvard makes its appearance, right after the discussion of the Yale Report, within the context of failed reforms at the University of Nashville, the University of Vermont, the University of the City of New York, the University of Virginia, and Amherst College. Harvard is the most important member of this group because it is the only institution among them where curriculum reformers were able to institute and sustain for almost a decade a significant alternative to the limited curriculum of Yale. In Nashville, Philip Lindsley's plans for a university that would be both utilitarian and scholarly succumbed to competition from neighboring colleges modeled on the curricular philosophy of the Yale Report. James Marsh was unsuccessful in his attempts at Vermont to depart from the Yale plan for reasons that Rudolph does not make clear. The forerunner of New York University made a brief attempt to move in the direction of an earned master's degree but soon returned to the ways of a classical college. Thomas Jefferson's attempts to incorporate certain practices from continental universities into the University of Virginia fell on "indifferent soil." By 1831 the institution he founded had "capitulated to tradition." At Amherst a faculty pamphlet of 1827 proposed a B.A. curriculum requiring neither Latin nor Greek, "but the institution lacked the will and the means to give it a respectable try."[14]

Harvard made the best effort of anyone in this group. Between 1835 and 1843, faculty reformers were able to enact academic regulations within which "virtually all courses beyond the freshman year were offered on an elective basis." Although the vision of reformers comparable to Lindsley, Marsh, and Jefferson played an important role, Harvard's experience seems especially instructive because the immediate motivation to change comes less from reformer idealism than from responses to signals sent by the general public.[15] Here is an example with apparently fine potential for reinforcing the traditional view of antebellum higher education.

The evidence offered is both scholarly and statistical. Rudolph cites Robert McCaughey's biography of Josiah Quincy. Upon assuming the presidency of Harvard in 1829, Quincy tried to pattern his college after the example of Yale. But Quincy, according to McCaughey, had to face some hard facts about public opinion. "Never had dissatisfaction [with colleges] been more general," and colleges in the 1830s were "on the defensive." A more specific and telling signal was the enrollment declines of the early 1830s. Reacting to these disturbing facts, Quincy endeavored to make Harvard more attractive and accessible to prospective students by instituting a primarily elective curriculum.[16]

But what is the evidence offered, in turn, by McCaughey? In addition to referring readers to a chapter in Rudolph's *The American College and University* (detailed analysis of which would overlap in large part with this analysis of *Curriculum*), McCaughey cites a chapter in Richard J. Storr's *The Beginnings of Graduate Education in America* as a persuasive source for "the general dissatisfaction with American colleges."[17] Storr detects "a general uneasiness over higher education in the United States" and considerable controversy in educational circles during the 1820s and 1830s. It is difficult, however, to find hard evidence of public dissatisfaction in Storr's chapter. We learn that the Yale Report expressed concern over the limited resources available for significant changes in American higher education at that stage of its development; that graduate education offered by the new, underfinanced, and poorly administered University of the City of New York attracted few students; that Congress decided against using funds from the Smithsonian bequest to found a national university; and that a letter printed in an 1830 issue of the *New York American* supported the Yale Report of 1828.[18] Does this add up to "general dissatisfaction" with American colleges?

More persuasive evidence might be found in the complete enrollment statistics in Harvard's catalogues for 1828 to 1860. McCaughey supplies totals for two years: 252 students enrolled in 1829–1830, Quincy's first year as president, and 210 students in 1834–1835, when it became necessary to make "an accommodation" to public opinion.[19] Yet the catalogues tell us that in the fall of 1834, before Quincy instituted reforms, Harvard admitted by far its largest freshman class in five years. One might also guess that as more course election was permitted, enrollments would show some increase. In fact, however, they fluctuate considerably from year to year and do not attain a level consistently higher than the early Quincy years until after what Rudolph describes as a movement back toward increased prescription, beginning around 1843. It would seem, therefore, that the Harvard experience suggests caution in seeking to connect the nature of the antebellum curriculum and changes in enrollment totals.

Yale may falter in educational imagination and Harvard in innovations that boost enrollments, but Union College steps onto the stage as "the best of all possible worlds." Under the clever and charismatic leadership of Eliphalet Nott, Union, according to Rudolph, "believed in young men" and "believed in itself." Nott introduced a parallel scientific course in 1828 that entitled students to the same B.A. degree awarded to those completing the classical course. "Where others failed," Rudolph tells us, "Union flourished." With "about a third of each class . . . enrolled in the scientific course," Union's enrollment "went merrily up." Throughout the 1830s, Union was graduating as many students as its closest rival, Yale.[20]

Evidence for casting Union in this heroic role is primarily drawn from the biography of Nott by Codman Hislop. From this source comes the important estimate that one-third of the students were enrolled in the scientific course.[21] Better evidence, it would seem, could scarcely be found concerning public demand for an attractive curricular alternative to the classical curriculum defended by the Yale Report.

There are several pitfalls, however, in using these data to draw such conclusions. Hislop probably based his undocumented estimate on a perusal of the so-called Merit Books in the Union archives.[22] A look at this source reveals the great difficulty if not impossibility of an accurate count of juniors or seniors enrolled in the scientific course. Nott was operating in the 1830s and 1840s with an unannounced elective system that permitted classical students to take scientific course listings and vice versa. Most students seem to have exercised their freedom of choice. It is very hard to find many students who can be designated purely scientific or purely classical. Blurring of these distinctions in practice may help explain why John Whitehead, in a book published two years after Hislop's biography, gives the undocumented estimate that one-fourth of all Union students were enrolled in the scientific course.[23]

Even if the higher of these estimates is granted, there is reason to ask whether it constitutes evidence for a nonclassical curricular option stimulating significant enrollment increases. In 1820 Union had 255 students. Giving the reforms of 1828 time to have some effect, a look at the statistics for 1850 shows a total of 266 students. For several of the years between these dates the enrollments topped 300, but the annual average between 1834 and 1850 was 278, giving little reason to conclude from the overall statistical picture that liberalizing requirements for the traditional bachelor's degree led to major enrollment gains.[24] Other causal variables may explain Union's attractiveness as well or better than a new curricular option. The chance to take the senior year moral philosophy course from Nott may have drawn many students. A flourishing system of social fraternities probably proved pleasing to others. Finally there is the question of academic standards. On the eve of implementing Union's new scientific curriculum in 1828, Nott, according to his sympathetic late-nineteenth-century biographers, was busy denying charges emanating from some New England educators that his college had become during the 1820s a "Botany Bay," where underqualified and unruly students denied access to other colleges could find ready refuge. One source of these charges was reported to be a recently departed member of the Union faculty, none other than Francis Wayland, the new president of Brown University. In a letter to his son-in-law written in September 1828, Nott found Wayland to be "misguided."[25]

This same Francis Wayland enters the drama sketched by Rudolph and others as an accurate observer of the collegiate scene only after he has been enlightened by experiences at Brown. His role is chiefly that of the prophet unjustly and unwisely spurned. It is through Wayland's eyes that we learn "of the isolation of the traditional colleges from the American people," a situation in which "each institution 'plods on its weary way solitary and in darkness.'" Rudolph finds him "suspicious of faculty psychology," and suggests that Wayland's reform efforts at Brown were thwarted by a "local elite." After a seemingly "endless quarrel with the Brown corporation," Wayland did, however, obtain an opportunity to try out his version of a more practical and attractive curriculum at Brown in the early 1850s.[26]

Although both Wayland and most of his reforms were gone within five years, a better than 60 percent jump in enrollments occurred between 1850–1851 and 1853–1854. Rudolph's figures are accurate, but is this a good indication of long-thwarted popular demand for nonclassical higher education finally finding an outlet? Rudolph suggests the additional 75 to 100 students enrolling annually during these years is an affirmative answer. The reforms lacked staying power, he explains, mainly because of insufficient funding to establish new departments of instruction in sufficient number or depth. Sources cited in support of this interpretation are Walter C. Bronson's *History of Brown University* and R. Freeman Butts's *The College Charts Its Course.*[27] Since Butts cites only Bronson in discussing Wayland and Brown, it might be interesting to see what other relevant information and perspectives on the data Bronson provides. Given the high level of industrial development in Providence and the entire state of Rhode Island, Bronson finds that the enrollment increase "though encouraging, was far from satisfactory." It did not, he argues, indicate a high public esteem for scientific education. The evidence points primarily to a market for lower academic standards in any subject studied.[28] Is this all that Wayland's perceptiveness as an observer of the contemporary collegiate scene really amounts to? After studying the information and assessments presented in Bronson's chapter on Wayland's "New System," one might reasonably arrive at such a conclusion.

Some of the details presented in this review of dramatis personae may be too obscure for a historian with general interpretive responsibilities to dig up. Little more than a mild curiosity or skepticism would, however, lead any scholar to readily accessible enrollment statistics summarized in most early-nineteenth-century catalogues and in some institutional histories. And even brief exploration of these most elementary of student statistics within their institutional contexts gives little support to the established interpretation of antebellum colleges.

Beyond the level of individual institutions are regional data frequently cited as a backdrop to the traditional drama of collegiate unpopularity. Wayland himself collected enrollment figures for the New England colleges.[29] Rudolph cites two other studies. The first was compiled in 1870 by the president of Columbia, F. A. P. Barnard. If statistical evidence for public disfavor with the antebellum curriculum cannot be found at Yale in 1828, Union in the 1830s, Harvard in the early 1840s, or Brown in the early 1850s, perhaps supporting data can be located with the help of a New York City perspective after the Civil War.

Rudolph tells us that Barnard's statistics "demonstrated that the enrollment capacities of a still growing number of colleges were increasing at a greater rate than the college-going student population," and that "Barnard had the wit to recognize the real difficulty: the classical course." Actually Barnard makes no survey of increasing enrollment capacities in this pamphlet and computes no growth rate for the total number of college students. Even if he did, it is difficult to see what such computations would mean for the popularity of classical curricula. Barnard does assert that the nation could be more efficiently served by fewer colleges and that Columbia could better serve the limited market for traditional college education in New York City if spared the competition from New York University and City College of New York. He further assesses the local market for college students by examining current enrollments of New York City residents at twenty colleges in nearby states and computes ratios of students to total population in these states for 1840, 1860, and the late 1860s. Connections between unencouraging enrollment data and a claim that this was a sign of declining public interest in the classical curriculum are made only in terms of a few suggestions from Barnard that Columbia might liberalize its curriculum, and in a reference to statistics presented in his annual report for 1866.[30] Flaws in this earlier report are serious and would require extended discussion. A second study cited by Rudolph was prepared by Professor Edward Hitchcock of Amherst in 1877. These statistics, Rudolph says, "demonstrated that the country's population had been increasing at twice the rate of college-going." In fact Hitchcock's pamphlet deals only with students from Massachusetts attending eleven New England colleges.[31]

Rudolph's book clearly indicates the elusive and at times gossamer nature of student statistics used to support long-established portrayals of antebellum colleges as being out of touch with their times. How much longer, then, will the period continue to be described in terms of "reactionary" early-nineteenth-century colleges overthrown by the university "revolution" after the Civil War? As Rudolph seems to realize at one brief point in the text, the hard facts suggest that changes in curriculum and enrollment growth were "incremental" rather than dramatic.[32] Historical analysis along these lines and consistent with what student statistics can support will probably have less drama but greater accuracy.

What new models and themes might emerge from such analyses? We can at least anticipate development of more sophisticated notions of how supply and demand operate in higher education. We might begin to see interesting interactions between the persuasive powers of colleges and the economic and other forces shaping individual and public responses. As colleges continue to encounter complex demographic and economic challenges, historians can contribute important analytical perspectives on the ecological issues of higher education.

The Rights of Man and the Rites of Youth
Fraternity and Riot at Eighteenth-Century Harvard

≈

LEON JACKSON

During the academic years 1788 to 1797, Harvard's Hancock Professor of Hebrew, Eliphalet Pearson, kept a very special diary. In it he sought to record each and every instance of tumultuous and disobedient behavior in the nation's oldest and most prestigious college. The years in question were evidently ones that kept the professor at his diary with depressing regularity. Day after day, and week after week, Pearson chronicled the assaults of young students on their putatively cherished mentors:

> Decr. 9 [1788]. . . . Disorders coming out of chapel. Also in the hall at breakfast ye same morning. *Bisket, tea cups, saucers,* & a *knife* thrown at ye tutors. At evening prayers the lights were all extinguished by powder and lead, except 2 or 3. Upon this a general *laugh* among the juniors— From this day to Decr 13 disorders continued in hall and chapel, such as *scraping, whispering,* & c.[1]

And so it went on, week after week, and year after year: emetics in the drinking water, dead dogs dropped into the well, stones thrown through windows, the chapel bell broken, candles stolen, drunken abuse of the tutors. Soon the onslaughts expanded to include not only verbal violence against faculty, but physical violence within the student body itself. Factions formed for or against the student agitators, and eventually these came to blows. Walking to chapel one morning in 1793, a college student recorded seeing "an Effigy hanging by a rope from a tree in the college yard representing *Judas,* or *Perkins,* a senior, supposed to be the founder of [an] informing club in the college, and today I have seen his Execution advertised."[2] Academic life became so fraught that one college proctor took to sleeping with a loaded pistol under his bed in dread anticipation of attempts on his life. He was probably not alone in his fears.[3]

Had Professor Pearson both the time and the temperament, he might have filled a dozen or more volumes, chronicling the increasingly violent tides of disturbance at Harvard and other colleges in the early Republic. And indeed many historians have stepped in to take on just such a task. A slew of recent books and articles has now made it quite evident that the fifty years between 1776 and 1826 were the most "dangerous" in the history of American higher education.[4] Disruptions ranged from surliness and noisy atheism, through acts of minor sabotage and vandalism, to arson, theft, and the public horsewhipping of unpopular tutors. If professors at the time scratched their heads in an attempt to explain the prevalence of such tumult, then their descendants in the academy have been no less perplexed. However, a variety of explanations have been forwarded. Some have argued that the disruptive elements were the children of the wealthy; others that they were the children of the poor or of parvenu entrepreneurs.[5] Some have seen the youth of the protagonists as a major explanatory factor; others have laid blame at the feet of older students held back from early admission to college.[6] Some have argued that there is an inherently confrontational element within the very structure of student life; and others have looked to very specific grievances such as poor food, poor teaching, and an inadequate curriculum as possible catalysts for disruption.[7]

The range of (often conflicting) theories offered should not suggest a lack of historical grip on the problem of student disturbances, so much as indicate that a variety of causes were at work simultaneously, goading some to violence while delimiting such pugilistic options for others. A sound account of student disturbances in the early Republic should certainly take account of all the above-mentioned factors, and by so doing might arrive at a relatively nuanced account of student life in this period. Historians badly need such a synthetic appraisal, but such an undertaking is beyond the scope of this chapter. The following work is simply a prolegomenon to such a study. In these pages I argue that any future account of college life will be fundamentally flawed and inaccurate in its findings unless it takes into consideration the role of student societies and cabals in the making and breaking of riotous occurrences. While a certain amount has been written about student fraternities in the early Republic, and an even more modest output has touched on eighteenth-century understandings of sociability and friendship, no one has yet put these strands of scholarship together to consider how such understandings impinged on the evocation of order and disorder in the antebellum college.[8]

It is the major argument of this chapter that the lines of division in the student body at eighteenth-century Harvard were drawn between two competing understandings of friendship and association prevalent during this period. The decision, or even the impulse, to riot was significantly shaped by how one understood friendship: in what it consisted, what it demanded, what it provided, where one sought it, and how one sustained it. Both visions of friendship grew out of a matrix of republican thought, yet one was a classical republicanism, the other a radical republicanism. Both envisioned a larger vision of society, yet for one it was corporate and institutionalized, and for the other individualistic and ad hoc. One vaunted the power of reason, the other the efficacy of will. Finally each conception of friendship was heavily inflected by the notion of ideal gender roles, yet for one the ideal was of brotherhood, while the other vaunted manhood.

This chapter seeks to reconstruct these visions of friendship as they existed at Harvard in all their rich and nuanced detail, before applying them to an analysis of social order and disorder in the college between 1788 and 1794. Through such an analysis, I believe it can be demonstrated that students who belonged to Harvard's secret societies—the champions of classical notions of friendship—were significantly less prone to riotous behavior than those who did not, even though they often shared the same grievances and frustrations as their nonfraternal fellow students. It is my belief that we will understand the dynamics of student life in this period only when we have fully assayed the modes and models of friendship available to the protagonists of these much-studied but little-understood disturbances, and charted how the adherents of each vision interacted with the other.

The Problem of Studenthood

The two decades that straddled the American Revolution were exceptionally difficult ones for Harvard College. A devastating fire in 1764 razed old Harvard Hall to the ground, destroying the library and its contents in the process; the Revolutionary War led to the removal of the college to Concord, resulting in a great loss of students and revenue; and after the Revolution it became apparent that the college treasurer and republican hero, John Hancock, had mismanaged the funds of the school, resulting in a loss of more than a thousand pounds.[9] The college's crippling financial problems were only partially mitigated by the institution of public lotteries; the lack of adequate teaching staff meant that, on occasion, subjects were never covered; the quality of the food and board was atrocious; and on one occasion, the college closed down for two months because of a lack of firewood.

All of these factors made the life of a Harvard student one of austerity and frustration. The quality and style of life at Harvard very often generated *casi belli* for student disorders: there were a rancid butter riot, a kitchen access riot, several riots protesting academic rules, and almost perpetual friction with respect to the rigidity and austerity of the college regime. Yet although one may list a variety of monetary and material problems that generated a sense of grievance among students at Harvard, it is important to distinguish between such *casi belli* and the principled grievances that underlay them. In other words the various causes célèbres vaunted by the students might never have become the explosive material they did, had there not existed deeper problems within the structure of the college itself. Just such an argument was made by one of Harvard's riotous students, Willard Phillips, in his manuscript "Anti-Don-Quixotism," where he argued that complaints about food were merely symbolic. The corporation, he explained, believed that the disturbances were to be attributed to students' "youth, inexperience, and want of consideration; or from the arts and influence of a few disorganizing spirits among them; and not from a general temper hostile to the government of College, and the rules of decency and decorum." But this latter cause was the real one, according to Phillips, for "when a general uneasiness prevails among the subjects all things are not right with the government."[10] At bottom the troubles at Harvard precipitated because the faculty had no clear sense of either the function of the college or the nature of the students they were attempting to teach. Or to put the matter somewhat more pointedly, the conceptions of studenthood they harbored were increasingly out of touch with the realities of New England in the late eighteenth century, and so exacerbated tensions that bedeviled the college itself.

To his great credit, Eliphalet Pearson, the anxious annalist of the student riots, realized this disjunction very early on. Even as he was recording the daily tumults at Harvard, he wrote a long and anguished letter to his friend Edward Holyoke in Salem, in which he explicitly addressed the question of the appropriate principles upon which a college government might be run. "I take it to be a maxim in politics," he wrote, "that that system of jurisprudence will be most satisfactory, & the most productive of good, which is best suited to the nature of society, for whose benefit it is established." The two dominant models of polity, he went on, were the civil/political and the familial/patriarchal, yet many were hard-pressed to say whether a college polity "ought to be denominated *domestic,* or *civil,* or *sui generis,* or *mixed.*"[11] Pearson's problem, and one of the fundamental causes of disturbance in the eighteenth-century college, lay in this realm of categorization. Professors were hard-pressed to decide what form a college government should take, only because they found it impossible to determine the precise nature of the college student they sought to govern.

The problem lay in the fact that the eighteenth century experienced an immense flux in its perception and understanding of human development. In both religious and legal treatises, it is true, distinctions between infants, children, youths, the middle aged, and the old were frequently made. Yet this terminological precision notwithstanding, the articulate early-eighteenth-century thinker was apt to make a more strictly binary distinction between childhood and adulthood. The rationale behind such a division was, as Joseph Kett has argued, primarily economic. A child was one who lived at home and depended upon family for subsistence; conversely an adult was one who lived away from home and maintained a relative degree of financial solvency and independence. In an age when parents frequently lacked the resources to feed and clothe family members without sacrifice, material criteria made more sense in separating boys and men than those based upon physical maturity.[12]

Students drove a wedge between this neat child-adult dichotomy. Their status can thus be usefully associated with what the anthropologist Victor Turner has called the liminal: a category of persons who "elude or slip through the network of classifications that normally locate states and positions in cultural space." Liminal entities "are neither here nor there; they are betwixt and between positions assigned and arrayed by law, custom, convention, and ceremonial."[13] Through the course of the eighteenth century, as more and more colleges were established and the student population burgeoned, a liminal period between childhood and adulthood came to be grudgingly acknowledged, institutionalized, and denominated "youth," yet youthhood itself remained charged with ambiguity.[14]

Almost by definition, students fell into the capacious and somewhat troubling category of youthhood. They were neither producers nor wholly dependent consumers; rather, they stood midway between the two. More than children, but somewhat less than adults, they occupied a sort of developmental gray area. College in the eighteenth century was, quite literally, a no-man's-land.[15] For just such reasons Pearson anguished over the precise form that college government should take. Nor was the debate purely academic. Questions concerning the nature of the student and structure of the college were informed by a practical concern for the future of the young nation. According to the prevailing tenets of republican political philosophy, only the economically independent were safe enough from bribery and corruption to be considered full citizens of the polis. Thus students were discouraged from political activities and self-determination out of consideration for the status quo of the country, to say nothing of the well-being of the campus. On the other hand, however, students were acknowledged to be the cream of America's youth and heirs to the political mantle; and to this extent their politicization and socialization were cautiously encouraged.[16]

Educational theorists of the eighteenth century sought to elide this problem by describing the course through college as a rite of passage from childhood to adulthood. As with other rites of passage, this one began with separation from former life (matriculation), passed through a marginal phase (student life), and led to a final aggregation into adult community (commencement). The purpose of college was to make men of boys and citizens of noncitizens.[17] Yet if college was designed to engender a transformative experience, then it still begged the question of student categorization and left an embarrassing and frequently rowdy *tertium quid* in its midst. "Too many are hurried to university, before they can estimate the value of a publick education," wrote John Clarke in discussing the tenuous ideal of youthhood. "Too young for reflection, and too old for the restraints of fear, they require all the wisdom of [college] government to keep them in tolerable subjection."[18] A lack of categorical precision and a concomitant lack of wisdom on the part of the college authorities led to the conditions that encouraged student rioting. Although liminality did not *cause* the students to riot, it did lay the foundations for a system that made public disturbance an attractive and effective means of protest.

The Problems of Students

To test the hypothesis that anxious liminality lay at the root of student misbehavior, we need only examine the writings of the students themselves. As befit liminal beings, they frequently complained of their marginalization in terms that suggested emasculation or arrested growth. In a rousing republican poem of 1769, a student implored "the sons of H******d then / to let them [i.e., the tutors] know, that they are sons of men." In reality, however, as another unhappy youth put it, the new student at Harvard was expected to "shake off the man, and assume the mere scholar," where the phrase "mere scholar" implied an unsatisfactory state between childhood and manhood. A third went further still, stating that the college rules tended to enslave students and "degrade them to the position of schoolboys."[19] Almost every aspect of the student's life at Harvard was shaped by the faculty's perception of student liminality, according to which college youths were, if more than schoolboys, still less than adults.[20]

The example of pedagogical theory is instructive. According to eighteenth-century philosophers, the basis of intellectual development lay in the faculty known as reason. Reason was the capacity that enabled an individual to discriminate between truth and falsehood, between the beautiful and the repulsive, and between right and wrong. As adherents of the school of "rational intuitionism," Harvard professors believed reason to be an inherent faculty of the human mind, yet one that needed to be nurtured, developed, and protected. A contemporary essayist put the matter this way: "cultivated and undebauched, reason discerns and approves the things that are excellent; applauds the exercise of piety and the practice of virtue, as highly befitting rational creatures; and condemns vice as unbecoming and mean." In short, the essayist argued, "Reason is the characteristick of man."[21] Yet what of those who were not quite men? In another essay the same author described studenthood in no uncertain terms as that "season in life when the spirits are in the briskest flow, and when the passions are the most indulgent, and the whole animal machinery is playing its pranks against reason, virtue and order."[22] In sum, and according to such thinking, lack of restraint meant that students could not qualify as men. The minds of children and youths were constantly under threat from the passions: those surly and disruptive feelings that focused on selfish and shortsighted gratification of the baser appetites. Neither children nor men, the students of Harvard hung in a developmental limbo. While they might readily be shaped into young republicans, they were equally susceptible to the blandishments of tyrants and infidels, fads, and factions.

Alive to the threats of passion and pride, Harvard's pedagogues sought to craft a curriculum that was at once rationalistic and moral, and that instilled discipline and rigidity.[23] Emphasis was placed on the classics, with Greek and Latin forming a large part of the curriculum. Some rudimentary attention was also paid to metaphysics, natural philosophy, and divinity. Appropriately enough the centerpiece of the eighteenth-century curriculum was the course in moral philosophy.[24] Ordinarily taught by the president of the college, the moral philosophy course emphasized the rational basis of right thought and right action. It was here, above all, that students were to learn the arts of restraint and probity. Optional classes were offered in both Hebrew and French, but other than those, there were no electives. The basic technique of teaching was the recitation of memorized passages from the various texts: a method that was held to discipline the faculties of the mind even as it instilled sound and moral wisdom. Students were also taught to declaim in public, since the skills of oratory were held to be vital to those who were to be the citizens of a republic. And public speaking competitions were instituted to encourage a sense of competitiveness among the students. The result of this republican zeal was a lifeless and uninspiring curriculum that failed to address the needs of either the preprofessionals or the scholastically inclined.

Student David Kendall lambasted the whole notion of the classical curriculum of Greek and Latin. At "venerable HARVARD," he wrote, "we behold thousands of dollars expended, and vast accumulations of time consumed for the attainment of—what? If we call it a species of coin, it is not in currency; it serves ne[i]ther the purposes of commerce, nor of domestic intercourse. Yet it is suffered to occupy one half the circle of academic studies; while many useful, pleasing and important sciences are scarcely admitted within the consecrated walls."[25] William Austin agreed. At Harvard, he wrote, "the votary of the belles-lettres and the lover of philosophy, the poet and the mathematician, the witty and the dull, are all expected, nay, obliged, to pursue the same course, to breath the same air, and be subject to the same discipline."[26] Even those who supported the classical curriculum were appalled by the methods of teaching employed and shared a contempt for what Joseph Dennie called "that nonsensical syllogistical mode of reasoning which the united *wisdom* of the President and Tutors prescribes."[27] John Quincy Adams, for example, pointed out the worthlessness of recitations in which a student regurgitated "the two first Lines" of a paragraph, leaving "the rest for the Tutor to explain, which he commonly does, by saying over again the words of the author."[28] To dull materials and an inane method of teaching them was added an excessively rigorous schedule that kept a student on his toes for hours at a time. John Quincy Adams described a typical day in his college diary for 1786:

> This morning at 6. we went to Prayers, after which we immediately recited. This took until 7 ¼. At 7 ½ we breakfasted, at 10 we had a Lecture on Divinity from Mr. Wigglesworth. . . . At 11 we had a Philosophical Lecture from Mr. Williams upon the mechanical powers. . . . At 12 ½, Dinner. At 3, an Astronomical public Lecture upon the planet Mercury. . . . At 4. again we recited, and at 5, attended prayers again, after which there are no more exercises for this day, but we are obliged in the evening to Prepare our recitation for to-morrow morning.[29]

Such was the academic regime held best by the faculty for the training of young minds, which were otherwise all too apt to stray into dangerous studies or general profligacy.

Concern to limit and shape the direction of intellectual inquiry is also seen in the college's library policy. Although Harvard possessed one of the largest and richest collections of books in the nation, access to its holdings was severely restricted. Only seniors and juniors were allowed to visit the library. Visiting times were restricted to two hours, once every three weeks, and the students were permitted to withdraw no more than three volumes per visit. The selection of freely circulating books was strictly limited to those on a faculty-approved list. Students who wished to withdraw books not on the list required a special letter from either a tutor or the president before being allowed to withdraw them.[30] The rationale behind both the approved list and the limitations on access was not so much a concern for the fabric of the books, but (as with the curriculum) for the fabric of the students' minds. As the introduction to Harvard's 1773 catalogue of approved books explained, most of the library's books were "above the comprehension of Younger Students." Hence the "briefer Catalogue, to wit, of Books which are better adopted to their use."[31] In 1791 the college government pushed this idea to an extreme by publicly forbidding any student to buy or read Edward Gibbon's *Decline and Fall of the Roman Empire.*[32] As if to ensure the hegemony of the college curriculum, the *Laws* also expressly forbade students from seeking any tutoring or instruction outside the college walls, on pain of a heavy fine, or in the case of repetition of the offense, degradation or rustication.[33]

Emphasis on restraint and control of student behavior extended beyond the classroom and the library and into the wider realm of student activity. One of the most striking features of college life in the eighteenth century was just how thoroughly well regulated it was. College in the eighteenth century very closely approximated what sociologist Erving Goffman has called a "total institution," this being "a place of residence and work where a large number of like-situated individuals, cut off from the wider society for an appreciable period of time, together lead an enclosed, formally administered round of life."[34] The college *Laws* laid out a schedule that defined a student's entire day from waking to retiring. Each day began at six o'clock with mandatory attendance at chapel, services beginning well before sunrise during the winter months; moved through a thirty-minute breakfast in the commons; and then proceeded to a full day of classes. Evening chapel and dinner in the commons rounded out the day, after which students were required to withdraw to their rooms to study. After nine at night, students were expected to be in their own residence and to curtail all activity. At no time was a student permitted to deviate from the schedule or its dictates. The ringing of the chapel bell was used to regulate and advertise the schedule and make sure that all members of the college community were aware of the time, and roving tutors were also employed to make sure that students obeyed the rules.

Because the rules of the college were unpopular, and because students could not be trusted to abide by them without threat of reprisal, the government instituted a variety of punishments for lawbreakers. For minor infractions of the rules, there were fines ranging from a penny for arriving late at chapel to twenty shillings for leaving town for more than a week without permission. More serious crimes demanded more serious punishments. These included (in roughly ascending order) private admonition and public admonition, degradation, suspension, rustication, and expulsion. Degradation entailed the lowering of a student's academic standing in his class. Those suspended were required to leave the school for varying periods of time and study with a minister, while those rusticated had, in addition, to receive a good report from their pater familias before they were allowed to return to college and were degraded upon returning to

Cambridge. Expulsion was reserved for the severest infractions. Among the many crimes for which strict punishments were offered, the *Laws* listed "contempt of the lawful authority of the College," "violence, or any heinous insult, to any of the Governours of the College," and bringing "dishonour and disturbance" to the college.[35]

Perhaps the most oppressive aspect of the college rules was their utterly non-negotiable status. The college government dictated its laws from on high, and student commentary on them was almost, by definition, considered an impertinence. Occasionally students presented petitions or made a deputation to the president or faculty. In December 1787, for example, a number of students visited President Willard to dispute "an unjust pecuniary punishment" levied against them for tarrying in the dining hall "a little while after supper." Although Willard promised the students a further "hearing," he defaulted on the promise, and the more than thirty petitioners were fined a hefty ten shillings each without further ado.[36] The faculty and tutors seemed to pay scant attention to the students at all, other than policing their minds and their movements.

Explicit rules delimited the nature and tenor of student-faculty interaction. "The President and the Professors were never approached," recalled one otherwise very content student, "except in the most formal way, and upon official occasions; and in the college yard (if I remember rightly) no student was permitted to keep his hat on if one of the Professors was there."[37] When President Willard was approached by a student, it was his unerring habit to ask, "Well child, what do you want?"[38] With a student body that included some "children" aged twenty-seven, this could not have been perceived as other than inaccurate and demeaning. Relations with the tutors were even more strained. Most of the tutorial staff were fresh out of college and were rarely more than a few years older than their charges. In some cases they were younger than the oldest seniors. Yet because of their salaried, independent position, they were considered men, while the students under their tutelage were deemed children or, at best, youths. To assert their authority and maintain a sense of differentiation from their charges, the tutors tended to adopt a crushingly supercilious attitude toward the students. In a letter to his friend at Harvard, Joseph Dennie commended a rare tutor, Thomas Thompson, "who disgraces himself, by descending from the heights of his genius and virtue, to associate with solemn blockheads."[39] The aloofness of the teaching staff has been explained by Robert A. McCaughey, who argues that professors and tutors at Harvard only slowly developed an ethic of professionalism. Even in the 1820s the majority of the teaching staff were insiders—locally born and Harvard educated, but with limited academic aspirations. Most tutors did not hold their position for more than a few years, while the position of professor was rare enough to be something of an anomaly. For both this led to status anxieties vis-à-vis the students and the larger community, and resulted in a harsher enforcement of the college regime.[40]

Failing to define specifically the nature of the students in their charge, the tutors and professors were scarcely able to construct a functional self-image. In this confused and confusing environment, student grievances were forced underground where they festered and where resentments grew to the point of explosiveness.

A Taxonomy of Student Resistance at Harvard

In his diary for 1793 student Daniel Appleton White recorded a particularly memorable encounter between a disorderly student and the college government. "This morning," wrote White, "Leonard, [a] junior, was rusticated, and after sentence read to him, he put on his hat and desired the President to proceed, who thereupon ordered him to leave the Chapel. But he replied 'By no means—go on Sir, and don't be so big, but tell me the whole story, &c.'"[41] Leonard's insolence and backchat were highly motivated, and displayed a clear contempt for the notion of students as children. By donning his hat, desiring to hear "the whole story," and demanding that the president be not "so big," Leonard was suggesting that he was socially and intellectually the equal of an adult such as Willard and his professoriat. Such encounters were rare, but we need not therefore suppose that the sentiments expressed were unique to Leonard alone.

Of course there *were* those such as Leonard who spoke their minds when they felt they had nothing to lose, such as when they were being punished or graduated. One student, upon being degraded, announced that "he should leave a society, the government of which is actuated by *malice,* & whose decisions are founded in *prejudice,*" while another seized a large cane and swung it around and around, shouting, "It is all a damned lie; you are a pack of devils, and I despise you."[42] Others felt comfortable expressing their frustrations to their fellow sufferers. Joseph Dennie, who was suspended in 1789, wrote to a college friend of the delights of rural life: "Here are no interruptions, no *unseasonable* morning prayers, no Abbots, and no damned fools."[43] And finally we have instances of anonymous written critiques: William Austin's *Strictures on Harvard College* (1798), which comprised the most systematic indictment of Harvard in this period; Willard Phillips's manuscript "Anti-Don-Quixotism"; and an anonymous poem, entitled *A True Description of a Number of Tyrannical Pedagogues* (1769). All make it clear that students harbored a variety of grievances against the Harvard regime. Topics of contention included poor food, poor teaching, an inadequate curriculum, rigid laws, haughty tutors, partial professors, and lack of redress for any and all grievances. Nor were the students lacking in solutions.

Benjamin Church wrote of an unpopular tutor in his Commonplace Book in the 1750s:

> If he attempts to box, let him attempt in vain,
> Or hold his Hands, or box ye Fiend again:
> Strike where he Strikes: to quit ye Battle scorn,
> But Stroke for Stroke and threat for threat return.[44]

Yet as sociologist James C. Scott has argued, a prevailing feature of oppressive institutions is their tendency to "deny subordinates the luxury of negative reciprocity: trading a slap for a slap, an insult for an insult."[45] To directly attack the college or its representatives was to face immediate and massive reprisals. It is more typical, according to Scott, for persons living under oppressive systems to express their feelings anonymously, in order to avoid recrimination, or to express them obliquely, veiling their true sentiments behind a facade of compliance and docility. The "weapons of the weak," as Scott has called them, typically include euphemistic criticism, anonymous threats, strategic sabotage, and foot-dragging, all of which one finds at Harvard in the eighteenth century. After a night of deliberate and destructive sabotage around the college, student John Henry Tudor confided to his diary: "I have been thought by the government a very *steady* fellow. But they have acted so infamously lately, that as the scholars always come off badly when they are independent, *sneaking* methods are justifiable."[46] Tudor was able to get away with his sabotage safely because he was so far above reproach in the eyes of his betters. The "sneaking" was always best perpetrated by the allegedly "steady."

The very gap between such anonymous acts and the public personae of their perpetrators makes the former hard to decode. Scott argues that "sneaking" acts become meaningful only when framed by the "hidden transcript" of subaltern grievance. And interpreting the students' acts in the light of their more obtrusive verbal criticisms, one can see both existing on the same spectrum and embodying the same ideological criticisms of the Harvard regime. Yet even when such a contextualizing frame is not readily available, one can discern a criticism of the official notion of studenthood, for as Erving Goffman has explained: "To forgo prescribed activities, or to engage in them in unprescribed ways or for unprescribed purposes, is to withdraw from the official self and the world officially available to it. To prescribe an activity is to prescribe a world; to dodge a prescription is to dodge an identity."[47] If we look closely at the disorderly behaviors of the Harvard students, it will become apparent that many felt the same way as Leonard, Austin, and Phillips, nursed the same grievances, and held the same ideals, but lacked the temerity or articulateness of their brethren.

Among the many varieties of obtrusive disorder at Harvard, we can identify four main categories: group rowdiness, individual acts of sabotage, material appropriation and theft, and specific violations of the rules, each of which can be interpreted as embodying an ideological critique of the governance practiced at the college.

Group disorders have often given the impression of being irrational or undirected expressions of anger. Daniel Appleton White, for example, supposed that they were the result of excessive drinking, while for other, older, interpreters they were held to be the result of a sinful disposition.[48] It seems much more likely, however, that the student disorders were the result of specific grievances, for they seemed to occur again and again at the same junctures: when unpopular edicts were handed down, when lectures were particularly dry, and when the food was especially unpalatable. Again, they tend to crop up at those points where the students as a whole felt themselves being overly dominated by the rules.

Group disorders had the advantage of relative anonymity and flexibility: several of a crowd could create brief disruption and then blend back into the throng without identification.[49] To assure their anonymity, agents provocateurs tended away from the verbal. When entering and leaving both the chapel and the commons, they resorted to jostling and pushing.[50] Sometimes the rowdiness verged on sabotage, as it did on the occasions when those within a room would deliberately block the door to impede ingress and cause havoc. More often, however, it seemed to be an expression of resistance to being herded in and out of buildings. In other shows of group disorder, students scraped their feet, dropped coins, laughed derisively, and whistled to show their boredom and anger. Doing more was unsafe. Students also developed a language of hoots and animal noises to convey their feelings. Tutor Alden Bradford was assailed with hisses and a "low *goose*-like manifestation of displeasure" whenever he prayed in the chapel, and Eliphalet Pearson reported "certain gutteral sounds . . . beside some whistling" when he stood to preach.[51] The use of these inarticulate noises, as mentioned, allowed the students to express their disapprobation quickly and safely from the relative anonymity of a crowd. The animal noises in particular carried a very specific and conventional set of meanings. As White records in his journal, they were sometimes used even when tutors were not present. One day in commons, he recalled, the lamb "was *strong* and *unsavory,* exciting all sorts of *animal* noises among the students in the Hall, in imitation of *sheep* & c—kicking legs of mutton about and throwing one into the College yard. When the tutors appeared, all of course, were careful to avoid detection, and the shameful transaction probably passed off, if not without investigation, yet without any notice adequate to a prevention in future."[52] In this instance, and possibly in others, we see a collective articulation of what James C. Scott calls the "hidden transcript" of the oppressed;

in this case the students' mocking suggestion that they were being fed food that was not fit for animals, let alone men. The point was more than metaphorical, for according to one student, "it seems almost to be a maxim among the Governors of the College, to treat the students pretty much like brute Beasts."[53]

These collective vocalizations of dissatisfaction were the result of and tended to reinforce a group mentality predicated upon shared grievances. Their infectious and spontaneous nature suggests a sense of frustration that was shared by many, if not all, who were present. Pearson referred on several occasions to nearly a whole class indulging in hooting and laughter, and the comparative safety with which such demonstrations could be made probably meant that they were the most widely participated in form of protest among the members of the student body.

In addition to the spontaneous disorders described above, one finds many accounts of sabotage. Like the crowd noises and jostling, sabotage was an anonymous form of resistance: an action in which the agent was always one remove from the scene of the crime. And again, as with the practice of mobbing and jeering, it was always targeted at specific areas of college life. The most frequent target for student saboteurs was the chapel in Harvard Hall. Symbolically the chapel was a locus of official power. There the students met every morning to pray according to the dictates of the college's congregational polity; there, too, the president, professors, and tutors appeared in what was a daily show of power; in the chapel the students were preached to by the college authorities and public punishments were handed down; the chapel housed the bell by which the daily schedule was regulated; and finally the morning chapel service was the first and hence most important event in the daily schedule. To the extent that the morning service or the operation of the chapel could be disrupted, the whole college routine could be delayed or possibly brought to a standstill. This point was hardly lost on the students. One popular act of sabotage included stealing or damaging the bell during the night, thereby ensuring that students could not be awakened for services.[54] On several occasions the chapel candles were stolen so that the predawn services had to be conducted in the dark; these also made yet further disorders easy to perpetrate and hard to ascribe to identifiable students.[55] When neither bell breaking nor candle snuffing was possible, students stole the chapel Bible so that the preacher was not able to offer a homily upon any given text.[56] At their most damaging, student saboteurs were able to accomplish all three at once; when those acts were not possible, students threw stones through the windows of the detested structure. Attacks on the chapel expressed a generally disruptive and destructive attitude on the part of the saboteurs, but also showed them striking out at the most visible manifestation of the college's power base.

A third form of disorderly behavior at Harvard was theft. Acts of student larceny in the eighteenth century were almost entirely confined to the theft of material provisions such as food and firewood, and such items were almost always stolen from the college or town rather than from other students.[57] The reasons for a high incidence of food theft were fairly self-evident. By common consensus the food served in hall was bland at best, and at worst completely inedible. Following a riot over bad butter in 1766, nine barrels of butter were deemed unfit for consumption and another three "allow'd for Sauce only." Fifty years later another riot was sparked by a dinner consisting of fish and rotten cabbage. "The provisions were badly cooked," wrote student Joseph Thaxter, "the Soups were dreadful we frequently had Puddings made of Flower and Water, and boiled so hard as not to be eatable."[58] Commons was seen as a focal point for establishing college decorum, however, and for this reason if no other, both students and tutors were forbidden to dine elsewhere without the permission of the president or professors. Even though there was a buttery where students could buy extra provisions, such as sugar, biscuits, butter, and cheese, the cost was often prohibitive, and credit strictly limited to twenty-four shillings per student per quarter.[59] Practically speaking, the hungry student had three options. He could tolerate the food in commons; he could sneak into town and take an illicit second meal at Bradish's or Blood's Tavern; or he could steal food from wherever it was available. Often a student did all three. To the extent that they had already paid for their board and were required to attend hall whether they ate or not, all students were, de jure, "in commons." The option of buying a second meal at Bradish's or Blood's, while appealing, was expensive, and doubly so if a tutor caught one and levied a fine.[60] Moreover it rankled to be paying two times a day for the privilege of eating well only once. In any case few students could afford to eat in town with any regularity. Most were fairly poverty stricken, as is made evident by the frequency with which they were granted absence from classes to teach school. Thus students took to theft. Harrison Gray Otis recalled that in the 1780s it was common for students to make snares out of wire to catch and cook geese. Others were less secretive. In February 1789 a group of students burst into a townsman's house, "insisted on his dressing a Turkey, & threatened to strike him for resisting." They then traveled to Menotomy (now Arlington) where they "exchanged their turkey for beef stakes." More commonly, however, students took food and wood from the college itself. In the 1750s tutor Henry Flynt's cellar was regularly raided for its beer and brandy, while in November of 1793, hungry students made away with 2 pounds of coffee, 20 pounds of beef, 220 pounds of butter, a pail of cider, and some plates. The plates were later returned.[61] Occasionally food theft must have been undertaken out of sheer starvation. It seems much more likely, however, that appropriation of food and firewood was a reflexive indication of what E. P. Thompson has called the eighteenth century's "moral economy," according to which one took what one had paid for by means fair or foul.[62]

Individual violations of college laws by individual students are the hardest to interpret in a political light because, in truth, they often lacked a political motivation. Virtually every student at Harvard incurred fines for missing chapel services, arriving tardily, skipping classes, and failing to complete academic exercises. Again, one finds in the faculty records innumerable instances of rowdy parties, drunkenness, and protracted absences from the college. It is quite likely that most of these represented little more than youthful exuberance, social exploration, and a testing of the boundaries of legitimacy. To the extent that the students could avoid detection or harassment by the tutors, they seemed content to keep their tumultuousness in house. Disturbances escalated, however, and took on a political tone at the point at which the tutors or professors intervened and sought to take action. What almost inevitably followed was a series of increasingly hostile reprisals on the part of the students, taking the form of sabotage, violence, and vandalism against the college. The faculty's zeal for order and restraint coupled with the students' excessive concern that they should be left to their own vices and devices led the college to a state of almost perpetual guerrilla warfare. Behind all this tumult one can see the students clamoring to establish their identity as men in the face of their official status as youths.

Four Disturbances at Harvard

The disturbances of the academic year 1788–1789 began innocuously enough with a drunken student party on the night of 4 December 1788.[63] There had been an exhibition that day, with students presenting disputations and orations for the faculty; most of the students were probably celebrating the passing of this event.[64] An especially boisterous gathering in the rooms of two juniors, Roger Vose and Benjamin Whitwell, led to a visit by tutor Samuel Webber, who asked them to quiet down. As soon as he had left, however, the noise greatly increased, compelling him to return again. Webber then asked the students to break up their party immediately, whereupon two students—James and John Sullivan—refused to leave. Two more tutors were called, and they too faced the righteous ire of the students. Names were taken and the tutors retreated. The small encounter was enough to trigger six months of protracted conflict that was little short of a guerrilla war. The day following the party, a snowball was thrown at Webber while he prayed in the chapel, and that evening another party, this time of sophomores, was closed down, leading to yet further friction between tutors and students. Because the tutors had had the misfortune to discipline members of three out of the four classes, they met uncommonly well-mobilized and unanimous resistance. Before the week was out, every tutor in college had his windows broken. The faculty met on 6 January to investigate the infractions, privately admonished

James Sullivan, and compelled John, who had been drunk, to sign a confession of guilt. The reading of this confession on 9 December in the chapel was the final straw for the students. Not only had their harmless fun been interfered with on two occasions, but one of their number was forced to submit to a ritual of public humiliation. During the reading of the confession, according to Pearson, "there was such a scraping" that the president "could not be heard."[65] At breakfast that day there was an all-out riot in which crockery and cutlery were thrown at the tutors, at chapel in the evening the lights were extinguished, and at night stones were hurled through many windows. The disorders continued all week. The following week the tempo increased: Professors Pearson and Wigglesworth were stoned in their lectures, and the chapel was ransacked by the students. On 20 December the faculty decided to crush the rebellion by suspending Jonathan Bowman six months for breaking windows, John Howard six months for blowing out the chapel candles, and by degrading Abraham Ellery to the bottom of his class for stone throwing.[66] Rather than cowing the students, however, the punishments provoked them to greater heights of disorder. Ellery stood up and denounced the president and faculty in the chapel (for which he was further punished), guns were fired in the yard at night, and more windows were broken. From its inauspicious beginnings at Whitwell and Vose's ill-starred party, the disorders spiraled out of control: for the next six months there were acts of violence and vandalism almost every day, and the fire was dampened only by the eventual suspension of two students (Benjamin Trapier and William Read), the rustication of a third (Daniel Russell), mass finings, and the timely arrival of summer recess. The pattern seen in this and almost every other disorder of this period was one of faculty discipline and student reprisal, followed by harsher disciplinary actions and more destructive retaliations by the students. As Willard Phillips put the matter: "it has always been customary among the Students to betake themselves to . . . disorders when they thought a Classmate injured."[67] The chain reactions engendered by faculty/student confrontation clearly suggest that the two groups were operating under almost wholly incompatible conceptions of justice, the enactment of one provoking the response of the other.

The disturbances of 1791, by contrast, began with the institution of an unpopular new college rule regarding public examinations. In an attempt to "animate the Students in the pursuit of literary merit and fame, and to excite in their breasts a noble spirit of emulation," the immediate government introduced a series of oral examinations for all classes, to be conducted by the professoriat along with the members of the corporation and the overseers. All subjects were to be covered, and those who excelled in the examinations were to be "recommended to the peculiar favours and honours of the University," which is to say that they would receive scholarships and commendations at graduation. Those who declined attending the examination were to be "fined a sum not exceeding twenty shillings, or . . . admonished or suspended."[68] The whole idea of the public examinations proved to be extremely unpopular with the students, but for two different reasons. In the first place it was held to be unseemly for the upper two classes to be examined in such a public way. It had never been done before, and as such it violated the unwritten traditions or customs of the college. Because students had no written rights or charter, college "customs" were an embodiment of liberties, and a violation of a custom such as this was, de facto, an infringement of liberties. Several earlier disturbances had begun in just such a way, for as Willard Phillips explained: "at College precedent is considered as weighty a consideration as expediency at other places."[69] There was also the issue of grandfathering. According to one student, it was "a very impolitic thing to enforce an examination upon classes, which entered before the law was in being."[70]

The second reason for student hostility toward the exams was more substantive. Many believed that the standards used by the faculty in evaluating student attainments were unnecessarily rigid and made no provision for individualism or, to use the students' term, *genius*. In what was essentially a protoromantic argument for creative originality, the students claimed that the academic award system forced those desirous of literary recognition into mindless conformity to outmoded aesthetic and intellectual standards. True creativity was crushed, while a debased literary form of pandering took its place. "Parts," or literary honors, became, in the words of one student, "the political engine of [college] government."[71] More practically the exams tended to be incredibly superficial. According to the calculations of President Willard's son, each undergraduate could be expected to undergo approximately two minutes of examination per subject studied; enough time to falter horribly and make mistakes, but not enough to show genius or talent.[72] By turning scrutiny on all students at once, the honors system provoked anguish and frustration among the literarily ambitious and the scholastically mundane alike.

Uniting as a collective, the senior and junior classes petitioned the overseers for exemption from the examinations, but the board overruled their plea, and the faculty forged ahead.[73] The students struck back. On 11 April, the day before the first round of the examinations were to take place, a plot was hatched by three juniors—Justin Ely, William Sullivan, and Benjamin Trapiert—to sabotage the proceedings by placing a powerful laxative in the commons water supply. This was done on the following morning, and the results were appalling; during the examinations, as the faculty records note, "a great number of those who breakfasted in Hall were puked, and some of them violently." About 150 students "left the hall, some in a slow, others in a hurried manner, but all plainly showing that their situation was by no means a pleasant one." In an attempt to avoid implication, the conspirators drank heavily from the tainted water, but one of them having been seen loitering near the copper boilers, the ruse was exposed and the culprits captured.[74]

The following day, sophomore Henry Jones threw a stone through the window of the examining room, showering the professors, president, and visiting dignitaries with an explosion of broken glass, and striking Governor Hancock's chair. The faculty were quick in responding. Jones was expelled the following day, Sullivan and Ely were suspended, Trapier (a persistent offender) was rusticated, and five other students were fined and admonished for window-breaking offenses and generally disorderly behavior.[75] The disturbance was rapidly quelled for two reasons. First, students were mindful of the severity of the punishments handed down: the college almost never expelled or rusticated a student where suspension or admonition would do. And second, the new rules clearly affected the student body unevenly. While some felt that their creativity was being unduly scrutinized, and others believed that their sloth was about to be publicly revealed, a substantial number were willing to work with the new system in the confidence that they would benefit from the awards promised them. Nevertheless, disturbances on this issue continued sporadically and often violently for the next five years, until the system was eventually abolished.[76]

The third example of disorder at Harvard also came about as the result of the institution of a new rule in 1791, this time concerning the arrangements for serving food in commons. The problem began when the steward complained that many students coming out of chapel in the evening were going directly into the kitchen and helping themselves to food rather than waiting to be served by the college waiters. Access to wholesome food in substantial amounts was, as we have already seen, a point of great contention among the college students, and no doubt their invasion of kitchen space was in part prompted by a desire to get the food they felt they deserved. Thus when the faculty determined that a new serving counter was to be erected that would stop students from getting into the kitchen area to help themselves, they encountered great resistance.[77] For the week following the imposition of the new rule there was great disorder in commons, with students throwing food, overturning tables, and literally forcing their way into the kitchen to get what they wanted. Again the college acted swiftly and severely, rusticating one (Thomas? Bowman), suspending two (Thomas Paine and S. Gardiner Whipple), and admonishing three (Charles Angier, John Appleton, and Francis Cabot Lowell).[78]

The fourth and final example of disorder at Harvard was the most complex and bizarre. The problems began on 6 November 1793, when three students smashed open a pantry window and stole coffee and sundry provisions from the college store. The following week a cellar was broken into and significantly larger quantities of food taken (described above).[79] Ordinarily food theft was not associated with nondietary grievances by the students, nor was it used as a punitive gesture, but in this case it seemed to represent wider issues of discontent. The date of the first break-in is a crucial clue for such an interpretation. In the first place the initial break-in occurred the night before Thanksgiving, and it is evident that the food was taken for the purpose of celebrating that event. Less obvious is the fact that the previous evening had been Guy Fawkes Night. By popular tradition, it was a day for revelry, bonfires, and general disorder, and among the students, it was a flashpoint for disturbances.[80] The college firmly forbade bonfires (which in any case were a customary gesture of student anger) and just before the fifth, the immediate government threatened dire consequences for anyone caught celebrating on Guy Fawkes Night. Unhappiness at the peremptory edict might explain the two break-ins; certainly it would go a long way toward explaining why the first two acts of theft led almost immediately to a far greater wave of disorder.

The problems began early on the morning of 18 November, when a basket of candles was stolen while the chapel bell was being rung, thereby forcing the students to attend services in the dark. That night a group of students broke into the chapel belfry, dismantled the bell, and heaved it out a window, causing it to crash through the library roof. On their way out, they stole the preacher's Bible, broke the clock, and for good measure smashed a window. The following night the replacement Bible, costing twenty dollars, was stolen, and the night following that, yet another disappeared.[81] Possibly because the provocation for the acts was not glaringly egregious, they failed to garner universal support. In any case many felt that they were an insult to the college and to the student body, and after the third Bible had been stolen, the members of the junior and senior classes decided to form a Society to Discourage the Perpetration of Crimes and put an end to the disorders.[82] The founder of the organization, Joseph Perkins, made up a subscription form that circulated among the junior and senior classes, getting forty-one names, at which point he presented the list and a statement of intent to the faculty.[83] At evening prayers on the twenty-third, President Willard announced the existence of the society opposing disorders and made known their "determination to expose in future as far as they may be able, the Authors and Abettors thereof, that they maybe brought to condign punishments."[84] The announcement was greeted with hisses and yells by some, and with silence by others. The existence of the society marked a wholly unprecedented and highly threatening rupture within the student body. Loyalty was among the highest of student virtues, and even those who disapproved of another's actions were bound by tradition against informing on them. Timothy Fuller Jr. wrote of another disturbance only five years later: "Custom has established it as a point of honor among students never to give information against each other, and although I felt inclined to contribute to the punishment of the violators of decorum in a sacred place, yet I felt that I must keep silent."[85] To organize an informing society was a total breach of student custom.

The dissident students were not to be intimidated, however. As if to show their intention of continuing the campaign, they stole two Indian artifacts from the yard of Professor Winthrop the following evening, and carefully booby-trapped a brass chandelier in the chapel. The following night the students were rowdy and unsettled, and when the heavy chandelier fell to the floor, mayhem broke loose. Following the service, dissident students blocked the chapel door from the outside and demanded that it be opened by the "informing club." The challenge was not taken up. The following morning the students were greeted by the gruesome sight of an effigy in the likeness of Perkins hanging from a tree in the yard, with the word *Judas* hung on a placard around its neck. At breakfast the effigy was carried into hall, and later that day an anonymous note was posted announcing Perkins's imminent execution.[86] The use of the effigy and execution was replete with meaning. As E. P. Thompson has explained, such "Charivaris" were customarily adopted in the eighteenth century to punish those guilty of violating community norms; in this case the violation of the custom of silence. The custom was taken in deadly earnest. Thompson writes: "To burn, bury or read the funeral service over someone still living was a terrible community judgement, in which the victim was made into an outcast, one considered already dead. It was the ultimate in excommunication."[87] Two days later, scuffles broke out leaving the chapel. The "high bucks," wrote one student, "when shut up in the Entry, thumped some of the informing society." Outside in the yard, senior Jesse Olds was savagely beaten by another student, and a huge crowd gathered to watch until the fray was broken up by tutor William Barron.[88]

Despite its setbacks, however, the informing society managed to do its work. On 1 December a rumor began to circulate among the students that the thieves had been identified. The day of reckoning came soon. For stealing food, senior S. Gardiner Whipple and sophomores Aspinwall and Wetmore were rusticated; and for abetting the crime, sophomores Russell, Lador, Charles Cushing, and Peter Thacher were suspended. For stealing Professor Winthrop's Indian images, blocking the chapel doors, punching a senior, and threatening others, sophomore Amory was rusticated and, upon protesting his punishment, was summarily expelled. For disturbances in the chapel, sophomores John Leighton Tuttle and Samuel Welles and freshman Thomas Fargues were suspended, and freshman George Wingate was publicly admonished. For punching a classmate who was trying to leave the chapel, student Appleton was suspended five months. For stealing three Bibles from the chapel, junior Leonard was rusticated, and for the original raid of 6 November, juniors Israel Eliot Trask, Thomas Cordis, and

Ebenezer Lawrence and sophomore David Smiley were suspended.[89] Thus ended what was possibly the most sustained and vicious spate of disorders at Harvard in the eighteenth century.

The Political Culture of the Harvard Students

To summarize thus far, there seem to have been two basic provocations for disorderly behavior at Harvard, underpinned by a single conceptual grievance. On the one hand, students resented the crass and authoritarian way in which the educational agenda of the college was forced upon them, especially insofar as their efforts to negotiate or petition the authorities were so singularly unsuccessful. On the other hand, they tended to lash out at the overly officious interference of the tutors and professors in their social and extracurricular avocations. The two were often hard to separate because both were predicated on the students' conviction that they should be treated as men and not children or animals. Men had rights and rights could always be violated. And from the point of view of the faculty, there was little difference between an academic and an extracurricular misdemeanor, since either one indicated a disregard for the due authority of the immediate government of the college and demanded instant punishment. Thus most disturbances, whether ideologically motivated or not, eventually took on a thoroughly political tone. The progression from pedagogy to politics was laid out with great clarity by William Austin: "Where a manly independence is construed into insolence and contempt of authority; and a meek spirit of passive obedience and non-resistance the only road to College honor . . . what are the State to expect? Courtiers or Republicans? Creatures or men?"[90] To students at Harvard, the issue became one of protecting their rights as men and citizens.

In mentioning "Republicans," Austin referred, of course, not to the Republican Party, but to the tradition of classical republicanism that functioned in eighteenth-century America as a powerful and cohesive language of politics and morality.[91] According to the tenets of this tradition, the well-being of the state depended on a virtuous citizenry; one that was willing to act publicly and place the interests of the polis above those of any individual or group of individuals. Virtue, so the argument ran, was based upon property ownership because only property owners were sufficiently independent to escape the blandishments of wealthy tyrants and self-serving factions; it was also predicated upon reason, since the ability to restrain the passions of greed and avarice was essential to the smooth functioning of the state. To be a courtier, on the other hand, was to eschew virtue, for courtiers placed their desires above those of the common good and sought to further these ends by selling their allegiance to the most promising power broker available. Austin's juxtaposition of republican and courtier with man and creature was not incidental, since the definition of a virtuous citizen (financially and intellectually independent) was also that of a man, while that of a courtier implied unmanliness.[92] Within the classical republican tradition, the state was seen as being under constant threat from the passionate, including both tyrants and mobs: the former indicated too much power in the hands of government, and the latter indicated its total absence. A delicate organism that comprised the sum of its constituents, the republic might succumb at any time to vice and corruption, and so constant vigilance was required. History was littered with stories of states that had given way to luxury, licentiousness, and vice, or to tyranny and despotism, and by so doing had spiraled into destruction. Such narratives formed the backbone of the Greek and Latin curricula at Harvard.[93] Austin was implying, in effect, that to rob students of their independence, and to shackle them to a system too enamored of rigid conformity, as Harvard had done—in short, to treat students as less than men—was to train up a generation who would lack the backbone, manly independence, and republican virtue necessary to sustain the state. Moreover it implied that the immediate government of the college was nothing less than a dictatorship.

Others were quite explicit. Students referred to an unpopular academic rule enacted in 1768 as a species of "Turkish Tyranny," knowing full well that the Turks were considered to be the consummately despotic nation. A year later another student published a scurrilous poem offering "A True Description of a Number of Tyrannical Pedagogues." A decade or so later another writer, possibly John Quincy Adams, referred to President Willard as a "tyrant," while later still Joseph Dennie denounced the college's "pigmy despotism."[94] A common meeting place for protesting students between Massachusetts and Harvard Halls became known as the Liberty Tree, and unpopular rules were deemed "unconstitutional."[95] The language of classical republicanism offered a powerful explanatory paradigm that placed the relationship of students and tutors in a charged moral and political context.

Yet the language of republicanism provided not only a model of the ideal society; it also laid out an elaborate justification for rebellion and revolution, in the name of social survival. The disorderly students saw themselves as men deprived of the rights of men, who were fighting for their independence from tyranny and domination.[96] Perhaps the most compelling evidence for the existence of a republican mentality at Harvard is the fact that by the time the century had turned, it had become the target of satire by those who felt the idea had been entirely overworked. With great sarcasm, Joseph Tufts ridiculed the students' rhetoric of republicanism and their talk of manhood:

> What student that has the least tincture of humanity, would not feel his blood boil within him, at seeing the most severe and despotic power of

the government exercised in sending into exile some of his comrads, for no other crime, perhaps, than drowning with a little noise the melancholy toll of the clock, striking the ghostly hour of midnight, and for just sallying out, and enlivening the dreary stillness of the night, by the cheerful tinkling, excited by the shattering to pieces a few glass windows. . . . The high resentment of some of the students at this horrid abuse in the government, was therefore just and manly.[97]

If students at Harvard tended to frequent acts of resistance and rebellion, then this can at least in part be explained by the fact that they lived in a society that explicitly sanctioned such acts; that had undertaken them at the national level; and that regarded them, mutatis mutandis, as nothing less than the very survival mechanism of a perpetually endangered political system. Thus when Joseph Dennie wrote to a Harvard friend, imploring him to "Inform me of the College affairs, the Revolutions in our class & c.," we know that his reference to Revolution was anything but tongue in cheek.[98]

It goes without saying that the dissident students appropriated the language of republicanism to their own ends. Their understanding of the rights of men resembled less that of an Adams or a Jefferson than a distinctly artisanal version of the republican tradition that had manifested in the works of Thomas Paine as well as in the mob actions in Boston in the 1760s and 1770s. Artisanal republicanism was an egalitarian, populist, rights-based radicalism that meted out summary justice to those who would deny its believers their privileges.[99] When denied these "rights of men," the students resisted on terms and in ways informed by a radical republican vision.

The Social Structure of Student Life at Harvard

Although we now have a clear idea of both how and why the students rebelled, the genesis, structure, and maintenance of the students' organization are much less evident. To come to grips with the nature of student disorder, it is necessary to address the following questions: In what ways did students mix at Harvard? What forms of friendship existed? What opportunities were there for association? What constraints, if any, shaped modes of student affiliation? How unified was the student body? And if there were competing forms of socialization at the college, how did they interact vis-à-vis the struggle with the immediate government?

One thing is certain: the newly arriving freshmen did not bring any substantially intact social networks with them. The admission books and faculty records suggest that incoming students were essentially strangers to one another. While a handful were educated together at the Latin School in Boston, most came from a generous scattering of towns and villages around Massachusetts and, to a lesser extent, Connecticut and New Hampshire, with a few hailing from the South and from the West Indies. Educated by local ministers and recent graduates, the new students arrived in Cambridge with very little social baggage.

For students at Harvard the primary social context was the class system. Although there were four classes constantly in residence at Harvard, casual socialization between them was limited. Almost from the moment a youth arrived, he was ritually isolated from the older students and defined as a member of the entering class. At the beginning of each academic year the sophomores challenged the new freshmen to a group wrestling match; they also practiced various forms of hazing, such as throwing water over the sleeping first years and stealing their sheets.[100] More generally there was a separation of the classes. Each class was assigned its own pastoral tutor; each class studied together, sat together in commons and the chapel, was examined together, and boarded together.[101] Students in each class, moreover, were immediately identifible by their differing dress. Freshmen wore jackets with plain buttonholes and no cuff buttons; sophomores, plain buttonholes with cuff buttons; juniors, buttonholes with frogs (braiding), except at the cuff, and cuff buttons; and seniors, cuff buttons and frogs on all buttonholes. After much resistance on the part of the students, the system was abolished in 1797.[102] Yet because of this de facto segregation, students socialized almost exclusively within their respective academic classes.

The academic class was the most powerful unit of social organization legitimately sanctioned by the college, and the *Laws* went so far as to allow class meetings to be held upon occasion.[103] Among each class, according to Sidney Willard, "there grows up a strong, centralized feeling, as of many members of one body. . . . The whole class meets in democratic mass, as occasion for legitimate object requires, and, duly organized, they conduct their proceedings by parliamentary rules; so that no faction is likely to be strong enough to destroy the unity of the body. The only danger is that of subordination to a higher power."[104] The solidarity of the academic class is well captured in William Biglow's 1792 poem, "Classology," in which the members of the class of 1794 are described partaking in a (drunken) party or "high go":

> Come on, merry lads, toss the bumper and bowl round,
> Throw follies and quarrels of schoolboys away;
> Let malice no longer becloud the glad soul round,
> But friendship enlighten the heavenly ray.
> With hearty compliance we'll form an alliance,
> And bid bold defiance to sorrow and wo;
> We'll ne'er be afraid, boys, though tutors parade, boys,
> Here's health to the blade, boys, who loves a HIGH GO.[105]

Certainly such sentiments reflected an important social reality at Harvard. It is noteworthy, for example, that the disturbances of 1793 polarized the students along distinctly class-based lines. The much-villified informing club was composed solely of members of the junior and senior classes (and numbered almost every member among its ranks), while the dissidents against whom they organized were comprised almost exclusively of freshmen and sophomores. It is evident, then, that class loyalties could pit student against student even as the undergraduates sought to do battle with the faculty. Equally significant to our examination of student mobilizations, however, is Biglow's unhappy allusion to "follies, quarrels, and malice," for in reality the classes were rarely as cohesive as the dissidents would have liked them to be. Rather, internecine squabbles and petty jealousies addled the student bodies, undermining their sense of unanimity and purpose as agents of resistance. If each class was a symbolic community, then it was one that more often than not failed to coalesce except in moments of great crisis.

Students took personal loyalty as a point of common reference and tended to remain within their own small groups of friends. Friendships seemed to be casual: based upon shared rooms, shared drinks, and shared exploits. If the dissident students' identity ideal was one of manhood, then their forms of socialization more nearly resemble what Anthony Rotundo has called "boy culture": freewheeling, amorphous, antiauthoritarian, and sometimes violent.[106] John Henry Tudor, who offered a disarmingly frank evaluation of his classmates in his diary for 1799, followed this pattern closely. He rated students most highly for their "generosity" and "independence," and then for their abilities, whether as a fighter or as a scholar. He despised the older and poorer students, and sneered at those from rural backgrounds as "dirty." Each semester he reevaluated his opinion, noting whether a student was "same," "better," or "different." His opinions changed often and drastically. Such fluctuations led to the formation of often violently hostile factions within each class. Evaluating the popularity of student Joseph Stevens Buckminster, for example, Tudor wrote that he was "very much fished after. He is admired by one party, hated by another, & envied by a third."[107] If power lay anywhere, it was to be found within such "parties" of students rather than within the classes or the student body as a whole. Yet the fragmented and fluctuating nature of these parties, and their tendency to indulge in infighting as much as resistance to the faculty, made them an almost helplessly centrifugal force at Harvard. Of course students perceived a shared sense of difference from the teaching staff—students who made friends with tutors were disparaged as "fishermen"—only that the difference did not give the students a corporate and oppositional identity. To use a Marxist distinction, the students were a group "in themselves," but only intermittently "for themselves." And this made intensive confrontations hard to sustain.

When students did unite, it was through loyalty to a wronged friend or, at best, as a whole class. Ironically, then, the individualistic manhood ideal in whose name, and for whose privileges, the dissident students protested made sustained corporate activism a near impossibility. Even more ironic is the fact that the largest, best organized, and most secretive student group on campus was also the most conservative, the most villified, and the most successful in its campaign against the faculty. This group was Phi Beta Kappa.

Phi Beta Kappa at Harvard

Outsiders knew little about Phi Beta Kappa. The internal workings of the group were shrouded in a well-designed and effective cloak of mystery. Nevertheless, it was common knowledge that the group opposed overt rebellion. The society made it evident that the good behavior of its members was a characteristic virtue. Timothy Bigelow wrote of the Harvard chapter of Phi Beta Kappa in 1796: "Fifteen years have already elapsed since its first establishment here; During all which time, irregularities of conduct, riot, tumult and disorder have uniformly been discountenanced; and due subordination and a regard to order have been enjoined and practiced."[108] While we may doubt the extent to which Phi Beta Kappa actually served as a social pacifier beyond its own membership, members and nonmembers alike *perceived* the society to be inherently opposed to student resistance, and the fraternity itself became the target of student opposition on a number of occasions. What, then, was the Phi Beta Kappa? Who were its members? And why did it seem to be so openly opposed to acts of student resistance at Harvard?

Phi Beta Kappa was founded in Virgina in 1776 by a group of students at the College of William and Mary for the stated purpose of promoting "social and improving intercourse." It was essentially a literary and debating society, tinged with Masonic ritual, and decidedly secretive in its operations. Members of the society met once a fortnight in the room of one of the members and presented forensic disputations, opposing compositions, and extemporaneous speeches on a variety of literary, political, and religious topics. Food and (nonalcoholic) drink were provided, and the society also had a small library of works of which members could avail themselves. Although a minor organization at William and Mary, the group established chapters at both Yale (1780) and Harvard (1781) that flourished long after the Virginian organization had disappeared. In passing on the mantle to Yale and Harvard, the founders outlined their social vision in describing their organization as a "scion . . . ingrafted on the stock of friendship, in the soil of virtue, enriched by literature." Here, they told new members, "you are to look for a sincere friend, and here you are to become a Brother of inalienable Brothers."[109]

If friendship was seen to be the fundamental form of socialization, then for many the club was, mutatis mutandis, the ideal form of society. Anthony Ashley Cooper, third earl of Shaftesbury, had sung the praises of the literary club as early as 1709 in his essay "Sensus Communis: An Essay on the Freedom of Wit and Humor." There he defined the "liberty of the club" as a "freedom of raillery, a liberty in decent language to question every thing, and an allowance of unravelling or refuting every argument, without offense to the arguer." Among friends, the possibility of easy debate gave access to the truth. "We shall grow better reasoners," wrote Shaftesbury, "by reasoning pleasantly, and at our ease; taking up, or laying down these subjects, as we fancy."[110]

The founders and early members of Phi Beta Kappa wholeheartedly agreed and believed that the society was ideally suited to promote the three attributes of virtue, literature, and friendship. Indeed Phi Beta Kappa member Thadeus M. Harris argued that literary societies tended to "strengthen reason, to confirm the judgement, and to excite emulation; to warm the heart with sentiment, and store the mind with information; and to lead philosophical precision, free from pedantry, and to complacency of manners, devoid of affection."[111] In short Phi Beta Kappa believed itself to be a microcosm of the ideal social arrangement.

Many societies and clubs at Harvard were based loosely or otherwise on such principles. These included a Singing Club, a Coffee Club, the Speaking Club, the Adelphoi Theologia, the Navy Club, and just a few years later the Hasty Pudding and Porcellian Clubs. In addition there were a military company known as Marti Mercurian Band, a firefighting company known as the Engine Society, and a Graduate Debating Society, to say nothing of the smaller and looser clusterings of students within the college. Victor Turner has argued that for those passing through a liminal phase of development, there is a great compulsion to form neophytic groups, to foster what he calls "communitas": that is, an affiliation based on "intense comradeship and egalitarianism."[112] His observation is borne out by the example of the Harvard students. In this closed and somewhat sterile academic environment, the "relish" for friendship, according to one graduate, was "like a violent appetite."[113] Yet this appetite was always justified on the strictest of moral grounds.

Although the immediate government of the college outlawed combinations and tended to look with suspicion on extracurricular gatherings as a whole, it tacitly condoned the student societies. Phi Beta Kappa came under official scrutiny during these years. In October 1789 a committee from the board of overseers noted "that there is an institution in the University, with the nature of which the Government is not acquainted, which tends to make a discrimination among the students," and it suggested "the propriety of inquiring into its nature and design." By the time this recommendation had been advanced, however, the eager-toplease organization had already handed a copy of its laws and constitution to President Willard for scrutiny.[114] The president found nothing objectionable in the society, especially inasmuch as several tutors had been members as undergraduates. A dour and antisocial man himself, Willard evidently still held the notion of social affections sacred enough to allow Phi Beta Kappa to continue.

Ironically enough, many students considered Phi Beta Kappa a pernicious organization. In 1787, members of the senior class boycotted the society's annual public exhibition, which was held in the chapel.[115] In 1791, members of the junior and senior classes presented a petition to the immediate government of the college, protesting the existence of Phi Beta Kappa on campus.[116] In a series of letters to the *Columbian Centinel* in 1793, a pseudonymous correspondent lambasted the society for having such an aloof and superior nature, and for letting loose a "spirit of faction and party" within the school.[117] And in 1796, the corresponding secretary of the fraternity, Samuel Shapleigh, requested that members of other chapters address their letters to him "to the College Librarian" to avoid their being intercepted and destroyed by hostile students.[118] Some of this hostility can be ascribed to jealousy on the part of those who had been refused membership, but more generally it seems to have been provoked by a conviction that the society was a traitorous outfit that did not have the best interests of the students at heart. At bottom the dispute was over two competing visions of social organization.

During the 1780s and 1790s, Phi Beta Kappa was condoned by the faculty and condemned by many students. Viewed from a limited, but nevertheless very important perspective, it was a conservative organization. Its unstinting emphasis on "good character in the litterary as well as [the] moral line," for example, made it congenial to the immediate government, even as it roused the opposition of the dissident students and the jealousy of the disappointed aspirants for membership. However, the members of Phi Beta Kappa acknowledged many, if not all, of the grievances expressed by the dissident students: they resented being considered children; denied that they lacked rationality; loathed the tedium of the classroom; detested the vile food served in commons; and rejected the authority of immediate government. John Henry Tudor, who spent his early years at the college as a dissident saboteur before joining the fraternity, clearly illustrates this continuum. In 1799 he wrote, "Our commencement this year was miserable & truly college degenerates. But [the] day after will retain its seat within me while reason, flesh & blood continue. That day the ØßK [celebrated] & one day is worth years of torment."[119] So far from being at odds with the dissident students, the Phi Beta Kappans were in perfect concurrence with them. Theirs, I would argue, was a dispute over means and not ends.

Where the dissident students sought to protest the inadequacies of the college in an attempt to gain reforms, the members of Phi Beta Kappa accepted things as they were and quietly instituted compensatory measures, constructing a social organization that consciously imitated, yet improved upon, the existing system at Harvard. Phi Beta Kappa had its own president and officers, its own library and curriculum, its own laws and disciplinary code, and even its own commencement exercises. To an extent that has not yet been acknowledged, Phi Beta Kappa was a parody of the eighteenth-century college regime, seeking to ridicule by reversal the shortcomings of the parent institution. More important, however, it sought to overcome these flaws: where the college organized itself along paternalistic lines, Phi Beta Kappa was both democratic and egalitarian. The society paralleled the wider college at almost every point, making up for the inadequacies and anachronisms, the exclusions and the coldness of the official regime, with well-stocked libraries and well-filled pantries.

Groups such as Phi Beta Kappa were, as James McLachlan has suggested, quite literally "colleges within colleges."[120] Of course, most of Harvard's societies and clubs functioned as partially compensatory organizations, making up for the failings of the college at large. Where Phi Beta Kappa stood apart, however, was in having a fraternal structure. Not only did the group offer an alternative and compensatory curriculum, it also offered a stable and determinate sense of male identity. The basis of this identity was not adulthood, but brotherhood.

The way in which a determinate male identity was constructed is clearly seen in the Phi Beta Kappa induction ritual.[121] After having been proposed and approved by the members, the candidate was blindfolded, handed a sheet of paper, and led by the proposing member to the door of the room where the society was meeting. At the threshold, the escort was switched, the candidate seated, and his blindfold removed. Before him sat the members of the fraternity. Reading from the sheet of paper, the candidate thanked the president and members for the invitation to join a society that "has Friendship for its Basis, Benevolence and Literature for its Pillars," and in response the president gravely swore the candidate to secrecy. There then followed a series of questions for the candidate:

> 1st If upon hearing you dislike the principles of this Society and withdraw, do you promise upon the word of a Gentleman to keep them secret?
>
> 2nd Is it of your own free choice unbiased by persuasion that you become a member of this Society?
>
> 3rd Will you approve yourself a worthy member of this Society by being a Friend to Morality & Literature?
>
> 4th Will you regard every worthy member of this Society as a Brother?
>
> 5th Will you assist them when in distress with your Life and Fortune?

If the candidate answered in the affirmative, then the president and society formally accepted him. The rules of the society were read, the secret handshake described, and the secret code used in writing the minutes explained. Finally the president offered a formal speech of welcome, which concluded with the following promise:

> Now then you may for a while disengage yourself from scholastic Laws and communicate without reserve whatever relations you have made upon various objects; remembering that everything transacted within this room is transacted *Sub rosa,* and detested is he that discloses it.
>
> Here too you are to indulge in matters of speculation, that freedom of inquiry which ever dispels the clouds of falsehood by the radiant sunshine of truth.—Here you are to look for a sincere Friend, and here you are to become the Brother of unalienable Brothers.

The key emphases of the Phi Beta Kappa ritual, as described above, were liminality, fraternity, secrecy, and rationality. Examined anthropologically, each can be seen as contributing to a determinate and corporate sense of male identity that differed substantially from that adopted by the dissident students at Harvard.

Liminality. The whole Phi Beta Kappa ritual is based upon the transition of a liminal being from one state of existence to another. According to Victor Turner, such rites of passage often involve a symbolic death and rebirth. In the Phi Beta Kappa ritual this is seen in the summoning of the candidate, the blindfolding, and the changing of escorts at the threshold of the meeting room, all of which suggest an ontological rite of passage.[122]

Fraternity. The new identity assumed by the initiate was definitively male, but stressed brotherhood rather than manhood. The significance of brotherhood as a masculine ideal was threefold. In the first place, it was a wholly egalitarian identity, and as such it militated against the hierarchical structure seen in the college at large. In the second place, it was an enduring status that existed through time in a way that age-determined identities did not. And in the third place, it created an immense bond of loyalty and stability among fellow members.

Secrecy. Secrets, according to Georg Simmel, have not only a substantive meaning but also a functional quality. The very sharing of secrets creates a bond of obligation and a "reciprocal confidence" between individuals.[123] By inviting the candidate to hear the rules of the society, the members of Phi Beta Kappa extended a trust to him, and an obligation, that joined him with those he was considering joining. By revealing the arcana—the secret handshake and the secret code—the bond was solidified. In point of fact the secrets themselves were of far less importance as information than as the ethical foundation of a neophyte community. In the words of Victor Turner, the special information revealed in rites of passage is always more than "an aggregation of words and sentences; it has ontological value, it refashions the very being of the neophyte."[124] Knowing was being, and special knowledge constituted a special form of identity.

Rationality. The ability to make an informed decision whether to join a fraternity, the capacity to keep privileged knowledge a secret, and the recognition that one was morally bound to one's brothers all bespoke, in the eighteenth century, the posession of a rational and ethical mind. And the purpose of Phi Beta Kappa was the exercise of reason in pursuit of a moral community. As the fraternity president's closing remarks made clear, Phi Beta Kappa did not believe that the college at large provided the resources for a free and impartial pursuit of the truth. Rather, exploration was impeded by "scholastic Laws." In part this was a result of the curriculum offered at Harvard, but more important it was a result of the fact that the college's teaching staff did not believe the students capable of fully rational inquiry. In true Enlightenment fashion, Phi Beta Kappa held that the club could provide an ideal forum for free debate.[125]

Conclusion: Dignity and Honor at Harvard

Phi Beta Kappa's vision of studenthood stood in sharp contrast to that prescribed by the immediate government at Harvard. The fraternity member was rational, loyal, and responsible. He was adult enough to make informed decisions and reliable enough to engage in organized decision making. And since the members of Phi Beta Kappa almost never incurred the wrath or disciplinary action of the immediate government at Harvard, we have reason to believe that the social identity fostered by the group served as an adequate alternative to the official vision of the student as youth.

Yet if Phi Beta Kappa quietly opposed the faculty, then the members were equally at odds with the dissident students. In almost every way Phi Beta Kappa's vision grew out of the same intellectual and social matrix as that of the dissident students. Both based their sense of aspiration on a hybrid mixture of republicanism and enlightened rationalism; both saw determinate male identity as pivotal to their organization; and both resented the structure and substantial organization of late-eighteenth-century Harvard. Yet to an astonishing degree, their solutions and alternatives differed. While Phi Beta Kappa members drew upon a rich heritage of Enlightenment social thought to institutionalize their vision in the form of a fraternity, the dissident students lacked a clear sense of organization or corporate self-identity. Their coalitions were ad hoc and functional, and tended not to survive beyond the immediate circumstances that gave rise to them. Where Phi Beta Kappa sought to introduce elaborately integrative rites of passage, the dissident students eschewed ritual altogether, stressing what they *were* rather than what they could become. Thus secrets for Phi Beta Kappa were a form of social cement, bringing the group together as initiates of arcane knowledge; while for the dissidents, secrets were items of knowledge that had to be kept from the immediate government for fear of reprisal.

At the greatest level of abstraction the distinction between these two groups may be summarized through reference to the conflicting cultures of "honor" and "dignity."[126] In a culture of honor, personal worth is entirely coequal with the worth another bestows upon one; in a culture of dignity, personal worth is inherent and wholly unalienable. In a culture of honor, the insulted are morally, indeed almost ontologically, obliged to attack their insulter to reestablish their worth; in a culture of dignity, the insulted rise above insult and concentrate on assertion and mastery of self. Edward L. Ayers has applied this distinction to the North and the South in the antebellum period, but it seems equally pertinent to the dissident students and the Phi Beta Kappans at Harvard. The dissidents' sense of manhood was so precarious, and so shakily dependent on the recognition of the immediate government, that they were compelled to respond to every insult (perceived and real) with an attack that would restore their standing in their own and in others' eyes. Theirs was a culture of honor. The Phi Beta Kappans' sense of worth, on the other hand, was ritually endorsed at the initiation ceremony, after which one became a "Brother of unalienable Brothers." Brotherhood was not something for which one had to contend in the same way one did one's manhood. This was a sui generis culture of dignity. The dissidents looked outward for their identity; the Phi Beta Kappans looked within. In this simple distinction we see the basis for disorder and order at eighteenth-century Harvard.

The last great rebellion at Harvard took place in 1834. Like so many others, it began with a violation of student customs regarding recitation. Classroom confrontations led to expulsions; petitions were met with polite but firm rejection; the entire sophomore class was suspended; and in a novel and wholly unwelcome gesture, threats of legal action were levied against the students. Like the unfortunate Joseph Perkins forty years earlier, President Josiah Quincy was hung in effigy in the college yard, while seniors printed a circular denouncing his want of consideration and ability. The 1834 disturbance was crushed by an awesome show of arms and by Quincy's stolid refusal to back down in the face of harassment.[127] It was to be the last major disturbance of the nineteenth century.

One reason for a decline in rioting after this time is the fact that a revolution in higher education was slowly taking place. This study began with the observation that much of the tinder for college conflagrations was a result of the fact that those who taught and administered America's eighteenth-century schools had an unclear conception of their institutional mission; lack of clarity led to a confused and provocative perception of the students whom they taught; and the practices upon which these perceptions were based were highly galling to generations of eighteenth- and early-nineteenth-century students. Ronald Story and a number of other historians have demonstrated that the 1830s and 1840s saw a marked tendency toward the professionalization of American education and a concomitant elitism within the student body.[128] Greater emphasis was placed on the training and development of professors; much deeper consideration was given to the issue of curriculum; and above all, a new understanding of studenthood began to emerge. Beginning with President John Thornton Kirkland, but even more strikingly under the administrations of Josiah Quincy and Jared Sparks, the barriers between faculty and students began to break down. Students began to receive the respect that they had spent the previous century lobbying for. Then, too, the students began to develop a new sense of identity that was largely fostered, as Story has shown, by an increasingly self-conscious sense of elitism. As the nineteenth century moved into its fourth and fifth decades, the "dirty" country students of whom John Henry Tudor had complained in the 1790s became rarer and rarer. Those who did enter Harvard at a material disadvantage were quickly assimilated in cultural if not in financial terms. Student culture did not disappear, and the barriers between student and faculty did not evaporate. Nevertheless, student life seemed to take on a significantly less combative tone after the 1840s. By 1851, when Benjamin Hall's *Collection of College Words and Customs* was published, the world he described, and from which so much of the historical evidence for this chapter was drawn, had become a violent and revolutionary era whose time had passed.

College As It Was in the Mid–Nineteenth Century

~

ROGER L. GEIGER WITH JULIE ANN BUBOLZ

avid Allmendinger begins his study of student life in nineteenth-century New England colleges by calling his subjects
"the silent people of higher education."[1] Yet by the end of the
antebellum years of which he wrote, those silent people had
found a distinctive voice. The previously unpublished mem-
oir of James Buchanan Henry and Christian Henry Scharff, *College As It Is, or, The
Collegian's Manual in 1853,* is but one exemplar of an unusual genre: descriptive
accounts by actual students of their everyday curricular and especially extracurricular experiences.[2] These works stand out in two respects.

First, student life held an abiding interest for American men of letters in the
nineteenth century. This interest was first expressed in moralistic tales, and later
in an outpouring of reminiscences by sentimental old grads.[3] College novels,
which began to appear in the 1880s, comprise another large part of this corpus.[4]
The works discussed here, however, were written by students during or immediately after attendance, apparently to provide a true picture of college life to the
public, pleasant reminiscences to alumni, or amusement for students much like
themselves.[5]

Second, these generally celebratory pieces appeared only a short time after
some of the worst student disorders in American history. During the first three
decades of the century, students at these same colleges thought themselves to be
in a perpetual war with their teachers, the immediate government of the colleges.[6]
By the 1840s a new generation of students regarded their college years with such

ardent nostalgia that they felt compelled to memorialize these experiences. This memoir thus provides an insight into midcentury Princeton (officially, the College of New Jersey), but also provides an occasion to examine this curious and ephemeral phenomenon.

Henry and Scharff appear to be representative, if not typical, Princeton students.[7] Both entered as sophomores, as did most midcentury Princetonians, and both appear to have been reasonably conscientious in their studies. Henry was graduated twenty-third among the sixty-seven men of '53, while Scharff ranked sixth. Both subsequently practiced law. Their memoir was composed in the last half of their senior year. Henry wrote a bit more than Scharff, and an anonymous third party apparently contributed a small section, but all assumed the voice of an anonymous narrator. They apparently intended eventually to give their work to the Princeton library. However, their principal motivation must have been their enjoyment in reconstructing the times when they "gloried in the name of Student."[8] Understanding how this happy state of existence came to pass probably holds the greatest interest today. It was a product of the interaction of the studies required of the students, the disciplinary regime imposed by the college, and the freedom available to students to fashion their own unique world.

On the surface the authors' course of study at Princeton conformed to the pattern that had existed in North America for more than two hundred years. The basic studies, especially for the first two years, were Latin, Greek, and mathematics; and students recited them almost every day. Three recitations were scheduled—at 7:00 A.M. (between morning prayers and breakfast), 11:00 A.M., and 4:00 P.M. The spacing was deliberate: students were expected to devote the intervening time to prepare for the next recitation and were required to be in their rooms in order to do so. In the junior year at Princeton, Latin and Greek were reduced, and rhetoric and belles lettres added; but emphasis was placed on mathematics through calculus, the most difficult subject of the entire college course. Seniors studied only a little Greek, while having lectures and recitations in chemistry, physics, astronomy, and philosophy. On paper this may appear to be a formidable course of study, but custom and usage made it otherwise.

By the 1850s (and undoubtedly earlier) a regime had evolved that was forgiving to both teachers and learners. The authors estimated that they needed only thirty minutes of "polling" (studying) to prepare for a Latin or Greek recitation. For the less conscientious, which would describe a number of their classmates, other stratagems lightened the burden. Students had a good idea of approximately when they would be called upon to recite, and thus could prepare quite selectively. If caught unaware, one could find pretexts to walk out of class. Examinations of varying seriousness were held, with junior mathematics being the most difficult, but cheating was common and tacitly condoned. Studies at Princeton were scarcely a farce: some students worked diligently; most respected their obligations even while cutting corners; and a minority performed the minimum needed to get by. Failure was theoretically possible, but no examples are mentioned. The course of study at Princeton was an unspoken compromise between the tempered expectations of teachers and the restrained exertions of students. Discipline in the college followed much the same pattern.

Students were expected to conform to an exacting list of college regulations that had changed little since discipline had been tightened early in the century. However, the faculty had largely lost the will to enforce these rules. "No shouting, loud-talking, . . . or any other boisterous noise shall be permitted in the entries or rooms of the college at any time" is one law the authors ridiculed as being a dead letter. Likewise, the rules against visiting taverns or eating houses in town would, if obeyed, have cramped the students' social lives. In some matters the erosion of control was palpable. Until 1851, absences from recitations were marked excused or unexcused, but in that year, absences began to be recorded and entered onto student report cards. Similarly the faculty made perfunctory passes through student living quarters during study hours, noting those not present for another report card entry. Nevertheless, the authority of the college, although invoked almost reluctantly, remained an awesome presence in the lives of the students, ready to strike anyone who transgressed the murky boundaries of approved behavior.

Excessive absences would trigger a letter notifying parents and, if continued, possible "dismission."[9] Perhaps least tolerated was public (or discovered) intoxication, which was likely to bring immediate separation from the college. The only professor who seemingly had the stomach to search out and occasionally apprehend miscreants was "Johnny" Maclean, soon to be president (1854–1868). Maclean was beloved by students, partly because of these ineffectual efforts, and pranks or "sprees" lost much of their attraction when he was absent from campus. The tacit limits of college authority were repeatedly tested. The class of '53, as juniors, rebelled against "disagreeable" assignments for rhetoric recitations, refusing in a petition to perform the work. They were quickly threatened with dismission and meekly forced to recant. Later, though, the assignments were changed.

In sum the Princeton students had only a modest and manageable amount of classroom assignments to perform, lived under a regime that was sufficiently authoritarian to challenge their anarchic ingenuity, and had fairly abundant free time with which to fashion a distinctive social regime.

While the institution made great claims on their minds and spirits, it left students to their own devices for most personal needs. They furnished their own rooms, most cheaply with used furniture sold by the servants, and they made all other arrangements for necessities. Because the system of dining at commons had broken down at Princeton, students boarded throughout the town. Although this practice fragmented the class, mealtimes were apparently occasions for intense conviviality. The most fashionable place to board for '53 was at the Princeton Theological Seminary. Besides having free time during and after meal hours, when students congregated at the post office or played organized games,[10] they had six hours per day ostensibly to study for recitations. This provided ample time for reading, conversation, country walks, or some of their other official and unofficial duties.

In addition to lectures (for juniors and seniors) scheduled at odd hours, students had to find time for various structured activities. Students in each class were required to deliver public addresses. Senior orations were the culmination of these exercises and were presented before an audience of townspeople, apparently bribed to attend by the accompanying musical performances. Students also must have found some time for the activities of the literary societies that, being secret, are not described. Still, compared with later in the century, the class of '53 had few sanctioned student activities. The only recognized organizations were the two literary societies, the *Nassau Literary Magazine* (f. 1842), and a religious association. Princetonians thus divided their time among academic, ancillary, or personal pursuits.

After 8:30 P.M. students were assumed to be safely ensconced in their rooms, preparing for the morning's recitation. In fact they were fairly free for whatever mischief they might devise. That was the time for hazing the "newies," clandestine whist parties, secret banquets, and various sprees. Fact and campus legend undoubtedly blend in the retelling of these manifestations of youthful exuberance. One notorious example was the sophomore horn spree: students climbed high into trees on a dark night and blew "tin horns and bugles . . . until forced to retire by the Faculty throwing off their dignity, and following the students up the trees."[11] As at most colleges, the sophomores had a reputation for being most rowdy, while seniors guarded their newfound dignity with somewhat more reserved behavior.

Overall, Henry and Scharff describe the class as the inviolable unit of college life, and the inexorable progression from freshman (or sophomore) to senior emerges as the most powerful psychological feature of the college experience. Each sphere of student life was affected—classroom duties, other structured activities, and of particular importance to the students themselves, a sense of self and campus status. College was thus an exceedingly dynamic experience for mid-century students, which may account for the intense feelings it generated. That such experiences were not limited to Princeton is apparent from the appearance of other student writings at this time.

Henry and Scharff probably got the idea for composing a memoir from reading other works of this type. In all likelihood the Cliosophic literary society, to which both belonged, would have possessed volumes of such direct interest to students. Editor J. Jefferson Looney notes a similarity to *Sketches of Williams College*, which appeared in 1847. This hundred-page volume is divided between "Williams College as It Has Been" and "Williams College as It Is." In the latter part the authors adopt a conceit of viewing the college experience sequentially through the eyes of a more or less typical student. This same form is much more fully developed by Henry and Scharff; the Princeton memoir represents a considerable advance in the emergence of a student voice.

Although written by students "yet in their teens," and "without the supervision of older and wiser heads," *Sketches of Williams College* has a semiofficial air.[12] Published in Williamstown shortly after the Williams College semicentennial, its avowed intention was to entertain the public and touch the sentiments of alumni. The first half of the volume is an informative history of the college's first fifty years. The presentation of the college "as it is" follows, providing largely descriptive information on the physical setting (always important for Williams), student excursions in the surrounding mountains, college buildings, organizations, and the course of study. Only the chapter "College Life" attempts to convey a student perspective and then with rather forced irony. The overall tone is earnest: the fictional narrator subscribes totally to the 1828 Yale Report's concept of mental discipline; regards his classmates as "brothers" by the time of graduation; and ends by lauding the Christian mission of the college.

The Williams College *Sketches* were clearly modeled upon *Sketches of Yale College*, published just four years earlier. The anonymous author (Ezekial Porter Belden) also assumes a pose of modesty, but hopes "his humble efforts" will be justified by recalling to alumni "those 'joyous happy days' of College life."[13] Two-thirds of Belden's volume provide a condensed history of Yale and a virtual catalogue of current information. The final third, however, presents an original account of a rather studious "Day in College," followed by numerous college customs and anecdotes that record the semimythic oral traditions of student culture.

In 1851 Harvard senior Benjamin H. Hall compiled an extensive "collection of college words and customs." He ostensibly published his collection to amuse other students, but also to "explain the character of student life."[14] This work was in all probability the inspiration for Henry and Scharff's second chapter, which is a similar alphabetical glossary of terms current among students at Princeton. The labor of collating Princeton slang with that in more general usage has been performed by editor Looney. In general this information shows Princetonians employing a distinctive idiom as well as being conversant with the wider student argot.

Looney also suggests that Henry and Scharff may have drawn inspiration for their project from the memoir of Charles Astor Bristed, *Five Years in an English Universi' y,* which also appeared in 1851. While the general idea of recounting college lif(may have appealed to the authors, it seems unlikely that Bristed's actual account would have. He was at once fawning toward the Cantabrigians, sanctimonious in his moral posture, and condescending toward American colleges. Only this last note is struck in *College as It Is,* and it is quite out of harmony with the rest of the book.

Americans with any acquaintance with European universities were well aware of the inadequacies of American colleges. Henry and Scharff, perhaps to establish their credibility or sophistication, begin their memoir by echoing the familiar plaints that the United States had too many colleges, inferior standards, and an absence of inducements for "Scientific and literary attainments."[15] They then offer the incongruous suggestion that the entire system be torn up "root and branch" to be replaced by one in which colleges would serve as preparatory schools for a few true universities. One can detect echoes in these passages of Bristed as well as Brown president Francis Wayland, whose radical *Report to the Corporation of Brown University* appeared in 1850. However, the telling argument that universities ought to supersede colleges came directly from Henry Tappan's *University Education,* published in 1851.[16] Henry and Scharff thus signal their familiarity with the current of informed criticism of American higher education before launching, in quite a different vein, into their celebration of student life at Princeton.

Had they published their volume for contemporaries, Henry and Scharff might well have had their own imitators. Instead, the tradition of student memoirs appears to have gone dormant, possibly because of the quickening growth of other forms of student publications. One remarkable specimen fits closely with the spirit of midcentury student memoirs while differing in form: *The University Quarterly: Conducted by an Association of Collegiate and Professional Students in the United States and Europe.* The *Quarterly* was organized at Yale in the late 1850s, but its association consisted of editorial committees at up to thirty colleges and professional schools. During 1860 and 1861 it managed to publish eight hefty issues of student writings, each consisting equally of literary essays and news articles contributed by the participating institutions.[17]

The premises on which the *Quarterly* was founded reveal much about its subsequent character. It sought "to record the history, promote the intellectual improvement, elevate the moral aims, liberalize the views, and unite the sympathies" of students and their institutions. It thus embraced the ends of the colleges themselves while also implying that they were not currently being achieved too well. As a supporter of the existing regime, then, it was able to garner testimonials from a who's who of contemporary figures; but its fundamental belief was that only students themselves, through intellectual exchange and mutual stimulation, could effect an improvement in their college experience. The founders set themselves to rectify a kind of blameless decadence: they saw half of students "doze through college," but did not fault the faculty; they disapproved of student pranks or misbehavior, but offered understanding rather than condemnation for miscreants.[18] The journal, above all, manifested an underlying confidence and independence similar to other student writings, but channeled this spirit explicitly toward moral earnestness and enthusiasm for literary culture. Moral earnestness was particularly evident in the literary essays. Perhaps a third of the essays addressed aspects of student life—literary societies, secret societies, skepticism in college life—and in every case endorsed orthodox views. The news articles were far more varied. Many submissions are devoted to current events. Among this ephemera can be detected a surge of interest in sports. Nearly every campus, for example, comments on its new or projected gymnasium. In more reflective comments, both Union and Hamilton Colleges remark favorably upon the increasing freedom and responsibility accorded to students. Noting the absence of student problems, the Hamilton editors no doubt echoed the view of most contemporary collegians: "being considered as gentlemen they naturally act as such."[19]

The *Quarterly* expired unexpectedly as a rising martial spirit engulfed many college campuses, although it seems unlikely that collegians would have been able to sustain so large and complex an enterprise for long. The very magnitude of participation is evidence that it struck a responsive chord among collegians of the day. The college experience was terribly important to the *Quarterly*'s many contributors. They expected to expand their literary powers, to learn to become gentlemen, and to pursue postgraduate studies here or abroad. To accomplish these goals, they looked less to the curriculum and more to the qualities engendered in their own student culture. They had asserted in their "Prospectus" that "Students in Colleges to-day are generally superior, both in age and acquirements to those in Colleges twenty years ago," and by all indications, so they were.[20]

After the Civil War, in 1871, George R. Cutting published *Student Life at Amherst,* a somewhat disjointed narrative with unclear institutional sponsorship. The manuscript was originally written as a history of the Amherst literary societies, but Cutting was encouraged to expand it for the college's semicentennial. The chief theme is the waning of the literary societies due to the rise of secret fraternities. However, Cutting provides additional information on the continual formation and dissolution of student societies, including athletic groups that organized the nation's first intercollegiate "base ball" game in 1859.

Also in 1871, the jewel of all student memoirs appeared: *Four Years at Yale* by "a graduate of '69." The author, Lyman H. Bagg, professedly sought to correct a general misunderstanding of college life by providing a close factual description of the entire college experience.[21] In more than seven hundred pages he detailed the operation of Yale's unique system of class societies, student life in each of the four classes, and relations between students and Yale college within the "official curriculum." Sixteen years and 150 miles removed from the Princeton of Henry and Scharff, Bagg's Yale exhibited difference in detail but similarity in spirit. Yalies endured a more formalized disciplinary regime in which all absences resulted in "marks" (demerits) and missed recitations had to be made up. But the system was easily accommodated, and ultimately entrusted Yale students with greater responsibilities. If students avoided failing grades or excessive marks, they were "left to their own devices. Where a man is, or what he is doing, outside the hours when his presence is required at recitation, lecture, or chapel, the faculty make no effort to enquire." Student autonomy at Yale by '69 had advanced well beyond Princeton of the "Johnny" Maclean era.[22]

Bagg offers considerably more than a student memoir. His historical accounts are the standard source for several aspects of Yale student life.[23] His depiction of Yale is minute and above all candid. When used to supplement Henry and Scharff, Bagg, and to a lesser extent the other works mentioned here, can refine understanding of the student experience during a transitional era for the American college.

In the mid–nineteenth century the colleges of the Northeast were still Christian institutions, but they had ceased to embody much of their former religious mission. One would not grasp this by reading their official spokesmen—President Noah Porter of Yale, or John Maclean, who "would make every other part of education subordinate to [the study of religion], and . . . imbue the minds of our youth with the principles of piety and virtue."[24] These testimonies, however, indicate that the realities of student life were otherwise. The mandatory religious services may have framed the daily routine of college students, but like so many other requirements, they were observed in a perfunctory manner. Students who lived their Christian commitments or were preparing for a religious vocation tended to be marginalized in the close community. They had their own societies that met on weekday evenings for voluntary prayers; but Bagg described such sessions as "thinly attended," while Princeton students spoke disparagingly of "religs" and "Seminoles" (seminary students). Henry and Scharff dutifully report that "a young man may become, or Continue religious, at this College," but clearly this was a minor concern for most of their classmates.[25]

Nor had college yet become an arena for social climbing. Bagg could speak about an individual's "social importance" as a fact of life—which it was, given the class structure of the Gilded Age. But within the colleges social homogeneity seemed to reign in spite of obvious differences in wealth. Henry and Scharff wrote of "Hyphenutes," who had elegantly appointed rooms, exhibited insouciant manners, and socialized with genteel townspeople. Bagg too mentioned a minority of wealthy students who partook of New Haven society. But such matters seem to have counted for comparatively little among classmates. Henry and Scharff depict Princetonians as a collection of varied types: the "poller" studied to achieve high honors; the "fancy man" sought constant social activity; the Hyphenute displayed his affluence; while the "spreer" devoted himself to drinking and cards. The "scientific man" projected an image of serious learning but actually knew little; and the "Chemist" was absorbed in fearsome experiments. Although the authors affirm the importance of character at several points, no single set of overriding student values emerges from their account. They even complain with some exasperation that the kind of meaningful competition that might stimulate and reward a student's talents was lacking. Studying hard for first honors merited no more distinction "than he who has passed his time in idleness and amusement."[26]

In contrast Yale sixteen years later comes much closer to embodying the values that would dominate eastern colleges by the end of the century. Bagg describes a unitary moral order based on "personal character"—"the thing by which a man stands or falls in college."[27] Student life consisted of a continual competition that brought forth and largely rewarded men according to their character and abilities. The driver behind this process was the Yale society system, in which students were evaluated and selected to successive freshmen, sophomore, junior, and senior secret societies—with the last constituting the real prize. The social life of the class, formal and informal activities, even academic standing—all fed into the ultimate judgment. Bagg regarded the most prized senior society as a true meritocracy, combining "the best of the good scholars, good literary men, and good fellows."[28]

Students who did not partake of "the full glory of student life at Yale" were to be pitied. This did not require joining the societies (Bagg was a "neutral"), but certain behaviors were beyond the pale. Students who would "dig for a stand" (study hard for high grades) were disapproved. Also ostracized were those who entered Yale too young or "green," and sought to compensate by "bumming." (Henry and Scharff offered the same argument against freshmen at Princeton— that their immaturity made them prone to dissipation and "injured moral character.") So important was proper socialization in one's class that Bagg recommended students attend the top boarding schools in order to "stand the best chance of having a successful career at Yale."[29]

Bagg's impulse to standardize the age and background of Yale students is evidence of a significant transformation under way. For most of the century American colleges harbored students ranging in age from their early teens to late twenties. By midcentury, however, the eastern colleges contained an increasingly homogeneous youth culture, which Bagg instinctively sought to reinforce with his recommendations.[30] Princeton would be little different from Yale by the end of the century, when the socially exclusive eating clubs were in full operation.[31] However, for the class of '53 these factors were clearly muted.

With respect to the curriculum, the testimony of students does not support the conventional wisdom. As Samuel Eliot Morison put it for Harvard: "almost every graduate of the period 1825–1860 has left on record his detestation of the system of instruction at Harvard."[32] Perhaps in later life its shortcomings were more apparent. For actual students, Morison's "stupid method of instruction" may have been dry (as Henry and Scharff concede), but it was also easily manageable. Charles Bristed is virtually alone in believing that the classics were of such value that additional years should be devoted to learning them well.[33] Henry and Scharff nevertheless complain that the classics were given insufficient weight at Princeton. Mathematics, in their view, received too much emphasis in classroom time and in determining class standing. In their ap-proach to languages and mathematics, Princeton students tended to favor one and neglect the other; but the authors found little evidence to support the prevailing belief that being forced to learn math trained the mind. Lyman Bagg offered virtually the same assessment for Yale. He would have had more classical studies because they might be more readily "choked down a man's throat" and still produce some lasting benefit. Mathematics, on the other hand, was inaccessible for many students.[34]

Bagg was actually a staunch defender of the traditional curriculum, believing it to be most effective for the real students he described, as opposed to those whom reformers imagined to be thirsting for knowledge. He objected to electives because they disrupted class solidarity, and he averred that modern languages, since they were taught badly, had no place in the college course. Henry and Scharff took the opposite position, considering modern languages badly taught only because poorly qualified part-time instructors were hired to teach them, and advocating a prominent place for them in the college course. They also complained that all instruction in physics and chemistry was crammed into the senior year instead of being treated in greater depth throughout the four-year course. Perhaps their strongest protest concerned the way grades were awarded. The evaluations of oral examinations could be capricious, and different instructors used widely varying standards. Numerical averages were nevertheless used to calculate a student's final class standing, where differences in rank might be determined by only tenths of a point.[35] In a narrative that is generally uncritical of "college as it is," these discontents reflect serious shortcomings in the Princeton course of study.

The memoir of Henry and Scharff, while not great literature, is an informative and sometimes entertaining account; and although idiosyncratic in some respects, it provides genuine insight into the student experience at a midcentury eastern college. Above all, the book provides evidence for the hard-won autonomy of the student estate in formerly repressive institutions—the precondition for the budding high-collegiate era. In this respect it provides a forceful reminder that the old-time or antebellum college was not the stagnant institution that it is generally portrayed to be, but was in constant, though not linear evolution.

"We Desired Our Future Rulers to Be Educated Men"

South Carolina College, the Defense of Slavery, and the Development of Secessionist Politics

~

MICHAEL SUGRUE

*I*n the wake of the election of 1800, South Carolina Federalists sought a bipartisan modus vivendi that would secure their property and political ideals against the new political power of the Jeffersonian upcountry.[1] The new Jeffersonian governor, John Drayton, sought to allay fears of "Jacobin" social change, a charge often leveled at the Francophile Jeffersonians. He worked with Federalists to erect one of the most important institutional bulwarks against the radical political possibilities of the "revolution of 1800": South Carolina College.[2] Governor Drayton supported the college because "the friendship of our young men would thence be promoted, and our political union be much advanced thereby."[3] Federalist Henry William DeSaussure, one of the legislators most closely associated with the founding of the college, stated, "We of the lower country well knew that the power of the State was thenceforward to be in the upper country, and we desired our future rulers to be educated men."[4]

Both Drayton and DeSaussure were gentlemen and slaveholders, and they had an interest in making Jeffersonian democracy safe for South Carolina. DeSaussure, a prominent Charleston lawyer, articulated concerns shared by many influential low-country gentlemen.[5] Chancellor William Harper ('08), in his memoir of DeSaussure, emphasized the political intentions of the founders:

This measure originated in the contest which had arisen between the upper and lower country of the state, with respect to representation in the legislature. The upper country, which at the adoption of the constitution of 1790, was comparatively poor and unpeopled, had allotted to it, a much smaller representation. It had now grown in wealth, far outnumbered the lower country in population, and imperatively demanded a reform in the representation. This the people of the lower country feared to grant, on the ground of general deficiency of intelligence and education in the upper country, which would render it incompetent to exercise wisely and justly the power which such a reform would place in their hands. It was to remedy this deficiency that it was proposed to establish a College at Columbia. The act was passed, not without difficulty, nor without the strenuous opposition of many who it was more especially intended to benefit.[6]

South Carolina College was a last gesture made by the wealthiest men of South Carolina's Revolutionary generation toward preserving their political ideals and elite status. The college was the Noah's ark of anachronistic political philosophy. Drayton, DeSaussure, and the other gentlemen who helped found the college gathered together conservative eighteenth-century political ideas so that they could be kept safe on campus while the rest of the world was flooded by the nineteenth century. The waters of time, alas, never receded, and as the century wore on, the education given to these planters' sons moved from old-fashioned to atavistic, from conservative to reactionary.

The college was located in the state capital, Columbia, just down the street from the state legislature. This close proximity both facilitated and symbolized the intimate connection between politics and education in South Carolina. The lavishly funded college was the most important political legacy of the post-Revolutionary era because it institutionalized the transmission of doctrines and standards of judgment characteristic of South Carolinian Federalists, long after Federalism had ceased to dominate state politics. South Carolina College helped keep alive a tradition of political discourse that borrowed heavily from Federalism and the deferential "gentleman's politics" that it legitimized.

Many themes stressed by South Carolina's Federalist elite, such as the pursuit of republican virtue by an independent squirearchy, strict insistence upon the right of property in slaves, the support for virtual as opposed to actual representation, the belief in natural aristocracy, the equation of democracy with demagoguery, and the abhorrence of factions and parties, were kept alive on campus and in the statehouse long after they became extinct elsewhere. When slavery was threatened, the social conditions that maintained their peculiarly virtuous (in the high Federalist sense of the term) society were jeopardized, and the gentry who dominated South Carolinian politics revived a remedy that had been threatened by South Carolina's politicians since the first abolition petitions were presented to Congress in 1790: secession.[7]

DeSaussure had hoped that the college would produce "able and worthy men for every department of government."[8] His hopes were realized. In 1836 the aged DeSaussure was elected president of the South Carolina Society for the Advancement of Learning (SCSAL), which began as the alumni association of the college, but became the SCSAL when the alumni association was opened to graduates of any college.[9] At the inaugural ceremony DeSaussure was introduced by Governor McDuffie ('10), who said, "we have only to look around us to see what South Carolina now is, and to consider what she would have been if the college had never been established."[10] As he spoke, one of the two senators, eight of the nine congressmen, more than half of the state judiciary, and more than a quarter of the state legislature were alumni. He also might have noted that two alumni already had served as governor of Alabama; alumni had been elected to Congress from Mississippi, Alabama, and Georgia; and alumni were prominent in the state judiciary of Alabama and Mississippi. The college had come a long way: from a political olive branch to the most important institutional mechanism for selecting South Carolina's political elite in the antebellum period.

By 1836, future governors of Georgia, Florida, and Mississippi, and future congressmen from Georgia, Alabama, Mississippi, and Louisiana, had already been graduated, as had the future president of the Florida secession convention. The alumni formed a regional elite, an old-boys network whose social, intellectual, political, and marital connections formed an elaborate network with a hub in South Carolina. Congressman James Dellett ('10) of Alabama corresponded with at least sixty alumni in five lower southern states. Senator James Henry Hammond ('25) of South Carolina corresponded with more than one hundred. The old-boys network formed by college alumni was both extensive and durable.

The formidable power of the attachments made in the college was political as well as personal. In 1833, during the nullification controversy, James Dellett was urged to run for Congress against former governor, and fellow University of Alabama trustee, John Murphy ('08), but declined. He had known Murphy in college, and even though they had considerable political differences, they reached an accommodation. In a letter Dellett revealed one node in his network of alumni political connections when he wrote that he had already confidentially agreed with Murphy not to run against him. Moreover, Dellett stated, he did not wish to go to Congress because he could not in good conscience act against the nullifiers—not because they were right but because they were South Carolinians: "although I am satisfied in my own mind that So Carolina is wrong—yet I cannot forget that she nourished me in my infancy, and taught lessons I learned in my youth and early manhood. I am proud to say that I love her in the midst of her faults. . . . I could not voluntarily give a vote or strike a blow which would lacerate the cheek of my mother state."[11]

The college forged lasting attachments both to the state and to its peculiar culture, but the South Carolina connection was sometimes as much a hindrance as a help. In December 1860 the governor of Florida, Madison Perry ('32), was attacked in the press as a "catspaw for South Carolina secessionists" who, like other Palmetto radicals, "thought more of South Carolina than of the state of their adoption."[12] South Carolina College provided many prominent southern politicians with a theory that later informed their political practice. Henry L. Pinckney ('13), congressman and nullifier, noted with particular approval that the college had prevented the undergraduates from "contracting any of these prejudices which so unhappily prevail in other sections of our country, in reference to the internal policy of the Southern states."[13] Their experience of four years welded together a consensus on political matters that grew narrower and more strident in the years between 1805, when the college opened, and the afternoon of 8 November 1861, when all of the undergraduates on campus left their studies to join the Confederate army.[14]

The college gave the young gentlemen a *liberal* education, in the original, literal, sense of the term: the curriculum of the college fitted a man to be a master rather than a slave. The college curriculum, which stressed classical languages and literature, was intended to train the students' minds in a broad, general sense rather than to prepare them for a specialized profession. The college gave the sons of the gentry an education designed to produce what Max Weber might have called the "ideal type" of a slaveholder. It was designed to take fourteen- and fifteen-year-old boys and polish them into young eighteen- and nineteen-year-old gentlemen. In their course work the students developed ideas; in their dormitory arrangements they developed friendships; and in their extracurricular activities they developed bad habits that often lasted their whole lives.

Reflecting on his college days, one student noted the effect of the college's educational regimen on the undergraduates:

By the time he had reached his senior year, he had evolved into a personage of great dignity, who would have been immensely shocked by the boyishness of the modern student, and could by no means have understood the modern interest in football and baseball, games to his mind belonging normally to schoolboy days. Almost the only athletic amusement in which any of the students participated was a grand tournament that took place at the Hampton racetrack near Columbia. Many of the students engaged in this, assuming each some chivalrous character and arraying himself in appropriate costume.[15]

The ideal of personal honor was sufficiently strong among these young men that by age nineteen or twenty these personages of great dignity could only disdain boyish games. Intramural sports for them meant jousting. Pseudofeudal posturing was a conspicuous element in the culture of South Carolina's elite, and the students could not ignore this ubiquitous influence. In an 1857 letter, one student wrote to his father that he had just heard a splendid lecture on "Chivalry," that several young men were expected to duel the next day, and that the architecture of the new statehouse "reminds as much of the Feudal ages as the frequency of duels does."[16]

The most important extracurricular activity was debate. Antebellum South Carolina was primarily an oral culture. As the first president of the college, Jonathan Maxcy, noted, "whatever the test in other lands, here a man must speak and speak well if he expects to acquire and maintain a permanent influence in society."[17] With only a few exceptions all of the undergraduates were members of the two literary societies, the Clariosophic and Euphradian, and with membership came the obligation to engage in regular debate and declamation. The college cadet corps was established in 1824, and it allowed the students to drill, learn the use of firearms, study military tactics, and pay homage to the military virtues. Preparing to be a soldier or legislator was the main leisure activity that did not violate college rules.

The debate societies ensured that the graduates of the college were effective public speakers, and even if their speeches lacked the austere rigor of the Roman orators they so admired, their bombastic, sentimental style of rhetoric served them well in court or in Congress. South Carolina College produced what contemporaries described as "the South Carolina school of orator-statesmen." The alumni of the college, such as Senator Louis T. Wigfall ('37) of Texas, were seen as icons of "southernness" largely because of their habits of speech. One contemporary described Wigfall as "a good type of the man that the institutions of the [South] produce ... a remarkable man, noted for his ready natural eloquence; his exceeding ability as a quick, bitter debater; the acerbity of his taunts; and his readiness for personal encounter."[18]

The fact that the student body was recruited from the most influential families in the state meant that as alumni, these men would often find that the road to political officeholding had been paved by their relatives. The alumni of the college shared a lasting esprit de corps, plus a sense of noblesse oblige or at least a sense of noblesse, which was both praised and inveighed against by contemporary observers. President Thornwell remarked in 1853, "to make any commonwealth a unit, educate its sons together. This is the secret of the harmony which has so remarkably characterized our state. It was not the influence of a single mind, great as that mind was—it was no tame submission to authoritative dictation. It was the community of thought, feeling, and character, achieved by a common education."[19] Thornwell could not have been referring to a common primary or secondary education for South Carolina's "sons" because wealthy boys were generally taught by private tutors; sons of the poor were restricted to a public school system that all acknowledged to be dreadful. Thus the college was effectively restricted to the sons of planters. With students drawn almost exclusively from the gentry, the college could hardly help but propagate a class based on the community of "thought, feeling, and character."

This community of thought and feeling was socially constructed and reproduced in the college. In the required course on moral philosophy the students studied the arguments in favor of slavery, and they emerged well versed in proslavery apologetics.[20] In addition the undergraduates were taught the laws of honor and the relation of these laws to their religious and civil obligations.[21] They were taught that strict construction was the only legitimate kind of constitutional interpretation and that secession was a constitutionally prescribed remedy to federal usurpation.[22] The students' extracurricular activities, their mores, and their sense of honor remained remarkably similar over time. A study of the wealthiest families in South Carolina showed that South Carolina College was without serious competition as the most popular institution of higher education for their sons.[23] Slightly more than three thousand students matriculated between 1805 and 1862, and they were overwhelmingly the sons of wealthy cotton and rice planters. At least nine in ten of the students grew up in South Carolina. Those that did not were usually sons of alumni that had moved to the lower South or the sons of prominent southern politicians attracted by the ideological bias of the college.[24]

One professor described his students as "the young lords of slaves" and as "young men of affluence or independence."[25] If by good fortune and steady application, a "poor scholar" were to get an education that would enable him to meet the strict entrance requirements, there was still the problem of tuition and associated costs.[26] One critic of the college estimated the cost of a year's education between five hundred and one thousand dollars, and while this was surely an exaggeration, it is clear that education at South Carolina College was beyond the means of most citizens.[27]

The alumni of South Carolina College shared many habits, particularly certain habits of thought, expression, and action. They were, for example, in the habit of marrying one another's sisters and cousins.[28] They habitually chose the same adult occupations: planting, politics, the learned professions. The students socialized in the same elite circles; moreover, as undergraduates did then and do now, they often got into trouble together.

The rules drawn up by the trustees were quite elaborate, and the faculty had the power to warn, admonish, reprimand, or suspend students for violations. The trustees reserved the power of expulsion for themselves, and when the faculty recommended incorrigible hellions for expulsion, the trustees often refused, especially for the sons of powerful public figures. This arrangement had the effect of eroding the faculty's disciplinary authority, and the professors often found it more effective to coax the students than to threaten them with a suspension not easily distinguishable from an impromptu vacation. One alumnus recalled, "colleges depend, for the most part, on the patronage of the scholars. The faculties are compelled to choose between discipline and bread."[29] It is thus not surprising that the most effective professors were those with keenly persuasive rhetorical styles.[30] It is even less surprising that after an investigation by the trustees of particularly conspicuous student misbehavior in 1813, it was found that college "discipline had been almost totally relaxed."[31] William Grayson ('09) remembered that

> The raw freshman is subjected to the influence of companions a little older than himself. He is anxious to emulate the high spirited example of his senior. He makes rapid advances in smoking, chewing, playing billiards, concocting sherry cobblers, gin slings and mint juleps, becomes an adept at whist and "Old Sledge," in champaign [sic] and hot suppers, to say nothing of more questionable matters, and takes degrees in arts and sciences about which his diploma is altogether silent.[32]

The same offenses, such as gambling, heavy drinking, brawling, carrying concealed weapons, discharging weapons on campus, dueling and threatening to duel, swearing, skipping class to attend cockfights or horse races or dances, seem to have been perennial favorites with the undergraduates because they appear with considerable regularity in the disciplinary records. The students of South Carolina College were not more unruly than fifteen- to twenty-year-old males were in other places and times, but the peculiar forms that their misbehavior took are noteworthy.[33] The pattern of their transgressions reveals much about the overall character and personality of the students. In fifty-seven years of college disciplinary records (1805–1862), there are many crimes of violence, self-indulgence, and pride, but very few of dishonesty. In particular drunken brawling and the physical abuse of the college servants (slaves) were common, but there are almost no records of theft, lying, or cheating on exams.[34]

The undergraduates shared a certain ethos; their behavior reflected in many ways a commonly agreed upon set of judgments of right and wrong. One alumnus said, "The College boys of that time seemed to draw a well defined circle, within which there were things counted mean and low. Into that circle very few students dared intrude. Unfortunately, the radius of that circle was rather short."[35] Breaches of honor and etiquette were not tolerated among the students. Of the few records of theft in the antebellum campus, most were settled entirely among the students. The campus debate societies conducted investigations and expelled the dishonorable thieves. No other students would have anything to do with such pariahs, and they inevitably left campus in disgrace.[36]

Violence was an important trope of cultural expression for South Carolina's males, and the students could directly observe the fact that many of the state's most influential figures publicly cultivated a pose of genteel defiance. A known propensity toward violence was something of an advantage in the rough-and-tumble world of South Carolinian politics. Far from disqualifying students from public office, developing a reputation for violently defending one's honor may have helped prepare the young men for political life by allowing them to threaten people convincingly. Many of the violent young men of the Maxcy era made their most conspicuous early appearances in public life by fighting duels.[37]

The second president of the college, Thomas Cooper, never fully appreciated the atavistic import of honor and dueling for his students, and his approach sometimes made discipline go from bad to worse. One alumnus noted, "He was an entire stranger to Southern society and he knew nothing of the peculiarities of Southern youth." Being a foreigner, Cooper never understood the "spirit" of slavery.

> . . . he had to govern Southern youth. Whether for better or worse, they have their peculiarities, which spring from the manners, customs and institutions of the country. In certain particulars he erred grievously in his estimate. . . . Dr. Maxcy, as Dr. Henry tells us in his eulogy, judged differently. He saw in Southern youth a conviction of independence and a disposition to assert and exercise it. He did not attempt to extirpate this elevated principle, but to modify it. He appealed to the honor of his pupils, and with generous minds the appeal was always powerful, and generally successful. If there be any among us who object to this—let them abolish the institution of slavery; for that spirit is born of it.[38]

The college gave to this nebulous "spirit of slavery" a behavioral form in the rules of etiquette and the code of honor. One of the "peculiarities" of the "Southern youth" who populated the college was a powerful desire for the maintenance of honor, which amounted to the recognition by others of patrician status in a society whose most prominent feature was inequality. The textbook that the students used in their classes on moral philosophy defined the law of honor as "a system of rules constructed by people of fashion, and calculated to facilitate their intercourse with one another. . . . this law only prescribes and regulates the duties betwixt equals; omitting such as relate to the Supreme Being, as well as those which we owe to our inferiors."[39]

Because its students often became politically influential adults, the college indirectly influenced the political culture of the whole state. Preston Brooks might have graduated with the class of 1839, had the nineteen-year-old not been expelled a week prior to graduation because of his fondness for liquid refreshments and his tendency, when excited, to threaten people with the dueling pistols he kept in his dormitory room.[40] In the 1850s when he served in Congress, he broke a cane over the head of Senator Charles Sumner of Massachusetts. Every graduate of the college knew that the laws of honor required satisfaction for disrespectful words between gentlemen—an apology or a duel. The "code" further held that a man who would not duel was no gentleman, and if a gentleman were offended by a social inferior, an honorable recourse was to publicly cane the offending scoundrel. Brooks, who was not excessively touchy by Carolinian standards, felt that etiquette obliged him to beat Senator Sumner senseless with the appropriate ceremonial instrument. Brooks was expelled again, this time from the House of Representatives; his constituents reelected him immediately and without opposition.

The students who were conspicuous for their misdeeds were great favorites among the student body if they managed to acquit themselves stylishly, and being expelled was not necessarily a problem, as can be seen in the case of Brooks. Professor Francis Lieber noted in his diary:

> February 14, Story from real life. I arrived here in October, 1835. In January 1836, W—— and another student were expelled on account of a duel. Since that time W—— has:—
> First. Shot at his antagonist in the streets of Charleston.
> Second. Studied (?) law with Mr. DeSaussure in Charleston.
> Third. Married.
> Fourth. Been admitted to the bar.
> Fifth. Imprisoned two months for the above shooting.
> Sixth. Become father of a fine girl.
> Seventh. Practiced law for some time.
> Eighth. Elected member of the Legislature.
> Now he is only twenty-two years old. What a state of society this requires and must produce![41]

The "state of society" was favorable to men like Louis T. Wigfall ('37), a bad-tempered, hard-drinking student, who was a flamboyant disciplinary problem during his collegiate years. He never went out in public without two loaded pistols, and people were generally very polite toward him. He was described as having a "monomania on dueling."[42] After graduation he killed one of his classmates in a street fight, dueled twice with Preston Brooks (both were wounded), then became a lawyer in Texas.[43] In January 1860, William Campbell Preston ('09), former senator from South Carolina who had been president of the college while Wigfall had been a student there, wrote Wigfall, his former student, reflecting: "poor Pres Brooks, your old adversary, was afterwards my friend when we were colleagues together in Congress. . . . life tumbles us together very oddly, and it seems to me as I jog on, that all the good boys have gone out of mind, while all the headlong ones, whose ruin was speedily predicted, are turning up as colonels, judges, and Senators."[44] Senator Wigfall was unable to reply to his teacher's letter, being occupied in Congress bringing Texas out of the Union.

The college initiated students into the rules of honor, particularly the violent folkways that validated a man's claim of being an honorable gentleman.[45] Dueling, caning, posting a man for cowardice, and the other violent customs were closely observed by the students while in college and later in life. Dueling was never eradicated regardless of the sanctions imposed. In 1834 one alumnus observed, "the frequency of challenges and duels amongst the students is very injurious to the College. I am informed that there have been two challenges to fight duels amongst the students within a few weeks past."[46] Neither of these is mentioned in the faculty minutes or local newspapers. Every student on campus either had a pair of dueling pistols or knew where a set could be quickly obtained.

The only duel between undergraduates that resulted in fatalities was fought in 1833 between juniors A. Govan Roach and James G. Adams:

> Both men were of fine families, and . . . they were very intimate friends; they sat opposite each other in the Steward's hall at table. When the bell rang and the door was opened, the students rushed in, and it was considered a matter of honor, when a man got hold of a dish of butter or bread, or any other dish, it was his. Unfortunately, Roach and Adams sat opposite each other, and both caught hold of a dish of trout at the same moment. Adams did not let go; Roach held onto the dish. Presently Roach let go of the dish and glared fiercely in Adams face, and said, "Sir, I will see you after supper." They sat there all through supper, both looking like mad bulls I presume. Roach left the supper room first, and Adams immediately followed him. Roach waited outside the door for Adams. There were no hard words and no fisticuffs—all was dignity and

solemnity. "Sir," said Roach, "What can I do to insult you?" Adams replied "This is enough, sir, and you will hear from me."[47]

One young man was killed; the other was wounded and drank himself to death two years later. In another case a teenage student formally challenged the sixty-seven-year-old Thomas Cooper to a duel.[48] However excessive and vainglorious, these lessons in status maintenance were significant. In the absence of bureaucratized political parties, dueling and the associated rituals of violence were more important than in other states in identifying those men who were legitimate bearers of political power. "Honor" was the bridge between the politics and the ethics of the slaveholding class, and the college homogenized and articulated the mores associated with honor.[49]

In other states, in the wake of especially regrettable results such as the death of Alexander Hamilton, dueling had gone into disfavor. Not so in South Carolina. One polite atrocity after another scars the annals of South Carolinian politics. Although gentlemen throughout the South occasionally had recourse to the code, nowhere was dueling a more important or conspicuous part of political life than South Carolina.[50] The reason for this may be that in South Carolina there was more of a need for it. Politics in antebellum South Carolina was not bureaucratic but charismatic. One alumnus noted, "Then politics were altogether of a personal character. There were no great principles at stake; it was simply whether this or that *man* should be elected; and the man who was the most popular, and had the most money, and could buy the most whiskey, was generally the man that carried the day."[51]

Every state, including South Carolina, needed to identify and promote political leaders on a regular basis. In other states during the antebellum period, political parties bureaucratically performed these functions. Whatever else dueling involved, an important function of dueling in South Carolinian politics was the "routinization" of charisma.[52] Politicians in the Palmetto State (and the students in the college) held fast to the atavistic antiparty ideals of the Federalist era, and in the absence of parties, dueling served as a marker of status; the duelist was the man of honor, and the honorable gentleman was the legitimate bearer of political power. Despite the rules against dueling, South Carolina College prepared its graduates to enter this unusual system of selection. Dueling benefited many alumni early in their political careers. Among those who had graduated during the Maxcy years, there were many prominent politicians who had proven themselves "gentlemen of the code." William Campbell Preston ('12), who eventually became president of the college, issued at least one challenge during the nullification crisis.[53] George McDuffie ('13) engaged in a series of spectacular duels in 1822, which helped make him nationally prominent.[54] The symbolism of the duel, with its ritual equalization of status by an aggrieved gentleman and the hazard of physical safety, would be revisited on the largest possible scale in 1861.

The college was as important in political theory as in political practice. The defense of slavery was taken up by the alumni, trustees, faculty, and students since early in the history of the college. Henry Laurens Pinckney ('13), editor of the *Charleston Mercury,* threatened secession in response to antislavery agitation as early as 1823.[55] He eventually was elected to Congress, but made sure that another alumnus, John Stuart ('17), took over as editor. One of the earliest and most influential defenses of slavery, the 1828 *Memoir on Slavery,* was written by Judge William Harper ('08), who also wrote the Ordinance of Nullification in 1832.

The secession movement, which originated in and around South Carolina College, had been actively promoted since the 1820s by Thomas Cooper and other conspirators, many of whom were connected with the college.[56] The development of secessionist politics was linked with free trade and the defense of slavery, and these doctrines were developed in the curriculum by a politicized faculty in the years following the Missouri Compromise.

At the founding of the college there were only two members of the faculty, and at no time before 1860 were there any more than six professors. The first president of the college, Jonathan Maxcy, served from the opening of the college in 1805 until his death in 1820. He was a Baptist minister and a New England Federalist who took almost no part in political affairs. Perhaps he had his hands full with the unruly students and the high turnover of faculty. Most of the professors of the Maxcy era left after two or three years, and none stayed more than five.

When the next president, Thomas Cooper, arrived on campus in 1820, politics moved from being a peripheral to a central concern of collegiate education. Cooper had been on the faculty only a few months when Maxcy died, yet he had sufficiently impressed the trustees to be appointed Maxcy's successor. Cooper remained on the faculty until 1834, when he was ousted by a heterogeneous coalition of political and religious enemies, but while he was on campus he was the dominant intellectual figure in the state. Cooper solved the problem of high faculty turnover by retaining on campus a group of cronies who shared his political enthusiasms. Under Cooper, the faculty formed an intellectual vanguard that advocated extreme antitariff, states rights, proslavery, and ultimately secessionist political views. The faculty was conspicuous within the state capital, a town of only three or four thousand people, and their views were no secret to the students.

Cooper, an expatriate Englishman, had been an agitator all his life. In 1819, just before he joined the faculty, he had been publishing newspaper articles against the protective tariff, against the Missouri Compromise, and in favor of the perpetuation of slavery.[57] Once ensconced in the president's chair, he redoubled his efforts. As one of his students recalled: "He loved excitement and would participate in it wherever it was to be found . . . he was a partizan *[sic]* of more than usual bitterness. . . . He had already reached conclusions on every possible question of morals, politics and religion. No man was more tenacious, dogmatic, or had a bolder or more uncompromising spirit."[58]

Cooper often posed as a defender of individual freedom, and occasionally he was, but it often appears that this was more a posture than a principle. With vast exaggeration, he painted himself as an unoffending advocate of civil rights, persecuted by ignorant sectarians. Cooper modestly stated that he had the misfortune of running "half a century ahead of the knowledge of the day; . . . if a man is bent on doing this, he should make up his mind to meet the consequences, and count the cost."[59] Cooper had no sense of proportion, and he often abused his opponents, both religious and political, in terms that are nearly slanderous. In 1828 he wrote to David McCord, an alumnus, a personal friend, and editor of the pronullification *Columbia Southern Telescope:* "All the tariff men rely on exciting a revolt among our slaves."[60] The same factual foundation and emotional equilibrium are found in his published remarks on the clergy. "Who ordained the Sabbath? Those avaricious, ambitious, fraudulent and impudent impostors, the Christian priests. For what purpose? To create business for themselves; to obtain influence; to get money; to make their services necessary to the ignorant."[61]

Many observers noted that his lectures were little more than propaganda for his self-indulgent political commitments. The *Camden Journal* complained that Cooper "has not only been engaged in inculcating infidelity and irreligion, but in inoculating our youth with the virus of Nullification."[62] An anxious father wrote that he sent his son to Princeton only "to avoid the infidelity and dissipation of S. Ca. College. . . . Many young men from the South since the College has gotten into infidel hands have gone to Northern institutions."[63] The tendentious content and gratuitously hectoring tone of his criticism are typical of his notorious "infidelity":

> To say that any member of society is not of the productive class does not imply that we have not been prodigal in recompensing by salaries or by reputation, classes of an unproductive character, greatly to the detriment of public morals, of public wealth, and of public expedience. Some one has observed that mankind pay best 1st. those who murder and destroy them; warriors and heroes. 2nd. those who cheat them; statesmen and the priesthood; 3rd. those who amuse them; singers, actors, dancers, fidlers, *[sic]* etc. 4th. those who instruct them. . . . The priesthood, a class of men who cost us at this moment between 12 to 14,000,000 of dollars annually have contrived to persuade us that they are absolutely necessary to our welfare. I know not in what respect.[64]

Once in South Carolina, Cooper repudiated the French Revolution at least insofar as it was a threat to slavery, but he held fast to aggressive anticlericalism, which he reformulated in the language of English political economy. Although eloquent and learned, he self-righteously insisted that his students accept his dogmas. He insisted on trying to teach his students what to think rather than how to think. In 1823, the year he began giving America's first course in political economy, Cooper published a tract against the tariff, which he sent to every member of South Carolina's congressional delegation. In 1824, when most of South Carolina's politicians, including Calhoun, were still nationalists, Cooper published a widely reprinted tract called *Consolidation* in which he took an extreme prosouthern, antitariff position. In 1826 he published a volume of his lectures on political economy. He stressed the danger that the tariff posed to the South and insisted that free trade and states rights were the only solutions. In the same year he published a tract, *On the Constitution,* in which he defended slavery and strict construction as well as argued that the Missouri Compromise was unconstitutional.[65]

Cooper wrote dozens of newspaper articles while publishing these books, but his most important contribution to secessionist politics came in a speech he gave in Columbia on 2 July 1827. At an antitariff meeting run by members of the college faculty, Cooper declaimed that on account of the tariff, "we shall be driven to adopt some decisive measure, when the power is gone from us. Wealth will be transferred to the North and wealth is power. Every year of submission rivets the chains upon us... before long we will have to calculate the value of our union.... The question is fast approaching the alternative of submission or separation."[66] Unlike the constitutional cobweb spinning of Calhoun, Cooper's speech was radical talk about tangible realities, like wealth. An enormous controversy erupted in the wake of this speech, which was reprinted all over the country and extensively cited in the Webster/Hayne debate.

It is remarkable that in 1827, before nullification had even been invented, the president of South Carolina College was issuing invitations to the American Civil War. Less obvious, but perhaps more important in the long run, Cooper took the intellectual high ground. He and the ideologues on the faculty pioneered in problematizing and thematizing the relation between the South and the federal government. This allowed them to formulate the terms of debate, and the dichotomy between "submission" and "separation" gained wide currency throughout South Carolina and eventually throughout the lower South. Taking the conceptual initiative gave secessionists, who were a radical minority, indispensable rhetorical leverage over the more conservative majority. Cooper wrote in 1829 that he expected that the tariff would cause South Carolina and Georgia to secede "toward the end of 1830 [and that] . . . I shall promote secession to the utmost of my powers."[67] Reflecting upon this crisis in 1850, one of Cooper's former students candidly stated, "only a few of the older Nullifiers regarded it as any more than a form of secession."[68] Cooper was consciously trying to create the politicians of the next generation. As he said in 1821 in an address to his first graduating class, "it is probable you will all become politicians of various grades."[69]

Three sets of student notebooks survive from this era, but none to Cooper's lectures. Only notes to Professor Robert Henry's class in metaphysics and moral philosophy survive in duplicate. These two notebooks, taken from lectures given three years apart, are verbatim identical.[70] This suggests that Professor Henry gave "canned" lectures. Henry, who was on the faculty from 1819 to 1856, informed his students that "it is absolutely necessary to keep the blacks in their present condition."[71] Moreover, both of the notebooks read like catechisms, with the notes dictated in a question-and-answer format for easier memorization. The notes from 1831 are indeed memorable:

Q: Can any state be called disloyal which will [not] submit . . . to the usurped powers of Congress?
A: No rather a friend of the Union.
Q: What would you say of acts passed by Congress which transcend its powers?
A: They are null and void. . . .
Q: What is necessary in order to be relieved of oppression?
A: Unanimity of the oppressed.
Q: What effect on the Union has the known right of secession?
A: It strengthens rather than injures it.
Q: What was the fault of the English with regard to her conduct toward us when colonies?
A: She confided too much in her own strength and in the supposed ease with which she could intimidate us.
Q: What was the consequence?
A: Separation.
Q: Will not the same causes produce the same effects now?
A: Certainly.
Q: Do you recollect what particular terms gave rise to the mistakes of the old royal and present federal government?
A: Englishmen and Americans.
Q: Can we be one people in interest and government?
A: No, because experience shows we are not one people.[72]

The whole process of education pushed the students toward political extremism. One of Cooper's students recalled that he and his fellows went down the street to hear a political speech. The students "left the hall detesting the tariff, and with the firm conviction that they would nullify or die."[73] Nationally known politicians attended mass nullification meetings held on campus.[74] The Nullification Convention of 1832 was held just down the street from the college; nine of the most important members were trustees; seven of these trustees were alumni. The Nullification Convention as a whole consisted of 39 percent alumni.[75]

The extremist political milieu permeating the college was described in 1834 by an English traveler, George Featherstonaugh. The Englishman had naively congratulated Cooper on the compromise that had narrowly averted civil war:

> [Cooper] rose from his easy chair, and . . . he seized the hearthbrush with eyes full of fire, and wielding the brush as if it were a broadsword denounced the compromise act as an ignoble measure he could never approve of; declared the Nullifiers had been quite in the wrong in making peace with the Union men . . . and that it would have been much better for them to have taken the field against General Jackson and all the force he could have brought against them. "We have lost a fine opportunity, sir, of bringing this statue into the highest renown," said this crooked little octogenarian *[sic]*; and then giving General Jackson a desperate cut with the hearthbrush, he went back to his easy chair again.[76]

The astonished Englishman wisely did not press the issue but noted in his journal that while he found Cooper's learning impressive, "some of his screws were uncommonly loose."[77] Featherstonaugh got a taste of the town's intellectual life at a dinner party the next evening. He wrote:

> Our party consisted of some gentleman of the place, Dr. Cooper, and a few professors belonging to the college. . . . What particularly struck me at this dinner was the total want of caution and reserve in the ultra opinions they expressed about religion and politics; on these topics their conversation was not at all addressed to me, but seemed to be a resumption of opinions they were accustomed to express whenever they met and upon all occasions. A stranger dropped in amongst them would hardly have supposed himself amongst Americans. It was quite new to me to hear men of the better class express themselves openly against a republican government and to listen to discussions of great ability, the object of which was to show that there can never be a good government if it is not

administered by gentlemen. . . . Something very extravagant having been said, I asked if they called themselves Americans yet; the gentleman [replied] . . . "If you ask me if I am an American, my answer is No sir, I am a South Carolinian." If the children of these Nullifiers are brought up in the same opinions, which they are very likely to be, here are fine elements for future disunion, for imbibing from their infancy the notion that they are born to command, it will be intolerable to them to be, in their own estimation, the drudges of Northern manufacturers, who they despise as an inferior race of men.[78]

One of the gentlemen who had been at the dinner party met Featherstonaugh the next day. The Englishman had tactfully waited until he was about to leave Columbia before he ventured delicately to ask this unnamed gentleman about slavery.

The line of argument he took up in answer to my observation was really very curious, and deserves to be recorded. He observed that the institution of slavery (so he dignified this bondage) was not understood outside of the southern states; that it elevated the character of the master, by comparison, made him jealous of his own, and the natural friend of public liberty; that the dignity of character which had belonged to southern gentlemen from Washington down to the present times was unknown to men of the northern states. . . . [The North lacked slavery,] and everybody knew that this generated a rapacious spirit, and made the accumulation of wealth the object of every man's life. This was not the case in South Carolina, where the planter, whatever might be his transactions, was careful not to encroach upon the character of a gentleman [he gave Calhoun as an example of a gentleman politician]. . . . All these great principles of action, he said were developed and strengthened by the institution of slavery; that the slaves were not an unhappy race of men. . . . If there had been a necessity for it in the late dispute with the United States government the slaves would have shown to a man their well known fidelity to their masters.[79]

This gentleman was obviously a practiced speaker, and it is also obvious that his proslavery oration was not an improvisation. It is equally clear that the English visitor had hit a nerve with even the most tentative inquiry about the justice of slavery. Blown back by this gentleman's verbal hurricane, Featherstonaugh made no retort, but he was silently appalled by the content of the argument. He noted:

I was struck with this justification of slavery, which, notwithstanding its excluding humanity, benevolence, and justice from the list of our duties to others would seem to qualify white men in a very high degree for the enjoyment of the compulsory labor of men of a different color. If it means anything it must mean that every man should be a slaveholder in order to [*sic*, ? foster] the successful development of his own inherent dignity.[80]

Evidence showing the influence of this radical milieu on the growth of proslavery, secessionist political opinions among the students can be found in the debates of the literary societies. The records of the debate societies are like a weekly opinion poll with questions chosen by students and answers in the form of votes by members. Prior to 1820, during the tenure of President Maxcy, the students were generally nationalistic. In 1809 one society voted a unanimous affirmation to the question "Would it be disadvantageous to the country for the several states to become independent?"[81] Ironically they adopted an even harder line in 1813 during the agitation for the Hartford Convention, affirming the proposition that "if one state of our union were to form a separate government, the rest [would] be justified in compelling it to reunite."[82] Moreover they were sanguine about the nation's prospects, and in 1819 they affirmed that it was probable that the government of the United States would survive a century.[83]

Slavery was the one topic debated at least annually and by every class of students, and it appears that the most popular topic of undergraduate discussion was the politics and ethics of slaveholding. Under Maxcy, the Clariosophics debated questions concerning slavery at least seventeen times in the first fourteen years.[84] The most striking fact about their debates on slavery was the ambivalence and lack of unanimity among the auditors. Their uncertainty about slavery during the Era of Good Feelings paralleled the lack of clarity and consensus on the slave issue in American political culture as a whole. The students were intelligent young men who could not help sensing the conflicting tendencies within American political life and the tension between the political traditions of South Carolina and those of other states. On issues other than slavery the trend of the students' thinking is reasonably clear, but their discussions of slavery, at least during the Maxcy years, were far more convoluted and contradictory.

In 1808 they decided that "the condition of African [was] meliorated by being brought to this country," but in 1810 they voted the reverse.[85] In 1809 they voted that the introduction of slavery had been disadvantageous to the state.[86] In 1816 they reversed themselves and voted that it had been advantageous.[87] In 1819 they reconsidered the introduction of slavery and found it to be disadvantageous.[88] Nonetheless, in 1820 they voted that Congress should not prohibit slavery in the state of Missouri.[89] In 1818 the proposition "Would a law prohibiting the introduction of slaves be politic, admitting it constitutional?"[90] was overwhelmingly rejected (24–2). However, in the same year, they resolved that "the colonization of slaves on the coast of Africa [would] be advantageous to America."[91] They agreed that simple justice required the manumission of slaves; yet they voted that free Negroes ought to be banished.[92] In 1819 they decided that it would be politic to address the grievances of a slave by law, but the next year they voted that slaves should not get an education.[93] The emancipation of the slaves was supported in 1812, but slavery was to be tolerated in 1813.[94]

One trend in the Clariosophics' debates on slavery is clear, however. At least five times in fourteen years human polygenesis (the theory that races are the products of separate creation, hence not members of the same species) was seriously entertained by the students. In 1806 the society debated the question "Were all mankind descended from the same origin?"[95] The results of this debate were not recorded, but it is likely that the vote was in favor of polygenesis because the next year, 1807, these same auditors rephrased the question to put the burden of proof on those who accepted polygenesis. This time the Clariosophics decided that they did not "have sufficient reason to believe that all mankind [were] not descend[ed] from the same origin."[96] Although polygenesis continued to be a controversial subject, the preponderance of student opinion remained the same, and human beings were affirmed to be of the same species in 1816 and 1817.[97] Although a consensus of the undergraduates' opinions on slavery had not coalesced by 1820, it is noteworthy that the implied apologies for slavery contained within their topics for discussion (such as polygenesis) were all secular rather than theological in their orientation.

In some respects the college debates can be seen as a reflection of public opinion in South Carolina. Between 1770 and 1820, there exists only evidence of secular defenses of slavery, founded on naturalistic or legalistic assumptions. Ministers were not held in especially high regard, and slavery was primarily defended by lawyers and politicians in terms of constitutional law, natural law, the law of nations, economic necessity, climate, and superior resistance to disease.[98]

The evidence of student opinion from the two debate societies shows a clear movement away from the qualified nationalism of the Maxcy era toward the sectionalism of Cooper and the other members of the faculty, while at the same time their views on slavery hardened. In 1821, at the very beginning of Cooper's tenure in office, the Clariosophic Society affirmed that the dissolution of the Union was "probable."[99] The Clariosophics affirmed as early as 1822 the proposition that "the causes of discord growing out of the localities of the different states, together with those which arrive from the relation of the states and the general government, threaten the existence of the union."[100] Moreover in 1826 the Clariosophics decided against the question "Should we send our youth to northern colleges for education?" So it appears that they understood that they were getting a "southern" education.[101]

Between 1821 and 1835, the justice of slavery and the expediency of emancipation were debated by the two societies at least twenty times.[102] While the students harbored some misgivings about slavery prior to 1820, and their votes were roughly equally divided between proslavery and antislavery positions, during the Cooper era, the students voted that slavery was justifiable and that emancipation was undesirable at least fifteen times out of twenty. Some traces of antislavery sentiment can be found in the debate society records, but these traces became fainter and more attenuated over time.[103]

Nullification and the tariff were debated at least fifteen times during the Cooper era, and both societies were heavily in favor of the nullifiers.[104] In the wake of the "calculate the value of the Union" speech, the Clariosophic Society debated the question "Was Dr. Cooper justified in using the language he did in protesting against the Woolens Bill?" They affirmed that he was. The Euphradians believed that they had "as good reason to resist the tariff of 1828 as our forefathers had to resist the tax on tea."[105] In his tract *Consolidation,* Cooper had argued that secession might be the only just response to federal encroachment. Given the choice, the Euphradians thought it better to nullify than to secede.[106] The Clariosophics, on the other hand, saw a different set of alternatives. They debated the proposition "Which is preferable to the United States: consolidation or disunion?" Like Cooper, they chose disunion.[107]

It is not surprising that disunion and secession, which were not controversial issues during the Maxcy era, became controversial under Cooper. The students spent a considerable amount of time calculating the value of the Union. During the Cooper years disunion was debated at least a dozen times by the two societies.[108] Although both societies had misgivings about disunion (the Clariosophics, in particular, voted against secession in 1828, 1829, and 1830), they generally agreed that at least in some circumstances, the tariff could "justify a rebellion."[109] The young men who repeatedly considered the option of secession in the 1820s turned out later to be exactly what Featherstonaugh predicted, "fine elements for future disunion."

The later political thought and action of the alumni closely paralleled their education at the college. Within the state legislature the alumni formed a particularly formidable voting bloc because the state had no organized political parties, and opposition was disorganized. The alumni were conspicuous for their support of one another and their support of the college, and through them the college wielded enormous influence on politics.[110] They often selected alumni to serve as governor or senator or presidential elector or state judge. The alumni in the legislature influenced legislation, policy, and patronage by controlling the speakership of the House and thus committee assignments. Between 1824 and 1860, the Speaker was an alumnus for all but six years.[111]

To a great extent the college took up the institutional slack left by the absence of a political party system.[112] The papers of Congressman, Governor, and Senator James Henry Hammond reveal the subtle sounding of collegiate acquaintances and careful planning with collegiate friends to secure the endorsement of local notables so important to election.[113] The pattern of officeholding in South Carolina through the Civil War suggests what contemporaries generally knew; the college was the intellectual and political crucible for South Carolina's elite. Between 1824 and 1865, twelve of South Carolina's twenty-one governors were alumni. After 1865, alumni were elected governor five more times. Between 1830 and the death of Calhoun in 1850, one of South Carolina's senators was an alumnus; thereafter, one or more were. Between 1820 and 1860, at least a quarter of the members of the lower house were alumni, and an average of 32.5 percent of the lower house was composed of alumni.

While most were agreed that the college had been a politically unifying force, the exclusivity of the college and the hauteur of alumni were often criticized by the unanointed. One member of the state legislature, whose proposals for the reform of primary and secondary school education had been thwarted by a voting bloc of alumni, stated bluntly:

> The College—the S.C. College—governs the state. Its Trustees are the Governor—the Judges—the Chancellors—the president of the Senate— the Speaker of the House—the Chairmen of certain Committees—distinguished and ex-distinguished personages of the land. Legislators talk of *the* College with undisguised scorn for all other pretenders to the name of College in the State, and most of those out of it.[114]

In a letter to a Columbia newspaper, another writer complained of the elitism of gentlemen who looked "upon those educated at South Carolina College as *alone* fit to fill the offices and control the destinies of the state."[115]

The alumni of South Carolina College constituted a privileged elite who had all of the advantages of wealth and education that the South could offer. They spoke a common political idiom, and they shared a consensus about the ends of public policy if not the means. A writer in the *Charleston Mercury* noted,

> If the College does [say] farewell to the unity of sentiment which has made South Carolina, small as she is, the centre and rallying point of

states' rights resistance; as Massachusetts has been, owing to the influence of Harvard, of the antagonistic principles of encroaching federal power. It is the educated intellect and the trained and developed morale of the state which gives it tone, character and direction.[116]

The "tone" taken by alumni was deeply influenced by the "tone" of their teachers. The alumni who matriculated under Maxcy, while predisposed toward slavery and the interests of the South, showed some diversity of political beliefs.[117] Since the alumni were an economic as well as an intellectual elite and rich men make unlikely revolutionaries, a substantial minority became conservative unionists opposed to nullification. Most of the Maxcy-era alumni whose political views are known did support nullification. Five of these nullifiers eventually represented South Carolina in the Senate, nine in the House, and four were elected governor. Most of these early alumni were dead or retired by 1860, but of those who were still active all except one were disunionists.

There are many possible indices for the influence of Cooper upon his students. One graduate of the class of 1831, William Boykin, named his son Thomas Cooper Boykin. Another former student, Nathaniel Gist, named his son not after Cooper, but after his political principles. The boy, who came from a prominent family and was himself graduated from the college in the class of 1850, could hardly avoid becoming a Confederate general with a name like "States Rights" Gist. The ultra views of Chancellor George Dargan ('23), who eventually became an ex officio member of the board of trustees, also seem to have been influenced by the beliefs he was exposed to in the college lectures. An associate recalled,

> He was a most devoted states rights man, nullifier, secessionist and disunionist. . . . his boast for many years was that he had never been beyond the limits of South Carolina, and hoped never to be under the necessity of going out of the state. . . . he regarded South Carolina as his country, his whole country, and all beyond her limits as aliens and foreigners! He was devoted to the state and the State alone, her honor and her glory. He once said to me. "You old fogies may be Union men, and glorify the Union, because you have been educated and brought up in that school, but the rising generation will scorn that Union and sever it into fragments. Mark what I tell you."[118]

The "rising generation" represented by the prescient Dargan did sever the Union into fragments, and this was at least partially caused by a faculty that "educated and brought up" South Carolina College students in a different "school" from that of the "Union men."

With a few exceptions the Cooper alumni were too young to take much of a part in nullification; however by 1860, they were the elder statesmen of South Carolina, and they were overwhelmingly secessionists. All of South Carolina's governors between 1858 and 1865 were Cooper's students, as were eleven of South Carolina's congressmen. Most important, South Carolina's Secession Convention was composed of 44 percent alumni, and the majority of them were Cooper's students. One alumnus remarked,

> More than a quarter century after Cooper's retirement from the College, Langdon Cheves [a member of the Secession Convention] . . . so prominent in civic and military life, late in 1860, when the question of secession was [considered] . . . spoke not of his illustrious father, nor Calhoun, nor Hayne, but referred to and cited the words of Dr. Cooper as having first given bent to his thought which assured him of the soundness of his political views.[119]

The fact that the college was the single most important influence on the politics of South Carolina's antebellum elite was common knowledge to contemporaries. One observer noted, "the South Carolina College has done more to make us one homogeneous people than all other influences combined."[120] An early alumnus stated, "the great merit of South Carolina College is that it tended to make the state one people."[121] Another alumnus stated that, "from its commencement, the College has become to a large extent the center, not only of education, but of political thought in the state, and is doubtless the institution which has done the most to mold and influence the character of the people of the state."[122]

South Carolina College also exerted a powerful influence on the newly admitted states of the Deep South. In 1851 Oscar Lieber ('49) wrote to his father (a professor at the college) while traveling in Alabama :

> Our College certainly holds the highest position among southern institutions of the kind and most men who graduate are above the average intellect of the country . . . they spread over the whole broad acres of the South and yet whenever you meet a graduate of our College, you can be sure, yes 50 to 1 that he is strong in his political faith and that that faith is of the right sort. It would be interesting if it could be ascertained, for instance, what number of her alumni were Know Nothings. I feel confident not more than 5% were of that party and not more than 20% were indifferent. So regular is this similarity of opinion that a priori I should never hesitate to speak to them, but as if they had already expressed it.[123]

Between 1830 and 1860, South Carolina led all states in the Union in percentage of outmigrant population.[124] Almost half of the alumni left the state, and nearly all went to the lower South. In the process these ministers, doctors, editors, and lawyers contributed to the development of a new political elite in these new plantation societies. One alumnus remarked, "The ideas instilled, the doctrines inculcated, the influence exerted by the College, were disseminated throughout the whole southern and southwestern country, not only by the students from these other states, but by the great numbers of native South Carolinian students, who, after graduation, emigrated there."[125]

College alumni served as antebellum governors of Georgia, Florida, Alabama, and Mississippi. More than a dozen alumni were sent to Congress from Georgia, Alabama, Mississippi, Louisiana, and Texas. When South Carolina seceded in December 1860, Mississippi, Florida, Alabama, Georgia, Louisiana, and Texas joined the state in a little more than a month. Alumni were in every one of these secession conventions. As one alumnus noted,

> To the College is very largely attributable the influence which has not only made South Carolina the prompt and determined champion of Southern rights and interests, especially state sovereignty, free trade, and the institution of domestic African slavery, but which has also deeply impressed the doctrines entertained, by South Carolina, on those subjects on the heart and mind of the entire South and Southwest. So great has been this influence as to give it historical significance.[126]

Agency, Denominations, and the Western Colleges, 1830–1860

Some Connections between Evangelicalism and American Higher Education

~

JAMES FINDLAY

R eligion, and more specifically evangelical Protestantism, has been recognized as an important factor influencing the small colleges that dominated American higher education prior to the Civil War. But the precise connections between evangelicalism and higher education during those years have not been studied very systematically. This chapter begins with a brief sketch of the new historiography and tries to suggest some of the interpretive strengths and weaknesses of the recent writings. Then follows a description of the "agency" system developed by certain midwestern schools to aid in fund-raising—a specific point of linkage between the general religious community and the colleges this community helped to found. This latter section seeks to redress in a limited way the interpretive imperfections of the recent historiography and to suggest something of the nature of the special relationships that existed between the small colleges of the Midwest and the evangelical Protestant churches during the middle decades of the nineteenth century.

New historiography has emphasized the functional roles the colleges played in a society dominated by local, decentralized institutions, suggested nonelitist characteristics among the students attending these schools, revealed expanding, not contracting, enrollments, which tend to reinforce the apparent functionalism of these schools, and pointed out curriculum innovations occurring behind a facade of conservatism.[1]

It is strange that the new interpreters of the nineteenth-century college have largely ignored or soft-pedaled the key role that religion played in the shaping of these schools. David Potts, a leading spokesman for the revisionists, has perhaps articulated their attitude most clearly. According to Potts the small colleges of the pre–Civil War era "were above all else *local* colleges." "Religious zeal" was not to be excluded "as one element of localism, but it does give secular forces their rightfully *predominant* role" (latter italics added). Potts went on to assert that the colleges "were closely tied with the local cultural and economic ambitions of citizens, parents and students; special religious interests became of major significance only in the unusual cases where these ties were weak or absent."[2]

Anyone who has worked extensively in the archival records of these colleges and the religious bodies closely associated with them would find Potts's statements difficult to accept. Secular forces affecting the mid-nineteenth-century colleges should not be ignored, but neither should the religious influences impinging upon these colleges. The collegiate system of the pre–Civil War era cannot be understood properly if it is placed outside the context of evangelical Protestantism, which served as one principal historical home of all those who founded and maintained institutions of higher education in America before 1870.

Timothy Smith has published a lengthy essay dealing with all the colleges founded by religious groups in Indiana and Illinois between 1820 and 1950. Over half this essay is devoted to a discussion of the quarter century between 1830 and 1855.[3] Like Potts, Smith emphasizes the importance of local interest and concerns in establishing and maintaining the colleges, but unlike Potts, he always views these developments within the broad framework of the churches and denominations representing evangelical Protestantism.

In one sense Smith's study represents a continuation of the efforts of American church historians of a generation ago to study the relationships between mainstream American Protestant groups and the westward movement. That work was centered at the University of Chicago, chiefly in the publications of William Warren Sweet and his students. Their interpretive biases no longer hold sway; however, they were deeply affected by Frederick Jackson Turner's all-encompassing view of the frontier's influence on American life. They were institutionalists who tended to ignore too often the theological dimensions of their story. And they wrote (with the exception perhaps of Sweet himself) too much out of the Presbyterian-Congregational framework influenced by the massive collection of letters of the American Home Missionary Society then in the library of the Chicago Theological Seminary. They never analyzed in any detail the many Protestant colleges established in the Midwest.[4] Nevertheless, the writings of these historians remain an important corpus that present-day students of the nineteenth-century colleges could read with profit.[5]

One result of Timothy Smith's study is that he points to the role that *intrade-nominational* conflicts—especially among Baptists and among Presbyterians—played in shaping the early history of the schools founded by these groups in Illinois and Indiana. The conflicts involved internal ecclesiastical and theological issues that have been ignored by other historians but are crucial matters to be understood in any effort to reconstruct the milieu of the colleges of the nineteenth century.[6]

This work is based on a study of seven schools in Illinois and Indiana: Knox, Illinois, McKendree, and Shurtleff Colleges in Illinois; Indiana Asbury (later DePauw) University, and Wabash and Franklin Colleges in Indiana. All of these schools were established in the late 1820s or the 1830s, and collectively they represented the four denominations that were at the core of the evangelical movement: Baptists, Methodists, Presbyterians, and Congregationalists. Within the general context of revisionist educational history, a regional study like this one can serve a useful purpose, shifting attention away from New England, which has dominated fact gathering and interpretations in American collegiate history for much too long. There are connections and continuities between East and West that must be recognized, but there are variations, too, that deserve the attention of historians.

In his attempts to analyze the pre–Civil War colleges David Potts has spoken of the need to assess "the consequences of efforts by college agents to create increased demand for higher education in various local and regional contexts."[7] Potts has put his finger on a key element in the structure of collegiate education, still largely unexamined by historians. Throughout the antebellum era, college agents served as the principal fund-raisers for their respective schools. They also became important people in interpreting the colleges' broad purposes to the larger community. Because they were nearly always ministers (faculty of the colleges or local clergy on leave from a regular parish) or laypersons widely recognized as associated with sponsoring denominations, agents reflected the characteristics of the religious groups that were the chief support of the colleges. The agents then served in a unique mediating role between the colleges and the churches. To compare the agency systems of the different schools as they evolved over time should suggest certain characteristics of both the religious bodies making up evangelical Protestantism and the colleges nurtured by those bodies. Such an analysis may also reveal some of the factors that enabled the colleges to function effectively in a local or regional milieu.

The records are clearest regarding the Methodists. In Indiana especially, the Methodists lavished a degree of attention upon their firstborn college that no other Methodist educational institution in the state ever received.[8] An extraordinarily close relationship existed between Indiana Asbury University and the Indiana Conference from the time of the school's founding, and this fact was fully reflected in the agency system devised to provide much of the financing of the school in its early years. The first two agents of the school were ministers appointed first by the annual conference and then approved by the college board of trustees. Late in the first year of operation the trustees suggested for the "favorable consideration of the conference" that "each member of that body" be constituted an agent of Indiana Asbury, in addition to the two formally appointed agents. In other words all the Methodist ministers in the state would "solicit funds, procure students, and collect what books the liberality of the public may bestow . . . for the use of the institution." This was a sweeping extension of the agency system, perhaps difficult to implement, yet highly revealing of the relationship developing between the school and the local denominational structure.[9]

A modified version of this proposal was soon after put into operation statewide. By order of the Indiana Conference, beginning in 1841 a general collection was to be made "in all our congregations . . . for the aid of our University." Pushing forward with a typical Methodist sense of direction and organization, the conference further spelled out its plans. "Each P[residing] E[lder]" was to "preach a special sermon" on the subject "annually in each station and circuit in his District," and the elder was also to make sure that "each preacher make collections." The conference went even further. It gave instructions to the preachers in local areas as to "the best method of collecting funds," that is, "not to depend on public collections alone, but in their pastoral visits to bring the subject before the members and friends of the church, individually." By this means, the conference concluded, "the entire strength of the church may be concentrated upon the great object we desire to accomplish, viz: the religious and intellectual improvement of the whole community."[10]

In these documents one can see how the agents of Indiana Asbury University, now all the ministers of Methodist persuasion in the state backed by the powerful organization of their church, could reach out and touch quite directly the lives of thousands of rough and largely unlettered Hoosiers. Through preaching and even more significantly though the pastoral visits of local preachers with individual church members, the message of the value of education as a key method of achieving "the religious and intellectual improvement of the whole community" was to be pressed home. No more concrete and dramatic illustrations can be found to reveal the evangelical Protestant community's commitment to higher education even in the most primitive of social situations and how they unhesitatingly utilized existing denominational machinery to implement their commitments.

The last-quoted words above also point to another important characteristic of the pre–Civil War colleges. Most were closely allied with specific Protestant groups or denominations, yet few fell into narrowly sectarian roles in public life. This was true in part because in the 1830s and 1840s the religiously controlled colleges were essentially the only system of higher education available. If a broad public role was to be played by the colleges of the time, those schools would have to do it. Religious leaders eagerly embraced this opportunity, especially in the Midwest, since control of the educational system from the primary level through college would enable evangelical Protestants to influence deeply the entire cultural and social system then developing in the region. Among all the church groups there seemed to be no disagreement that strong support of their specific colleges ultimately had the widest implications.[11] This explains why exhortations for Methodists to give generously to Indiana Asbury University could be seen as a way of working toward "the religious and intellectual improvement of a whole community." Perhaps there were times, however, when the scarcely hidden power of the larger community of Methodists to affect their fledgling colleges was a limiting and not a liberating influence. On a variety of matters conference boundaries were considered all but inviolate. Thus it is not surprising that over the years the regularly appointed full-time agents of Indiana Asbury seldom ventured outside the state to raise money. Even the president of the school, the most important of the fund-raisers, was directed by the conference as to time and place for soliciting money, usually just within Indiana. These organizational constraints were one more way to reinforce the localistic nature of the college enterprise in the Midwest. These constraints also imposed a certain lack of flexibility on a Methodist college that was not so true of Presbyterians or Baptists or perhaps even of Methodists in other states.

McKendree College, the first Methodist institution of higher education established in Illinois (1828), like its sister school in Indiana was watched over closely by the state denominational organization. In their earliest meetings the founders of the school appealed for help from the Illinois Conference, and by 1830 McKendree had cemented formal relations.[12] Yet McKendree never was able to assume the position of primacy in the hearts and minds of Illinois Methodists that Asbury did in Indiana. A partial explanation is that at the time of the school's founding, the Illinois Conference embraced portions of Missouri and Indiana as well as Illinois, and from the beginning there were competing interests seeking to create Methodist seminaries and colleges in such a large area. By the time Asbury was established in 1837, a separate Indiana district had been created, which concentrated exclusively on its own educational concerns.

Illinois Methodists also adopted tactics of building colleges that differed from those in Indiana. As the rapidly expanding population moved into the northern half of Illinois after 1830, the Methodists began to think about another college to serve the newly settled areas rather than concentrating their energies on McKendree, located one hundred miles farther south near Saint Louis. Finally in 1849 they founded Illinois Wesleyan at Bloomington, almost at the center of the state, and immediately placed the competing school under the protective wing of the Illinois Conference.[13] Whatever the reason, McKendree's financial agents did not experience the tight supervision exerted over Indiana Asbury by the Methodist system in Indiana. Free to act on its own, in its early years McKendree sent agents in search of gifts to the South (down the river all the way to New Orleans), to nearby states, occasionally to the East Coast, and once even to Great Britain.[14]

The Illinois Conference also seemed more willing than the Hoosiers to exhort its followers to contribute to McKendree rather than to devise specific organizational means to make sure money was collected. The vaguer arrangements in Illinois in relation to the statewide Methodist organization—traditionally the center of power in the Methodist structure—may partially explain the severe financial difficulties McKendree experienced in the late 1830s and early 1840s. Asbury had its ups and downs economically in the same period, but it never went through as prolonged a crisis as did McKendree.[15]

Only "*system, system, system*" could assure success in fund-raising for colleges, asserted a writer in a local Illinois periodical in 1848.[16] Wesleyan colleges seemed to be prime exemplars of this rule. Thus despite some differences in institutional development, system remained the key term that explained the unusually close and effective relationships that developed in the 1830s and 1840s between Methodist college agents in the West, their supervisors in the local Methodist administrative structure, and their clientele in scattered circuits and small churches in a frontier society. Ultimately it was a superior system that set apart Methodist colleges in Indiana and Illinois from similar schools nurtured in the same area by other denominations.

The Presbyterians (with powerful assistance from Congregationalists in Illinois) also founded colleges very early—Illinois College in 1828, Knox College in 1837, and Wabash College in Indiana in 1832. The founders almost immediately appointed agents to help in financing these schools. Like those of the Methodists, the fund-raising techniques of the Presbyterians reflected the broader institutional arrangements that evolved between the three colleges and the sponsoring denominations.

In trying to understand these complex institutional arrangements, one must begin with the Plan of Union, a compact signed in 1801 between Congregationalists and Presbyterians in New England, New York, New Jersey, and Pennsylvania, which enabled these two evangelical groups to cooperate in all missionary work in the West. Colleges founded under this agreement officially were nonsectarian, yet unofficially many people viewed them as Presbyterian institutions, since at least initially everyone in the western areas operating under the Plan of Union was expected to join a local Presbyterian church. As time passed, however, doctrinal and ecclesiastical divisions rooted in the Congregationalism and Presbyterianism of the eastern states sometimes made it difficult to sustain the formal and informal affiliations in the West that the Plan of Union sought to encourage. Open conflicts occurred at Illinois College and at Knox. Wabash seemed much more clearly a Presbyterian school; it experienced no major internal divisions. All this was true primarily because New England Congregationalists migrated in much greater numbers to central Illinois than to the upper Wabash Valley in Indiana in the 1830s and 1840s—the formative years of the three colleges.[17]

Thus these "Presbygational" schools were never as directly and intimately linked to local and regional denominational structures as were Methodist institutions. The agency systems of the Presbygational colleges differed in important ways from those of the Methodist schools. For example, the statewide Presbyterian synod exerted much less direct influence over the agents of Wabash College than did the Methodist Conference over the agents of nearby Indiana Asbury University. In selecting fund-raisers and assigning them their duties, the board of trustees at Wabash never felt compelled to seek approval for their actions from denominational officials as did Methodists.[18] The majority of the fund-raising efforts of the Presbyterians probably occurred locally as was the case with the Methodists, but the Plan of Union institutions also maintained constant contact with centers of Presbyterian and Congregational strength on the East Coast. That fact also enhanced the flexibility of their agency system.

The connections of Wabash and Illinois Colleges with key elements of the fostering denominations on the East Coast were especially strong from the outset.[19] Both schools sent agents to New England, New York, and Pennsylvania in search of financial support almost as soon as they opened their doors. The first presidents of both schools had been ministers in major cities on the East Coast, highly qualified as presidents in part because they could ask for substantial sums of money without embarrassment from friends and former associates within the Presbygational power structure in the Northeast.[20]

In 1843 the Presbyterians and Congregationalists organized the Society for the Promotion of Collegiate and Theological Education at the West (SPCTEW), designed to systematize the fund-raising in the East in support of Plan of Union colleges in the Mississippi Valley. Through this national benevolent society, denominational leaders were able to plan more carefully with the colleges how and when money was to be raised, to control the agents' visits to the East, and to end potentially destructive competition or proliferation of agencies that eventually would exhaust eastern donors' interest and ability to give. Officials of both Wabash and Illinois Colleges were intimately involved in the planning and implementation of the SPCTEW, and the two colleges received significant financial support from the society over many years.[21] Under the auspices of the SPCTEW, the presidents, faculty members, and other agents of the two schools regularly trekked eastward to the "money frontier" in the manufacturing cities and towns of the northeastern United States. Knox finally received some support from the society, but the relationships there always remained somewhat strained, reflecting both personal and ideological differences between the leaders at Knox and the directors of the SPCTEW.[22]

The Western College Society was one of the later examples of the vast benevolent empire of voluntary societies organized by the evangelicals in the nineteenth century for the purpose of Christianizing first the Middle West and then all of the nation. Early in the century the Plan of Union churches, especially, had begun to harness the wealth and activist temperament of their congregations in the East to this task of home missions. Formal education controlled by the churches came to be viewed as a key instrument to be used in that missionary task.[23] Thus it seemed but a matter of time before the pressing financial needs of western colleges such as Wabash, Knox, and Illinois Colleges, coupled with the previous experience and peculiar ideological bent of both local and national denominational leaders sponsoring such colleges, would lead to the creation of a fund-raising agency like the SPCTEW.

The work of this society underscored again how the Presbyterian leaders of western colleges never neglected their connections with sources of denominational strength on the East Coast. Like the Methodists, they developed local support systems that were crucial to the colleges' continuing existence; but for the Presbyterians at least, Timothy Smith's claim that the western colleges were essentially the products of "local initiative and personal commitment" cannot be sustained.[24] More than any other group, western Presbyterian (or Presbygationalist) educational leaders developed denominational affiliations of great importance that both spanned the continent and were rooted in the soil of states like Indiana and Illinois.

The western Baptist schools also quickly developed agency systems with characteristics that seemed almost a hybrid form of Methodist and Plan of Union practices. Baptist fund-raisers made their primary appeals for funds through the Baptist associations at the county and statewide levels. There were parallels in this structure of organization to the Methodist system of local districts and statewide conferences. But because of traditional Baptist skepticism about hierarchies and centralized authority, the relationships between Shurtleff College in Illinois and Franklin College in Indiana and their respective state associations were never as close as those between Wesleyan schools and their statewide conferences. Appeals for aid appeared regularly in the records of the annual meetings of the numerous associations, and agents were sometimes appointed within each small administrative unit to raise funds for the colleges. Yet it is clear that the denominational hierarchies never possessed any ultimate control or supervision over the colleges. The power to raise money really rested with the colleges, with voluntary help being offered by the overarching Baptist associations whenever possible.[25] Of course, this arrangement more closely resembled Presbyterian practice than that of the Methodists.

Shurtleff and Franklin both represented the missionary wing of the national Baptist movement, in large part an extension of the evangelical activism of New England Baptists.[26] From the beginning the founders of Baptist colleges in Indiana and Illinois maintained their connections, like the Presbyterians, with the East Coast; but these links to the East were much weaker and less effectively exploited than was the case among western Presbygationalists. Only Shurtleff really profited financially from associations with Baptists in New England, chiefly from wealthy Boston supporters of the Massachusetts Baptist Missionary Society, and then only in the earliest years of the college's existence.[27] The Baptists, then, like the Methodists, were forced to rely finally on people and churches in surrounding areas for most of their financial support.[28]

The agents of these western colleges engaged in a wide variety of fund-raising activities. They conducted special drives for new buildings or endowments of faculty positions; they served as representatives of the college in securing donations of land and other special gifts from wealthy individuals. But primarily their job was to appeal to broad segments of the evangelical community for the small gifts that would keep the colleges going on a day-to-day basis. It is next to impossible to gauge precisely the effectiveness of these efforts. Many variables determined the results. Sometimes direct competition for the attention of churchgoers occurred among agents of various causes sanctioned by churches. Antimission Baptists kept hands in pockets when missionary agents for the Baptist colleges arrived and asked for help. In times of prosperity the money collected was often substantial. When hard times arrived, there were difficulties. Edmund O. Hovey, an experienced Presbyterian agent, reported after one discouraging visit to Madison, Indiana, in 1839 that tight-fisted merchants in the midst of the recession had given him "a little," but that they had made the effort "what I call up-hill work." The effectiveness of agents varied greatly, and their salaries and expenses, often substantial, were deducted from sums collected. The conclusion must remain impressionistic, but probably John Peck, well-known Baptist educator in Illinois and one of the first agents of Shurtleff College, was correct when he asserted in 1852 (after eighteen years' experience) that "from 40 to 60 percent" of funds gathered actually reached college coffers.[29]

By mid-twentieth-century standards of collegiate financing, it took a mere pittance to keep those institutions of the nineteenth century going. Until the Civil War nearly all of those schools could survive on annual budgets of $10,000 or less. Thus the several thousand dollars that agents collected annually for a college were crucial to that school's continued existence.[30] But perhaps the most significant long-term benefit accruing to the colleges was something more intangible: the creation of broad public support for the colleges and for education generally.

Denominational connections in particular enabled the western colleges, almost immediately after their founding, to develop local and regional networks of support in small towns and cities.[31] Hundreds of people in local churches heard the messages about higher education and then gave money and moral support over the years to specific colleges that signified concrete and impressive commitments to formal education. They were real grassroots sources. This fact can best be demonstrated by what the documents tell us about patterns of giving. College agents collected regularly gifts of one hundred dollars or more (sizable sums for that day) from a small number of well-to-do laypeople and from less wealthy yet strongly committed ministers. But the great majority of the donations came from average churchgoers in small to medium contributions of twenty dollars or less per person.[32]

One should also emphasize the importance of the more general educational role the financial agents played among their constituencies in the churches. Agents made their rounds, preaching or talking again and again about higher education to local congregations. In such moments they spoke about the need for the general populace to commit itself to colleges that would provide teachers, ministers, lawyers—many of the leaders of the new society of the western states; to schools that would offer new avenues of mobility to poor young men into a rapidly expanding middle class; to institutions that would serve as important centers of cultural and moral guidance for communities left uneasy and uncertain because of extreme social fluidity and flux. The colleges were to serve both as social conservators and as a liberating influence on the body politic. Perhaps this paradoxical image the colleges projected, meaningful to a wide variety of groups, explains in part the enthusiasm and broad public support the schools seemed to be generating for themselves.[33]

This examination of the work of the fund-raising agents for seven midwestern colleges has stressed first the importance of denominational affiliations in determining the institutional methods and techniques developed by these schools as they struggled to solve perennial financial problems. Methodists, Presbyterians, and Baptists seemed to develop distinctly different arrangements for fund-raising that reflected long-standing denominational characteristics as well as the unique sense of time and place that impinged upon each school.

Unlike older interpretations of the antebellum college, which stressed the highly competitive, almost self-destructive aspects of this denominationalism, the intent here is to view these sectarian characteristics within the broader context of evangelical Protestantism. The aims and motivations of these schools grew out of religious and cultural impulses that received widespread support in all of the major Protestant denominations. Religiously sponsored colleges were to provide teachers and especially preachers for an expanding America; they were also to be centers of religious propaganda and moral instruction and gathering points for the conversion of young people just as much as local churches were. The colleges were to be a key institutional support of the vast evangelical effort to Christianize America in the nineteenth century. This combination of the specific and the general may help to explain the fierce devotion to specific institutions that denominational loyalties generated and yet the broad community support these schools also maintained, which reflected their position within the larger evangelical community. And thus perhaps the educational historians' recently discovered insight concerning the widespread popularity of these antebellum colleges can be better understood by placing these schools within precisely such a religious context.

The regional bias of this study has also developed into an important perspective. It is a regional bias still influenced by the old New England centers of culture, however. From the moment of their founding, the midwestern colleges maintained continuous connections with the eastern seaboard. Many of these colleges could not have survived the early years without drawing upon the East for wealth, personnel, and ideas. Religious institutions made this kind of outside support possible. Through the denominations and their respective agency systems flowed the necessary support from east to west. And in such a context the colleges in Indiana and Illinois activated the missionary and benevolent energies of hundreds of churchgoers both eastern and western, thereby creating some of the most powerful and distinctive impulses characterizing nineteenth-century evangelicalism in America.

Yet we must not forget that schools like Indiana Asbury, Shurtleff, and Knox were also creations of western conditions and that they sought primarily to respond to the needs of the people of Indiana and Illinois. The schools also depended upon local resources to survive. Large groups of alumni, an important source of support for private colleges today, did not yet exist. Students had to be recruited from the surrounding regions, with their small yet essential tuition and so-called boarding fees; regular donations of land, scholarships, and gifts of money from local supporters of the colleges had to be secured, state governments solicited for financial aid, and the continuing support of evangelical churches in the area maintained. The educational aims and purposes of the colleges had to be

explained and made meaningful to the farmers, small shopkeepers, and trades-
men of the Midwest. Both agents of the colleges and denominational connections
were crucial in facilitating the never-ending quest for support in local communities. The midwestern colleges possessed strong links to long-established religious
institutions and cultural traditions that implied order and a degree of stability.
Those same institutions and traditions when extended westward proved adapt-
able and resilient enough to survive and then to flourish in a turbulent and disor-
dered frontier society. They shaped to a considerable degree the cultural context
of the new communities springing up in the West. Around such strengths the
Protestant colleges of the Midwest organized themselves and made their unique
and important contributions to American life in the nineteenth century.[34]

The Era of Multipurpose Colleges in American Higher Education, 1850–1890

∽

ROGER L. GEIGER

*T*he decade of the 1890s in American higher education is properly seen as marking the "Emergence of the American University."[1] Stanford opened in 1891 and the University of Chicago the following year, touching off what Laurence Veysey called "the academic boom of the early nineties." Even Harvard president Charles Eliot, a longtime skeptic, was finally ready to admit the American university had become a reality.[2] But if the future lay with these new educational enterprises, they were still the exceptions as that fateful decade began. In 1890 the majority of students attended denominational colleges, the number of these colleges was still growing, and the majority of men and women students attended single-sex colleges. By 1900 none of this would still be true. The rise of universities and the pressures of standardization displaced the traditional American college from its accustomed central role. The 1890s—more precisely the first half of that decade—thus stand as a major turning point in the evolution of American higher education.

The historiography of American higher education has, not unnaturally, emphasized the rising new elements—research, graduate education, the new disciplinary knowledge base.[3] This study takes the opposite approach. It seeks to explore the "old order" that began to form as early as the 1850s and found itself in a deepening crisis after 1890. More than antiquarian curiosity motivates this inquiry; these developments constitute an unwritten chapter in the history of American higher education.

For the generation following the Civil War, the denominational college was still the characteristic institution of higher education. This institution, however, could no longer be equated with the "oldtime" classical college. The majority of existing colleges (and almost all newly founded ones) implemented some or all of the items on a standard menu of innovations: nonclassical degree courses (bachelor's of science, letters, literature, or philosophy), partial courses for part-time students, varying numbers of electives, and coeducation. In addition significant numbers of colleges innovated further by entering entirely new markets: the education of teachers; separate schools of science, engineering, or agriculture; and short courses for commercial subjects. Further linkages were forged—and broken—with professional schools of theology, law, or medicine. The modal institution of higher education thus existed in a fluid educational marketplace in which it competed not only with other colleges, but also with other types of schools, including high schools, normal schools, institutes of technology, and commercial colleges. In a time of accelerating educational change, the colleges were forced to make crucial decisions about how to use their generally meager resources to achieve a mix of offerings that would meet the needs of sponsors, traditional constituencies, potential new students, and their own treasuries.

This institution—the multipurpose college—is the missing link in the evolution of American higher education.[4] By the 1850s many of the country's colleges were expanding the scope of their offerings and assuming such a guise, even as classical colleges of the traditional type continued to be founded. In the succeeding decades the balance turned decisively in favor of multipurpose colleges (which also describes the new state universities). New and old colleges adapted their degree courses in the face of an expanding academic knowledge base, eclectic student constituencies, and emerging markets for practical, vocational skills. The pace of change varied by institution as well as across regions. However, the inflection point of the early 1890s signaled the onset of a pervasive crisis for these colleges.

In economic terms the crisis had to do with economies of scale and scope. As these economies began to yield huge payoffs after 1890 for the expanding universities, they essentially ceased to work to the advantage of the smaller multipurpose colleges. The colleges consequently had to redefine their missions, a process fraught with internal conflict and instability.[5] The resolution of the crisis of the 1890s was a long-term development by which the colleges gradually conformed to one of several viable models. Overall, however, they had to assume a new, complementary role as a component rather than the centerpiece of American higher education.

The analysis of this transitional era will start at the endpoint rather than the beginning for two tactical reasons. First, while the denouement definitely lies in the 1890s, its origins are diffuse. Thus identifying and charting the elements of higher education in this era is an analytical task in itself. Second, abundant data for the later years are available in the annual *Reports of the Commissioner of Education* (RCE).[6] Judiciously interpreted, these data provide a relatively solid depiction of the essential features of the educational system as it was perceived by contemporaries. This foundation, then, permits the structuring of more fragmentary and eclectic information about earlier decades.

"Higher Instruction" in the 1880s

The Bureau of Education was created in 1866, and by 1870 it was able to compile and report statistics for colleges (including women's colleges) and professional schools. It identified 369 colleges, but it noted that "there is very little known" about 80 of them.[7] During that decade, higher education grew considerably, as did the completeness of the data that institutions supplied to the bureau. By 1880 a credible depiction of the entire system was available, even if certain details remained elusive. A decade later this information was being reported in voluminous detail, and the inevitable omissions were largely marginal institutions. The contours of the system can thus be depicted with some confidence for the 1880s (see table 1).

The many categories of table 1 are part of its message. Just as the terms employed today, such as *postsecondary* and *research university,* reflect the nature and structure of our current system, the different institutions enumerated by the bureau mirrored realities of that day. Here, though, relations among the parts are more amorphous. Universities, for example, reported separately as colleges, scientific schools, and various professional schools. The different categories of institutions overlapped in some respects, as did the activities they represented.

A relatively fixed point in this array was the undergraduate programs of degree-granting colleges and universities. But land-grant colleges were recorded both separately and as parts of universities, and non-land-grant schools of science were listed apart. Colleges for women generally possessed the right to grant degrees, but contemporaries regarded most of them as inferior, often straddling secondary education in their offerings.[8] Professional schools were more alternatives to colleges than destinations for graduates. Normal schools were clearly below college grade at this date, but some teachers were also trained in high schools and in colleges. Academies, on the other hand, were relegated to secondary education, although they sometimes taught portions of the college curriculum. Given this tangled picture, the Bureau of Education merely tabulated institutions within categories that were self-evident to contemporaries.

The figures in table 1, imperfect as they are, reveal a significant dynamic. The number of students in all colleges and professional schools grew barely more

TABLE 1

INSTITUTIONS AND ENROLLMENTS IN HIGHER EDUCATION, 1879–1880 & 1889–1890

Type	1879–1880		1889–1890	
	Institutions	Students	Institutions	Students
Colleges & Universities (UG)	364	32,142	415	44,414
Resident Graduates, C&U		411		1,717
Schools of Science/Technology (inc. Land Grants)	80	*6,637	63	**7,577
Colleges for Women	227	11,626	179	11,992
SUBTOTAL		50,816		65,700
Schools of Theology	142	5,242	145	7,013
Schools of Law	48	3,134	54	4,518
Medicine		14,006		20,714
Regular	72	9,876	93	13,521
Eclectic	6	833	9	719
Homeopath	12	1,220	14	1,020
Dental	16	730	27	2,643
Pharmacy	14	1,347	30	2,811
TOTAL HI ED ENROLLMENTS		73,198		97,945
Normal Schools, Teaching Programs		25,736		34,814
Commercial Colleges	162	27,146	263	78,920
Population, 15–19		5,011,400		6,557,600
HI ED Enrollments		1.46%		1.49%

*adjusted
**adjusted for double counting

than the increase in the 15- to 19-year-old population (+30.9 percent).[9] Graduate and professional school enrollments all expanded at a greater rate, accounting for about 11,000 of the 24,000 additional students. The numbers of normal students and those taking business courses (although not part of higher education) also grew relative to the population. Only collegiate enrollments lagged. A closer look reveals a more intriguing finding: when the male/female breakdown is estimated, the number of women in coeducational colleges increased by more than 80 percent, but male undergraduates merely matched population growth.[10] Even preparatory students in these institutions increased by 51 percent. Thus Americans in the 1880s increased their relative commitment to advanced education in most every category save male undergraduates, traditionally the staple of the American college.[11]

Population Dynamics of the Colleges

No convention governed the nomenclature of the central institutions of American higher education—universities and colleges. While some of the "universities" possessed the same professional faculties that were the hallmark of those institutions in Europe, others taught only at the collegiate level. Most colleges, on the other hand, consisted of more than one part. Except in the Northeast, the great majority maintained preparatory departments, which in 1890 enrolled just 5,000 fewer students (39,415) than the colleges proper. There was one clear standard for the college course—four years of graded study in Latin, Greek, mathematics, science, and philosophy, leading to an A.B. degree. But a closer look discloses a vagueness about its beginning, duration, and end. Students were admitted according to their proficiency, so that those with strong training entered the sophomore, junior, or even senior classes. One of the liveliest questions of the day concerned the possible shortening of the college course (discussed below). Catholic colleges, on the other hand, considered "college" to consist of an unbroken six- or seven-year course. Nor was it evident why students should persist to graduation, since there was nothing that could be done with a bachelor's degree that could not also be done without one. The term *college* in the latter nineteenth century conjured up definite images, but the actual permutations of this ideal were many and varied.

The "universities and colleges" reported in the RCE were either male or coeducational (women's colleges being a separate category). In 1890 the majority of men enrolled in single-sex institutions, as did their female counterparts. This situation was not destined to persist: gender separation was the rule along the populous eastern seaboard, but throughout the country, nearly two-thirds of the colleges were coeducational. An even larger proportion were associated with a denomination. Just 99 of the 415 colleges in table 1 lacked formal church ties, and roughly half of those were publicly controlled. In contrast, 74 colleges were associated with some form of Methodism. Roman Catholics operated the next largest number of colleges (51), but this was a particularly volatile group that should be considered a sector in itself (see below). For Protestant colleges, sectarian doctrines were presumed to be banished from the curriculum, and the influence of the church, exerted through president and trustees, varied from traditional association to outright ownership. For all these colleges, however, daily chapel and a religious ambiance were ubiquitous traits of college life. The colleges of 1890 were remarkably young: the majority of institutions in table 1 were less than thirty years old.

The latter decades of the nineteenth century, far more than the antebellum years, were the era of proliferating colleges. Any effort to enumerate college foundings, however, confronts an imposing obstacle: many of these institutions were discontinuous—in function (operating level), operations, name, and/or location. Precision is thus an impossibility. Table 2 represents a conservative estimate of when and where colleges appeared.[12]

According to Colin Burke, 50 new colleges opened in the 1830s and enrollments grew by 79 percent. The 1840s experienced a lull that produced only 29 new colleges while enrollments virtually stagnated (+19 percent). The 1850s then witnessed the largest antebellum net increase of colleges (73) and substantial enrollment growth as well (67 percent). Table 2 reveals that the dynamics of the 1850s persisted through the next decade, apparently unfazed by the Civil War. The founding of new colleges continued at a lesser but still robust pace for the next two decades, even though enrollment growth probably slowed in the 1870s.

Viewed in this way, the period from about 1850 to 1890 constitutes a distinct era in American higher education. Its hallmark was the proliferation of colleges at nearly as rapid a rate as student enrollments (table 3).

Three aspects of this situation are noteworthy. First, although traditional historical treatments of this period emphasize the major new departures in higher education—MIT, Cornell, Johns Hopkins, Eliot's Harvard—the vast majority of new institutions were denominational colleges. Second, the relative stability in average size indicates that the educational technology or modus operandi of the colleges was—again, for the vast majority—largely fixed. Third, the shape traced by the increase in the number of colleges is that of a logistic curve (figure 1). That is, exponential growth during the 1850s and 1860s gave way to decelerating growth in the following decades, and ceased altogether after 1893—the peak year for traditional colleges.[13] This pattern occurs when the conditions responsible for growth are, in the first phase, self-reinforcing, and in the second phase, self-limiting.[14]

TABLE 2

COLLEGE FOUNDINGS, BY REGION, 1850S TO 1890S

	1850s	1860s	1870s	1880s	1890s	Total Founded 1850–1900	Total 1900	Founded before 1850
New England	1	2	1	2	1	7	22	11
Mid-Atlantic	11	14	7	2	2	41	72	26
South Atlantic	8	6	7	11	6	38	63	21
North Central	28	20	14	6	6	74	96	34
South Central	9	14	12	3	4	42	57	22
West Central	21	24	13	34	20	112	121	8
Western	6	12	7	11	12	48	42	4
TOTALS	84	92	61	69	51	357	473	131
Burke, ACP	88							129
Technical Colleges	1	9	8	9	11		43	5

SOURCES: 1850s-1870s: RCE, 1880;
1880s: RCE, 1895;
1890s, Total 1900, Technical Colleges: RCE, 1900;
Colin Burke, *American Collegiate Populations*, 15–17.

TABLE 3

AVERAGE COLLEGE SIZE, 1840–1890

	1840	1850	1860	1870	1880	1890
College Enrollment	8,328	9,931	16,600		32,142	44,133
Colleges	107	136	209		364	415
Average Enrollment	78	73	79		88	106

SOURCES: 1840–1860: Burke, *American Collegiate Populations*, 54;
1889–1890: Table 1.

FIGURE 1

LOGISTIC GROWTH OF COLLEGES, 1850–1890

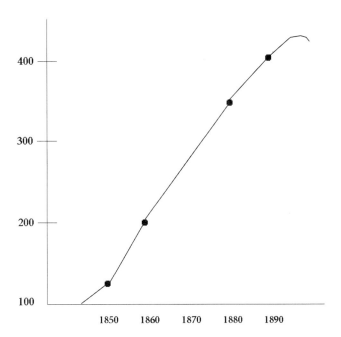

What happened during this era, in the most general terms, was that a variant of the classical college—the multipurpose college—encountered geographical and religious conditions that induced exponential growth during the 1850s and 1860s but became increasingly restrictive thereafter. The potential for growth was entirely exhausted after 1890, when conditions favored the expansion of different kinds of institutions and produced a crisis for the old order of multipurpose colleges.

The growth of colleges after the Civil War, it might be argued, was affected by exogenous events such as the Morrill Act (1862) and the establishment of the historically black colleges (HBCs) for freedmen in the South. Both effects turned out to be small, however. Before 1890 the Morrill land grants and the formation of new western states produced only 15 additional flagship universities (plus Cornell) classified with the colleges. All of these institutions can be considered smaller or larger versions of multipurpose colleges, differing chiefly in lacking denominational ties and, by the end of this period, in possibly receiving public support. Only 3 of them—the Universities of California, Minnesota, and Illinois—counted more than 300 college students in 1890.

Most other public, land-grant colleges were classified during this era with the schools of science. Here a different dynamic prevailed. A linear pattern of steady expansion is evident in table 2.[15] As for the HBCs, 20 of these colleges were operating by 1890. They nevertheless fit the profile of denominational provision of higher education to underserved populations. Inherently multipurpose, they had only small collegiate enrollments in 1890 (averaging 26). In addition one might note the founding of "idiosyncratic" institutions in this era—the University of Cincinnati, Johns Hopkins, and Clark.[16] There nevertheless remains a fundamental underlying pattern of logistic growth of, overwhelmingly, denominational colleges.

The distribution of college foundings presented in table 2 is the product of the interaction of geographical and denominational factors. Geographically, colleges followed settlers into the trans-Mississippi West, but they also increased in density in many settled areas. Two different processes were involved—"extension" and "elaboration" of the collegiate matrix—propelled by the interests of different sets of churches.

The extension of colleges across the trans-Mississippi West resembled in some ways the push across the Appalachians a generation earlier. A difference was that the education of ministers was less urgent a consideration in this era, that task being largely fulfilled by some 140 theological seminaries. These colleges were intended to bring civilization, in the form of advanced Christian education, to the western settlers. The initial wave of colleges, often begun as seminaries or academies, was often the product of missionary zeal. The early leader of Colorado College, for example, the Congregationalist Edward Payson Tenney, espied a population of Native Americans, Mormons, and Spanish-speaking Roman Catholics, in addition to the boisterous young men of the minefields, all to his mind desperately in need of Protestant culture.[17] A second pattern of founding, usually at the initiative of individuals, occurred largely on what geographer D. W. Meinig has termed "the speculative frontier."[18] In this case initiatives to found colleges were part of the competitive development of rival settlements—a kind of prospective boosterism. In either case the founding of colleges in the West was led by the principal denominations. Colorado's first colleges, for example, were Methodist and Congregational, but the Presbyterians too sponsored four institutions, all of which failed. Presbyterians were particularly active in spreading the college gospel in the West, but apparently experienced more failures than successes. Dismay at these results led to the establishment of a central Board of Aid in 1883, which carefully evaluated the prospects for future colleges and achieved better results. All told, 16 enduring Presbyterian colleges were established in the West in the three decades after the Civil War, 11 by direct initiative of church bodies.[19]

East of the Mississippi (roughly speaking) the proliferation of denominational colleges was principally driven by the increasing density and religious fragmentation of the population. The figures in table 4 can provide only a rough idea of the changes in denominational sponsorship because many colleges were only loosely associated and changes occurred. The principal denominations, in fact, attempted to exert more direct control over their colleges during the latter decades of the century, causing a good number of the older colleges to lapse into nondenominational status.[20] Thus the figure of 265 Protestant colleges understates the actual situation for 1890. Nevertheless, the contrast indicates the effects of religious fragmentation.

Some 44 of the additional colleges represent independent branches of the main denominations. These churches too felt the need for colleges and added to the overall number. Even when the split was ostensibly regional, the effects could be far-reaching: the 6 colleges of the Cumberland Presbyterians stretched from Pennsylvania to Texas. The growth of a distinctive immigrant population accounted for 14 additional Lutheran colleges. Another 34 colleges were founded after 1860 by smaller denominations, including Friends, United Brethren, and Disciples of Christ. These sects in some ways retraced the experience of Baptists

TABLE 4

PROTESTANT COLLEGES BY DENOMINATION, 1860 & 1890

	1860	1890
Presbyterian	40	35/14*
Methodist Episcopal	35	52/22
Baptist	29	36/8
Congregational	17	22
Protestant Episcopal	15	6
Disciples of Christ	6	20
Lutheran	5	19
United Brethren	2	10
Others	9	21
TOTAL	158	265

*Main church/other branches

SOURCES: 1860: Burke, *American Collegiate Populations*, 25;
             1890: RCE, 788.

and Methodists in belatedly embracing higher education. Their concern was less the training of a learned ministry than it was to protect their social base. Repeatedly they expressed concern that young men who attended the colleges of other denominations were lost to the church. The remedy, then, was to establish colleges of their own. Thus religious fragmentation was the chief impulse behind the elaboration of the collegiate pattern in settled regions.[21]

A definite pattern of college founding emerged in this era, employed by virtually all denominations. Once a church, through its regional body, decided upon the desirability of establishing a college, it solicited bids from interested communities. The church itself usually contributed some funds, but it expected that the future home of the college would donate land, perhaps buildings, and a certain amount of endowment. The most lucrative offer almost always took precedence over other considerations such as transportation or population.[22] While this procedure gave the town a certain stake in the new venture, the churches retained fairly close control through the right to name the college trustees. This process of founding colleges had several consequences. It favored small or medium-sized towns, in which pure boosterism could be most readily mobilized, rather than the larger and more heterogeneous cities. The combined resources of church and town gave most of these colleges the vital financial margin for survival, but at the same time, by identifying them with a particular constituency and placing them among a limited population, these arrangements constrained their potential size and scope. Finally the interests of the churches were clearly paramount in the founding of such colleges.

These two dynamics—geographical extension largely in the West and denominational elaboration elsewhere—underlay the logistic pattern of college expansion in this era. During the 1850s and 1860s, college founding through denominational elaboration was in full force, particularly in the mid-Atlantic and north central states, while geographical extension was accelerating in the Great Plains and the Far West (table 2). The confluence of both patterns made the 1860s, surprisingly, the most fecund decade for new colleges. The self-reinforcing nature of this growth was undoubtedly due, on the one hand, to the rapid extension of the railroad network and the real estate frontier, which created communities eager to host colleges. On the other hand, the reciprocal effects that denominations had upon one another produced an implicit or protective competition. The momentum behind this dynamic may well have been diminished by the panic of 1873 and its aftermath. In any case denominational elaboration continued afterward at a much slower pace (although it has never stopped), but most of the foundings of the 1880s and 1890s were due to geographical extension—principally in the Dakotas (7 colleges), Texas (10), Kansas (9), Nebraska (6), Missouri (7), and Florida (5).

Both these processes were self-limiting or, in extreme cases, self-destructive. Where religious fragmentation was high, as in Tennessee, Kentucky, and Missouri, excessive elaboration resulted in the founding of numerous weak and non-viable colleges. Extension also resulted in high mortality rates, as founders often wagered on what turned out to be poor locations. Generally where population density remained low, colleges faced difficult conditions. In the Midwest, by way of contrast, extension in the 1820s through the 1840s was followed by elaboration as the population grew. For most of the West, however, overextension precluded much subsequent elaboration before the nature of higher education began to change after 1890.

Catholic Colleges

The creation of Catholic colleges contributed to the overall logistic pattern, but differences from their Protestant counterparts made them a kind of parallel system with even less stable population dynamics.

Catholic colleges were founded for essentially the same motives as Protestant ones. Before 1850, Edward Power has noted, they were chiefly founded out of the need to perpetuate the clergy, in this case by preparing students for the seminaries, out of missionary zeal to bring Catholicism to the spreading population, and out of a desire to provide Catholic moral education shielded from hostile doctrines. After 1850, Catholic interests shifted like other denominations toward educating a learned laity—providing higher education appropriate for a Catholic community.[23] Both sets of motives gave Catholics powerful incentives first for extension of their educational complex and then for full territorial elaboration of colleges. However, whereas each Protestant college was an independent corporation, Catholic colleges were emanations of permanent organizations—extensions of the universal Catholic Church.

The two key entities were the Catholic dioceses, each headed by a bishop and entrusted with authority over education, and the religious orders. Many of the enduring colleges represented some combination of effort by both, since it long proved difficult for a diocese to mobilize the resources needed to sustain a college. Catholics further complicated matters by adopting a variant of the Jesuit seven-year plan of studies. This heavily classical course began with "Rudiments" and proceeded through three years of "Humanities," followed by single years of poetry, rhetoric, and philosophy. This arrangement largely duplicated the preparatory classes and four years of the standard classical A.B. course, but the rigidity of a single course demanded a larger educational enterprise while making such a commitment more formidable to students. Many colleges compromised this pattern out of necessity.[24] Thus the church was at once ambitious in terms of the elaboration of colleges to serve all Catholics and in curricular requirements, but starved for the resources to sustain such efforts. One might expect large numbers of foundings accompanied by a high rate of failure; indeed that was what occurred. But the permanence of the church was also a factor. Numerous insolvent Catholic colleges were shuttered, reduced to preparatory schools or seminaries, only to reopen again under more hopeful conditions. Catholic colleges sometimes flickered in and out of existence.[25]

Catholic colleges began to be founded at a rapid rate around the mid-1840s, and this process continued for the next seventy years. From 1850 to 1890 an average of 33 were started each decade, 70 percent of which ultimately closed.[26] This effort of elaboration persisted longer than that of Protestant denominations, and planted Catholic colleges in all but the most sparsely settled western states (Idaho, Nevada, Wyoming). In keeping with the pattern of logistic growth, however, the final efforts were the least productive: Catholic colleges founded from 1890 to 1910 expired at the astonishing rate of 85 percent.

The Nature of Multipurpose Colleges

Multipurpose colleges can be understood only with reference to the classical colleges that preceded and to some extent coexisted with them. The classical denominational college may trace its lineage back to seventeenth-century Harvard, but its early-nineteenth-century form nevertheless represented a particular variation of that venerable species.[27] As offered in numerous colleges, the classical course was infinitely varied but essentially the same. The first year was devoted to perfecting the student's skills in Latin, Greek, and mathematics—the subjects required for entry. The ancient languages were employed thereafter in the study of literature (belles lettres) and rhetoric. Natural philosophy (science) was emphasized in the third year, and mental and moral philosophy in the fourth. Interspersed were a variety of classes in history, logic, ethics, and religion. Each year's class studied the entire curriculum together. Students were expected to prepare their lessons on their own and then called upon to recite them in the classroom. The extent to which lectures were employed in the advanced classes depended on the college and the capabilities of its instructors.[28]

The ways in which the classical college might be altered were recognized by contemporaries. Parallel courses might substitute science or modern languages for Latin or, particularly, Greek. Optional courses could be inserted into the fixed curriculum, or a more radical approach was that students might be grouped by proficiency into more and less advanced courses. Students also might be allowed to study only subjects of their own choosing (partial course). During the 1820s, all of these approaches were tried, but met with little success.[29] Instead the clamor for reform provoked an imposing defense of the classical course—the Yale Report of 1828.

Four essential points are argued in the report. First, the classical college course was not intended for specific intellectual or practical ends, but was the foundation for subsequent professional study and public life. Second, this foundation consisted above all of mental discipline, formed from the "vigorous, and steady, and systematic effort" that the colleges coerced from their students. Third, the study of the classics was superior to all other subjects for acquiring mental discipline and cultural refinement for later life. Fourth, the report thoroughly disparaged all alternate forms of education, establishing in effect the indubitable superiority of the classical course.[30] All four of these points seemed plausible to contemporaries and were repeated almost verbatim for the next sixty years. Only the last, however, was confirmed in an important way by social practice. The reforms of this period foundered due to a variety of circumstances, but they were invariably weighed down as well by the invidious distinction that contemporaries made between the classical course and its alternatives.

Classical colleges nevertheless had distinct drawbacks. In an age when boys of about twelve assumed an economic role and semi-independence from their families, attending college most likely meant the prolongation of dependence and control. Semi-independence harmonized with intermittent forms of schooling, the pattern for most youths, but collegians were expected to undertake thorough preparatory study, followed by a continuous four-year course. And while most young people enjoyed considerable personal freedom, collegians were constrained by myriad rules, enforced in the spirit of petty but inefficient despotism.[31] Considering these traits, a college education probably did produce superior powers of mental application as well as conspicuous verbal skills. Even so, its cachet appealed to a definite but delimited constituency: sons of more affluent families pursuing the genteel route to professional status; aspirants, often mature young men, to the ministry; and a trickle of rural youths defying sociological description who sought better lives through education. For such a clientele, the classical college for long had few rivals.

Although most new colleges of the 1830s largely replicated the classical model, they often began by incorporating reformist ideas. Randolph-Macon College modeled itself after the University of Virginia, for example, and Wesleyan College opened offering a partial course and some electives; but both were brought back to orthodoxy.[32] The few departures from the classical college largely stood alone: Union College—offering nonclassical electives in its A.B. course; Jefferson's University of Virginia—a complete departure from the American college; and West Point—inspiration for a growing number of military academies. In the extension of higher education beyond the Appalachians, however, denominational colleges took the training of a learned ministry as their most urgent mission and clung to the classical course as the surest means to emulate the intellectual standards of the East.[33] Slowly, however, new departures appeared, and by the 1850s the colleges being founded increasingly resembled a new subspecies.

As its primary orientation the multipurpose college embraced the education of a learned laity rather than a learned ministry. At its core there remained the classical college, typically most highly esteemed, but now surrounded by additional courses of the type specifically condemned in the Yale Report. Besides the ubiquitous preparatory departments, these would include nonclassical (or non-Greek) degree courses in science (B.S.) or modern languages (B.Litt. or B.Phil). In addition these colleges might offer nondegree courses for teachers or for commerce. An inverse scenario frequently occurred when prospering academies upgraded their offerings by obtaining college charters. Academies were already multipurpose in nature, so that a classical course might merely be appended to existing offerings.[34] Finally, and perhaps most characteristic, the multipurpose colleges tended to admit women.

These traits of the multipurpose college are mutually consistent. Usually located in towns that had lured them with an attractive offer, they joined settled communities that had undergone the social and economic effects of the "market revolution" rather than the rudimentary frontier outposts where earlier colleges had begun.[35] They could thus appeal to a proto-middle-class constituency. Their local supporters (and some denominational sponsors) might appreciate the prestige of a classical education, but consistently expressed a desire for more practical and accessible nonclassical courses as well. Teacher and commercial courses might be offered if a demand existed. Such courses would make some financial contribution for these invariably hard-pressed institutions that depended not only on student tuition but on the goodwill of the local community as well.

Coeducation was entirely consistent with these traits, but it was notably antithetical to the spirit of the classical college. Given the prevailing doctrine of separate spheres, women had no need for an education that prepared for professional training or public life. Nor did they require the coercive tactics used to instill mental discipline into recalcitrant boys. College education for women had not yet been contemplated at the time of the Yale Report, but well before midcentury, advanced education in various forms was expanding rapidly in academies, seminaries, collegiate institutes, and ultimately women's colleges.[36] This movement was incorporated rather naturally into multipurpose colleges, in either separate or coeducational departments. Still, higher education for women evoked strong feelings, and thus the incidence of coeducation varied greatly by region and denomination. In the South, colleges or seminaries for women alone were the rule, and in the Northeast, coeducation made only selective inroads after the Civil

War. From western New York across the Midwest, however, conditions fostered by the market revolution favored coeducational colleges; and in the Far West, they were the rule. Roman Catholics were most adamantly set against mixed colleges, but the main branches of the Presbyterian, Episcopal, and Lutheran Churches also favored segregation of the sexes. The more populist and evangelical denominations, on the other hand, were far more open to the inclusion of women. These were the denominations, moreover, that were most active in the elaboration of colleges. Although coeducation cannot be considered the litmus test for multipurpose colleges, it is a frequent and telling correlate.

Elaboration of Colleges in Ohio

The market revolution created the conditions that nourished multipurpose colleges. It engendered the prosperity of the towns and countryside that harbored the denominational communities chiefly responsible for this new generation of colleges. Thus the territories most affected by these forces were the first to sprout such institutions. Nowhere was the transition from a frontier to a market-driven society more rapid and far-reaching than in Ohio. Driven by a boom in canal building in the 1830s and railroad construction during the next two decades, the state in 1860 had the third largest population, the most miles of railroad, and the largest number of colleges.[37]

Oberlin Collegiate Institute, which opened in 1833, was something of a bridge between the classical and the multipurpose colleges. It was founded by evangelical Congregationalists, and its missionary zeal almost immediately pushed it toward a larger role. Its stated purposes were, first, to educate ministers and teachers for the vast lands of the Mississippi Valley; second, to elevate female character through education; and third, to extend a useful and affordable education to all classes of the community. The first goal called for the classical A.B. course, capped by a theological department. The latter was greatly enlarged in 1835 by the defection of a group of abolitionists from Lane Theological Seminary and the arrival of famed evangelist Charles Grandison Finney. So important was theological education that provision was soon made for a short, non-Latin Bible course for impatient preseminarians, who were also permitted to take partial courses in the college. The second goal was met initially by a separate ladies' department, but soon women were admitted to any course. Oberlin graduated the first female A.B.'s in the country in 1841. In order to meet its third goal, Oberlin maintained a large preparatory department and also adopted the manual labor plan, like many colleges of the 1830s. Besides preparing students for the college, the preparatory department offered courses for teaching and commerce. Oberlin was considered radical during its early years, but it also became Ohio's largest antebellum college, attracting many of its students from outside the state. When it was rechartered in 1851 as Oberlin College, the institution was clearly a multipurpose college, although by that juncture it was no longer alone.

After 1840 the college matrix was gradually elaborated in Ohio as each church pursued independently its own denominational interests. Patterns of college founding were diverse or even idiosyncratic, but in total they represent a process that occurred throughout much of the country.

Perhaps most common was the concern of evangelical churches about losing the allegiance of young men educated by rival denominations. Ohio Methodists chafed at Presbyterian control over the two nominally state universities, Ohio and Miami. Their response was to found Ohio Wesleyan College in 1842. Although in the center of the state, Ohio Wesleyan offered little succor to Methodists in the northeastern section who wished to counter the lure of Oberlin. A wealthy layman, John Baldwin, worked with the North Ohio Conference to found an eponymous institute. Raised to collegiate status in 1854, Baldwin College soon surpassed Oberlin in the wide spectrum of its offerings. A third Methodist college, Mount Union (1858) was entirely the work of laymen. Beginning as a seminary in 1846, it also quickly sprouted additional departments. In governance Mount Union resembled earlier colleges in being firmly associated with a church, but not formally affiliated.[38]

Both the United Brethren and the German Reformed Churches were moved to found colleges for the same professed motives as the Methodists. The Brethren had eschewed colleges until they felt pressured into launching Otterbein in 1847. For the German Reformed Church, the long distance to their seminary in Mercersberg, Pennsylvania, was the decisive factor in starting Heidelberg College (1850). The founding of Antioch (1852) might be considered another variation on this theme. Liberal "Christians," who opposed denominational distinctions, sought to found a nonsectarian college of a high rank. They consciously sought the best local offer in New York and Ohio before accepting the bid of the small town of Yellow Springs.

Developments within denominations also generated colleges. Ohio Lutherans were divided between an English branch and a more traditional German branch that controlled the Evangelical Lutheran Seminary in Columbus (f. 1830). After cooperation between the two groups ended in 1840, the English Lutherans protected their interests by organizing Wittenberg College (1844). The German branch countered by founding Capital University (1850).

Presbyterian hegemony over Ohio's first two colleges may have offended other denominations, but it failed to satisfy the church's increasing desire for closer control. The contrasting fates of the two resulting colleges well represent the changing environment. Central College of Ohio (1842) resembled other early colleges in being founded by local Presbyterians acting independently. This institution garnered little support, producing just a single graduate before the Civil War. The two Ohio Synods of the church resolved in the mid-1840s to found a church-sponsored institution, but they apparently felt little urgency. For years they failed to agree on a location, and then the Civil War caused further delay. When the University of Wooster was founded in 1866, however, it had relatively solid underpinnings from both the church and the town.

These colleges in many ways mirrored the denominations they represented. Large denominations, like the Methodists, could support relatively large colleges. Ohio Wesleyan was generally the second largest college in the state (table 5) and would later harbor university aspirations. Otterbein, which depended almost entirely on the Brethren, remained small and impecunious. Urbana College, founded by the Swedenborgian Church (1850), remained tiny and imperiled throughout the century. Capital University, despite its name, reflected the conservatism of the German Lutherans and remained essentially a classical college into the twentieth century. The more liberal English Lutherans, however, transformed Wittenberg into a multipurpose institution after the Civil War.

Antioch, Otterbein, and Heidelberg were all coeducational from the time of their chartering, and each graduated women from the college course. They reflected support within their respective denominations for the advanced education of women. Muskingum, a United Presbyterian college, adopted coeducation early in contrast to the main church. Methodists generally were conspicuous supporters of women's education. Baldwin, Wilberforce, and Mount Union were coeducational, while Ohio Wesleyan was accompanied by a women's college, with which it merged in 1877. With at least seven antebellum coeducational colleges, Ohio was clearly in the vanguard of this movement.[39] Much the same could be said in curricular matters.

A historian of these colleges has observed that "none of Ohio's antebellum colleges limited itself to the narrow concepts outlined in the Yale Report of 1828."[40] While Capital University might be the exception to this rule, among other traditional institutions Kenyon taught engineering for a time, and St. Xavier offered commercial subjects in evening classes. Nonclassical degree courses in science or literature were the most common additions to the A.B. in these years, and some colleges offered courses for teaching or commerce.

Colleges that developed from academies (however named) tended to be the most innovative. Baldwin and Mount Union have already been noted, but both were remarkable in this respect. Among its many offerings Baldwin started an extensive commercial course in 1859 that, unlike some others, was never discontinued. In 1858 it started a German department, which met with such success that it was separated five years later as German-Wallace College. The two schools remained closely associated, and later reunited as BaldwinWallace University. By the 1880s Baldwin alone counted eight different schools. The founder of Mount Union, Orville Hartshorn, anticipated Ezra Cornell when he stated his intention "to found for the people a cosmic college, where any person may economically obtain a thorough, illustrative, integral instruction in any needed studies."[41] Even as a college, Mount Union operated more like an academy in encouraging students to take elective courses. Hartshorn also seems to have anticipated William Rainey Harper by offering a summer term, largely for teachers.

Fitting into this same mold was Hiram College, chartered in 1867. It was founded by the "Christians" or Disciples, who sought an educational institution for all the usual reasons, but originally opted against starting a college. Instead they opened the Western Reserve Eclectic Institute in 1850, which fast became a thriving academy offering a wide slate of electives up to and including collegiate course work. This same character was retained after full collegiate courses and degrees were instituted, as Hiram continued to teach large numbers of irregular students.

The most radical departure of the antebellum years was the Farmers' College (f. 1852) located outside Cincinnati. It too was preceded by a prosperous academy, but the founders wished to provide a practical collegiate education for business and farming. Ten years before the Morrill Act they established the functional equivalent of a land-grant college. It offered both a classical course and a scientific course with wide allowance for electives. It also organized an agricultural course with three professors and a model farm. The intent of Farmers' College was to teach the new practical curriculum in association with traditional classical subjects. The college appeared to thrive initially, but it faced continual problems after the war and ceased collegiate operations in 1888.[42]

Looking beyond the Civil War, these same tendencies remained prominent. The matrix of denominational colleges was further elaborated with additions from smaller denominations, but the pace clearly slowed as new possibilities were exhausted. By 1890, nine more Protestant colleges (including Wooster and Hiram) were operating as well as another Catholic college (table 5). In addition several more "eclectic" colleges (to borrow a term from Hiram's predecessor) emerged from academies and normal schools. The traits characteristic of multipurpose colleges became more widespread. By 1890 only four Protestant colleges remained confined to men, and fewer than half of the regular college students were enrolled in the classical course.

A new note in the postbellum era was the distinctive role played by philanthropy as the growing fortunes of the Gilded Age began to affect higher education. Some major gifts produced conventional results, such as denominational

TABLE 5

Ohio Colleges in 1889–1890, by Collegiate Enrollment

College	Year Opened	Denomination	Men	Women	All Departments
Oberlin	1833 #	Congregational	253	356	1,713
Ohio Wesleyan	1844 #	Methodist	266	218	1,117
Scio	1866	Methodist	200	108	402
University of Wooster	1870 #	Presbyterian	173	62	750
Ohio State University	1873 #	state	186	35	425
Mount Union	1846	Methodist	145	30	568
University of Cincinnati	1873 #	municipal	89	31	900
Heidelberg University	1850	Reformed	90	25	347
Wittenberg	1845##	Lutheran	89	26	285
Buchtel	1872##	Universalist	67	42	361
Marietta	1835 #	Congregational	100	*	171
Denison University	1831 #	Baptist	96	*	207
Baldwin University	1846 #	Methodist	57	37	344
Western Reserve	1826 #	Congregational	67	5	198
St. Xavier	1840 #	Roman Catholic	71	*	419
Capital University	1850	Lutheran	71	*	154
Muskingum	1837	United Presbyterian	53	18	119
St. Joseph's	1871	Roman Catholic	50	*	225
Ohio University	1809 #	nonsectarian	50	16	171
Franklin	1825	United Presbyterian	54	12	118
Otterbein	1847 #	United Bretheren	35	25	238
Hiram	1867 #	Disciples	40	19	324
Miami University	1824##	nonsectarian	44	1	72
Findlay	1886	Church of God	29	12	302
German-Wallace	1864	Methodist	36	5	110
Kenyon	1828 #	Episcopal	38	*	129
Wilmington	1870	Friends	18	17	113
Calvin	1883	Reformed	19	10	143
Twin Valley	1886	Methodist?	12	8	63
Rio Grande	1876	F.W. Baptist	11	7	33
Ashland	1879	United Brethren	9	3	96
Urbana	1851	New Church (Swedenborgian)	6	4	37
Hillsboro	1857	Methodist	4	5	110
Richmond	1835	Congregational?	8	1	110
Wilberforce	1855	A.M.E.	4	3	177
Antioch	1853 #	Christ/Unitarian	— 20 —		146
Farmer's	1852	Methodist	0	0	51
		TOTAL	2,540	1,141	11,197

*men's college
\# named members of the Association of Ohio Colleges (1878)
\#\# nubsequent members of the Association of Ohio Colleges

SOURCES: RCE, 1889–90, 1892–95; and diverse sources.

colleges for the Universalists (Buchtel College) and the Free Will Baptists (Rio Grande College). However, a few acts of philanthropy produced institutions that clearly would not otherwise have appeared when they did. Four examples stand out, which in time produced institutions that transcended the model of the multipurpose college.

First, Charles McMicken left a bequest to the city of Cincinnati in 1858 for establishing a men's and a women's college. Implementation was delayed, but grew into a grander conception. The University of Cincinnati (f. 1870) aspired to consolidate all the city's institutions of higher education under its umbrella. Initial progress was slow, with only the School of Design and the Observatory being incorporated by 1890. The next decade saw the addition of professional schools, however, and with them the efflorescence of a unique municipal university. Second, the gift of Leonard Case led to the opening of the Case School of Applied Science in Cleveland in 1881. The school endured numerous difficulties during its first decade, but its substantial endowment assured its eventual success. Third, the Case gift helped to prod Amassa Stone to provide the funds that brought Western Reserve College to Cleveland in 1882. Hitherto a hidebound early college, mimicking Yale and maintaining the classical course "in almost pristine integrity," Western Reserve was propelled toward becoming a true university.[43] Finally, although it may be stretching to regard the land script given to Ohio under the Morrill Act as a gift, its effects were similar to those just described. A new type of institution with an assured income was thereby created, Ohio Agricultural and Mechanical University (f. 1873), which by 1890 would be poised for explosive growth.[44] Each of these four institutions represented new departures for the modern era. As late as 1890, however, they had more features in common than in contrast with the multipurpose colleges.

The Multipurpose Colleges in Ohio

The enrollments noted in table 5 suggest that Ohio colleges had not yet evolved beyond the multipurpose era in 1890. The great majority of colleges were small and precarious operations. The average collegiate enrollment of the 35 institutions equaled 105, compared to a national average of 106. The situation in Ohio appears representative of the dynamics governing multipurpose colleges.

The multipurpose colleges depended for their vitality or subsistence on some combination of student fees, endowment income, and timely support of benefactors. In practice each college had to determine for itself how to optimize these potential resources (although there is no evidence they thought systematically about such things). While some students sought the highest standards for the B.A., others might search out the most lenient or inexpensive option. Catering to nondegree students could be an uncertain endeavor. And benefactors might look to reward either traditional high standards or departures from tradition. At any moment debt, calamities, or inexplicable fluctuations in enrollment might drive a college to the wall. The Ohio colleges during this era appear to have tested myriad possibilities, and thus their experiences provide a laboratory for the complex interactions of academic, market, and external forces.

For an important sector of potential collegians, strong academic standards may have been the paramount consideration. From the earliest foundings an implicit standard existed that was defined by the practices of the New England colleges. The standard itself was strongly contested, wedded as it was to the classi-cal curriculum most vigorously defended by Yale and Princeton. But for some colleges such an approach fulfilled the expectations of their constituency. This standard in practice called for well-qualified students and faculty, something that all colleges would ostensibly desire, and it was traditionally linked with a con-trolled residential setting. It also tended to be joined with a commitment to piety and education for the ministry. The oldest denominational colleges largely embraced this formula. Western Reserve, Kenyon, Denison, and Marietta were highly traditional in curricular matters, but so too was Oberlin in its classical course. Such a profile apparently allowed these schools to charge higher tuition and appeal to wealthier families. As of 1880 (before the impact of the new philan-thropy) their endowments were the largest among Ohio colleges ($150,000 to $250,000).[45]

If the years surrounding the Civil War were fertile with challenges to the existing order, a conservative reaction became apparent in the mid-1870s. Its vehicle was the Association of Ohio Colleges, which formed in 1867 as a rather informal discussion group among presidents and professors who attended the Ohio State Teachers' Association. Common topics were relations with the high schools and the thorny problem of Greek (discussed below). In the 1870s the association began to meet on its own, and its interests focused on "elevating the standard of the colleges in the State."[46] They first turned to the matter of regulat-ing the requirements for the bachelor's degree and devised a standard requiring "4 years of solid work with 15 recitations per week." In addition they sought to defend the A.B. as a classical course representing the study of both Latin and Greek. They also stipulated that colleges offering the degree should have a mini-mum of ten professors.[47] Their disdain for the B.S., on the other hand, was evi-dent. Their reporter remarked: "Nothing probably did so much to cheapen the degrees given by the colleges of Ohio, a few years ago, as the frequent granting of degrees of B.S. for very inadequate and inferior courses."[48] Once degree standards were agreed upon, the association limited its membership to those colleges meet-ing them (see table 5). The definition of quality taken by the Ohio Association did not necessarily exclude other kinds of courses, as was common in the East, since most of its approved members were multipurpose colleges with large irregular enrollments. Rather, it chose to man the barricades for the imperiled classical A.B., which throughout the era of the multipurpose college retained its preeminent status.

The general lack of success among colleges that aggressively entered the market for practical subjects is more perplexing.[49] Such programs were the signature of the multipurpose college, but most adopted them selectively and opportunistically. If popular, they boosted enrollments and revenues, but they were often dropped as quickly as they were added. The colleges that placed greatest emphasis on such programs had checkered histories. They tended to thrive from the late 1850s to the 1870s, but faced difficulties by the end of this era. Farmers' College was anemic after the war, eventually converting to a military academy. Scio declined somewhat later and was forced to merge with Mount Union (1911); and that institution, which styled itself a "people's college," barely survived the 1880s.[50]

One explanation is valid but beside the point. The kinds of curricula that reformers had been demanding since the 1820s were scarcely viable prior to 1890. The B.S. may have been an easier route to a college degree, but it did not signify systematic training in science and there was no identifiable demand for such graduates in the American economy. The lack of a knowledge base for agriculture education became painfully apparent after the Morrill Act, and was not appreciably mitigated until well after the Hatch Act (1887) established Agricultural Experiment Stations. The teaching of engineering slowly matured during these years, but even a proponent had to admit that the supply of trained engineers eventually created a demand, not the reverse.[51] Such training, it became apparent, could not adequately be appended to small denominational colleges. Thus the lack of fit between college, curriculum, and careers may have contradicted the visions of reformers, but it scarcely affected the market-driven programs of multipurpose colleges. These institutions faced a different problem.

As the colleges offered an increasing variety of programs, they tapped into the huge market for intermittent education by irregular students. This was the characteristic pattern for education beyond the common school in mid-nineteenth-century America, and it was met largely by academies and similar institutions.[52] Students mixed periods of education with periods of employment, sometimes into their early twenties. They sought education that would expand their intellect, dignify their social standing, or possibly get them a job. The colleges that developed out of thriving academies were already serving such a clientele, and devised flexible college programs to meet further needs. Other colleges capitalized on their prestige to dabble in these markets. However, results were often disappointing. Students seeking practical instruction attended irregularly and rarely completed degrees. This phenomenon had doomed Francis Wayland's 1850 reforms at Brown; and Cornell opened in 1868 with more than 400 students (332 freshmen), but the attrition rate for the first class approached 90 percent. The industrial classes, whatever their educational aspirations, did not relish spending four consecutive years in cloistered study.[53]

An additional complication was becoming apparent in the last decades of the century. Although the practice of admitting special students was widespread, even in the East, their presence became less compatible with the strengthening collegiate peer culture. Yale president Timothy Dwight was especially blunt: "the special and short course men demoralize the others more than they benefit themselves." If it were true generally, as one conscientious inquiry concluded, that irregular students on the whole were "a drag upon the improvement of the regular students," then their presence in significant numbers would inescapably tarnish the prestige of a college.[54] Such factors may explain why serving irregular students tended to produce substantial enrollments but impecunious institutions.

The colleges of this era are commonly imagined to be tuition dependent, but student fees were seldom adequate to sustain them because they charged so little. In Ohio tuition ranged from $24 per year at Heidelberg to $75 at Kenyon, with most colleges charging $30 to $45 (1890). If there were 15 students for each teacher (a rough average), a full $40 tuition from each would yield $600, or about half an instructor's salary.[55] Finding the other half of that salary was a continual challenge. Nationally, colleges in the 1890s derived about the same amount of revenues from endowments and other sources as they did from student fees. In Ohio endowment earnings exceeded income from students. All colleges probably desired robust enrollments, but for financial security they looked above all to productive funds.

In 1900 the majority of colleges reported endowments large enough to support one or more instructors ($25,000). The 171 colleges reporting no endowment were made up largely of public institutions without land grants, Catholic colleges, and most of the small colleges in the South. A similar number (170) reported $100,000 or more, but fewer institutions fell between these two groups.[56] For private colleges to better themselves in the postbellum years—to hire more and better qualified instructors—almost invariably meant accumulating productive funds. Institutional prestige was, as a rule, the critical factor for attracting bequests and benefactions. The distribution of endowments in 1900 indicated a widening distance between have and have-not colleges.

The third and most uncertain element of college financing in this era was deficits. Colleges apparently had only vague notions about their likely income and expenditures. Given good intentions and congenital optimism, colleges over-spent virtually every year, ending with a shortfall that had to be somehow met. Trustees at many schools customarily passed the hat; sometimes assets were drawn down; and many colleges actually borrowed funds, deferring the day of reckoning.[57] These perennial deficits, in effect, constituted part of college finance, but they also underlined the colleges' ineluctable dependence on outside support.

Other kinds of support for the colleges changed over time. One frequent recourse was the selling of subscriptions, presentable in lieu of tuition for a set number of years or in perpetuity. This practice was quite widespread in the 1850s and caused subsequent embarrassment to numerous institutions, includ-ing Antioch and Ohio Wesleyan.[58] Local enthusiasm for founding a college usu-ally brought an infusion of funds, but this feat generally proved difficult to duplicate. Direct support from the churches was always problematic. The denominations constituted natural networks for fund-raising, and college agents exploited them. However, actual church organizations were hard-pressed by other needs with higher priorities. The organization late in the century of special boards to coordinate aid to the colleges indicates that such support had to be carefully allotted.[59]

Existing essentially as mendicants created one source of uncertainty for the colleges, but they also found themselves operating in an increasingly competitive marketplace. Although the population and the demand for education were both growing in the late nineteenth century, so too were the alternatives. In offering programs for teachers, colleges competed with the burgeoning normal schools; commercial courses were offered in private business schools as well as high schools; and courses in music and art in all likelihood duplicated the offerings of private teachers. Competitive pressures came from other colleges in the form of rising standards. Hiram College had to extend its degree courses to meet the guidelines of the Association of Ohio Colleges; Mount Union was excluded from the association before 1890 because of its summer term and liberal policy on electives—precisely the features geared to local needs.[60]

As Colin Burke has emphasized, the multipurpose colleges were peculiarly suited for meeting the needs of educationally underserved communities. These were the "island communities" that Robert Wiebe has identified as characterizing the United States of the mid–nineteenth century.[61] The multipurpose colleges were an integral part of small-town America, and they spread across the land at roughly the pace that island communities were formed. They provided the kind of general education that in untold tacit ways permitted enterprising young men to dignify their presence and thus better themselves in commerce, the profes-sions, or public life. For just these reasons the colleges found the growing cities to be barren ground.

There was not a single urban occupation that required a bachelor's degree, and few where it might be an asset in finding employment.[62] Moreover, the cities were thick with competing institutions. High schools developed from an early date, providing general education as well as entree into commerce or teaching. A myriad of private schools taught anything for which customers would pay. In Ohio, as elsewhere beyond the Appalachians, the cities tended to be graveyards for nineteenth-century colleges. Cincinnati College was one of Ohio's earliest, but it operated intermittently and closed in 1846. Woodward College failed there too, and the Protestant University of the United States (chartered 1845), whose grandiose vision seems to have been lost in the mists of time, apparently never opened. Farmers' College also foundered on the outskirts of Cincinnati. The single exception was St. Xavier's, which served a well-defined population of Roman Catholics. Cleveland University was launched in 1850 with impressive sponsorship, but was soon defunct. Only private philanthropy gave Western Reserve (after its move) and the University of Cincinnati the staying power to persist into a new and more favorable era.[63]

The other side of this coin is that professional education in law and medicine was located exclusively in Ohio cities. Cincinnati by 1890 had four regular medical schools and four other kinds. Cleveland, Columbus, and Toledo each had two regular medical schools. Law schools were found only in Cincinnati and Cleveland. Large cities, it would seem, were as prolific in sprouting professional schools as the countryside was in breeding colleges. By 1890, however, such compartmentalization was disintegrating along with America's island communities. The multipurpose college, as a result, faced both internal and external challenges.[64]

The Rise and Fall of Useful Knowledge

Higher Education for Science, Agriculture, and the Mechanic Arts, 1850–1875

∾

ROGER L. GEIGER

. . . to the endowment, support, and maintenance of at least one college where the leading object shall be, without excluding other scientific and classical studies, and including military tactics, to teach such branches of learning as are related to agriculture and the mechanic arts . . . in order to promote the liberal and practical education of the industrial classes in the several pursuits and professions in life.
MORRILL LAND-GRANT ACT, 2 JULY 1862

S ince its enactment in 1862, the Morrill Land-Grant Act has meant different things to different people.[1] Some believed it promoted access to higher education for the common man, or what contemporaries called the "industrial classes." Others interpreted the act as specifically intended to elevate farmers and advance the practice of agriculture. The third principal association has been with service, the commitment of land-grant universities to link and apply academic learning with practical affairs. Justin Smith Morrill himself encouraged all of these associations. In fact his very vagueness about the institutions he sought to create was undoubtedly a factor in their ultimate success.

Historians of higher education have more often celebrated these assumed intentions than evaluated them critically.[2] The legislation had a determinative influence on the shaping of American higher education, but because that shape is now taken for granted, its precise role is difficult to perceive today. Its most far-reaching consequences were tangential to access, service, or agriculture. Rather, the Morrill Act was the key to combining within the same institutions technical or applied forms of higher education and the "liberal" arts and sciences. For this purpose the awkward prepositional phrase in the middle of the act's key provision—"without excluding other scientific and classical studies"—assumes crucial importance. Morrill clearly meant to elevate practical, and particularly agricultural, education to the level of liberal, collegiate studies, but he wisely did not trouble himself about precisely how this might be done. As he said later, "the bill fixes the leading objects, but properly . . . leaves to the States considerable latitude in carrying out the practical details."[3]

The unification of scientific, technological, and liberal studies in the United States was hardly foreordained. American higher education in 1860, although dominated by the classical colleges, contained a bewildering array of institutions. A clear separation between liberal or literary education, as offered in the classical colleges, and instruction with practical or utilitarian objectives was nevertheless maintained. The open-ended terms of the Land-Grant Act almost assured that this issue would become a major arena for contesting the future structure of higher education. Development in the years immediately following the Morrill Act largely followed established precedents, and thus tended to widen rather than narrow that separation. However, during this formative period, the legacy of the Morrill Act established and sustained a tenuous link between these two domains. A full generation was necessary not only to reconcile forms of education that were viewed as distinct alternatives, but also to bridge a huge gap between differing conceptions of scientific and practical education.[4]

Schools of Science before the Morrill Act

Congressman Justin S. Morrill, sponsor of the Land-Grant Act, and the many others whose agitation helped to prepare its way, acted from a populistic impulse to provide both liberal and practical education for the industrial classes: *liberal*—because they wished to overcome the prevailing social gradient distancing educated professionals from those who worked in the productive economy, in agriculture, manufacturing, or commerce; *practical*—because that was the conspicuous lacuna in the educational system. These notions were linked under the rubric of "useful knowledge," a venerable set of ideas that looked to education in science to directly enhance the productivity and social standing of mechanics, artisans, or farmers.[5]

In the useful knowledge tradition there was no distinction between pure and applied science: scientific knowledge by its very nature was considered to be inherently useful. MIT founder William Barton Rogers, for example, provided a classic statement of this tradition in his 1851 formulation of plans for a polytechnic school:

> . . . there is no branch of practical industry, whether in the arts of construction, manufactures, or agriculture, which is not capable of being better practiced, and even of being improved in its processes, through the knowledge of its connections with physical truths and laws, and . . . there is no class of operatives to whom the teaching of science may not become of direct and substantial utility and material usefulness.[6]

As early as the 1840s the conviction spread that useful knowledge ought to be purveyed by institutions of higher learning, but just how was anyone's guess.

The earliest institutions to teach scientific/technical subjects were sui generis. Engineering was first taught seriously at West Point after 1817 when Sylvanus Thayer instituted reforms inspired by French military education. A somewhat different approach to engineering and military education was pioneered by Alden Partridge at Norwich, Vermont, beginning in 1819 and extended on the collegiate level when his academy became Norwich University (1834).[7] In these years information on practical science was usually presented in public lectures rather than in classrooms. Hence the first experiment in agricultural education was the Gardiner Lyceum, which operated in Maine from 1822 to 1832. Similarly the Franklin Institute of Philadelphia began offering lectures on scientific and technical subjects in 1824, and for a short time it conducted a high school as well.[8] The same year the Rensselaer School was opened by Amos Eaton, a tireless lyceum performer, and for a decade it taught a one-year course in science. In 1835 the course was shifted to civil engineering, and the school changed its name to Rensselaer Institute.[9] In addition colleges had experimented intermittently with a parallel "scientific course," which allowed various subjects to be substituted for Greek and sometimes Latin.

By the 1850s, three distinct institutional forms for scientific/technical education had emerged, in addition to the parallel scientific course: (1) "schools of science" attached to some of the foremost colleges and universities; (2) colleges of agriculture; and (3) "polytechnics" devoted to engineering and the mechanic arts (table 6). Whether they were different parts of the same great endeavor to create "industrial education" or fundamentally different undertakings would long remain unclear.

The new schools of science were distinct alternatives to the Bachelor of Science courses that were increasingly being offered by colleges in conjunction with their regular classical course. In practice, however, a continuum ran between science courses and the more or less autonomous schools of science. At one extreme

TABLE 6

INSTITUTIONS FOR HIGHER EDUCATION IN APPLIED SCIENCE

Schools of Science or Engineering Affiliated with Colleges	Date of Opening	Non-Land-Grant Schools for Agriculture or Engineering
Union College, Engineering School	1845	
Yale College, Sheffield Scientific School	1846	
Harvard University, Lawrence Scientific School	1847	
	1851	Renssalaer Polytechnic Institute
Dartmouth College, Chandler Scientific School	1852	Farmer's College (open)
University of North Carolina, School of Application of Science to the Arts Norwich Univ. 3-yr. Engineering Course	1853	Polytechnic College of the State of Pennsylvania
	1854	Polytechnic Institute of Brooklyn Farmer's College (chartered)
	1857	Michigan State Agricultural College
University of Virginia, Dept. of Applied Chemistry	1858	Maryland Agricultural College
	1859	Farmer's High School (Pennsylvania)
Columbia College, School of Mines	1864	
	1865	Massachusetts Institute of Technology
Lafayette College, Pardee Scientific Department	1866	Lehigh University Illinois Agricultural College
	1868	Worcester County Free Institute of Industrial Science
Dartmouth College, Thayer School of Civil Engineering Harvard University, Bussey Institution (agr.)	1871	Stevens Institute of Technology
Univ. of Pennsylvania, Towne Scientific School	1872	
Princeton College, Green School of Science Columbian University, Corcoran School of Science	1873	
Boston University, School of all Sciences	1874	Colorado School of Mines

stood the Sheffield Scientific School at Yale, whose evolution dates from 1846, the Lawrence Scientific School at Harvard (1847), and to a lesser extent the Chandler Scientific School at Dartmouth (1852).[10] Despite the common name, these schools were quite different. The Yale school evolved as a separate teaching unit before being strengthened by the benefactions of Joseph Sheffield. It was established explicitly for the instruction of "graduates and others not members of the [Yale College] undergraduate classes." During the 1850s, the Scientific School organized distinct two-year courses in chemistry and engineering, as well as provisions for postgraduate study in languages, philosophy, and science. In the 1860s the course of study was extended to three years—a first year of general scientific and linguistic grounding, followed by two years of specialized study in one of seven fields.[11] Although distinctions are difficult to draw in this incremental process, these studies plausibly represent the first advanced undergraduate science course organized on a regular basis.

The Lawrence School failed to take this last step. As originally proposed by President Edward Everett, the "Scientific School of the University at Cambridge" would have included instruction in practical science and postgraduate study, much like Yale. However, the gift of Abbott Lawrence and the hiring of the renowned Swiss scientist Louis Agassiz tilted the balance toward pure science. Its students largely studied independently with a single professor, and they could earn a B.S. by studying and being examined in just one subject.[12] Dartmouth's Chandler School more closely resembled the scientific courses at numerous other colleges. It initially taught a three-year course to students who were generally younger and less prepared than those in the college, and it was accordingly compared disdainfully to the A.B. course.[13] As at Yale the students at these scientific schools formed a separate body from the students of the respective classical colleges.

The other so-called scientific schools or courses of the 1850s did not separate students in this way. Sometimes a single professorship might be declared to be a school, but in practice such instruction was usually integrated with the regular college. The University of North Carolina, for example, appointed professors of civil engineering and agricultural chemistry and formed the School for the Application of Science to the Arts (1853), but these subjects could be elected only during a student's senior year.[14] Many of the parallel scientific courses organized at this time were essentially designed as alternatives for students unwilling or unable to study Greek and/or Latin. They offered instead some instruction in modern languages and additional classes in science, but not in more advanced scientific subjects. Initially most of these B.S. courses lasted three years.[15] Colleges that wished to teach applied science were obliged, like North Carolina, to employ special instructors in applied chemistry and/or civil engineering. Such authentic science and engineering courses existed in the 1850s at Union College and the Universities of Michigan and Virginia, among others.[16]

Perhaps the best-known reform effort of the day, that of Francis Wayland at Brown, should be seen as an effort to achieve similar ends. His well-publicized critique of the classical college gained him the opportunity to restructure the Brown course of study in 1851. Wayland sought to attract more students to college and to make education more relevant to industrial pursuits, much like Congressman Morrill; but he was motivated more by notions of efficiency drawn from political economy than by a devotion to useful knowledge. Brown's "New System" promised courses in civil engineering, "application of chemistry to the arts," agriculture, and "didactics" (teaching), among others. These subjects could be taken for two years as a special course or three years for a Bachelor of Philosophy degree. The Ph.B. course was integrated with the classical course so that Brown to some extent combined liberal and technical education. This experiment essentially failed. The New System had some initial success in terms of enrollments, but was declining noticeably when Wayland retired in 1855. He had expected the curricular freedom of the New System to encourage greater student learning, but just the opposite occurred. Lower standards in the literary courses soon tarnished the college's reputation, while poorly prepared students and low rates of graduation plagued the special courses. In 1858 Brown reverted to a more conventional structure.[17]

Agricultural education was not entirely neglected before the Morrill Act, since at least four fully organized colleges of agriculture operated in the 1850s. Those in Pennsylvania, Michigan, and Maryland were organized under the auspices of state agricultural societies and thus had quasi-public sponsorship. The organization of similar institutions was under way by 1860 in Massachusetts and Iowa, but a parallel effort in New York ultimately foundered.[18] Jonathan Baldwin Turner's campaign for an industrial university in Illinois was deflected toward support for a normal school.[19] Probably the most vigorous institution in the 1850s was the privately organized Farmers' College outside Cincinnati.[20]

It is difficult to assess these inchoate institutions because the Morrill Act soon altered almost everything about them. They were clearly emanations of the bucolic version of useful knowledge, which had long inspired visions of agricultural education. That such aspirations finally began to be realized in the 1850s was due principally to the efforts of state agricultural societies.[21] These institutions sought the cachet of conferring college degrees, while rejecting most other traits associated with classical colleges (except possibly Farmers' College). The Farmer's High School of Pennsylvania disdained even the title of college, but nevertheless sought a form of instruction that would—to invoke a code phrase—"afford a good mental discipline" as well as "practical knowledge peculiarly adapted to the necessities and calling of a farmer." The result was a combination of academic courses and manual labor on a model farm. Initially most agricultural colleges offered a three- or four-year B.S. course with an option for agricultural subjects.

As with science and engineering (below), these focused institutions scarcely represent all the efforts to introduce agriculture into higher education. Lectures on agricultural chemistry were offered widely as that subject acquired substance and popularity. Applied or organic chemistry was an important stimulus behind the establishment of scientific schools as well, where agricultural lectures were usually offered.[22]

The teaching of civil engineering in antebellum colleges was not uncommon. Surveying had been taught in the previous century, and West Point after 1817 provided an updated model. But aside from West Point, and perhaps Norwich University, early efforts in the colleges tended to be weak and intermittent. Only civil engineering was taught before 1850; engineering lectures were offered as a partial course or a two-year certificate course, and they were often suspended. Signs of vitality appeared in the 1840s when the U.S. Naval Academy (f. 1845) began teaching the new subject of steam engineering, and Union College instituted a regular course in civil engineering (1845).[23] As with agriculture, developments accelerated in the 1850s.

Rensselaer became the first true engineering college in 1851, when it instituted a three-year degree course in civil engineering and renamed itself a Polytechnic. An urban tradition of useful knowledge soon surfaced in the founding of additional polytechnic institutes. These institutions focused on the mechanic arts and superseded earlier mechanics institutes organized by or for mechanics and artisans. The Polytechnic College of the State of Pennsylvania was launched in Philadelphia in 1853. It offered several two-year courses for engineers and a three-year course leading to a Bachelor of Industrial Arts. A similar institution opened in Brooklyn two years later. The small number of more-or-less permanent institutions scarcely reflects the enthusiasm for this type of education existing before and after the Civil War. In Pennsylvania alone, five ephemeral engineering schools were chartered between 1860 and 1871.[24]

The school that soon set the standard in this area, however, was the Massachusetts Institute of Technology. Incorporated in 1861 after a lengthy campaign by founder William Barton Rogers, MIT was originally conceived as part of a grandiose four-part scheme for bringing science to the industrial classes through a learned society, a museum, instruction for regular students, and a night school for workers. The hallmark of Rogers's educational philosophy was the argument that a solid grounding in science should be the foundation for the applied "arts." He also felt initially that the intended clientele should be not the "comparatively few" who could avail themselves of "complete and comprehensive training" in the colleges, but "a large number whom the scantiness of time, means, and opportunity would exclude from the great seats of classical and scientific education."[25] Rogers thus endorsed both a modern conception of technical education and the romantic chimera of useful knowledge. Most important, he secured sponsorship from among the industrial and intellectual elite of Boston and used this backing to secure public support as Massachusetts's land-grant engineering school. MIT from the outset had the resources to implement the more orthodox part of Rogers's visionary plan.

In sum at the time of the Morrill Act, the country already possessed a host of institutions in which "the leading object was education in agriculture or the mechanic arts," and others were on the drawing boards. However, no template was yet accepted for organized instruction in useful knowledge. Each of these exemplars was unique. No wonder historians have had difficulty characterizing these schools: they were puzzling to contemporaries as well.

Daniel Coit Gilman and "Our National Schools of Science"

As soon as the guns of war fell silent, the task of realizing the terms of the Morrill Act began in earnest. Nor were these the only such efforts. Laurence Veysey has written that "during the ten years after 1865 almost every visible change in the pattern of American higher education lay in the direction of concessions to the utilitarian type of demand for reform."[26] The emerging educational leaders of this era sought to define, and thus shape, this powerful yet inchoate movement.

In contrast to the useful knowledge tradition, scientific and technical education was viewed quite differently at this juncture by two well-placed teachers, who were soon to become the most important university presidents of the era— Daniel Coit Gilman, professor of geography at Yale's Sheffield Scientific School, and Charles W. Eliot, professor of chemistry at the recently opened Massachusetts Institute of Technology. Both men envisioned liberal and practical learning being joined at a higher level, intellectually and professionally. Gilman in 1867 waxed enthusiastic over the prospects for "Our National Schools of Science," but he did not think it likely or desirable, as Morrill and Turner apparently did, that their graduates would "go back and labor with the hoe or the anvil."[27] Both Gilman and Eliot envisioned the new types of schools as forming scientific professionals who would "take charge of mines, manufactories, [and] the construction of public works." For such roles they advocated a substantial base of liberal education, ideally including Latin.[28] Beyond this common perspective, however, the two future leaders made different contributions to the ongoing debate.

When Gilman wrote "Our National Schools of Science" for the *North American Review* in 1867, he envisioned the proliferation of institutions much like his own. For him the crucial feature of these schools, their common denominator, would be "the study of natural science in its applications to human industry." Such study, as noted above, was for aspiring managers, not workers. He realistically pointed out one fallacy of useful knowledge: "experience seems to show that the sons of farmers in this country, if they spend three or four years in acquiring an education . . . will almost always choose to enter other callings, than to be educated farmers handling the scythe and tending the cattle." Gilman favored the provision of useful knowledge to workers, but consigned that task to "industrial schools of a lower grade," which of necessity would have to await the formation of the "central" schools of science.[29]

Gilman seconded Morrill's liberality toward the form that land-grant institutions might take, although he objected that the already common rubric of "agricultural college" was too narrow. Gilman offered the possibility that the grants might form "even a university with all its faculties," but warned that this model would require far greater revenues. Fundamentally, though, he conceived the schools of science as separate institutions. Their existence, he predicted, would allow the older colleges to concentrate "more vigorously than ever [on] the established disciplines of Latin and Greek." The "National Schools of Science" would thus allow "both classes of institutions [to] flourish side by side."[30]

As the acknowledged expert in this field, Gilman was asked by the commissioner of education in 1871 to report on the state of the emerging land-grant institutions. The realities he found in this survey proved rather different from the idealistic hopes of his original article. "The end to be gained [by the Land-Grant Act] was better understood than the means which should be employed," he wrote, "in other words, . . . the theory of agricultural education was vaguely worked out." The exemplars he encountered caused Gilman to refine his general conception of these institutions. He saw three distinct social needs for such education to fulfill.

> First, and most easily recognized is the need . . . for able, educated, trustworthy technologists, such as well-informed engineers, architects, mechanicians, manufacturers, miners, agriculturalists, and the like; . . . Secondly, the country needs more skillful laborers [acquainted] with the natural laws underlying manufacturer's processes: for them, industrial or trade schools are requisite—the more the better; Thirdly . . . even a greater want . . . in order to carry forward scientific investigations and to contribute to the advancement of knowledge, on which all useful arts depend, the country requires a great many men of science.[31]

Gilman saw the new land-grant institutions as dedicated to the first of these wants—technologists. In some cases they addressed the second need through shops, model farms, and compulsory manual labor. But as for scientists, he could point to only one institution "where the presence of post-graduate students studying science for its own sake, is regarded as of the highest good." That was obviously his home institution, Yale's Sheffield School. In sum the land-grant colleges at this early stage failed to conform to Gilman's previous hopes for national schools of science. Instead they were intently focused on applied science, particularly agriculture.

In the early 1870s the immediate fruits of the land grants were a distinctive group of institutions. Six simply adopted the name of Agricultural College[32] (see table 7). The most common title, adopted in sixteen states, included Agricultural and Mechanical (A&M). Some of the A&Ms were separate entities while others had varying degrees of connection with existing institutions. Some institutions that later developed into comprehensive universities began life with land-grant titles: for example, Illinois Industrial University; Ohio Agricultural and Mechanical College. Generically all the land-grant schools were popularly referred to as "agricultural colleges," a designation that strengthened the proprietary claims of farmers and their supporters, while exasperating the champions of academic "schools of science." A dozen of the land-grant recipients were units of existing or refurbished colleges or universities (often vehemently attacked for neglecting agriculture).[33] The degree of separation of A&M education and the literary course varied in these institutions from little to total. Seven new state universities were fashioned with land-grant funds. Three of them were in small states where more than one institution could scarcely be justified, but flagship state universities emerged in Minnesota and California.[34] At least one of the new universities, Purdue, wholeheartedly embraced the mission of an A&M school. The closest initial exemplar of an integrated land-grant university was Cornell—an institution possessing both great resources (the precondition foreseen by Gilman) from the patronage of Ezra Cornell and a university vision from its president, Andrew Dickson White.[35] With its strong promotion of liberal scholarship, Cornell was a beacon to those educators who wished to integrate technical and academic studies. But given its philanthropic foundation, it was hardly a feasible model. Outside a few avowed universities, literary or liberal studies obtained only a toehold in the new land-grant colleges.[36]

During these same years the founding of separate private schools of science or engineering continued unabated in the East, and then later in the West.[37] From 1864 to 1874, ten science or engineering schools were added to eastern universities (see table 6). Among them, the Columbia School of Mines, which was organized like the scientific schools, pioneered and long dominated its field.[38] Independent institutes of engineering also were founded. Besides MIT,

TABLE 7

LAND-GRANT INSTITUTIONS & UNITS IN 1875, BY YEAR OF OPENING*

Yale College: Sheffield Scientific School	1846
Michigan State Agricultural College	1857
Maryland Agricultural College	1858
Pennsylvania State College	1859
Kansas State Agricultural College	1863
Rutgers College: Rutgers Scientific School	1864
Massachusetts Institute of Technology	1865
University of Vermont: State Agricultural College	1865
Kentucky University: A&M College	1866
University of Wisconsin: Engineering Departments	1866
Illinois Industrial University	1867
West Virginia University: Agricultural Department	1867
Massachusetts Agricultural College	1867
Dartmouth College: New Hampshire College of A&M Arts	1868
Cornell University: College of A&M Arts	1868
Corvallis State Agricultural College	1868
Iowa State Agricultural College	1869
University of California: Agricultural Mining & Mechanical Arts College	1869
Brown College: Agricultural & Scientific Department	1869
East Tennessee University: Tennessee Agricultural College	1869
Delaware College: Agricultural Department	1870
University of Minnesota: Colleges of A&M Arts	1870
University of Missouri: Missouri A&M College	1870
University of Mississippi: School of A&M Arts	1871
Alcorn University (Mississippi): A&M Department	1871
University of Missouri: School of Mines & Metallurgy	1871
[Alabama] State A&M College	1872
Arkansas Industrial University	1872
University of Georgia: Georgia State College of A&M Arts	1872
University of Nebraska: Agricultural College	1872
Virginia A&M College	1872
Hampton Normal & Agricultural Institute	1872
Ohio A&M College	1873
Purdue University	1874
A&M College of Louisiana	1874
Maine College of A&M Arts	1874
University of Nevada: College of Agriculture	1874
University of North Carolina: A&M College	1875
South Carolina A&M Institute	1875
A&M College of Texas	1876

* Titles and date of organization taken from RCE, 1875, 749–51. N.B. this table provides a
contemporary picture of the land-grant colleges. Nomenclature and land-grant
designation changed, and reported dates of organization were often inconsistent.

engineering schools were opened at Worcester (1868) and Hoboken (Stevens, 1871). Lehigh University (1866) too was launched as a polytechnic college.[39]

The difficulty of combining A&M training with serious study in science, as well as a literary course, was ironically demonstrated in Gilman's own career. In 1872 the University of California finally persuaded him to assume its presidency. Gilman fully embraced the cause of building a true university, dedicated to advancing the arts and sciences and to meeting the needs of its state. However, this comprehensive vision—essentially the same as in "Schools of Science"—was too academic for many Californians. During his brief tenure (1872–1874) the most serious, and ultimately demoralizing, problem confronting the university was a rebellion of the supporters of agriculture, who nearly succeeded in securing the land-grant revenues for a separate college of agriculture. This battle was won only after Gilman's departure, when a new state constitution shielded the university against such political pillage.[40] The episode nevertheless reveals that the obstacles to an integrated university were more than political: they also reflected the uncertain organization and pedagogy of the entire area of technological education.[41] This was a topic to which Charles Eliot had given much thought.

Charles W. Eliot and the "New Education"

When Eliot published "The New Education: Its Organization" in the *Atlantic Monthly* early in 1869, he was, much like Gilman, interpreting the utilitarian movement in education from the comfortable perspective that he knew best—in this case Boston and Cambridge.[42] His views were nevertheless well informed about existing institutions, although far from prescient about their evolution. Posing the questions of a concerned father seeking a practical education for a son, he analyzed the schools of science, engineering schools, and parallel scientific courses largely in terms of the congruence between the instruction offered and the students served. He omitted the agricultural colleges as being too immature to be judged.

The scientific schools, Eliot began, had been originally intended as professional schools suitable for students who had completed a regular college course.[43] At the time 12 percent of the students at the principal schools were college graduates.[44] But for Eliot this minority was insufficient. The schools had in fact seen their rolls filled with poorly prepared and often part-time students. The Sheffield School had dealt with this situation best, although it had taken more than a decade to institute an effective three-year course of study, having a first year of general preparation for the specialized courses that followed.[45] In addition Sheffield had imposed more stringent admission standards. Sheffield had thus elevated the scientific course toward the higher, collegiate level of work, while the Lawrence School and the Columbia School of Mines were still forced to accommodate special students with varying levels of preparation. Thus Sheffield, Eliot hoped, had indicated the future direction of scientific education. In praising Sheffield, Eliot was forwarding his own views. As an assistant professor of chemistry at the Lawrence School in 1862, Eliot had attempted, unsuccessfully, to institute a required two-year introductory sequence as well as meaningful admission standards. When he joined MIT, he was instrumental in establishing just such a structure there.[46] By the time he wrote "The New Education" undertaking one or two years of preparatory study was becoming the standard pattern, but institutions with weak enrollments were still obliged to tolerate "specials" who wished to study only technical classes.

The mixing of classical and scientific students in parallel but overlapping curricula had no future in Eliot's eyes. It had failed in Europe, he declared, and was doomed to failure in the United States because of the "incompatibility of the practical spirit with the literary spirit." Thus the mixed courses at Union, Brown, and Michigan (and by implication, numerous other colleges) were in his eyes, "temporary expedients during a transition period."[47] Here again, Eliot was reasoning from the supposed educational objectives of students, which he assumed to be pure learning in the classical course and practical skills in the scientific course.

Like Gilman, Eliot believed the scientific course and the classical course provided mental training that was different in nature but of similar worth—a controversial proposition in 1869.[48] The critical features for attaining such equivalence were the quality of the teachers and, for students, a regular course of study. Eliot felt that these conditions were achieved more readily at independent polytechnics simply because their energies were more focused than those of university-related schools of science. "The number and quality of teachers actually employed in a school are the best tests of its real character," he averred. By this standard his own MIT had already achieved preeminence with a course of study comparable with those given at Sheffield and Rensselaer Polytechnic Institute (RPI). The greatest problem for the New Education were those students outside the regular course—those partial or special students who studied only a single subject, or—even worse—students who chose the science curriculum as an easier alternative to the classical. Eliot regarded the presence of these "shirks and stragglers" as the bane of the scientific and technical schools, although he asserted, somewhat wishfully, that "this evil is a temporary one."[49] The actual clientele of scientific courses, circa 1870, was heavily weighted with underprepared, practical-minded, irregular students. The New Education had only begun to wrestle with the dilemma of how to provide both accessible, basic instruction for the many and rigorous, advanced technical education for the few.

Before the year was out, Eliot was president of Harvard and in a position to impose his stated views on the Lawrence Scientific School.[50] The course of events, however, belied Eliot's basic premise in "The New Education" of the inherent separateness of practical and literary education. His first gambit was to seek a merger with MIT. Such an arrangement would have given Harvard a distinctly separate unit for applied science, not unlike the Sheffield School in New Haven. This idea must have had a strong appeal for Eliot, because he explored this possibility on two succeeding occasions, but satisfactory terms could never be negotiated. Instead, faute de mieux, Eliot induced the school in 1871 to organize the kind of regular course that he had so strongly advocated. Given the few, specialized faculty members of the Lawrence School, this course could be realized only by having students take basic math and science subjects in Harvard College. Over the next five years an entrance examination was required (1873), and all courses of study were extended to four years. An attempt was made to divert the special students into a one-year teachers' course, but it soon disappeared. The Lawrence School became integrated into Harvard College despite Eliot's earlier strictures against such arrangements. Besides the common courses in math and sciences, any student could take advanced courses in science or engineering as electives. In addition the Lawrence faculty were given appointments in the college, and in 1890 most meaningful distinctions were obliterated with the creation of a single faculty of arts and sciences.[51] Harvard thus evolved toward an integration of pure and practical studies and the modern university model, but elsewhere in the country this issue continued to be contested.

The Demise of Useful Knowledge

The post–Civil War explosion of utilitarian forms of education exhausted its expansive force by the mid-1870s. The panic of 1873 ended the postwar economic boom and dampened the mood of the country. These changes were particularly apparent in agriculture, where falling prices and related worries engendered a powerful movement concerned with the plight of the farmer. Very quickly these interests concluded that the agricultural colleges contributed little to alleviate the farmers' woes. The rebellion of the agriculturalists that undermined Gilman at the University of California was repeated across the country. In 1875 the Grange launched an investigation of the colleges that termed them a "farce" and demanded that total control be given to farmers. According to the farmers' movement, Justin Morrill's great initiative had failed to provide them with useful knowledge.[52]

The disaffection of the farmers reflected a fundamental incompatibility between the useful knowledge tradition and the academic embodiments of technical education. During the 1870s and 1880s, the tensions that Eliot had identified were slowly resolved within these institutions, but the general movement was toward convergence rather than separation.

The general confusion about mission, clientele, and standards in technical education was reflected in the history of these institutions before 1890. Most of the institutions in the Northeast sooner or later adopted the academic outlook and thus aspired to bolster standards and respectability. Elsewhere the tradition of useful knowledge remained endemic as institutions sought to be broadly accessible and to teach job-related skills. Whichever the orientation, staying power was a significant factor in this volatile realm. For private institutions the indispensable resources were largely provided by endowments or sponsorship. In the public sector, first land-grant revenues and later state support sustained institutions through meager times. The institutions that were most dependent on irregular students, such as the urban polytechnics, faced the greatest difficulties in making the transition to a more stable model of technical education.

As Eliot had foreseen, the most significant curricular development among the schools of science was the adoption of a common one- or two-year set of courses that provided grounding in mathematics, physics, and languages.[53] This common course gave the institutions some control over standards for admission, but more important it became the gatekeeper for entry to the specialized advanced courses. The price of high standards, given the immature state of secondary education, was very high attrition.

Whether students sought only job-related skills or were unable to perform the work, only a small fraction actually graduated. About one-fifth of the matriculants at MIT were graduated in its first two decades, and the same was true at Lehigh in the 1870s. Cornell is celebrated for opening with the largest freshman class yet assembled—a result of both vast publicity and tolerant criteria for admission. But just 10 percent of its large early classes stayed the course through graduation. As standards were raised, the freshman class at Cornell shrunk to less than a third of its 1868 size, but graduation rates rose to nearly 50 percent.[54] Before the 1880s the academically oriented schools had difficulties implementing the standards they desired. Almost all suffered a downturn in enrollments during the late 1870s or early 1880s. But then conditions seem to have changed. Student numbers began to increase in the mid- to late 1880s. Not only were the engineering schools attracting more students, but they were getting the kind of regular students that they had been seeking for a generation. Increasing demand for engineers was undoubtedly a factor, but so dramatic a change also reflected improvements in the educational preparation of incoming students.

This development, conversely, signaled the obsolescence of the useful knowledge approach. The most conspicuous relic of this tradition had been embodied in the notion of "shop culture," which held that engineering was best learned inside a simulated machine shop. This approach was exemplified in the Worcester County Free Institute of Industrial Science (1868; later, Worcester Polytechnic Institute), where beginning students spent thirty-seven hours per week in shop work. Georgia Institute of Technology (f. 1885) was initially patterned after the Worcester model. Worcester also influenced some land-grant colleges where the idea of the mechanic arts was often taken literally. In agriculture an equivalent to shop culture existed in the model farm. Cornell nevertheless became the most important arena for sorting out these conflicting notions, since useful knowledge was favored by both the founder, Ezra Cornell, and the patron of the engineering school, Hiram Sibley. This orientation changed, however, when Robert Thurston was hired from Stevens Institute in 1885 to direct the engineering college. He resolutely imposed an academic model, raising admission standards and implementing a solid base of course work for the first two years. Practitioners would resist these developments until the end of the century, but the scientifically trained mechanical engineer inexorably displaced the schooled mechanic.[55]

University-affiliated schools of science followed a similar path as they increasingly resembled literary colleges in student recruitment and length of degree course. Where these schools were separately governed and financed, as at Yale and Columbia, distinctions died hard. The process of homogenization was ultimately most thorough at the state universities spawned by the Morrill Act. Student enrollments gradually swelled in those departments of letters or science that, by the grace of a prepositional phrase in the original legislation, had not been precluded. Over time, as well, institutional loyalties took precedence over the separate identities of the many individual units. In the Northeast no new science schools were founded after the early 1870s, but what really undermined their existence, at Harvard and elsewhere, was the gradual adoption of the elective system. Unlike previous systems of optional studies, which allowed students to substitute specified subjects within a rigid curriculum organized by class year, true electives allowed students to take almost any course they wished. Under those conditions there was no longer a rationale for separate scientific schools.

After 1890 the capacious American university placed science, engineering, agriculture, and a host of other fields on the same footing as literary studies. The university's overweening presence in the American system of higher education has made it difficult to appreciate that shortly before, in the third quarter of the nineteenth century, the situation had been otherwise. Then the predominant belief held that liberal studies and useful knowledge were intended for different kinds of students and ought to be organized separately.[56] In a twist of fate the Morrill Act, which was a product of this milieu, was ultimately instrumental in undermining this limited and limiting vision.

"A Salutary Rivalry"

The Growth of Higher Education for Women in Oxford, Ohio, 1855–1867

∽

MARGARET A. NASH

*H*istorians have written about the opening of Vassar College in 1865 as a turning point in higher education for women, giving the impression that little of importance in the women's college movement occurred before then. Other historians argue that the progression from seminary to college "exhibits no major-watersheds"; rather, the decade prior to the founding of Vassar represented a significant quickening in the transition from seminary to college education for women.[1] In the 1850s there were probably more than forty-five degree-granting colleges for women.[2] The idea of women attending college, though not without its detractors, clearly had become widely accepted. Schools for women proudly wore the name "college" in a way that would not have been feasible in the Northeast during the 1830s and 1840s.[3] However, the transition from seminary to college did not occur in a simple linear progression, and the lines between colleges and seminaries were long blurred.

Developments in Oxford, Ohio, a small town in the southwestern part of the state, illustrate these blurred boundaries. Oxford was home to three female educational institutions from 1855 to 1867, and they exemplify the variations existing in higher education for women in the middle of the nineteenth century. Western Female Seminary did not become an accredited college until 1894, yet like many other seminaries, it offered college-level courses from its inception in

1855. A second school, the Oxford Female College, called itself a college without initially offering a truly collegiate curriculum. A third school, the Oxford Female Institute, offered a collegiate department along with its primary and secondary departments. Competition for students and for the support of local church members resulted in each school setting increasingly higher academic standards, while also assuring parents and the community that graduates would be prepared to assume their duties as women. The conception of those womanly duties varied according to socioeconomic class. Relatively wealthy students, who were more likely to attend Oxford Female Institute and Oxford Female College, received ornamental education in addition to academics; they learned music and embroidery along with Latin. Less-affluent students, who attended Western Female Seminary, participated in an arrangement in which they performed all of the household labor in addition to their academic work, thereby demonstrating that learning Virgil did not make them unfit for the kitchen.[4] Exploring the interactions and relationships among the three Oxford schools reveals how class differences and local competition shaped the development of higher education for women.

One of the three schools in Oxford, the Western Female Seminary, was a "daughter" school of Mount Holyoke Female Seminary. Although Mount Holyoke had many imitators, it officially claimed a connection to just five U.S. schools: Cherokee Female Seminary (Oklahoma, 1851), Western Female Seminary (Ohio, 1855), Lake Erie Female Seminary (Ohio, 1859), Michigan Female Seminary (1867), and Mills Female Seminary (California, 1871).[5] Although scholars have written extensively about Mount Holyoke and other schools in the Northeast, their counterparts in the West or South have received little study.[6] The case of Oxford, in addition, exemplifies the close and formative ties between one "daughter," the Western Female Seminary, and the "mother," Mount Holyoke Female Seminary.

Like its English namesake, Oxford, Ohio, was associated with education. A federal land grant to John Cleves Symmes in 1793 stipulated that land be set aside and held in trust as a site for a college. In 1803 the General Assembly of Ohio appointed three commissioners to locate a college within the Symmes purchase. They chose a hilltop in an uninhabited area near the navigable stream of Four Mile Creek. Miami University was chartered in 1809 as an all-male, land-grant school. It opened its doors in 1824 to 20 students, and by 1854, enrollment had increased to 266.[7]

Oxford's schools for women were founded from 1849 to 1856. Several faculty members at Miami University helped organize the first academy for girls in Oxford in 1830, including Robert H. Bishop, Miami's president; John W. Scott, a professor of science; and William McGuffey, who later became famous for his readers.[8] The academy had a succession of "lady principals," each of whom stayed one or more years until marriage. Each time the principal left, the school was temporarily suspended. Desiring something more permanent, Oxford citizens formed a stock company to finance a female institute, and in 1849 the academy became the Oxford Female Institute, headed by John Scott.[9]

By 1852 the institute enrolled more than 170 students and already was overcrowded. Frustrated by the trustees' refusal to expand the institute, principal Scott resigned and founded the Oxford Female College, at the opposite end of town from the institute (1856). Between the foundings of the institute and the college, Western Female Seminary was launched by Daniel Tenney, a local Presbyterian minister, who looked to Mount Holyoke Female Seminary as a model. The Mount Holyoke model combined advanced academic work with evangelical Christianity in an institution that was affordable to students of limited financial means. Expenses were minimized by a plan known as the "domestic system," in which students and faculty grew most of their own food and did all of their own cooking and cleaning. Chartered in 1853 and opened in 1855, the Western Female Seminary became a Holyoke "daughter" school.

The Western Female Seminary differed from the other two schools in several ways. Western's curriculum emphasized academics over the more ornamental accomplishments, such as needlework, that were taught at the institute and the college. Western, through its cost-saving domestic system, geared itself toward a less-affluent population of students. In addition, because it was associated with an evangelical group of Presbyterians, religion at Western held a more prominent place than at the other schools.

Oxford Female College soon became the largest of the three women's schools: in 1856–1857, it enrolled about 200 students and had 18 faculty members. In 1855–1856, Western, with 11 instructors, enrolled just over 150 students, while Oxford Female Institute, the smallest of the three, had just 8 faculty members and an unknown number of students.[10]

All of these institutions—Miami University for men and the three schools for women—were decidedly Presbyterian. Each of the first seven presidents of Miami University was a Presbyterian minister, and by 1854, 175 of the 532 graduates entered the ministry.[11] Oxford Female Institute, Oxford Female College, and Western Female Seminary all were sponsored largely by Presbyterians, but the church was divided. The Presbyterian Church in Oxford had split in two in 1841. Some of the reasons for the split were specific to Oxford, and some followed the national divisions among Presbyterians. One divisive issue was joint missions. Since the Plan of Union in 1801, Presbyterians had sponsored joint missionary societies with Congregationalists, in addition to supporting solely Presbyterian missions. By 1840 some Presbyterians wanted to end this practice. Joint missions were supported by the more evangelical New Light or New School faction, who believed that salvation could be gained through submitting one's will to Christ and experiencing conversion. On a national level Presbyterians were also divided over the issue of slavery. Generally both sides saw slavery as a sin, but Old School Presbyterians were willing to let the South deal with the problem in its own way, while New School members were more likely to be active abolitionists.[12] Oxford followed this national pattern, creating New School and Old School congregations.[13]

In Oxford the church split was reflected in the different institutions for female education. Oxford Female Institute and Oxford Female College were sponsored by Old School Presbyterians, while Western Female Seminary was a New School initiative.[14] The ideologies of each religious division were reflected in the tenor of education at the institute, the college, and the seminary. Western Female Seminary founders intended it to be an institution where religion was not "taught in a fashionable manner," but "where the old and tried Christianity of ancient times shall again be received."[15] The emphasis on religion led to numerous revivals at Western. Neither the institute nor the college was engaged in this sort of evangelism. In fact the institute's catalogue stated that while "religious culture . . . will not be neglected," there would be "no workings of a narrow and proselyting [sic] sectarianism."[16]

"Mother" and "Daughter": Western Female Seminary

The founding of Western Female Seminary was largely due to the efforts of Rev. Daniel Tenney. Tenney had studied at Lane Seminary in nearby Cincinnati under Lyman Beecher, one of the most prominent evangelical ministers of the era. Tenney chose Mount Holyoke Female Seminary as a model for the school he founded because his goals for female education were so similar to those of Mount Holyoke.[17] At the outset Tenney made it clear that Western would offer a practical and affordable education to young white women. In an Executive Committee Report in 1855 Tenney made note of the niche he intended Western to fill. He commented that the "West is indeed crowded with 'Seminaries' and 'colleges' and Institutes for the education of young ladies," but that many of them are merely "fashionable" or seek to educate "in some one art—or accomplishment—leaving all other branches of education out-of-view." He may have been obliquely expressing his disapproval of the Oxford Female Institute, which listed three teachers of piano, one of guitar, and one of wax flower work.[18] "The result" of such programs, he said, "is that it is exceedingly difficult to find thoroughly educated, practical young ladies."[19] Two years earlier Tenney had written in his journal of his desire "to check the frivolity and wrecklessness [sic] of our young ladies."[20] Tenney sought an institution in which students "shall learn that woman had a work to perform of amasing [sic] magnitude."[21]

Tenney knew of Mount Holyoke through several sources. One was his sister-in-law, who had been a student of Mary Lyon at the Adams Academy in Dover, New Hampshire. A second source was Mary Smith, the wife of Tenney's fellow Oxford clergyman Henry Little. Smith had studied with Lyon at Ipswich and then started a female academy in Chillicothe, Ohio, with another Ipswich student before moving to Oxford. Henry Little served as one of Western's trustees for many years. In addition Tenney personally visited Mount Holyoke in 1854, seeking a recommendation for a principal for Western and making "an earnest plea" for some of Holyoke's teachers to come to Western.[22]

Tenney wrote that he wanted a seminary "modeled somewhat" on the Mount Holyoke plan.[23] In its early years Western was nearly a carbon copy of Mount Holyoke. Faculty, curriculum, domestic arrangements, schedules, and even menus came from Holyoke. The principal of Western, Helen Peabody, and all of the original teachers were graduates of Mount Holyoke, and some had taught there as well. When these women moved to Oxford, they brought all the details of Mount Holyoke with them. The very first entry in the institutional journals kept by faculty members at Western stated the similarities between the schools explicitly:

> Every day we find ourselves forgetting that our school is not Holyoke itself. All the arrangements of the family and school are the same; many of the public rooms have the same names with yours; the young ladies' rooms, and their furniture—the domestic and dining halls,—the wash room—and in short everything bears a decided resemblance to the Holyoke pattern. From the time of rising in the morning until the hour for retiring at night, our bells ring (difference of longitude excepted) simultaneously with yours, and for precisely the same purposes. Our family devotions, our sections and general exercise, and our recess meeting are just the same.[24]

At the first anniversary of the founding of Western, in July 1856, Rev. Samuel Fisher from Lane Seminary stressed the importance of education for women. There once had been debate about the need of education for women, Fisher said, but this was no longer the case. Among "thoughtful" people, "the full, the free development of the intellect of woman is just as well settled as any other axiom of education."[25] Western was "unique" in "the extent to which it combines the intellectual with the practical." Comparing types of education available for women, Fisher said, "If any man wishes his daughter to be a fashionable doll, let him not send her here; we cultivate no such plants. If any man wishes his daughter to shine only in the light of artistic accomplishments, let him not send her here." Western, Fisher said, is for the "earnest minded woman, inspired with lofty aims, conscious of power for good . . . no longer a passive recipient or a partially developed flower, but part of the active forces which work for a grand end."[26]

Preparation for God's service did not preclude preparation for financial self-sufficiency. Fisher's 1856 address also commented on the positive effects of economic independence. Rather than calling a woman's femininity into question, Fisher said that self-support "gives dignity to her step" and makes clear that "she is not a plaything nor a loiterer," but a "true woman."[27] This position was restated several years later by a Rev. Field of New York. In his 1862 address to Western, Field said that it is "the duty of every woman" to have "some profession, art or trade that could be made available for her support."[28]

In addition to the emphasis on an education that was both practical and religious, Tenney further aligned himself with Mary Lyon and her desire to help the "middling classes." When Tenney discussed the need to secure a large endowment, he compared women's duties—and therefore their needs—with men's, saying, "for as with young men, who are studying for the ministry, so with young ladies, who wish to fit themselves for usefulness and for the call, they are generally in indigent circumstances and cannot secure a thorough course of instruction without aid."[29] Several years later this theme was repeated in an article about Western in the *Christian Herald:* "no daughter of our Republic" should "lack the means of self-culture," and therefore the cost of an education at Western was such that "any healthful, energetic American girl can command, though self-dependent."[30] Although the primary purpose of the "domestic system" that had been copied from Mount Holyoke was to make education affordable, the rhetoric surrounding the system emphasized other advantages. These included the healthful benefits of physical activity and the fostering of a homelike environment.[31]

Mary Lyon's system of domestic work was greeted with mixed feelings when she first instituted it at Mount Holyoke in 1837, and it was controversial in Oxford twenty years later. The system tended to be misinterpreted: hearing that students performed all the work, some outsiders assumed that the school taught domestic sciences. Dire results were imagined for the poor, overworked students. Regional gossip during Western's first year had it that eight or ten students already had died due to the domestic chores, and that "many had gone home only to breathe their last." One father, visiting his daughter at Western, said to Miss Peabody that he expected to find his daughter "looking pale and thin, for it is reported abroad that the young ladies are half-starved." Instead he found that she had "grown fat <u>right smart</u>, and she looks a <u>powerful heap</u> better than she did when she came"[32] (emphasis in original).

Faculty at Western were pleased to demonstrate that education could go hand in hand with domesticity. "Is not a service rendered to female education," one teacher wrote, "every time it is demonstrated anew, that the library and the kitchen are to be found in the same sphere?"[33] They intended to show that education could be incorporated into the "woman's sphere" without disrupting the stability of domestic life. Students at Western engaged in serious academic work, but not at the expense of other, more domestic, duties. Western, like Holyoke before it, pushed the boundaries of female education. The goal was to broaden women's sphere, but not to question the underlying assumption that men and women had separate spheres.

The first flyer published to promote Western made explicit the desire for the seminary to be a home for its students. Students and teachers were to live, eat, work, worship, and study together. Teachers were to serve "in the place of parents," and "family government and home privileges" would be enjoyed.[34] The Western journal is filled with references to Western as "the dear house," "our house," and our "hearts' home," and to students and faculty as our "beloved family." Students referred to Helen Peabody, the principal, as "Mother" and "Mother Teacher," and she referred to students as her children.[35]

Faculty at Western thought of the connection between their school and Mount Holyoke as that of a family relationship as well. Western, in its first journal entry, described itself as "a young sister of Holyoke; scarcely out of frock and pinafore to be sure, but a very promising child for all that. She already shows a most striking and daily increasing resemblance to her Eastern sister."[36] Journal entries throughout Western's first decade repeatedly mentioned "our Holyoke sisters."[37] Western faculty regarded receipt of the Holyoke journal as "getting a letter from home."[38] An 1857 Western journal entry thanked Mount Holyoke for its "motherly benediction" upon its "Western child."[39]

Religion was very important at Western, just as at Mount Holyoke, and it was the most frequent topic covered in the Western journal. The journal described revivals and conversions and made frequent requests to Holyoke for prayers on behalf of unrepentant students at Western. Western expected students to attend church services in Oxford on Sunday morning, study their Bibles on Sunday afternoon, and attend evening services at Western on Sundays and Thursdays. In addition the school held "monthly concert" events at which letters from missionaries were read or visiting missionaries spoke.[40]

Western faculty were deeply concerned about the salvation of their students. They regarded the conversion experience as "passing from death unto life," and as the "birth-day of the soul."[41] The most dramatic revival came at the end of the 1863–1864 school year. In late January 1864 typhoid fever hit the school, which appears to have been the catalyst for mass conversions. At one meeting held by

Miss Peabody, "voluntary prayers were offered and every heart overflowed with prayer, twenty seven prayers were offered at one time before rising from the posture of prayer."[42] This led to the "great event," during which students prayed "with the gushing love of those whose hearts God had touched." After an evening assembly led by Miss Peabody, "there was no need to ask of what subject any were talking as they walked together, for every one knew. As the teachers went around the house at night, they found the girls together praying and weeping silent tears, alone as they tried to come to Christ. . . . Those were days never to be forgotten."[43] Some years the conversions were quiet and occurred steadily throughout the year, "not with 'mighty rushing wind' indeed, filling all the place; but with that great influence of sunshine and shower which has made the good seed spring up in some hearts."[44] One year, "from the first week of the year one and another and another quietly and humbly yet firmly and openly avowed herself changed in heart and hope."[45]

As a self-proclaimed daughter of Holyoke, Western sought to mirror precisely the values, ideals, and plans of Mary Lyon. Faculty and students at Western cherished their connection to Mount Holyoke and used familial language to express their relationships. Because of the domestic system, attendance was affordable to the "middling classes," and the practical education offered by Western prepared women for the possibility of self-sufficiency. Combining the value of hard work with an evangelical mandate, Western sent young women out into the world invested with the spirit to be active and useful.

"Polite Education" and "Thorough Training": Three Institutions for Women in Oxford

Until Vassar (1865), Smith (1875), and Wellesley (1875) opened, Mount Holyoke was widely regarded as the preeminent institution of higher education for women.[46] As more Holyoke graduates entered the teaching field, they propagated Holyoke ideals in schoolhouses and seminaries across the country and throughout the world. But not all institutions followed the Holyoke pattern. Oxford, Ohio, provides an example of alternative visions of education for women coexisting in the same time and place. Western differed from the other two Oxford female schools in significant ways, and the schools consequently appealed to different groups of students. Western Female Seminary drew students from less-affluent families than did Oxford Female Institute and Oxford Female College, and had a heightened emphasis on both academics and evangelical religion.

Financially the institutions differed in the cost of the college buildings as well as the cost of tuition. John Scott had grandiose plans when he withdrew from the

Oxford Female Institute to establish a college. Rather than a simple edifice, he built on a grand scale. The 1857 catalogue for Oxford Female College assured students and parents that the accommodations were "all that our friends could desire. No pains or expense has been spared."[47] The building cost nearly $100,000, and included the newest and most expensive advances in steam heat and gas lighting. Students were attended by uniformed servants, and the staff included cooks, laundresses, and maids.[48] The opulence of the college was in stark contrast to the ideals of Mount Holyoke and of Western Female Seminary. Western's building cost half as much as the college's, and as noted above, students and faculty did all of the cooking and cleaning.[49]

The cost of study also reflected different institutional expectations of students' economic backgrounds. Western charged $100 for the 1855–1856 school year; the fee was lowered to $60 for ministers' daughters. This fee paid for tuition, room, and board; students needed to provide their own fuel for the stoves to heat their rooms. That same year Oxford Female Institute and Oxford Female College both charged more than $160, exclusive of heat; instruction in music and drawing cost an additional $100 per year at the college.[50] Clearly Western, true to Mary Lyon's concern for the "middling classes," was more affordable than either of the other colleges for young women in Oxford.

The academic offerings at the schools also differed. Western's first circular stated that the "intellectual privileges of young ladies should be much greater than are commonly afforded them." Western, the circular went on, would emphasize intellectual and reasoning powers, and would do so in a serious way, "not by ornamenting the surface with the mere tinsel of accomplishments."[51]

One indication of Western's higher academic standards was that entrance examinations were required. To be admitted for first-year study, applicants had to demonstrate competency in English grammar, modern geography, written and mental arithmetic, and U.S. history.[52] In 1862, the annual catalogue warned, "If any are not well prepared for examination in the preparatory studies, they are requested to withdraw their names."[53]

The 1854 circular outlined a three-year course of study. In the first ("junior") year, students reviewed grammar, arithmetic, and geography and studied ancient geography, natural philosophy, algebra, geometry, Latin grammar, botany, and history. The second ("middle") year was comprised of studies in history, botany, rhetoric, geometry, Latin (exercises and Virgil), trigonometry, mensuration (systems of measurement), bookkeeping, chemistry, astronomy, physiology, and evidences of Christianity. During the final ("senior") year, students took Latin (Cicero and Tacitus), geology, natural theology, mental philosophy, political economy, Butler's analogy, logic, and English classics. The course of study required composition in all three years.

The curriculum changed over the period of this study. By 1860, second-year studies in geometry and botany were dropped (although they continued as first-year subjects), as were mensuration and the third-year course in political economy. Bookkeeping was taught to individual students "as necessary," and not as a required course. In practice bookkeeping of a kind was encouraged as students were required to present weekly expense accounts to their teachers, recording money spent on books, shoe repair, pens, stationery, fuel, and other items.[54]

Greater curricular changes were in store. By the 1865–1866 school year, the course was lengthened to four years instead of three, thereby resembling those in men's colleges. Three years of Latin were required, and Bible study became part of the academic program as well. Greek was offered as an optional subject from the beginning; it was not required. During Western's first ten years, the curriculum became more collegiate, changing from a three-year to a four-year course and including more Latin.

In contrast Oxford Female Institute began with a much less rigorous curriculum. In 1853–1854 it included two years of Latin, compared to Western's three years. Several of the institute's first-year courses covered material that was required for admission to Western. The institute changed dramatically over the decade as well. The 1853–1854 catalogue describes its course as offering a "polite" female education.[55] But just two years later, faced with the competition of Western and Oxford Female College, the institute's catalogue observed that "a superficial course has been one of the serious defects in the system of Female Education," and that "the times require a more thorough training."[56] Not only did the institute's prescribed course of study now include three years of Latin, it also required one year of either Greek or a modern language. Conspicuous additions were courses that had appeared in Western's catalogue the previous year, including political economy, geology, natural theology, Butler's analogy, and bookkeeping.

The institute continued to teach ornamental subjects but by 1863 apparently felt the need to comment on and defend the practice. That year's catalogue asserted that "a lady's education is incomplete without something additional to mere literary acquirements," and added that many of "the Ornamental Branches are useful as well as beautiful."[57] Students were required to take music or some other ornamental branch.

Oxford Female College adopted a four-year course of study from its inception in 1856, the first of Oxford's three women's schools to do so. An 1857 circular indicated that the school wanted to be taken seriously as a college, arguing that "No respectable male college, now pretends to graduate a class under four years." Yet the claim to serious academic work was undermined in the next sentence, which stated that women needed at least as long as men because they "are expected to devote so much more time to . . . ornamental branches." The college so emphasized ornamentals that in 1857 there were nine teachers of music, painting, and needlework, and eight teachers for all of the other subjects.[58]

Western, too, offered the ornamental subjects of drawing, painting, French, and piano. Rather than including these subjects as part of the required course of study, though, Western listed this type of instruction in a section called "Miscellaneous Items" and noted that these subjects would be available "to those who desire . . . and can attend to [these subjects] without serious detriment to their standing in the regular studies of the course."[59] Not only were ornamental subjects not required, but some students were not even permitted to take them. For instance, not everyone was allowed to take instruction in music; teachers selected those students who exhibited talent and allowed them to pursue study of piano. Studying piano, however, lengthened the time students needed to complete the academic course. The emphasis was on academics, but to some extent Western also accommodated a desire for ornamentals.

Another example of dissimilar expectations for students is reflected in policies regarding the minimum age required for entrance. In 1855 no Western student could be younger than fourteen, and only those fourteen-year-olds "possessing unusual maturity from previous mental discipline" were admitted.[60] In 1856 the minimum age was raised to fifteen, and each catalogue thereafter stated a preference that students be at least sixteen or seventeen. Western did not want students "too young for sober reflection."[61] Oxford Female College, on the other hand, opted not to establish an "arbitrary limitation" with regard to either age or academic preparation, but then expressed a desire for no one under age twelve.[62] Oxford Female Institute apparently had no policy on age.

The three schools, accordingly, evolved differently. Oxford Female Institute basically was a secondary school, although before long it began offering collegiate-level courses. Oxford Female College called itself a college and offered many college-level courses, yet highlighted ornamentals and admitted children as young as twelve. Western Female Seminary preferred not to take the name college, yet offered a curriculum that was similar to that of many men's colleges.

The school that chose to call itself a college was the same school that set out to appeal to wealthier constituents, an intent that was apparent from its expensive building and uniformed servants. This implies an acceptance as early as the mid-1850s among the more well-to-do of the concept of college education for women, at least in southwestern Ohio. In order to stay competitive, though, the school steadily increased the rigor of the academic courses; taking the name college without offering the correspondingly challenging course work was not enough. Oxford Female Institute's catalogue for 1857–1858 commented on this, noting that the three schools "produce a salutary rivalry, in which, each trying to excel, education may be expected to be carried to a high pitch of perfection."[63]

Competition among the schools was not always friendly. Evidence of tension surfaced in an anonymous letter to the editor of the local newspaper, the *Oxford Citizen*, in 1857. The writer maintained that "For some time past efforts have been made to allay the unpleasant feeling existing between the different [schools]." Those efforts were called into question by the "attempt, by a Principal of one school, to prejudice the mind of a pupil recently connected with another school and thus get her to <u>change</u>" (emphasis in original).[64] Who wrote the letter, which principal is referred to, and whether or not any students actually switched schools are not known.

Oxford Female College was continually in financial trouble. Scott's insistence on expensive buildings and maintenance created an unsustainable burden. The Presbyterian Church soon withdrew its support in favor of helping to finance the new coeducational Wooster College in north-central Ohio that was chartered in 1866. Insolvent by 1867, Oxford Female College sold its building (which later became a men's residence hall for Miami University) and joined forces with the Oxford Female Institute, which also was having difficulties. The new Oxford College persisted until 1928, continually burdened with fiscal difficulties. Ultimately it closed and sold its property to Miami University. The building has been used as a women's residence hall ever since.[65]

Western thrived throughout this period, in spite of having to rebuild twice after fires destroyed the seminary building in 1860 and 1871.[66] Although it long had offered college-level courses, Western did not offer a course of study leading to a Bachelor of Arts degree until 1893. Accordingly it became Western Female Seminary and College in 1894 and just Western College in 1904.[67] Mount Holyoke had become "Seminary and College" in 1888, and eliminated "Seminary" from its name in 1892.[68] Western ended the domestic system in which all students shared in the work of the school in 1916. As the cost of attendance increased, Western became less accessible to the "middling classes" for whom Mary Lyon had created the system. In 1973, after 118 years of educating women, Western became an interdisciplinary coeducational college within Miami University.[69]

Oxford, Ohio, and Women's Higher Education

The women's schools of Oxford, Ohio, reveal several facets of antebellum women's education. First, the story of Western Female Seminary demonstrates that Mary Lyon's plan for women's education had a broad appeal that transcended regional and temporal limits. Mount Holyoke was not successful merely because of one charismatic leader; rather, the plan was successful decades after its initial implementation, and far from its birthplace in the Northeast. Western faculty followed the blueprint of Holyoke as precisely as they could. Given the different geographical settings, one might expect to see major differences between the two schools reflecting regional variations. That there were no such obvious differences is remarkable. Frequently in the antebellum period, when the head of a seminary left (for marriage, illness, or other reasons), the institution closed down. This was not the case with Mary Lyon and Mount Holyoke. The replication of Holyoke at Western demonstrated that the plan had wide appeal and that its success was not dependent on the power of one strong personality.

Second, Western was significant for its impact on women's colleges of the post–Civil War era. Studies of women's seminaries and colleges tend to focus on the Northeast as the origin of advancement. Yet Western played an important role in the development of the Eastern college movement. Henry Durant, founder of Wellesley, was inspired by Mount Holyoke. However, he turned to Western's principal for assistance in planning and designing Wellesley, and a Western faculty member, Ada Howard, presided over the new college. At least three other Western faculty members became teachers at Wellesley, and a Western alumna became Wellesley's first physician. Several graduates of Western went on to earn college degrees there. One of them, Leila McKee, came back to Western to serve as its second principal, ushering in the change of Western from a seminary to a college.[70] Ideas and resources did not flow unidirectionally, east to west; rather, there was an exchange of ideas and expertise through which Western contributed to the growth of eastern women's colleges.

The history of these three Oxford schools provides a glimpse of contested ideals of white womanhood based largely on class. The emphasis on either ornamentals or academics varied according to the schools' expectations regarding students' later roles. Oxford Female College, with its ornamental subjects and uniformed servants, and the institute, with its course work in wax flower making, connoted a passive and protected view of womanhood that could be attained only by the relatively wealthy. This view is in sharp contrast to that projected at Western, where women studied hard, scrubbed floors, literally served each other, and were expected to put their talents to use in the world after graduation. The evangelical foundation of Western nourished the ideal of utility. The Western philosophy was that any sphere of action was appropriate for a woman, as long as the work she did was "for God."[71] At Western, students learned to unite "womanly thinking to womanly acting" and were encouraged to "labor successfully in the field of the mind" or pursue other occupations.[72] Yet all three schools raised their academic standards, illustrating that female scholarship became more acceptable for women of both the middle and the upper classes. In fact offering collegiate-level course work became imperative for an institution's survival in Oxford.

The years from 1855 through 1867 were crucial in the transition from seminary to college education for women. Rather than the college movement beginning with Vassar in 1865, the situation in Oxford provides an example of the ways that women's schools grew toward collegiate status, in both name and curricula. The competition for students encouraged the growth of increasingly academic schools. If Western Female Seminary had not been established there, perhaps Oxford Female Institute and Oxford Female College would not have strengthened their academic offerings as quickly as they did. Western demonstrated that young women were capable of higher academic work, and its popularity demonstrated that some young women and their parents demanded that degree of rigor. The "salutary competition" that took place among Oxford's educational institutions contributed to the emergence of a truly collegiate curriculum for women in the United States.

The "Superior Instruction of Women" 1836–1890

~

ROGER L. GEIGER

Contrary to widespread impressions, advanced education for women developed rapidly in the mid–nineteenth century. A transitional point, when the education received by women began to approximate collegiate education for men, occurred in the 1830s. In 1836, Georgia Female College was chartered in Macon, and the next year Mary Lyon opened Mount Holyoke Female Seminary in South Hadley, Massachusetts. At Oberlin Collegiate Institute, male and female students were taught together in the same collegiate classrooms beginning in 1834, and in 1837 four women enrolled in the classical course. However defined, higher education for American women was a reality by the end of that decade.[1]

In 1890, just two generations later, more than 20,000 women were enrolled in collegiate courses (see table 10). Nearly half of these students attended institutions that the Bureau of Education had recently classified as "Division B Colleges for Women," which were actually or in spirit the lineal descendants of earlier women's schools. Founded in large numbers before the Civil War, these first women's colleges were feeling increasing pressure even before the government pronounced them second rate. All but ignored in the historiography of American higher education, they were one of the most characteristic institutions of the 1850–1890 era and can be aptly considered analogues to the multipurpose colleges.[2]

Female Seminaries, Institutes, and Colleges

Prior to the 1830s (and long afterward as well) academies provided the chief means for girls to attain education beyond the primary or common-school level. "Female seminaries" (or "institutes") were established with the belief that women should be instructed in at least some of the collegiate curriculum in order to prepare them to become teachers as well as good wives and mothers. Seminaries aspired to a higher level of studies than academies, but they occupied a rather ill-defined educational stratum. The early seminaries usually taught a three-year course that included many of the subjects required for admission to men's colleges. They also taught some subjects belonging to the college curriculum, having particularly broad offerings in science, English literature, and modern languages. The conspicuous difference lay with Latin and Greek. Latin was at best started in the early seminaries, while Greek was almost unknown. To encourage domesticity, the seminaries taught young women hygiene and embroidery, and to cultivate refinement, they often taught supplemental courses in drawing, music, and dancing. Students taking the entire academic course would receive a broad, but not deep, education; those preparing to teach might benefit from just a selection of substantive courses; and numerous special students enrolled in only ornamental subjects.

The opening of Mount Holyoke brought a new standard to women's education. Drawing inspiration from early pioneers of women's education, Joseph Emerson and Zilpah Grant, Mary Lyon resolved to create an institution for serious and substantive instruction. Her motivation encompassed no less than four kinds of goals: (1) evangelical—to provide a deeply pious educational setting; (2) social—by keeping costs low through the domestic system, to allow largely middle-class women to prepare themselves as teachers; (3) institutional—to establish adequate facilities on a permanent basis for the education of women; and (4) curricular—in the words of the seminary's prospectus, to teach "an elevated standard of science, literature, and refinement." In this era of separate spheres and the cult of true womanhood, the idea of imitating the course at male colleges seems to have held little attraction. Rather, Mary Lyon and the other pioneers of her generation sought a distinctive path to broaden and elevate the women's sphere. Thus the seminary curriculum overlapped only partially with the subjects taught in the colleges. Mount Holyoke students were required to take seven classes in science, for example, including nine weeks instruction in chemistry from Mary Lyon herself. More telling perhaps, after ten years of operation she added Latin to the regular course.[3]

Despite good intentions, the majority of female seminaries were probably more conspicuous for their weaknesses than their resemblance to Mount Holyoke.[4]

They were typically operated by a proprietor with the help of a few assistants. Given their proprietary nature, seminaries seldom had adequate facilities, libraries, or equipment. Like academies, seminaries also spread themselves thin by teaching numerous subjects, which invariably meant poorly qualified teachers and superficial coverage. Dependence on student fees also tended to encourage fashionable subjects and discourage rigorous standards. Catherine Beecher railed against just such structural impediments, based on the experience of her own failed schools in Hartford and Cincinnati. While holding that the women's course should be distinctively female, she strenuously urged that women's institutions be given the resources and consequent advantages of men's colleges.[5] Women had even less incentive than men to finish an entire course, so completion rates were exceedingly low.[6] Thus abundant evidence existed, if one looked for it, for contemporaries to dismiss the female seminaries as decidedly inferior to education in the colleges.

The broad variation in the quality of female seminaries poses a difficulty in interpreting the earliest women's colleges. As the idea of collegiate education for women gained acceptance, many seminaries sought a higher status by converting to "collegiate institutes" and then colleges. By the 1850s such institutions were being chartered in large numbers. Nomenclature remained wholly inconsistent, however.[7] Female colleges were more often than not an advancement over female seminaries (if only in self-image), but they were beset with the same fundamental shortcomings. The question inevitably arose, how did the course of study at these new or newly named institutions compare with that followed by men?

This question dominates Thomas Woody's discussion of women's colleges in his comprehensive *History of Women's Education in the United States* (1929). Woody wrote at a time when such comparisons had preoccupied women's colleges for a half century. Subsequent historians of women's education, being more eager to highlight the achievements of nineteenth-century women rather than their shortcomings, have followed Woody in dismissing these antebellum institutions as falling short of "true" collegiate studies.[8] However, considering the tacit acceptance of the ideology of separate spheres, one might doubt if this question is the proper one to ask. Only recently have a few historians tried to view the early women's colleges on their own terms.[9] Seen in this light, it becomes clear that curricula were in a state of continuous development, influenced by the availability of textbooks, teachers, and the example of men's colleges.

In the 1850s the first credible efforts were made to emulate the classical course in colleges for women. Both Mary Sharp College (1853) in Winchester, Tennessee, and Elmira Female College in New York (1855) were founded with the explicit intention of offering women a true collegiate course. Such equality had already been achieved, at least in token numbers, in coeducational settings at religiously "radical" colleges like Oberlin and New York Central College (1849–1858).[10] Mary Sharp's flamboyant president, Z. C. Graves, left no doubt about his institution's (and his own) place in history: "The Mary Sharp College for Young Ladies, was founded to supply a great and daily increasing want of the South, that of a School of a higher grade than any previously in existence—in fact, a College where ladies may have the privilege of a classical education."[11] The New York State Regents recognized Elmira Female College as offering a full classical course. Elmira also offered a scientific course without Latin or Greek. Mary Sharp conferred its first A.B. degrees in 1855 and Elmira in 1859. Thomas Woody considers these to be the first "real" college degrees conferred by women's institutions, by which he means that all preceding women's colleges had not attained this standard.[12] This harsh judgment undoubtedly slights the actual progress that had been made by this date.

By 1860 many women's colleges had taken steps to transcend the most obvious marks of inferiority by establishing a four-year course and teaching classical languages. Generally the classical course at women's colleges contained less Latin, and Greek was typically offered at a rudimentary level, if at all (modern languages could almost always be substituted). In addition they retained the three-year English or ladies course, often leading to a Mistress of English Literature diploma/degree.[13] These offerings approximated those at coeducational colleges, where women could take a three-year female or English course, or elect the more rigorous classical course. The results were similar too: far more women chose the shorter, less-taxing route. A rough parallelism thus existed between the opportunities for women in the early women's colleges and in coeducational multipurpose colleges.

Such comparisons held little interest for contemporaries or historians. Rather, the standard of reference typically has been the "better men's colleges"—equivalent to the New England colleges that midwestern colleges sought to emulate.[14] By that measure, of course, the great majority of American colleges fell short, but this fact offered little consolation to those who sought or expected equality in women's education. When one looks beyond the ancient languages, however, the women's colleges appear in a better light. Math was taught at least through trigonometry, and women had classes in all of the sciences taught to men. They also had similar offerings in history, philosophy, and religion. All of these subjects were identified by the textbooks used, which were often the same in both types of college.[15] Women's colleges had some advantage in modern languages. French (and later German) was regularly taught to women when it was at best optional in men's colleges. Women also were likely to devote more time to English language, literature, and composition, whereas men stressed rhetoric and speaking. Viewing the entire curriculum, one is struck with the irony that women's colleges were judged inferior because of their failure to measure up in those subjects—ancient languages—in which the men's colleges were criticized as most sterile and obsolescent.[16] This alleged inferiority nevertheless played no small role in their development.

The *Report of the Commissioner of Education* for 1881 listed 232 institutions for the superior instruction of women, but table 8 tabulates just those reporting a charter to award collegiate degrees. However, the chartered and uncharted populations are similar. Many chartered institutions still called themselves seminaries or institutes, while some noncharted ones were called colleges and reported collegiate enrollments. The noncharted group nevertheless appeared to contain more schools offering at best a semicollegiate curriculum, including 14 Roman Catholic "academies." Before 1900, Catholics generally resisted the idea of collegiate education for women. Still, 9 of their academies reported collegiate charters in 1880 and are included in table 8. Whether the more inclusive or more restricted populations are examined, the two principal findings are the same.

First are the antebellum origins of most nineteenth-century women's colleges. Probably about half of the 97 colleges founded before 1860 actually had college charters before the Civil War.[17] Clearly, as Thomas Woody wrote, "by 1855 the idea of college education for young women, in an institution like those established for men," had spread throughout the country.[18] The 1850s emerge in table 8 as the most prolific decade for foundings, but the activity is if anything understated. In Pennsylvania, for example, only 4 of the 7 colleges chartered in the 1850s survived to 1880. But undoubtedly the largest discrepancy occurred in the South, where numerous institutions failed to survive the destruction and dislocation of the war years.[19]

TABLE 8

DEGREE GRANTING COLLEGES FOR WOMEN IN 1880
BY FOUNDING DATE AND REGION

	<1850	1850S	1860S	1870S	TOTAL
New England	4	1		2	7
Mid Atlantic	5	9	4	2	20
South Atlantic	10	12	5	10	37
North Central	4	8	3	1	16
South Central	9	22	9	10	50
West Central	3	9	5	7	24
West		1			1
	33	59	26	32	155

Source: Report of the Commissioner of Education, 1881.

The second glaring fact in table 8 is the concentration of women's colleges in the South. When Missouri (13) and Texas (7) are combined with the south Atlantic and south central states, 107 of the 155 women's colleges are found in that region. Separation of the sexes in education was a powerful cultural norm in the South, but it was also heavily favored in much of the Northeast and universally endorsed among Roman Catholics. Coeducation became prevalent as one moved westward. Excepting Missouri and Texas, only 5 women's colleges existed in 1880 beyond the Mississippi (3 of them Catholic). In fact two distinct variations of the multipurpose women's college existed for the North and for the South. Each reflected fundamental differences in culture and social structure.

Advanced education for women in the North was long associated with preparation for teaching. Although educators strenuously maintained that higher studies did not lessen but in fact strengthened women's role as wife and mother, education also provided an often-needed livelihood. As such, first the seminaries and then the colleges served a largely middle-class clientele drawn heavily from small towns and farms.[20] This vocational role gave northern seminaries and colleges a strong mission that was functionally, if not ideologically, independent of any need to emulate men's colleges. Probably for this reason, some of the stronger seminaries in the North resisted transforming themselves into colleges. Mount Holyoke held off until 1888; Rockford Female Seminary until 1891.

In the South, higher education aimed to contribute literary and artistic refinement to women who expected to marry but not to work. Before the Civil War women's colleges catered to southern planters and professionals who did not expect their daughters to have to support themselves.[21] This situation made the South peculiarly receptive to women's education, since it in no way challenged the social order but accentuated social distinction. Linguistic skills complemented this role, and the teaching first of French and then of Latin was welcomed. The southern colleges thus incorporated Latin more readily, and hence more commonly adopted "college" in their title. This fact alone may account for the predominance of women's colleges in the South before the Civil War. Some southern colleges may have deserved the derisory label of finishing schools, since teaching the "feminine accomplishments" was integral to their mission (and perhaps too strongly emphasized by male commentators). Some sense of the full mission of a southern female college may be had from a glimpse of Greensborough College on the eve of the war. Its 351 students included 102 studying piano and another 37 devoted to guitar or painting; on the other hand, 57 students studied Latin in the classical course, 118 pursued the English course, and 37 were in the preparatory department. A finishing school for some, perhaps, it also provided a fairly extensive education for this period for the 15 to 20 young women whom it graduated each year.[22]

In other respects the multipurpose women's colleges were similar across the country. Nearly all had preparatory or academic departments. They also offered both a three-year English course and a four-year course that by the 1850s generally included some Latin. Although the shorter course was more heavily enrolled, relatively few students completed either. The women's colleges were also characterized by large enrollments of irregular students. In the South such students largely enrolled in the music and art classes that were outside the regular curriculum and required separate fees. Although these subjects were central to southern notions of refinement, they also played a large role in northern colleges. The latter also experimented with truncated normal courses, but more commonly allowed teachers to enroll as special students. The multipurpose women's college thus offered a broad range of educational services to both local and resident students.

College "in the Proper Sense of the Word"

For the multipurpose women's colleges, the Civil War stands as a watershed in at least one respect: the subsequent appearance of an additional set of institutions widely recognized as having higher status and aspirations. Matthew Vassar's goal in launching the first of these was unequivocal: "To build a college in the proper sense of the word, an institution which should be to women what Yale and Harvard are to young men, receiving them after suitable preparation at the academies and seminaries, and furnishing them with the means for a true liberal education."[23]

The intent was no different for Sophia Smith in endowing Smith College and William Durant in founding Wellesley College, both of which opened in 1875. This condescending view, that existing women's schools were not real colleges and did not provide a true liberal education, was the prevailing opinion along the northeastern seaboard. Once in existence, however, the new colleges found that they had to grapple with some of the same realities that handicapped their predecessors. That they eventually surmounted these problems has helped to make their retrospective image fit the prospective goals of their founders. But before 1880, the budding Seven Sisters bore a family resemblance to their unacknowledged stepsisters.[24] Planning the curriculum for Vassar presented the dilemma of offering a course of study that was suited for women but also equivalent with that offered at Yale and Harvard.[25] After considering diverse possibilities, the trustees resolved upon three principles: (1) the course of study must be truly liberal and collegiate; (2) a complete domestic system had to be included; and (3) in adapting the course to the needs of women, time would be allowed for the study of music and art. In this last respect, Vassar mimicked, but far surpassed, existing women's colleges. It opened with thirty-one pianos and a collection of more than five hundred artworks as a basis for supplemental courses. Later, Sister colleges would take credit for incorporating the fine arts into the regular curriculum, but these subjects had existed at women's schools from the start. The urge for domesticity was frustrated by the absence of curricular models or appropriate instructors, and was consigned to a single freshman class on hygiene. Thus the principal challenge was to fashion a true liberal education.

The chief obstacle to equaling the standards of male colleges was the dearth of young women with the "suitable preparation" that Matthew Vassar had assumed to exist. When the first potential students were examined, few were found ready for college work, particularly in the ancient languages. It was thus necessary to establish a preparatory department—something common enough throughout the country but regarded as bad form in the Northeast. At the end of the second year, 116 Vassar students were in collegiate classes, 71 were preparatory, and 165 were "specials." Wellesley had the same experience in 1875, when only 30 out of more than 300 aspirants passed the entrance examination and it too was forced to establish an unwanted preparatory department. Smith, which was strongly influenced by Amherst faculty, some of whom taught there, earned the approbation of Thomas Woody by being the first "to provide a course of study almost identical with that of the best men's colleges." By this he meant that it required equivalent Greek and Latin preparation for admission, and offered a single classical course. Only 14 students qualified for its first class and a like number for its second. Smith resisted any temptation to establish a preparatory department, but then compromised by relaxing admission requirements and admitting specials. Within two years (1879) Smith's enrollment topped 200.[26]

Vassar and Wellesley operated in their initial years as multipurpose colleges, having both classical and scientific courses, preparatory departments, and (along with Smith) numerous special students. Some of the specials undoubtedly came principally to pursue the fine arts, but a sizable number were teachers seeking higher studies. Wellesley soon embraced this mission, and even constructed a residence for its teacher-specials. It gradually discouraged other specials, however, and tried to induce them to take a five-year bachelor's course in music or art. Wellesley was able to spin off its preparatory department to a private school in 1881, and Vassar was finally able to dispense with this embarrassment in 1888.

For Vassar and Wellesley, at least, the initial failure to meet the admission standards of the men's colleges placed them in a position where they had to ratchet up classical studies if they were to achieve their avowed goal. As Vassar president John Raymond stated somewhat quixotically: ". . . while the education for boys has outgrown the old college system . . . that for women has but just grown up to it, and needs for a season the bracing and support of its somewhat narrow forms."[27]

Vassar made Greek a requirement for the A.B. in 1867, but weak enrollments may have influenced the decision to institute a B.S. degree without Greek.[28] In partial compensation Latin requirements were made increasingly rigorous until they equaled those of the most stringent male college by 1890. Wellesley followed much the same pattern. In 1881 it introduced a classical course with required Greek, while also retaining a non-Greek option in the scientific course. Smith, on the other hand, was able to relax its standards somewhat, establishing nonclassical courses in science and literature in 1886. In sum the new colleges at first experienced great difficulty, just like their stepsisters, in emulating the standards of Yale and Harvard, particularly where Greek was concerned. By the end of the 1880s, though, they had largely attained their goal: admission standards, degree requirements, and course offerings all rivaled those of the eastern men's colleges.

If the new women's colleges achieved respectability by imitating the worst features of men's colleges, they also improved significantly upon the best features of women's colleges. They offered a full range of courses in the natural sciences, including biology, which tended to be neglected in male colleges. Moreover their facilities for teaching science far exceeded all but a handful of existing colleges anywhere in the country. They also had superior offerings in English composition and literature, as well as extensive course work in modern languages. Initially at least, these colleges slighted the social sciences and advanced mathematics. As enrollments and faculty increased, course offerings multiplied, leaving them well situated to adopt a full elective system by the late 1890s. Thus once past the frustrations of their founding years, they were precocious in curricular expansion. This development was largely a consequence of what contemporaries regarded as their most distinctive feature—their considerable wealth.

Raymond described the opportunity seized by Matthew Vassar: "Millions had been spent in colleges for young men, while not a single endowed college for young women existed in all Christendom."[29] In the years that followed, endowment became linked ever more closely with academic respectability. The commissioner of education in 1890 approvingly quoted the sweeping judgment that "no institution of learning can preserve a high standard of scholarship and present an extensive course of studies for selection unless possessed of a permanent endowment, so as to be wholly or partly independent of the fluctuations of patronage."[30] For contemporaries an endowment signified institutional wealth and resources. Compared with other women's colleges, the new institutions possessed not only endowments, but also magnificent physical facilities, large numbers of students paying high tuition, and an intermittent flow of additional gifts.

Both Matthew Vassar and William Durant used most of their original gifts to build enormous single structures that accommodated the entire college and all its students. Vassar had rooms for 400 students, a figure it had difficulty attaining;

Wellesley could house 300 students and 30 faculty, levels it soon exceeded. Both institutions were envisioned to be larger than any existing women's college. Size was a considerable advantage. The expenditures for the original campus left both colleges with little endowment, so that tuition revenues were vital. They charged $100 per year (plus about $250 for room and board)—about the same as leading men's colleges and far more than most colleges in the country. Vassar and Wellesley had a pecuniary incentive to accept underprepared applicants. Vassar opened with a faculty of 8 professors (2 women) and 20 women instructors; Wellesley started with 7 professors and 11 instructors, all women. As they grew and added professorships, they retained this pattern of having large numbers of poorly paid women serving in various instructional and supervisory capacities. By 1890 the preponderant size and resources of these colleges clearly set them apart. Wellesley had 660 students and a faculty of 79; Smith had 541 students and 32 faculty; and Vassar had 323 students with 35 faculty. By way of comparison only two Ohio colleges exceeded Vassar's collegiate enrollment, and none bettered Wellesley.[31]

Division A and Division B

The emergence of the Seven Sisters colleges was an awkward challenge to the other women's colleges. These schools had been afflicted throughout their existence with invidious comparisons with men's institutions. Their response, for the most part, was steady, incremental improvement. In the postbellum North, for example, almost all degree courses were upgraded to four years. Now, however, they were judged to be inferior by a new standard—that of the endowed women's colleges whose size and affluence they could scarcely hope to rival. Hierarchy, status, and reputation are indelible features of the decentralized American system, but in 1887 the Bureau of Education made these distinctions official.

Record keepers at the bureau had long been frustrated by the heterogeneity of "institutions for the superior instruction of women." They somewhat reluctantly included in this category all institutions chartered by states to grant collegiate degrees, and then felt compelled to add institutions offering equivalent work. They regretted that the resulting list failed to distinguish those institutions doing "true" collegiate work. This difficulty was avoided for the five women's colleges recognized as part of the University of the State of New York, which appeared in the regular college list. But the prominence of the Sisters made this problem acute by the 1880s. In 1887 it was resolved by placing women's colleges in A and B Divisions (table 9).

The original list of Division A is quite straightforward: it consisted of the Sisters plus the legacies from the University of the State of New York. Wells College (f. 1868) was a respectable endowed college, although not quite in the league with the Sisters; Elmira was missing, having temporarily fallen off the bureau's radar screen, as had Rutgers Female College; and long-struggling Ingham University was a multipurpose college on the brink of closing (d. 1892).[32] The enlargement of the list in 1890 shows more clearly the nature of those institutions that were judged to be first rate. Four of the additions were perceived to be coordinate colleges (Baltimore, Evelyn, Barnard, and Cleveland), and thus derived the patina of quality from their male partner; Mount Holyoke and its "daughter" Mills were conceded A status when they upgraded from seminaries to colleges. These criteria seem to have persisted until the divisions were abolished in 1910, limiting Division A to no more than 16 schools. Aspiration to meet the standards of men's colleges was clearly more important than any actual level of achievement. Evelyn College, for example, was a feeble effort that lasted only a decade (1887 to 1897). In the twenty-three-year history of the classification, the only Division B schools to earn a higher grade were Mount Holyoke and two "daughters."[33]

The bureau's low opinion of the Division B schools was an explicit judgment of their multipurpose nature:

> . . . on the one hand they have endeavored to meet the general demand with respect to women's education. On the other they have sought to maintain that higher ideal which [is] best for mental discipline and culture. When to this double purpose is added responsibility of preparatory work it is obvious that some part of the scheme must fail of satisfactory results.

TABLE 9

WOMEN'S COLLEGES OF DIVISION A, 1887 & 1890

1887	1890
Radcliffe College	Radcliffe College
Smith College	Smith College
Wellesley College	Wellesley College
Wells College	Wells College
Vassar College	Vassar College
Ingham University	Ingham University
Bryn Mawr College	Bryn Mawr College
	Mills College
	Women's College of Baltimore
	Mount Holyoke Seminary & College
	Evelyn College
	Elmira College
	Barnard College
	Cleveland College for Women

The bureau in 1888 felt that this unstable combination had kindled a process of selection across the country. Some of the schools would develop into "colleges proper"; some would become only preparatory schools; and some would cater to "that very large class of young women to whose wants the customary college training is not adapted."[34] On the whole, and despite the jaundiced view of women's higher education, this was a prescient observation.

The multipurpose women's colleges entered the 1880s at their apogee in terms of numbers and relative importance, but by the end of the decade they had begun an inexorable decline. Few new colleges of this kind were founded, and after mid-decade Division B began to shrink. Compared with 232 women's colleges reported in 1880, Division B counted 165 in 1890 and 119 in 1901. Nearly 60 percent of Division B schools disappeared from higher education in the 1880s and 1890s. Given the bureau's opinion of these institutions, it assiduously culled from the list those that no longer seemed to be credible colleges. Record keeping in this case mirrored a real process of differentiation. After aspiring with little success to offer a collegiate course, many multipurpose colleges reverted to more feasible roles as academies or junior colleges. But many colleges simply expired, including some of the more reputable ones: Ingham University (1857–1892) has already been mentioned; pioneer Mary Sharp College (1853–1895) could not survive either;[35] Delaware's only exemplar, Wesleyan Female College (1841– 1885), likewise expired after more than forty years of operations, as did Pittsburgh Female College (1854–1896).

In general the multipurpose women's colleges were fragile organizations with little capacity to withstand crisis or prolonged adversity. They lacked the

TABLE 10

FEMALE ENROLLMENTS IN COLLEGES AND NORMAL SCHOOLS

1880–1900

	1880	1890	1900
Division B Colleges	10,977	10,013	11,006
Division A Colleges	800	1,979	4,872
Coeducational Colleges	3,933*	8,782	21,892
Normal Schools	14,500*	26,923**	45,424

* estimated

** 1891

stabilizing force of significant endowments and were often in debt. Despite nominal church affiliations, they lacked dedicated boards of control or the degree of community support that other colleges could sometimes muster. Many depended upon the efforts and skills of a single individual or family. But behind the myriad stories of decline and dissolution that might be told lie deeper structural reasons for the obsolescence of the multipurpose women's colleges.

A stark picture of relative decline is portrayed in table 10. College-bound women increasingly flocked to coeducational colleges and universities, and the 14 or 15 colleges in Division A grew apace in the 1890s (+150 percent). Even larger numbers of women pursued the teacher training courses of normal schools. Division B colleges, however, failed to participate in the growth of either market. Instead, their clientele stagnated from 1880 to 1900 (and even to 1910 when the classification was abolished). With more than two-thirds of these colleges located in southern states, the survivors were probably remote for the time being from the mounting competition from normal schools, coeducational universities—or even high schools. But such locales reflected the past rather than the future of American education.

As the number of these colleges was almost halved from 1880 to 1900, average enrollments grew to near 100 at the end of the century. But this was no longer an adequate size for an institution of higher learning. Measured by prevailing standards, these colleges were probably more inadequate at the end of this era than they had been at the beginning. The obsolescence of the multipurpose women's colleges arrived sooner and more abruptly than the crisis that afflicted multipurpose colleges in general after 1890. Even more than their coeducational counterparts, they were an artifact of the third quarter of the century. Some, of course, made the difficult transition to modern colleges; many were absorbed by other, more robust institutions, but as a class, the multipurpose women's colleges were crowded out by institutions exemplifying the emerging structure of twentieth-century American education.

Noah Porter Writ Large?

Reflections on the Modernization of American Education and Its Critics, 1866–1916

~

PETER DOBKIN HALL

We have yet to fully grasp the reasons why and how colleges and universities came to function as the central institutions for recruiting and training the managerial and technological cadres essential to the modern state and economy and, at the same time, as the outposts of those who criticized and resisted their power.[1] For more than a century historians have explored the ways in which the Civil War ratified the central state as the dominant force in the American polity. Since the 1960s, scholars have broadened this theme, examining the emergence of large-scale economic and political enterprises, focusing on the bureaucratization of institutional life. Despite the provocative work of Robert Wiebe, Laurence Veysey, Martin Sklar, and others, we are finding that American intellectual culture and the institutions that sustained it fit less easily into the ideal typologies of modernization.[2]

In portraying the transformation of American higher education after the Civil War as a conflict between tradition and modernity, between religious and secular forces, between localism and nationalism, between institutional authority and academic freedom, chroniclers have more or less unanimously aligned themselves with the emergent new order and, almost without exception, identified those who resisted it with the backward-looking sensibilities that held back educational development while the new nation's economic and political institutions moved relentlessly forward. Scholars singled out Yale as the chief promoter of the parochialism and sectarianism responsible for the "Great Retrogression" in higher education, pointing in particular to the influence of the Yale Report of 1828, which advanced a persuasive rationale for prescribed classical curricula, and to its perverse reaffirmation of educational conservatism even after the Civil War through its leadership in the struggle against lay governance and the elective curriculum.[3]

I have argued elsewhere that the Yale Report, read rightly, was actually a forward-looking manifesto for educational reform and that its focus on the "discipline and furniture of the mind," rather than being an attempt to perpetuate an obsolete curriculum, was in fact a bold effort to frame an educational process intended to mold character—to engineer behavior and values in a manner peculiarly suited to the conditions of an economy and polity in which external mechanisms of maintaining public order had largely broken down.[4] In this chapter I would like to advance the view that Yale's role in the post–Civil War struggle over the secularizing of higher education—in particular its resistance to lay governance and the modernization of the curriculum—was more than an effort to perpetuate backward-looking sectarian parochialism. Rather, it actually looked forward to the very real dilemmas facing the agendas of intellectuals and cultural institutions in the emergent national economy and was, as such, the starting point of an effort to demarcate institutionally a domain of cultural authority insulated from the forces of mass markets and politics.

Yale was hardly alone in its opposition. Influential secular writers, such as Henry Adams, John Jay Chapman, and Charles Eliot Norton, set forth a "genteel" critique of the shortcomings of capitalism and its culture, some even yearning, as Brooks Adams did, for the return of a time when "the wealthy, learned, and respectable united to crush the ignorant and vicious."[5] But Yale's opposition, I will argue, was less framed by nostalgia than by a pragmatic recognition of the limits of the marketplace and those who presided over it.

Denominationalism, the Colleges, and Cultural Nationality

Richard Hofstadter was correct in suggesting that New England–based "denominationalism" had cast a broad net: in cities, towns, and villages in the Old Northwest and, to a lesser but still notable extent, the South, graduates of Yale, Princeton, and other Congregationalist-Presbyterian colleges taught, preached, pled, and presided at bench and bar, and steered enterprises through the turbulence of a growing economy.[6] In the 1830s Alexis de Tocqueville pointed to the fact that one-eighth of the members of Congress had been born in Connecticut—a state whose population comprised only one forty-third of the national population.[7] He compared New England's astonishing national influence to "a beacon lit upon a hill, which, after it has diffused its warmth immediately around it, also tinges the distant horizon with its glow."[8]

However pronounced and unmistakable its national cultural leadership, New England's relationship to the rest of the nation was distinctly colonial. Tocqueville spoke of New England's efforts to extend its "influence beyond its limits, over the whole American world."[9] Dr. Oliver Wendell Holmes put it less poetically in dubbing Boston the "hub of the solar system" and describing it as a place that "drains a large watershed of its intellect, and will not itself be drained," a center that placed other cities in its "suction range" in order to draw off their promising young authors, rising lawyers, large capitalists, and prettiest girls.[10] Through the 1860s and into the early twentieth century, Harvard remained a definitively Boston institution, keeping control of the institution firmly in the hands of the city's Brahminate.[11]

In contrast Yale was a more genuinely national institution in terms of the origins of its students and ultimate destinations of its graduates. By 1830 less than half of Yale's graduates had been born in Connecticut (in contrast to the 75 percent of Harvard graduates who had been born in Massachusetts) and barely 25 percent remained in Connecticut after graduation, most settling in New York, Pennsylvania, Ohio, and other trans-Appalachian states.[12] Despite this diaspora, Yale graduates remained firmly tied to their alma mater either through involvement in one aspect or another of the evangelicals' "benevolent empire" of lyceums, missionary, tract, and education societies or, after the disestablishment of the Congregational Church in Connecticut, through the college's efforts to nurture alumni as a source of financial support.[13]

The "Old-Time College" under Fire

As the authority of established churches declined in the second half of the eighteenth century, clerically controlled colleges like Yale and Harvard had come under pressure to liberalize and secularize their curricula. These demands originated in their respective state legislatures and were evidently part of a broader effort to disestablish religion.[14] When the ministers who ran the schools resisted and government support slowed to a trickle, the colleges attempted to seek support from coreligionists—a hopeless effort in the face of declining support for religion generally and bitter factionalization within religious communities. In the 1740s, Connecticut Congregationalism had fragmented into New Light and Old Light factions over the Great Awakening—then split again in the 1780s as the more extreme New Divinity followers of Jonathan Edwards challenged both the ecclesiastical and the political leadership of religious moderates.[15] While Yale managed to maintain its monopoly of higher education in Connecticut until after 1820, it did so only by assuming a stance of political activism that damaged its intellectual and spiritual authority.[16]

Less united to begin with than their counterparts in Connecticut, Massachusetts Congregationalists had long been divided between theological liberals, who were tied to the interests of the merchants and professionals of the coastal towns and cities, and theological conservatives, who still hewed to the old Calvinist "Congregational Way."[17] The legislature had accommodated this division by chartering other colleges, while Harvard drifted into the hands of the Unitarians. Despite this, Trinitarians regarded Harvard as a public institution, and when Unitarian Henry Ware was appointed to the college's Hollis Professorship of Divinity, open political warfare broke out between the factions, which eventually widened into a sectarian battle for control of all of the state's houses of worship and eleemosynary institutions that ended only with the disestablishment of religion in 1833.

Despite almost continuous turmoil over the composition, roles, and responsibilities of its governing boards through much of the nineteenth century, the laicization of Harvard governance was, in the end, relatively painless. Laymen had dominated its primary governing body, the president and fellows (the Harvard corporation), since the 1780s and, to a significant extent, the secondary body (the overseers) since 1812, when the legislature amended the charter to include among its number the senior members of its own upper house. In addition Harvard was only one of several colleges in the Commonwealth—the legislature having chartered Williams in 1793, Bowdoin (when Maine was still part of Massachusetts) in 1794, Amherst in 1821, Holy Cross in 1848, and Tufts in 1852, as well as a half dozen theological seminaries, medical schools, and normal schools.[18] Because donations from the rising merchant class had supplanted government grants as major sources of financial sustenance at Harvard by the 1820s, the question of who controlled the university became of only passing interest to most citizens.[19]

The situation at Yale, however, was quite different. The "Standing Order" of Congregational merchants, ministers, and magistrates was severely tested by demands for disestablishment in the 1770s and 1780s. But alarmed by grassroots challenges to constituted authority (particularly Shays's Rebellion), the excesses of the French Revolution, and the emergence of a national coalition of political and religious dissenters led by Thomas Jefferson, the state's leaders abandoned their differences and formed a united front against the rising tide of "Infidelity."

For fourteen years after assuming the presidency of Yale in 1778, Ezra Stiles fought a running battle against legislative leaders who demanded submission to government control as the price for continuing support. As late as March 1792, prospects for maintaining Yale's independence seemed grim, as Stiles foresaw either "a total Abolition & Surrender of the College Constitution, & wresting it out of the Hand of Ministers into the Hands of Civilians" or, as political hostility to the clergy intensified, the chartering of a rival institution—which would defin-itively dash Yale's hopes for further government support.[20] Suddenly the political winds shifted. Political leaders, who had, only months before, been threatening to destroy the college, offered a huge financial grant in exchange for minority ex officio representation on the college's governing board—and with no other con-ditions that might impair the clergy's continuing authority over the institution. Stiles immediately recognized the political implications of closely binding together the interests of political and religious conservatives:

> . . . the Clergy will have a particular & special Reason now to preach up
> for & recommend the Election of religious & undeistical Counsellors; &
> tho' now & then an unprincipled Character may get into the Council,
> he may be hunted down in a future Election. It may be mutually bene-
> ficial by preserv^g a religious Magistracy & a more catholic Clergy. It will
> unite Moses & Aaron. It will extinguish the Jealousy of the Civilians
> towds the Clergy; and promote a friendly Disposition towds College
> throughout the State.[21]

The Act of Union was part of a far more ambitious conservative agenda. The legislature, which had for thirty years resisted chartering corporations of any kind, suddenly began issuing charters to banks, insurance companies, bridges, turnpikes, manufacturing ventures, and eleemosynary enterprises—including a missionary society whose major energies were to be focused domestically.[22] Placed in the hands of loyal Federalists and Congregationalists, these became components of a tightly centralized machine not only for maintaining political and religious orthodoxy in Connecticut, but also for fighting the rising tide of "Infidelity" throughout the new nation.

The election of Thomas Jefferson to the presidency in 1800 and the ensuing breakup of the Federalist Party ensured the electoral impotence of the "wealthy, learned and respectable." Conservatives turned to nonpolitical means of securing public influence. Forming a national coalition of religious, charitable, educa-tional, and moral reform associations (the "evangelical united front") that exceeded the scale and scope of any political or economic enterprises of the time, the conservatives sought, as Tocqueville put it, to "diminish the moral power of the majority" and, by discovering "arguments that are most fitted to act upon the majority," to draw "the majority over to their own side, and then [to control] the supreme power."[23]

Thus Stiles's optimism about the alliance of conservative politicians and orthodox clergy proved unfounded. In the end the conservatives' united front could not hold the line against social and cultural forces that were breaking people out of old habits of deference and subservience. Jefferson's election not only rallied dissenters everywhere; the new president's willingness to appoint his allies to public offices gave them a strong power base for pursuing their efforts to separate church and state. In 1815 after years of bitter struggle, Connecticut's Federalist/Congregationalist machine was swept out of power. Subsequently the Congregational Church was disestablished, and the legislature chartered Episcopal and Methodist colleges (Trinity and Wesleyan), breaking Yale's monopoly on higher education.

Rather than abandoning its religious ties, however, Yale began to look on them as a source of potential strength. An early effort to raise funds for a professorship of divinity proved so successful that, by the 1820s, friends of the college were proposing a more ambitious national fund drive, drawing on Congregationalists and the school's alumni. Although the effort to raise $100,000 took four years to complete (1831–1835), its success demonstrated that Yale no longer had to depend on government and could look to a new constituency—its nationally dispersed body of alumni—for financial support.

Perhaps the most important by-product of the success of the fund drive was the effort to organize systematically the alumni as a support group. In 1828 Yale encouraged the formation of a Society of Alumni and began encouraging classes to appoint class secretaries, to publish class books, and to hold regular reunions. This created an infrastructure of support on which the college would regularly draw through much of the nineteenth century—without, however, offering these faithful donors a voice in the management of their alma mater.

The ex officio representatives of government—eight of the nineteen members of the Yale corporation—remained on the board, but permanently in the minority, they seldom attended meetings. This situation became a major irritant to generous alumni who were denied a voice in governing the college in spite of its increasing dependence on their largesse.

Thus, as noted, Hofstadter was correct in assigning to Yale the leading role in promoting what he called denominationalism in American education, but he erred in so roundly condemning it as a reactionary force, for there really was no viable secular alternative source of support for higher education until the passage of the Morrill Act in 1862. His suggestion that nondenominational institutions had any possibility of flourishing in the ages of Jefferson and Jackson is not supportable by the facts. Although Federalist territorial governors in the Northwest Territory had chartered a number of public institutions, Jeffersonian state legislatures—despite their wielding the power to appoint their governing boards—declined to provide them with financial sustenance, forcing them into dependence on local and/or denominational constituencies.[24] Jacksonians in Congress opposed the government's accepting the Smithson bequest and, when forced to do so, proceeded to squander it in investments in "pet" state internal improvement bonds.[25] In 1854 President Pierce turned back Dorothea Dix's campaign on behalf of the insane by vetoing a bill that granted 10 million acres of land to the states as endowments for asylums.[26]

In the antebellum decades eleemosynary enterprises that promised to benefit minorities—whether the educated or the disabled—inevitably fell victim to the majoritarian constraint, leaving primary responsibility for education and charity to religious groups.[27] By the 1860s American higher education and charitable enterprise generally had been thoroughly localized and denominationalized—so much so that when war broke out, the federal government contracted with the United States Sanitary Commission, a private corporation with significant religious ties, to provide relief and public health services for its armies rather than turning to its own agencies.[28]

"The Awful Problem of Self-Government": Alumni and the Control of Higher Education

Because private entities had become so central to the provision of public educational and cultural services by the 1860s, postwar demands by alumni for a voice in institutional governance at Harvard and Yale took on a visibility that commanded national attention, becoming in effect a dramatized struggle between traditional forms of authority—exemplified by the leadership of the clergy and local political elites—and the emerging national order that was increasingly identified with aggressively secular translocal control of wealth. Because Harvard's alumni achieved voice without significant opposition (in part because the college's primary governing board, the president and fellows, had been dominated by laymen since the beginning of the nineteenth century), it attracted little attention. But the efforts of "Young Yale," led by nationally prominent business and professional leaders and stalwartly opposed by no-less-well-known clergymen and academics, produced dozens of articles in the leading New York newspapers, many of which were reprinted elsewhere; letters for and against the proposed reforms dominated the letters columns in such national periodicals as the *Nation* for months; and "serious" journals such as the *New Englander* and the *North American Review* carried essays that argued for one view or the other.

The uprising of Yale's lay alumni began innocently enough. It was sparked by a review in the *New Englander* written by Yale's president, Theodore Dwight Woolsey, of an address on the reform of Harvard's charter delivered to a meeting of alumni in July of 1866, the text of which had appeared in the *Atlantic* in September of that year.[29] In the address Harvard Professor Frederic H. Hedge had reviewed the history of Harvard's relationship to the state, presenting Josiah

Quincy's highly partisan account, which demeaned the state's contributions to Harvard and exaggerated the contributions of private donors.[30] This was by way of justifying recent changes in the college's charter, which substituted for ex officio overseers representatives elected by the alumni.

Woolsey's review of Hedge's address, while observing the important differences between Harvard's and Yale's governance structures (Harvard having two boards, the fellows and the overseers, and Yale having one, the corporation) and criticizing Hedge's advocacy of curricular and disciplinary innovations (Hedge favored a broadening of curricular offerings, an elective system, and a system of discipline that placed the burden on students' sense of honor), commented favorably on the substitution of alumni representatives for state officials and suggested that the Yale corporation would do well to consider instituting such a change.[31]

After reviewing what he considered to be long-standing defects in Harvard's governance, Woolsey turned his thoughts to Yale—specifically to the question of "whether a similar plan of graduate election, can be engrafted on its charter with advantage."[32] While asserting that the 1792 inclusion of eight ex officio government officials as members of the corporation had worked to the benefit of the college, he criticized the bylaw requiring that a quorum of the board be based on the attendance of all nineteen members. The irregular attendance of meetings by the ex officio members made it difficult for the corporation to do its work. "In this state of things," Woolsey mused,

> we cannot but feel that the connexion between the College and the State is, as far as the deputation from the Senate is concerned, a mere form—a form which does no harm to the College that we know of, but which adds nothing to the efficiency and dignity of its corporation. Men are wanted in that place who will feel it their duty to be present, but it is idle, we conceive, to expect punctuality from the Senators, as the Senate is at present constituted. They change every year, so that the same man rarely reappears in the council of the College. They have no time to learn what duties are expected from them, nor to become acquainted with the condition and wants of the institution. They are in some cases men who take very little interest in the higher seminaries of learning, or perhaps even question their utility altogether. Neither sympathy then, nor knowledge, nor power to uphold a permanent policy belongs to them to any great extent.[33]

Then came the shocker: "let the voters be all masters of arts and graduates of a higher, or an equal rank, together with Bachelors of all the Faculties of five years standing," Woolsey suggested, and let that part of the Board now elected from the Senate of the State give place to graduates, who shall hold their offices for at least six or eight years, and be reeligible, when their term expires; let the elections be held not every year, but every other year, or even less frequently;—will not the result be greater interest, punctuality, knowledge, sense of responsibility, and devotion to the welfare of the institution on the part of the new members; will they not, if well elected, be a new strength of their Alma Mater; will they not bring with them views at once enlightened and conservative?[34]

Woolsey's comments galvanized Yale's alumni who, as they anticipated the president's retirement (he had served since 1846), began pushing actively both for a change in the college's charter and for curricular reforms akin to those proposed at Harvard (abandoning the prescribed classical curriculum for an elective system). Alarmed, Yale conservatives, led by Rev. Noah Porter, professor of mental and moral philosophy, began to mobilize against the laity and their supporters within the faculty.

The battle was fully joined in January of 1869 with the first meeting of the Yale Alumni Association of New York at Delmonico's, one of the city's most elegant restaurants. Chaired by U.S. Attorney General William Maxwell Evarts (a graduate of 1837) and attended by such notables as inventor S. F. B. Morse (class of 1810) and President Woolsey, along with some 250 other wealthy and successful alumni, the tumultuous conclave received national attention and was covered by reporters from the *New York Tribune* and the *New York Times*. "We have come here tonight," Evarts declared,

> to consider the prosperity and the prospects of the College. How much this College has done for us and how little we have done for it! How much this College has done for the country, and how much some of our countrymen, for whom personally the College has done nothing, have done for the College—SHEFFIELD, of New-Haven, and PEABODY, of London. [Cheers.] Among the sons of Yale who have benefited the country, I will mention WHITNEY, whose cotton gin has done so much for our comfort, by giving us cheap cloth, and MORSE, [cheers.] who has put it in the power of the poor man to send messages and receive information which kings and armies could not have collected before.... [Three cheers for Prof. Morse.] And we must not forget those who, without earning fame, have spread the influence of learning through the country—the common soldiers of learning. [Cheers. ...] To keep alive the interest of graduates different alumni

associations must be represented in the college government, as the President has suggested. [Cheers.] Nothing is required but a statute of the State of Connecticut, and now we come to a tract—no, a song—no, a treat. . . . "Yale College"—our college, of whom the President a hundred years ago said: "*Esto perpetua, Alma Mater Yalensia.*"[35]

President Woolsey, with a clear awareness of the political storm breaking around him, responded to Evarts's rousing speech with a cautious affirmation of his confidence in the corporation as then constituted. The proposal to "place alumni on the corporation did not originate in any want of confidence in the present Board," he declared.

So far as the management of the finances of the College is concerned and the proper exercise of their powers, perfect reliance is to be placed in the corporation of Yale College. They never have lost a single cent— that is to say, every dollar ever given to that College is now in their treasury. Here is a body which has such confidence in the faculty that it never undertakes anything affecting the practical working of the College without its having been previously discussed by the faculty and by a committee of the corporation.

Still, he suggested, the disadvantages of having nearly half the board made up of men who took little or no interest in the college—and seldom even bothered to attend meetings—needed to be weighed against the advantages of knowledgeable and committed trustees. Nonetheless, Woolsey pointed out the strength of the alumni's commitment was far from obvious. "The graduates have never done much for the college," he lamented. Only "thirty-six graduates have ever given it over $5,000; and a gentleman here present, not a graduate, has given more than all put together. Is it likely, then, we asked ourselves, that we can move our College, and provide suitable buildings for it, and that endowments can be raised which are more important than brick or marble?"[36] Without demonstrating their commitment, changing the constitution of the college to include alumni was likely to be "a thing impracticable."

The gathering forces of Young Yale elicited ever more vehement responses from faculty conservatives. An unsigned essay in the *New Englander* in April 1869, reviewing the meeting of the New York alumni, detected more than a little anticlericalism in the comments of those in attendance.[37] Many alumni evidently wanted to go beyond merely replacing the eight elected officials who served ex officio on the corporation—and were pushing for opening the whole board to the laity.

The conservatives' most coherent and concerted response to the alumni came from Professor Noah Porter, who defended the old order in a series of articles, "American Colleges and the American Public," which appeared in the *New Englander* in 1869 and were published in book form the following year under the epigraph "it is not necessary that this should be a school of three hundred or one hundred and fifty boys, but it is necessary that it should be a school of Christian gentlemen."[38] (In response faculty moderate Timothy Dwight published a series of essays, "Yale College—Some Thoughts Respecting Its Future," which welcomed the transformation of Yale into a university.)[39]

Porter defended the clergy from Young Yale's charge that the clergy were unworldly. Not only had they more or less single-handedly created and managed America's literary institutions, they had been at the forefront of social change in America:

> It is said, that ministers are likely to be slow or behind the age. Some of them are so, no doubt, but so are some lawyers and a good many other laymen;—and that ministers, as a class, are behind the age, and are not as ready for every wise progressive step, in morals or education, as any class of men, is a charge which all the recent history of New England disproves, and which the discussions of the great questions of reform which have lately agitated the country ought forever to silence.[40]

Porter likewise defended the clergymen on the corporation from the charge of parochialism. "In order to its having a national character," Porter argued, the college "does not need to be governed by representatives from Missouri or California." Indeed, he suggested, making the corporation geographically representative could make it more, rather than less, parochial. Responding to the suggestion that each of the "Associations of Alumni in the various larger cities of the country" be permitted to elect members of the corporation, he declared that

> these bodies, being much smaller than the one which assembles at the College at Commencement, would be even more likely to be hurried or engineered into the adoption of ill-judged measures, or the election of unsuitable men. But there are further weighty objections against this scheme. . . . Moreover they, all together, include only a section, and even a small section of the whole Alumni.[41]

The very nature of their training and work, Porter suggested, not only ensured that the clergy were better educated than most laymen and more in touch with the broad range of activities and issues that engaged the public, but also—and this was a telling point—better acquainted *as professionals* with the problems of managing educational institutions than the laity could possibly be.

> The graduates of Yale are as intelligent a body of persons, no doubt, as the country contains. They are possessed of wisdom and knowledge and high character, as much as any men. Their opinions, on many subjects, are worthy of high regard. But comparatively few of them, after leaving the College at their graduation, are able to know anything of its interior life. They are widely removed from it in space. They are busily engaged in pursuits which draw their thoughts away from it and which give them little opportunity for reflection on the great subjects of education. At the end of five, or ten, or twenty years, therefore, they have, by the very necessities of life, lost their powers of passing an intelligent judgment on questions which arise in regard to the progress or interests of the institution with which they were once familiar as students. They have become unqualified, for the same reason, to decide intelligently who are the best persons to be chosen for the management of its affairs.[42]

Porter's most vehement remarks were reserved for the suggestion that lay trustees elected by the alumni would be more disinterested than the clergy. Making implicit reference to the lurid political corruption involving prominent lawyers and businessmen being daily exposed in regard to the Tweed Ring, he suggested that lay involvement in governance could introduce similar kinds of corruption into higher education. The annual meetings of the alumni, he noted, could

> be very easily "packed"—to use the language of politics—in favor of particular candidates, or even by the candidates themselves. They would be liable to have their harmony and good feeling—so large a part of the usefulness and enjoyment of such meetings—broken up by the pressing of "party-tickets," and by the "excitements and ill-feeling."[43]

Further, Porter argued, politicizing the alumni would create opportunities for alumni driven by personal ambition or covert agendas:

> It is the restless and dissatisfied men who are most active on all such occasions. Those who are content to "let well enough alone," and see no special change of management to be necessary, will either be absent or will generally be inactive. And the field is thus free for the operations of

the former class. Who can doubt that they will, most likely, be successful wherever the conservative section is not roused, as it will not often be, to an earnest opposition?[44]

Under such a system, "the hasty reformers and more selfish among them" would be

> very often successful in pushing their way into the management of affairs. . . . The election of one noisy agitator, or of a single individual who was disposed to think, in accordance with the declared views of one of the prominent Trustees of a prominent College in New York, that the reading of the American Encyclopedia would be as good a way of educating the mind as the usual course of College studies, might be an incalculable injury to any institution devoted to the cultivation of sound learning.[45]

Finally he suggested—somewhat disingenuously perhaps—that the past history of the institution gave little reason to believe that the alumni could be counted on to follow through on their promise to generously support the school, not only because most were not in the habit of giving charitably but also—and more to the point—because few laymen possessed experience in "raising money by contributions." "Why," Porter asked, "have the graduates not made larger contributions?"

> There are several reasons why they have not. One is, that most of them have always been men of moderate means, and, until quite recently, almost none of them have been possessors of ample fortunes. Another is, that, in this imperfect world, very few persons give very largely to any object entirely of their own impulse, or except as they are impelled to it by the solicitations of others; and the graduates of Yale do not, like those of Harvard, live in its immediate neighborhood, but are scattered all over the country, where they have never been reached by persons soliciting in behalf of the College. . . . We do not doubt that the number of gifts, and of large gifts, from the graduates, as well as from others, will increase in the future. We believe it, because the graduates, as well as other men, are growing richer constantly, because the habit of giving is extending itself and becoming more settled everywhere in the country, and because there will doubtless be more systematic arrangements hereafter to solicit such gifts. But we do not believe the proposed change in the corporation—whatever other advantages may result from it—

will result in any willingness, or increase materially the willingness, of the graduates to give to the College. Money for benevolent causes is gathered in only by hard work. The gifts to Yale College, during the past ten, not to say the past forty, years, have been obtained, in very large measure, because the officers of the College have earnestly and patiently solicited them. The same thing will be true in all time to come, and it will mainly be in answer to their personal and patient solicitations that money will ever be obtained. And the mere fact, that the Alumni are represented in the corporation by a few honorable gentlemen, will not change the great law of the world. Men will not be inspired by this fact to give largely. They will, in general, give largely, if at all, just as they have done, because the College Faculty—the men who have given themselves to the College, and who live in it every day—go out among them, with all the influence and earnestness which they possess, and tell, as no one else can tell, the story of its wants.[46]

Whether or not we agree with Porter, it is difficult not to be swayed by the power of his arguments. Yale, unlike Harvard, *was* a national institution. Because of this, Yale could not count on the support of a geographically concentrated metropolitan elite, as Harvard could. Moreover, as he ably pointed out, merely tinkering with the mechanisms of representation—whether by introducing geographical or other criteria of eligibility—did not assure meaningful representation of the public interest. Rather, if anything, it created opportunities for special interests. The notion that worldly success gave trustees the broad fund of knowledge or the understanding of education needed to run an institution was false on the face of it: the very capacity for specialized application that made them successful deprived them of the intellectual breadth that made good trustees. Only informed and conscientious professionals could assure that the colleges served the best interests of the public.

Porter's articles to the alumni provoked predictable outrage. At the June 1870 commencement, when hundreds of graduates assembled in New Haven for their annual alumni dinner, their anger boiled over. One speaker, William Walter Phelps, a graduate of the class of 1860, candidly expressed the feelings of the younger alumni. Phelps was no minor player: the only son of John Jay Phelps, cofounder of the Phelps-Dodge copper fortune and son-in-law of Joseph Earl Sheffield, Yale's greatest single benefactor, Phelps was a successful corporate lawyer and Republican politician.[47] "I speak for the Class of 1860," Phelps began.[48]

We are gathered from country and city, north and south; we are lawyers and clergymen, physicians and capitalists, judges and editors, representing all the interests of the varied civilization, from whose fiercest current we step for the moment aside. We are here to testify to our love for each other, and our interest in Yale College.

"We have a message," he declared, "the message of young Yale to old Yale, it is what the graduates of the last fifteen years think and say to each other; what they have not yet had opportunity nor courage to say to you." And then he took off his rhetorical gloves:

> . . . the younger alumni are not satisfied with the management of the college. They do not think that in any thing, except scholarship, does it keep progress with the age. They find no fault with the *men;* they find much fault with the *spirit* of the management. It is too conservative and narrow. . . . The college wants a living connection with the world with-out—an infusion of some of the new blood which throbs in every vein of this mighty Republic—a knowledge of what is wanted in the scenes for which Yale educates her children—this living connection with the outer world—this knowledge of the people's wants, can be acquired only from those who are in the people, and of the people. This great want can be supplied only by the Alumni. Put them into your govern-ment. Get them from some other State than Connecticut—from some other profession than the ministry. Call them, and they will gladly and eagerly come—call them, and with the reform will pass away every appearance of alumni coldness and indifference. . . . Believe me, men who sit on the Supreme bench, who control the cabinet of the execu-tive—who in all moral and intellectual reforms are the leaders of their countrymen; Yale men, who got their training here, and are as able to manage its affairs as Rev. Mr. Pickering, of Squashville, who is exhaust-ed with keeping a few sheep in the wilderness, or Hon. Mr. Domuch, of Oldport, who seeks to annul the charter on the only railway that bene-fits his constituency.

Very much in the brash competitive spirit of Gilded Age entrepreneurialism, Phelps suggested that the clergy's otherworldly resistance to change placed the college at a decided competitive disadvantage, pointing to the decisions by the sons of Lincoln and Grant to attend Harvard rather than Yale. "Don't let Harvard, our great rival, alone have the benefit of it," Phelps demanded,

> let Yale condescend to be worldly wise. The son of a President is a young gentleman about to enter college. Yale says—it is worldly to secure him.

We will make no effort to secure him. Saintly Yale folds her arms in true dignity of saintliness, and young Vicksburg goes to Harvard. The press, in a telegram carries the fact to hamlet and prairie, and the fame of Harvard enters a thousand households, for the first time. . . . Harvard takes great poets and historians to fill its vacant professorships—Yale takes boys, who have proved their qualifications by getting their windows broken as tutors.

At this open challenge to the conservatives, all civility dropped away. The debate over Yale's governance became a national issue—the subject of newspaper editorials and endless letters in national periodicals.[49] The attention devoted to the issue is not surprising; the stakes involved nothing less than the question of who should control American culture—the ministers who had reigned basically unchallenged ever since the establishment of the first colleges, or the emergent class of businessmen and professionals who, as alumni, felt closely tied to the colleges and, as the people being asked to support them, felt that they were owed a voice in them. Moreover Yale held a particularly important place in the American institutional imagination because so many colleges throughout the South and West had been founded by Yale graduates and because the college's widely dispersed alumni tended to be the leaders of benevolent ventures of every sort in the cities, towns, and villages outside New England. The outcome of the struggle at Yale would serve as a paradigm for the control of higher education in America and, more broadly, for a redefinition of the boundaries between the public and private domains.

For the most part the debate followed predictable lines, with conservatives defending the prerogatives of the ministers and older notions of "Christian education," and liberals advancing the idea of broad-based secular university training. A few exceptional offerings, which broke new ground, emerged from the controversy. One of the most interesting of these was written by William Graham Sumner, who went on to become one of the founders of American social science. A graduate of the class of 1863, Sumner had served as tutor at Yale between 1866 and 1869, while studying theology. Ordained as an Episcopal priest, he took charge of a congregation for three years, before returning to the college in 1872 to teach political economy.[50]

The struggle for control of Yale provided Sumner with an opportunity to critique traditional models of educational finance and governance in the pages of the *Nation*. In sketching out his "business plan" for college governance, Sumner added conceptual flesh to Phelps's bare-boned assertions of the superiority of practical men as leaders. Pointing out that no graduate had ever "paid in full what it cost the college to educate him," Sumner suggested that the alumni had a very tangible interest in seeing to it that "the college might hold the same relative position to future generations which it held in their own"—and that this "sense of gratitude . . . of responsibility" constituted a "resource which has never yet been tried, but which would yield richly" if tapped.[51] "If every graduate who could afford it should give the college ten dollars," he suggested,

> and others should give more in proportion, we should enter on a plan whose financial soundness is unquestionable. We should be paying a debt which we all owe. We should be applying principles which are thoroughly in sympathy with the ideas of this popular and democratic age, and we should reach results which we never can attain by waiting for the tardy generosity of a few men of extraordinary wealth.[52]

Sumner carefully avoided explicit reference to the proposed change in the Yale corporation, but his ideas about systematically cultivating the generosity of alumni pretty clearly implied the inclusion of graduates in the government of the college.

Sumner was an active sympathizer with the Young Yale movement and later one of its heroes—when Porter, after being elected president, tried to purge the young dissenter from the faculty, ostensibly because Sumner had assigned the works of atheist Herbert Spencer—and his plan attracted considerable attention. While never adopted as a model for university finance, it helped to provide a rationale for the Yale Alumni Fund. Established in 1890, the fund was a departure from the practice of "waiting for the rich man's thousands" and involved a shift toward systematically "taking the poor man's dollars." Recognizing that "there was more money to be made out of the pennies of the million than out of the dollars of the upper ten thousand," Sumner suggested "an annual drive directed at all Yale alumni," which would allow alumni, according to their means, to repay the subsidy their education had received from the endowment. Controlled by the alumni—not the Yale corporation—the fund became a powerful instrument for driving the college toward the modernity it so resisted.[53]

The resolution of the struggle for control of Yale was a less than satisfactory compromise. The corporation agreed to seek a charter revision from the legislature, which, while retaining the governor and lieutenant governor as ex officio members, would replace the senators with six trustees elected by the alumni and serving six-year terms. The ten "successor trustees"—the self-perpetuating part of the board—was opened in theory to the laity, but laymen would not succeed in achieving a majority on the board until 1910. The price the alumni paid for this concession was the election of Porter as president, which ensured continuing resistance to the curricular changes that were already transforming Harvard into America's leading university.

But the laity took revenge in 1871, when Yale initiated a major fund drive. Reassured by Porter's confident claims that Young Yale represented only a handful of self-seeking troublemakers, the college sought to raise $500,000. The effort was an abysmal failure: only $172,452 was subscribed.[54] Quite clearly Young Yale, outraged by the conservatives' maneuverings, had closed its pocketbooks to the college. In marked contrast Harvard's newly enfranchised alumni celebrated the election of Charles W. Eliot—the university's first lay president—by giving $2.2 million in a single year.[55]

The conservatives' grip gradually loosened. After a decade and a half, Porter stepped down and was succeeded by the younger Timothy Dwight, who had taken a moderate position in responding to Young Yale's demands. The graduates greeted his election by organizing the Yale Alumni Fund. But only when Yale took on a business-oriented president, with the election in 1899 of railroad economist Arthur Twining Hadley, did the university finally gain the full confidence of its more worldly wise graduates.[56] They rewarded the corporation's shift by raising a fund of $1.1 million to celebrate Yale's 1901 bicentennial.[57]

The displacement of clergymen from controlling positions in higher education and charity was a hallmark of American institutional life after 1870. While ministers and denominational groups continued to hold sway over many smaller colleges and community-level eleemosynary organizations, by the turn of the century all the major universities and most of the national associational enterprises had come under laycontrol. The final blow was Andrew Carnegie's offer to fund pensions for college and university faculty—on the condition that faculties' institutions sever their religious ties. Laicization was more than anticlerical, however. It was, more centrally, an effort to replace guildlike forms of professional self-government with decision making by "disinterested" businessmen and their allies. As such it can be seen as an effort to create a new kind of public accountability—accountability not to the public as represented by government or by professional authority, but to the public as represented by the most economically successful.

Beyond Lay Governance

"Plato's classic scheme of folly, which would have the philosophers take over the management of affairs, has been turned on its head; the men of affairs have taken over the direction of the pursuit of knowledge," wrote political economist Thorstein Veblen, who would emerge in the early years of the twentieth century as the most perceptive and bitter critic of lay governance—and, more broadly, of capitalist civilization. Veblen honed his critical skills at Yale, where he received his doctorate in 1884.[58] He was a protégé of Noah Porter, and it seems clear that he was profoundly influenced by his mentor's views on the laity and its appropriate role in university governance.

When *The Higher Learning in America* was completed in 1916, Veblen had the benefit of hindsight in understanding the implications of business control of universities. When Porter wrote "Universities and the Public" in 1869, business-men had only begun to acquire representation on governing boards, and their financial influence was insignificant. By the turn of the century they dominated the boards of most colleges and universities and, through the establishment of grant-making foundations, created powerful instruments for shaping the priori-ties and policies of a wide range of cultural institutions. The power of founda-tions would become evident following the publication of Abraham Flexner's Carnegie-funded *Medical Education in the United States and Canada,* which, fueled by investments of more than $70 million from John D. Rockefeller, became the basis for a revolution in American professional education. The Flexner Report helped to create an integrated complex of universities, research institutes, teaching hospitals, and grant-making foundations operating under the ultimate authority of wealthy businessmen.[59]

Veblen articulated explicitly the notions of professional authority implicit in Noah Porter's earlier arguments against lay governance. Like many members of the "new middle class" of university-trained managers and professionals that came to prominence with the rise of public and private bureaucracies after the turn of the century, Veblen believed that expertise, not money or other forms of ascriptive authority, legitimated power, but he differed from them in a number of important ways. Where most "progressives" of the new middle class were willing to forge alliances with business leaders who demonstrated allegiance to concep-tions of corporate social responsibility, Veblen was unwilling to make such Faus-tian bargains.[60]

"For a generation past," Veblen wrote in *The Higher Learning in America,* "there has gone on a wide-reaching substitution of laymen in the place of clergy-men on the governing boards. . . . The substitution is a substitution of business-men and politicians; which amounts to saying that it is a substitution of businessmen. So that the discretionary control in matters of university policy now rests finally in the hands of businessmen." Lay control of university budgets, in Veblen's view, created a situation in which "men of affairs" were able to decide "what the body of academic men that constitutes the university may or may not do with the means in hand; that is to say, their pecuniary surveillance comes in the main to an interference with the academic work, the merits of which these men of affairs on the governing board are in no special degree qualified to judge."[61]

Lay trustees did not bring their business acumen to bear on the actual day-to-day management of university finances—this task was delegated to a growing cadre of administrators. "These governing boards of businessmen commonly are quite useless to the university for any businesslike purpose.... Their sole effectual function," Veblen declared, was "to interfere with the academic management in matters that are not of the nature of business, and that lie outside their competence and outside the range of their habitual interest."[62]

Veblen tied his dark view of university governance to a more sweeping critique of American civilization, in which the public had irrationally entrusted control of its most central activities to men who, in his view, were little better than criminals.

> The spirit of American business is a spirit of quietism, caution, compromise, collusion, and chicane.... Success in business affairs ... comes only by getting something for nothing. And, barring accidents and within the law, it is only the waiting game and the defensive tactics that will bring gains of that kind, unless it be strategy of the nature of finesse and chicane. Now it happens that American conditions during the past one hundred years have been peculiarly favourable to the patient and circumspect man who will rather wait than work; and it is also during these hundred years that the current traditions and standards of business conduct and of businesslike talent have taken shape and been incorporated in the community's common sense. America has been a land of free and abounding resources; which is to say, when converted into terms of economic theory, that it is the land of the unearned increment. Putting aside the illusions of public spirit and diligent serviceability, sedulously cultivated by the apologists of business, it will readily be seen that the great mass of reputably large fortunes in this country are of such an origin; nor will it cost anything beyond a similar lesion to the affections to confirm the view that such is the origin and line of derivation of the American propertied business community and its canons of right and honest living.[63]

Corrupt and exploitative, capitalists grew wealthy on the ideas and energy of the genuinely talented and learned. Pecuniary standards replaced standards of craft and quality. And the market ethos eroded universities' commitment to intellectual excellence. The undergraduate curriculum came to be viewed as "introductory to those social amenities that devolve on the successful man of business," and "university training" came to mean those "practical" branches of knowledge (law, politics, accountancy, etc.).[64] These shifted the primary goals of higher education from the pursuit and diffusion of knowledge to the acquisition of wealth. Veblen saw little hope for reform because this "perversion" of education was grounded in the indisputable hegemony of private enterprise over every aspect of American life.

Though some might argue that "business principles do or can pervade the corporate management of the universities in anything like the degree here implied," Veblen believed that this view underestimated the extent to which "effective surveillance of the academic work is exercised through the board's control of the budget. The academic staff can do little else than what the specifications of the budget provide for; without the means with which the corporate income should supply them they are as helpless as might be expected."[65] Business values, he believed, led boards to prefer short-term tangible returns over

> those intangible, immaterial uses for which the university is established. These uses leave no physical, tangible residue, in the way of durable goods, such as will justify the expenditure in terms of vendible property acquired; therefore they are *prima facie* imbecile, and correspondingly distasteful, to men whose habitual occupation is with the acquisition of property. By force of the same businesslike bias the boards unavoidably incline to apportion the funds assigned for current expenses in such a way as to favour those "practical" or quasi-practical lines of instruction and academic propaganda that are presumed to heighten the business acumen of the students or to yield immediate returns in the way of a creditable publicity.[66]

To those who claimed that strong presidential leadership could effectively counteract the anti-intellectualism of the laity, Veblen pointed out the importance of the board's role in selecting academic leaders:

> . . . where the power of appointment lies freely in the discretion of such a board, the board will create an academic head in its own image. In point of notorious fact, the academic head of the university is selected chiefly on grounds of his business qualifications. . . . New incumbents are selected primarily with a view to give the direction of academic policy and administration more of a businesslike character. The choice may not always fall on a competent businessman, but that is not due to its inclining too far to the side of scholarship. It is not an easy matter even for the most astute body of businessmen to select a candidate who shall measure up to their standard of businesslike efficiency in a field of activity that has substantially nothing in common with that business traffic in which their preconceptions of efficiency have been formed.[67]

Nor did he see the alumni as a significant counterforce. "It follows as an inevitable consequence of the current state of popular sentiment," Veblen wrote,

> that the successful businessmen among the alumni will have the decid-
> ing voice, in so far as the matter rests with the alumni; for the success-
> ful men of affairs assert themselves with easy confidence, and they are
> looked up to, in any community whose standards of esteem are business
> standards, so that their word carries weight beyond that of any other
> class or order of men. The community at large, or at least that portion
> of the community that habitually makes itself heard, speaks to the same
> effect and on the same ground, viz., a sentimental conviction that pecu-
> niary success is the final test of manhood. Business principles are the
> sacred articles of the secular creed, and business methods make up the
> ritual of the secular cult.[68]

The result, Veblen argued, was that business trustees invariably delegated acade-mic leadership to "one of their own kind"—"a businesslike 'educator' or clergy-man, some urbane pillar of society, some astute veteran of the scientific demi-monde."[69]

Though Veblen's critique of lay governance may have been intemperate, it was symptomatic of the growing distrust between increasingly professionalized acade-mics and the businessmen and corporate lawyers who had come, during the previ-ous generation, to control and finance American higher education. In part this was an expression of resentment by the scholars and clergymen—the pillars of the "genteel tradition"—who had been displaced by the business takeover of the nation's central economic, political, social, and cultural institutions: as aesthetes like John Jay Chapman would sneer, "Eliot [Harvard's president] goes about in a cab with Pierpont [Morgan], hangs laurel wreaths on his nose, and gives him his papal kiss. Now . . . what has Eliot got to say to the young man entering business or politics who is about to be corrupted by Morgan and his class?" His contemporary Henry Adams would bemoan his student's belief that "the degree of Harvard Col-lege is worth money to me in Chicago" as yet another example of the decline of the civilization.[70] The Left, with which Veblen was more identified, had its own reasons for denouncing business control of the universities. But connecting both was a common conviction that "men of learning . . . ought to occupy the strategic loci of social control" in the emerging institutional order of modern society.[71]

By the turn of the century, scholars had been pushed aside, as "hand in hand with the dollar, the businessmen marched into the control room of Academe": between 1860 and 1900, the percentage of businessmen on university boards increased from 23 to 26 percent; of bankers, from 5 to 13 percent; of lawyers, from

21 to 26 percent—while the percentage of educators increased from only 5 to 8 percent.[72] A measure of faculties' loss of voice is their diminishing contribution to university fund drives: in the Yale fund drives of 1830, 1854, and 1870, faculty were leading contributors, giving nearly 10 percent of the whole amount raised, often as lead donors. By the 1926 drive, in which two-thirds of the $21 million raised came in the form of subscriptions of more than $5,000, faculty contributions were insignificant. In the larger universities, faculty had become employees and increasingly regarded their boards—not without good reason in many cases—as hostile to the academic enterprise.[73] However exaggerated the criticisms of Veblen, Upton Sinclair, Scott Nearing, Harold Laski, William H. Allen, Horace Coon, Eduard Lindemann, Gustavus Myers, and Ferdinand Lundberg, they were a portent of the adversarial spirit that would increasingly characterize board-staff relationships in the twentieth century.[74]

Conclusion

It seems peculiarly ironic that mid-twentieth-century public intellectuals like Richard Hofstadter chose to identify themselves—and the cause of academic freedom—with the businessmen who seized control of America's cultural institutions after the Civil War. His doing so is symptomatic of a deep confusion of the liberal sensibility of the time that, in its construction of "modernism," tended almost irresistibly to conflate a number of seemingly incompatible cultural, economic, and political forces. This version of modernism curiously combines two unlikely strands: the first, characterized by a radically individualist rebellion against traditional ideas, forms, and standards (evident in the abandonment of classical literary, architectural, and decorative forms for the sake of a more "functional" aesthetic); the second, an ethos that placed individuals and their skills in the service of the corporate state (evident in the extent to which modern art and literature benefited from the patronage of the wealthy and its products were collected and enshrined in institutions that uncompromisingly—if not brutally—asserted the pride and confidence of those who controlled economic life).

In his 1869 articles on the New Education, Charles W. Eliot's manifesto for the reform of American higher education, the man who would shortly become the most powerful figure in the nation's institutional life wrote admiringly of the relationship between universities and business in the advanced industrial economies of Europe. "Sixty years ago, in France, the first Napoleon made great changes, mostly useful ones, in methods of education," he declared.

> For more than a generation the government schools of arts and trades, arts and manufactures, bridges and highways, mines, agriculture, and

commerce, have introduced hundreds of well-trained young men every year into the workshops, factories, mines, forges, public works, and counting rooms of the empire. These young men begin as subalterns, but soon become the commissioned officers of the army of industry.[75]

"The American people are fighting a wilderness, physical and moral . . . for this fight they must be trained and armed," he continued, suggesting that only a similar set of relationships between education and economic life would enable the nation "to work out the awful problem of self-government" and develop the "prodigious material resources of a vast and new territory."[76] He would amplify this theme in his inaugural address as Harvard's president, on the one hand calling for the application to "mental activities the principle of division of labor," and on the other warning that educators' "lack of faith in the prophecy of a natural bent, and in the value of a discipline concentrated upon a single object, amounts to a national danger." Challenging the model of educational prescription that had dominated American higher education since the Yale Report of 1828, he declared that "the civilization of a people may be inferred from the variety of its tools. There are thousands of years between the stone hatchet and the machine-shop. As tools multiply, each is more ingeniously adapted to its own exclusive purpose. So with the men that make the State."[77]

Eliot fostered an educational method that placed an almost religious emphasis on the development of an individual's intellectual calling. "When the revelation of his own peculiar taste and capacity comes to a young man," Eliot wrote in explaining the elective system, "let him reverently give it welcome, thank God, and take courage. Thereafter he knows his way to happy, enthusiastic work, and, God willing, to usefulness and success." But he framed that intensely individualized calling with an ethos of service and located it within a corporate command structure. "For the individual, concentration, and the highest development of his own peculiar faculty, is the only prudence," Eliot proclaimed. "But for the State, it is variety, not uniformity, of intellectual product, which is needful."[78]

In 1869 Eliot had begun his essays on the New Education by asking, "what can I do with my boy?" Forty years later "commissioned officers of the army of industry" like Harvard-trained Herbert Croly would echo both the question and the answer that attested to the power of Eliot's vision. "What the individual can do" to fulfill the American national promise, Croly wrote in the progressives' sweeping blueprint for social transformation, is

to make himself a better instrument for the practice of some serviceable art, and by so doing he can scarcely avoid becoming also a better instrument for the fulfillment of the American national Promise. To be sure, the American national Promise demands for its fulfillment something more than efficient and excellent individual instruments. It demands, or will eventually demand, that these individuals shall love and wish to serve their fellow-countrymen, and it will demand specifically that in the service of their fellow-countrymen, they shall reorganize their country's economic, political, and social institutions and ideas.[79]

It was this tradition of corporate liberalism, which so curiously but effectively consolidated radical individualism with powerful institutional mechanisms for collective action, that Hofstadter, the preeminent spokesman for the academic liberalism of the mid–twentieth century, would defend in his paradigmatic accounts of American educational history.

The institutional order that Hofstadter and his contemporaries defended against the New Right of the 1950s and 1960s now lies shattered. *Modernism,* once a term that in its heyday connoted not merely an aesthetic orientation, but a "best and brightest" worldview that summarized the consolidated powers of science, economic freedom, the marketplace of ideas, and leadership of the free world, is now almost as much of a curiosity as Victorian manners and mores were to the modernists/liberals. Divorced from the power complex for which it served as legitimating myth, modernism is just another of many isms. This paradigm shift enables us to reexamine the development of central institutions—including the institution most central to the rise of the "modern" state and economy—and empowers us to view it critically rather than compelling us to accept it as a canonical representation of irresistible progress.

Viewed through postliberal conceptual lenses, seeming evolutionary dead ends like Noah Porter's educational ethos, which sought to equip young men to understand that rationality was bounded, that there were sources of truth besides the marketplace, and that the idea of duty in one's calling could be more than the ghost of dead religious beliefs, take on a peculiar resonance. Porter's legacy may not have been—as Hofstadter and other progressivist scholars believed—the last stand of Protestant parochialism, but the critical tradition represented by his student Thorstein Veblen.

The German Model and the Graduate School

The University of Michigan and the Origin Myth of the American University

≈

JAMES TURNER AND PAUL BERNARD

*T*he origin of the American university, the graduate school in particular, has a kaleidoscopic quality.[1] The pieces are all familiar—the early-nineteenth-century colleges with their tiny faculties, small student bodies, and limited curricula; the catalytic example of the great German universities; the takeoff of research; emergence of graduate training; professionalization of academic disciplines; expansion of curriculum; growth in numbers and infrastructure. Put these bits together, and there appears Cornell or Chicago or Michigan. But *how* to fit them together? Where, especially, to put the German example, the piece around which others often appear to coalesce?

Something like a standard pattern has taken shape in university history—one not so much wrong as oversimple. It can be briefly summarized.[2] Before the Civil War, American colleges mostly devoted their energies to controlling unruly students, their curricula to rote learning of classical languages, rhetoric, and simple mathematics. In today's terms they resembled high schools more than colleges—and certainly not universities—for the best of them aimed only to transmit the existing culture; the expansion of knowledge lay utterly outside their purpose. But the very defects of antebellum colleges provoked reform. Deepening discontent with their intellectual decrepitude inspired efforts to breathe new life into these dry bones; college reform became a persistent issue from the beginning of the nineteenth century. It finally achieved success in the decades after the Civil War.

The key innovations came from a cadre of academics who looked at colleges from a common point of view, deriving from a shared educational experience. Since early in the century, aspiring young Americans had embarked for Germany to pursue studies unavailable in their own country.[3] Returning, they imported more than *Wissenschaft;* they brought back a new idea of higher education. These German-trained professors were at first voices crying in a wilderness. But their influence magnified after midcentury, when leading college presidents went on pilgrimages to study European education, especially the celebrated German universities.[4] These lessons were swiftly applied. From the failed attempts of the 1820s to pull Harvard out of its slumbers to the invention of the modern American university at Cornell and Johns Hopkins in the 1860s and 1870s, it was the example and personal experience of German universities that commonly inspired reformers and shaped their vision.[5]

Americans saw four principal elements in the German model. First, the Germans clearly distinguished preparatory studies, appropriate to the *Gymnasium,* from the higher learning, proper to the university. Second, German universities assumed as their mission the advancement of knowledge and training in original research. Third, the universities gave both professors and students the independence needed to pursue knowledge (*Lehrfreiheit* and *Lernfreiheit*). Fourth, this research ideal took flesh in distinctive institutional arrangements—notably the seminar, to train researchers, and the Ph.D. degree, to certify their competence. American reformers seldom wished to duplicate exactly the German university in the United States, and German influence ultimately had little direct effect on undergraduate colleges. But these four elements shaped advanced studies. More specifically the German research ideal and the institutions linked with it led directly to that American invention, the graduate school.

No one believes that German influence tells the whole story. For instance, many scholars see professionalization as an independent force driving the move toward research universities.[6] And as historians have long pointed out, American university reformers borrowed selectively from Germany.[7] For example, *Lehrfreiheit* translated fairly well into the American practice of academic freedom; but *Lernfreiheit*—the German custom by which a qualified student could enroll at any university, in any course[8]—never habilitated itself in the United States. And what Americans did borrow, they reworked. The Ph.D. degree functioned quite differently in the two countries. In American universities the Ph.D. from the beginning usually entailed much more substantial research than in Germany. And in America the degree served almost exclusively as the gateway into the professoriat, in Germany chiefly as a ticket into the civil service or secondary school teaching.[9] Most strikingly the Americans concocted a novelty never imagined in Germany: the distinction between undergraduate and graduate studies.

Yet if German example does not explain everything, it explains a lot. If native social changes fed the deepest roots of the American research university, Germany still provided the "research ideal." If the German university had little to offer the American undergraduate college, it still was the main influence on advanced training. If Americans picked and chose among German practices, they still got from Germany the characteristic concepts and institutions of graduate education. So the story goes, and it is a plausible one.

Yet on closer reading, the tale begins to unravel. To begin with, by no means every university reformer waxed lyrical over Germany. Invocations of German example are in some cases peculiarly sparse. President Charles W. Eliot, the architect of modern Harvard, in his inaugural address in 1869 gave one fleeting mention to Germany in almost thirty printed pages (France got more attention).[10]

The story grows still more tattered. German influence accounts clumsily even for the changes, it is supposed to explain in American higher education between 1850 and 1900—even in graduate education. There are too many ill-fitting connections, too many outright gaps. Why did the requirements for and uses of the Ph.D. change so drastically in the United States? Why did the seminar, a semiautonomous institute in Germany, become a one- or two-semester class in America? Where did Americans get the unheard-of notion of distinguishing "undergraduate" from "graduate" schools? The glaring disparity between Teutonic example and American practice may explain why historians put so much emphasis on Johns Hopkins, the one well-studied American university that demonstrably did try to emulate the Germans.[11]

How often did reformers actually follow German patterns? Perhaps even more to the point, *how* did they follow them?

I

An adequate reply to that question requires the writing of a very large book. But the starting point is easy to find. It lies in recognition that the German model came in many versions. Different Americans impressed with German education drew differing lessons from its achievements. Their responses varied, less because of ignorance of German practices (as some historians suggest) than because of awareness of American problems.

Americans naturally picked out as the salient features of German universities not what a German academic might have chosen, but what rubbed hardest against their own discontents with American higher education. Joseph Cogswell, for instance, was particularly struck by the specialization and diligence of Göttingen's scholars, George Ticknor by the size and currency of its library, John Lothrop Motley by its library—and the absence of dormitories.[12] This last impression (which also figured in Henry P. Tappan's specifically Prussian ideal) comes alive when one recalls how much energy antebellum American professors had to pour into merely custodial supervision of the youngsters in their charge. And this peculiarly American reaction makes the point; the motive of reformers was not to emulate Germany, but to improve their own colleges. Thus the origin of the *research university*—Germanic influence and all—comes into focus only when viewed as one outcome of a century-long struggle to redefine the American *college.*

This effort began not long after 1800. From their seventeenth-century beginnings, American colleges had offered an education inherited from the English Renaissance.[13] In early-nineteenth-century colleges, teaching still centered on Greek and Latin, rhetoric, natural philosophy, and mathematics of a fairly practical sort. This was a training nicely suited to prepare teenage boys for life as seventeenth-century gentlemen or even for further study of theology or medicine in seventeenth-century universities.

Its relevance to nineteenth-century America came increasingly into doubt. The celebrated Yale Report of 1828 defended the classical curriculum as providing "the *discipline* and the *furniture* of the mind."[14] But other studies seemed equally able to discipline the mind, while furnishing it to more modern purposes. Ultimately two new paradigms came to compete for control of the colleges.[15] One (appearing in some institutions as early as the 1820s) stressed modern languages, mathematics, and the sciences and claimed to offer an education somehow useful in a modern commercial and technological world. The other developed more gradually out of the old classical education, often claiming the classical mantle. It continued to emphasize Latin and Greek, adding history, literature, and the fine arts; it prized the formation of character and intellect rather than usefulness and by the 1880s had evolved into what we now call "the liberal arts ideal."[16]

The "utilitarian" paradigm moved toward specialization of knowledge. The examples of increasingly arcane scientific expertise, of newly insistent professional claims to authority, of greater division of labor in the economy all pulled in this direction. Inside and outside the college, division of *intellectual* labor promised efficiency and progress. Utilitarian reforms were thought to link the college or university with the "real" world outside it. In this sense they belonged with contemporary innovations like the agricultural experiment station and the teaching hospital; they anticipated such early-twentieth-century phenomena as the "Wisconsin Idea" and the industrial research laboratory.

The liberal arts paradigm resisted specialization, insisted on broad grasp and integration of knowledge rather than expertise. It drew strength from the pervasive integrating influence of Scottish common sense philosophy in antebellum colleges and, later in the century, from idealist philosophy infiltrating from Germany. The liberal arts movement also gained salience from the Victorian crisis of religious faith, which encouraged the search for new sources of cultural unity and spiritual vision to replace the loosening glue of belief in God. In 1895 Charles Eliot Norton summed up the animus of the liberal arts paradigm: "The highest end of the highest education is not anything which can be directly taught, but is the consummation of all studies. It is the final result of intellectual culture in the development of the breadth, serenity, and solidity of mind, and in the attainment of that complete self-possession which finds expression in character."[17] The analogy with the German *Bildung* ideal appears strong, but in fact advocates of the liberal arts looked more to Matthew Arnold than to Wilhelm von Humboldt.

No one drew neat lines between the utilitarian and liberal arts paradigms. The same college president often urged both ideals in a single speech; advocates of each never hesitated to borrow notions native to the other. These labels identify the two major directions of reform, not two warring camps. If these clusters of ideas rested ultimately on incompatible principles, consistency has never been the hobgoblin of academic minds. The baffled offspring of this mixed marriage still bless our campuses today. But to understand the uses of German example, one must realize that college reformers felt tugged toward these two distinguishable, if seldom clearly distinguished, goals.

II

Amid this swirl of conflicts over the shape of American higher education, the University of Michigan took form. Michigan's young life powerfully influenced the evolution of the research university—and not merely because it became the largest American university by the 1870s. Henry P. Tappan's much-discussed innovations at Michigan in the 1850s and early 1860s provided the first American model of a modern university. Andrew Dickson White, "perhaps the most significant of the university builders in the United States," spent a decade at Michigan absorbing Tappan's ideas before becoming the first president of Cornell.[18]

Such trailblazing was not much evident in the university's beginnings. At its start Michigan had combined some organizational innovation with a very traditional curriculum. The effective history of the university began with its founding in Ann Arbor in 1837. Lacking any clear American precedent for the role of a state university, the state's constitution writers turned to the French philosopher Victor Cousin's celebrated 1832 report on Prussian education—the most systematically developed and, thanks in large part to Cousin, the most admired of the German educational systems. Following Cousin, Michigan's lawgivers declared the university the capstone of a unified system of public instruction—capstone, to be sure, with only dreams under it. The example of the Prussian rectorial system (reinforced possibly by sheer parsimony) also apparently suggested a rotating chancellorship, taken each year in turn by one of the professors.[19]

Prussian influence went no farther. The university's internal workings, leaving aside its revolving chancellorship, mimicked faithfully the old-fashioned American collegiate model. Lacking any distinctive idea of what curriculum ought to be, the university's regents copied the traditional classical pattern. The faculty even adopted the language of the 1828 Yale Report, insisting that "mental discipline" was more important than "mental furniture."[20]

Tradition did not bring stability. Cramping poverty disfigured the university's first several years, domestic bickering its next few. The state's political leaders soon felt the need for a steadier hand at the helm than a one-year chancellor's; and the new constitution of 1850 mandated a permanent president. The regents finally hired one in August of 1852.

III

The man they got—having failed to lure more prominent candidates—was Henry Philip Tappan.[21] A Congregational minister, sometime professor at New York University, writer on philosophic subjects, and great fan of Victor Cousin, Tappan offered as his chief recommendation for the Michigan job that he had recently stamped himself an authority on higher education. In 1851 he published a book called *University Education,* devoted largely to praising the Prussian system *à la Cousin:* "acknowledged to be the most perfect in the world." Indeed Michigan's halfhearted visions of building a New Berlin in Washtenaw County's green and pleasant land probably helped to persuade this New Yorker to come west.[22]

Tappan wanted "a University worthy of the name," by which he meant a Prussian one. He, like the Michigan constitution, imagined the university as capping a unified state system of public instruction. However, Tappan regarded the existing curriculum at American colleges, including Michigan, as like "that of the Prussian Gymnasium." Ultimately he wanted college work to hive off into the state's secondary schools, which would then assume the current role of American colleges—that is, become gymnasia. This shift would eliminate the solecism of "a University Faculty giving instruction in a College or Gymnasium."[23]

Tappan realized, however, that for the present the university must continue to give collegiate instruction; so he set as his "first object . . . to perfect this gymnasium."[24] To this end Tappan immediately instituted within the Department of Literature, Science, and the Arts "a scientific course parallel to the classical course," with English, history, and additional mathematics displacing Greek and Latin.[25] Tappan stretched the Prussian analogy pretty far here: the gymnasium was resolutely classical. Yet he felt the appeal of the utilitarian paradigm, especially in a frontier state.[26] There was to his mind nothing auxiliary or second rate about utilitarian studies at the "Gymnastic" level.[27]

These reforms expanded the German ideal into what Tappan called "the comprehensive idea of a University." Here a student was supposed to find any instruction desired, including schools of agriculture, fine arts, industrial arts, and pedagogy (though, in fact, the student would have looked in vain for these at Tappan's Michigan). This comprehensive ideal would later resurface in the founding of Cornell by Tappan's disciple Andrew Dickson White. It would exercise decisive influence on the structure of American universities, especially state universities. Yet Tappan insisted that such schools could not form part of the university "properly speaking." This august entity by definition comprised only faculties of theology, law, medicine, and philosophy.[28] Rather, adding various subuniversity studies simply patched up deficiencies of American colleges, considered in their role as quasi-gymnasium. And "after all that can be done to perfect it," the "Undergraduate course" or "Gymnastic department" is "still limited to a certain term of years, and, necessarily, embraces only a limited range of studies."[29]

These limits seemed to Tappan a crippling defect, for "a system of Public Instruction can never be complete without the highest form of education."[30] Tappan was scarcely alone in recognizing the essentially propaedeutic nature of American colleges. Even the 1828 Yale Report declared the purpose of collegiate training *"to lay the foundation of a superior education."*[31] Tappan's distinction lay not in recognizing the need, but in trying to meet it—and in invoking a particular version of the German model to do so. A real university must, like Prussian ones, offer "those more extended studies in science, literature, and the arts, which alone can lead to profound and finished scholarship." Following "Prussian principles of education," Tappan regarded such advanced study not as an ornament of the university's work, but as "the culmination of the whole."[32]

He proposed, therefore, "to open courses of lectures" in which college graduates and others prepared "by previous study" could pursue "the highest knowledge." He intended this "University Course," as he called it, to "form the proper development of the University, in distinction from the College or Gymnasium now in operation." All this, he assured his readers, was "in accordance with the educational systems of Germany and France." The course included twenty subjects of study, ranging from "Systematic Philosophy" through "Ethics and Evidences of Christianity," "Chemistry," and "Philology," to "The Arts of Design."[33]

In keeping with its character as true university work, the University Course discarded altogether the method of instruction by class recitation still common to all American colleges. Teaching was instead to "be conducted exclusively by lectures." The student would also have "full opportunity" to use "the library and all other means that can aid him in literary cultivation and scientific researches."[34] These "researches" probably did not mean what we now call original research (though that was not excluded) but something closer to looking up information independently, as an undergraduate is now said to "do research" for a term paper. Study in the University Course, unbounded by specified time limits, aimed at the achievement of erudition rather than the fulfillment of requirements. Otherwise, in method and level of teaching, the closest analogy in our present universities is probably to upper-level undergraduate lecture courses.

More to the point the University Course resembled instruction in German universities. "This Course," Tappan wrote, "when completely furnished with able professors and the material of learning, will correspond to that pursued in the Universities of France and Germany."[35] Despite his pretensions, Tappan was at this date hardly an authority on the "German system."[36] Yet he had learned its broad structure and absorbed his own version of its ideals. Independent learning based on lectures and reading, rather than recitation; pursuing the latest knowledge, rather than imbibing traditional learning; concentrating on a few chosen fields, rather than following a standard and rigid curriculum—in all these respects Tappan's program borrowed heavily and self-consciously from the German universities of his day.

Yet Tappan did *not* borrow the elements that loom so large in the received history of German influence and the rise of graduate education. He shied away from narrow specialization, avoiding even the German pattern of examination in one major subject and two minors. He ignored the German Ph.D. degree.[37] Increasingly aware of the prominence of research in German universities, he never incorporated it into the University Course. Far from hostile to research, Tappan urged it on his faculty.[38] But discovery of new knowledge never figured as a substantial *educational* ideal in his programmatic statements. Tappan believed lectures and independent reading entirely adequate to convey the "highest learning" and apparently never mentioned the seminar, already the symbol of erudition in Germany.[39]

The most persuasive explanation for this pattern of selective adaptation is the simplest. Tappan's immersion in the problems of American collegiate education had decisively shaped his understanding and uses of the German university. This is not to deny his genuine and uncolored admiration for German education. But his Prussian enthusiasms inevitably filtered through his concerns about the inadequacies of American colleges—and the filtered remains made up his program for the advanced education of college graduates.

Thus Tappan's "German" system at Michigan was very much part of the confused struggles to reshape the American college. Like Wayland at Brown, whom he much admired, Tappan had considerable sympathy with the utilitarian paradigm. He worried, not so much that the old classical course had grown irrelevant, but that its relevance had grown too limited. With the increasing importance and complexity of science and technology, colleges—especially those responsible to the public at large—needed to add such useful training to their curricula. These concerns led Tappan to the "scientific course" in the "Gymnastic department" and, more generally, to his astonishingly broad construction of the Prussian gymnasium and his refashioning of the Prussian system into a "comprehensive university."

Yet Tappan's deepest educational loyalties lay with the liberal arts paradigm. This informed both his view of the German model and his "University proper" in Ann Arbor.[40] For Tappan, the culmination of education was the integrative culture that he associated with "the highest learning." Hence he quite naturally placed ideals like independent minds, thirst for knowledge, and breadth of learning at the intellectual core of the German university. (How much Tappan's notions actually owed to Humboldt's *Bildung* ideal is not clear.) And he isolated as the key institutions of the German university those arrangements that appeared to him to support such ideals, such as the lecture system. By the same token Tappan's preoccupations blinded him to the salience of other features of German universities—including the careerism and narrow specialization that had smothered Humboldt's dream in its cradle.

German influence on Tappan was authentic. The pedagogical structure of the University Course and, to some extent, even the liberal arts ideals underlying it really were borrowed from Germany—but from a Germany itself seen through the lens of the liberal arts paradigm.[41] *Tappan's* Prussian university, just as his University Course, aimed to produce erudition grounded broadly in "truth, knowledge, beauty, and culture."[42]

Yet the University Course was not a direct ancestor of the liberal arts college any more than of the graduate school. It offered education at a much higher level than any mid-nineteenth-century college in terms of both what it taught and how it taught it. Tappan despaired of the youngsters then entering college mastering such a curriculum. Those who wished *either* the preparatory classical studies of the gymnasium or a simply utilitarian education would find it in college. True liberal education awaited those who had made it through college. Yet though postgraduate, the University Course was hardly graduate school in the later sense: it lacked both narrow specialization and focus on research training. Although Tappan's University of Michigan was the most celebrated German-model university in midcentury America, it resembled no mature form in the American university. German influence in American higher education followed a more tortuous path than historians have generally allowed.

Tappan's vision of university studies amounted to little more than a pipe dream when he left Ann Arbor. Why he failed is a matter of conjecture: perhaps chiefly for lack of clientele. Michigan instituted several "postgraduate" lecture courses toward the end of his tenure; but who populated them is a mystery, since there were never more than two or three resident graduates in arts and sciences.[43] Still, in proposing to turn college graduates into learned Germans, Tappan began the serpentine movement that eventually led to graduate training at Michigan. In the process he also stepped on too many toes. The wonder is that he survived for more than ten years. In 1863 the board of regents, unjustly, foolishly, inevitably, fired him.

IV

Tappan's successor was Erastus O. Haven, who spent his six years in office scowling at innovation.[44] In his haste to restore the good old days, Haven immediately expunged from the catalogue the very Prussian statement on the "Organization of the University" that had appeared throughout Tappan's term; eventually he even dropped the word *undergraduates.* Nevertheless Tappan's University Course had taken on a life of its own, even if a feeble one, as the route by which aspirants to the master's degree prepared for their examinations. On average, about six graduate students seem to have attended each year during the Haven interregnum—actually an increase over the Tappan years.[45]

When Haven resigned in 1869 to become president of Northwestern, it took the regents two years to find a replacement. In the meantime Henry Simmons Frieze, professor of Latin, served as acting president. Frieze had come to Ann Arbor in 1854 and immediately caught Tappan's Germanophilia. The next year he traveled in Europe, apparently attending lectures at Berlin during the winter term. "What he saw with his own eyes more than confirmed his previous impressions of the great excellence of the German gymnasium and university training, and after his return he never ceased to commend the application of German methods" to American schools and universities.[46]

It was therefore no surprise that Frieze revived Tappan's project of turning the state's high schools into gymnasia. He even looked forward ultimately to replacing the A.B. with a certificate of proficiency, to be granted by the high-schools-become-gymnasia. This would have amounted to an American version of the Prussian *Abitur,* though apparently minus the standardized examination required of gymnasium graduates in Prussia.[47] Frieze actually inaugurated a scheme of admission-by-diploma for graduates of high schools inspected and approved by University of Michigan faculty, eventually including schools as far away as New York and New England.[48] (This idea evolved into the now universal American practice in which high school transcripts replaced the old, widely varying entrance examinations given by every college.) But outside the university at least, Frieze's ambitions seemed never quite understood. The high schools never became gymnasia. College studies remained in college.

V

Serious development of graduate education took place after James B. Angell arrived in Ann Arbor in 1871.[49] Angell held the presidency until 1909. During his first two decades, all the distinguishing marks of today's graduate school appeared at the university: the distinction from both undergraduate education and postgraduate professional studies; the focus on training in original research; the entrenchment of the seminar as the characteristic method of such training; the awarding of the Ph.D. as the research degree; and finally in 1891–1892 the formal organization of the graduate school.

James B. Angell was the chief architect of the modern state university, a giant of the founding era of the research university. But he was almost entirely marginal in the story of graduate education. Unlike Tappan or Frieze, he cherished no broad vision of the future. Though fond of uttering appropriate pieties on public occasions, Angell really operated as promoter, fund-raiser, manager. In exercising these skills extraordinarily well, Angell carved out the niche that university presidents fill today. His diverse interests, humane sympathies, and genius for compromise made him effective and popular. He had a good eye for talent: hired it, nurtured it, and gave it a free hand. He often welcomed innovation, usually let others do the innovating—particularly in graduate education, for his heart lay with the college.[50] The graduate school evolved less under Angell's direction than under his benign smile—and under the long shadow of Henry Philip Tappan.

The key players were Henry Frieze and Charles Kendall Adams. Frieze was not only Tappan's most ardent disciple; he also enjoyed a friendship with Angell stretching back over twenty-five years. This long-standing amity, together with his own experience running the university, gave Frieze probably more leverage than any other member of the faculty. After stepping down as acting president in 1871, Frieze embarked on his second European journey, this one of two years' duration. He renewed his admiration for the German university during a term at the University of Tübingen "diligently studying Sanskrit under that great scholar, Professor Roth."[51]

The other major actor, Charles K. Adams, imbibed Tappan's ideas directly from the source as a Michigan undergraduate. A second critical influence was the professor of history Andrew Dickson White. White had arrived in Ann Arbor in 1857, Adams's freshman year, and immediately proved a rousing teacher. He "sent a sort of historical glow through all the veins and arteries of the University," Adams later recalled.[52] White introduced a vaguely German mode of instruction (possibly inspired by his own brief attendance at Berlin), replacing recitations with lectures and encouraging students to read beyond the textbook. His reliance on lectures soon spread to other professors—an enduring and substantial innovation. White also proposed somehow to "exercise" students in "original investigation," though this ambition vanished from the catalogue after his first year.[53]

Adams, graduating in 1861, continued his study of history under White, receiving in 1862 one of the first earned master's degrees. In that same year Tappan appointed him a junior faculty member. When White became president of Cornell in 1867, Adams replaced his mentor as professor of history.[54] Upon appointment, Adams immediately took a year's leave, to travel and study in France, Italy, and Germany. This *Wanderjahr* evidently stoked an already warm enthusiasm, inherited from Tappan and White, for the German university. Adams returned fired with the idea of extending, along German lines, White's reform of college history teaching.

This urge vented itself in a new course for seniors in 1871–1872—"something akin to the *Historische Gesellschoft [sic]* of the German universities." That is, a seminar: by some definitions the first taught in the United States. Adams sent his students off to write papers, armed with lists of assigned topics and of "the best authorities in the University library"; and each week class discussion centered on one of these student essays.[55] The seminar method struck a chord among students.[56] It soon popped up in a few other fields. It is hard to know exactly what Adams's imitators assumed they were imitating, but occasional hints suggest self-conscious discipleship to Germany.[57]

Yet were Adams and his colleagues really teaching seminars, properly called? In terms of the received history of graduate education, the answer is "no." The Michigan seminars catered mainly to advanced undergraduates, not graduates. Nor did the students in them pursue original research as now understood in American Ph.D. programs.[58] Adams's seminar (evidence is lacking for the others) centered on carefully directed exercises in the use of sources. Students wrote fairly short papers, typically using printed collections of excerpts from original sources and following a "pamphlet of 'questions' with references" prepared for them by Adams. Far from pursuing independent projects, each week all students in the seminar studied the same subject. To be sure, the seminar involved "a higher grade of historical investigation" than lectures; but Adams never hinted that it looked toward original research or even preparation for it (though presumably a student who intended a career as historian would have enrolled in the seminar).[59]

Not any desire to train professional researchers, but dissatisfaction with the rote learning, recitations, and elementary instruction of the old college curriculum, pushed the university's faculty toward the seminar.[60]

Yet these Ur-seminars probably resembled more closely than their descendants the practice of mid-nineteenth-century German universities. German universities, after all, had no "graduate" students, simply students. Seminars provided advanced training for those who intended to make a career in the field of the seminar—but not usually a career of original scholarship. Most students probably aimed to become gymnasium teachers.[61] Until well after midcentury, training for pedagogy seems explicitly to have dominated the purposes of seminars.[62] German seminars did train students in research techniques, on the assumption that in this way a student achieved a sophisticated grasp of the subject matter. But something like Adams's small-scale exercises in using documents was probably much more common than the original research projects on which American seminars soon came to center. If the early Michigan seminars now look more like undergraduate than graduate study, this was not because they were unfaithful to their German models.

The seminar was only one of a batch of changes at Michigan in the 1870s meant to raise the level of college work. The lecture method continued gradually to infiltrate instruction; the credit-hour system was introduced; and in the late 1870s the university expanded the number of electives permitted in undergraduate programs. Unlike the seminar, none of these had German associations (the lecture method having been around long enough at Michigan to lose its Teutonic coloration).

Yet like the seminar, they had the unintended consequence of laying a firmer basis for postgraduate education. They freed faculty to teach more sophisticated and specialized courses and to devote more attention to advanced students. This upgrading of undergraduate education thus made realistic two changes in higher degrees introduced in the mid-1870s: the toughening of requirements for the master's and the awarding of the Ph.D. And by 1880, twenty-one candidates for advanced degrees were enrolled in Ann Arbor. Not all were postgraduates: a reminder that "graduate education" had not yet jelled.[63]

The university followed the German model in its Ph.D. requirements: awarding it "on examination" for "special proficiency in some one branch of study, and good attainments in two other branches." A first degree and two years' residence were prerequisites. Research was probably from the beginning associated with the new degree in many cases, if not most. In 1879 the university formally declared that "faithful and industrious work" did not suffice; the candidate must also evince "power of original research and of independent investigation."[64] But it is not at all clear that the Ph.D. was primarily meant for researchers or even specialists; nor does research (as distinct from independent reading) seem always to have bulked large in Ph.D. work, especially outside the natural sciences.[65]

Frieze and Adams warmly supported all these innovations. Frieze hoped that they would lift Michigan "out of the narrow ruts" of the local college, make it "a national University."[66] But such scattershot changes did not create a true university. "It is manifestly difficult, if not impossible," Frieze wrote in 1880, "to change the Gymnasium into a University by merely building up a system of post-graduate courses, as a sort of annex to the old established curriculum of four years; for the post-graduate work will thus continue to be a mere subsidiary appendage, and the so-called Collegiate Department will still be the central and characteristic part of the institution."[67]

Frieze had long hungered for the day when Tappan's dream might take flesh in Ann Arbor. He wanted collegiate studies, pending their relegation to the high schools, pushed back into the first year or two of the Michigan course, leaving three years for university studies proper—explicitly on the model of the German universities.[68] Frieze found a zealous second in Adams. Angell, while not hostile to such ideas, was hardly the man to transform Michigan into Tappan's notion of Berlin. But in 1880 Angell left Ann Arbor on a diplomatic assignment, and Frieze once again became acting president.

Acting presidents are not supposed to revolutionize their institutions. They do, however, have to respond to emergencies. In the spring of 1881 Frieze discovered a convenient pair of them. Judge Thomas M. Cooley, the star of the Law School, threatened to quit unless he could shift his teaching to constitutional law and history. Frieze agreed, even proposed that Cooley lecture in the arts faculty as well as the Law School. Cooley replied that his courses might then be grouped with kindred subjects in a complete program. Frieze saw in this suggestion the means to douse another fire. Charles K. Adams's old teacher Andrew D. White was wooing Adams for Cornell, promising to let him organize a school embracing historical and political studies. Frieze offered to make Adams dean of a similar new outfit at Michigan—and trumped White by putting the celebrated Cooley on Adams's faculty. Thus was hatched the School of Political Science.[69]

Its presiding deity was Henry Philip Tappan. Adams, presumably in consultation with Frieze, designed the program to correspond to Tappan's vision of the true university—hitherto found only east of the Rhine. Students would enter the School of Political Science after completing their "secondary or gymnasium training" in the ordinary "required studies" of the first two years of college (at Michigan or elsewhere). Once admitted to the school, students learned through the methods proper to a university: lectures and seminars. After a minimum of three years' study, they became eligible to present a thesis and take oral examinations. The thesis had to show "elaborate study of the subject considered" and, "so far as is practicable . . . original research." The orals tested "special proficiency" in one branch of knowledge and "good attainments" in two others. A sufficient degree of "excellence" on both thesis and examinations earned the Ph.D. The three-year term, the lectures and seminars, the thesis and examination, the major field with two minors, the Ph.D. as the ordinary university degree were all familiar features to German students. The School of Political Science was as close a replica of a German university as anything that had ever existed in America—or ever would.[70]

So close that it puzzled most of the university's faculty. The School of Political Science as such roused no notable opposition, but the awarding of the Ph.D. to its graduates ignited an explosion. Angell's son reported to his father a "quite warm" dispute pitting "Frieze & Adams vs the crowd." The crowd feared that awarding the Ph.D. after only five years of study "would cheapen the degree."[71] Frieze called them old fogeys, simply afraid to do anything differently from Harvard.[72] In any case the faculty established a committee to report on the questions—a committee that included Frieze and Adams among its five members.[73]

Both men conceived the School of Political Science in the larger context of reforming the traditional American college. Two months before Cooley suggested the new program, for example, Adams had written to Angell about allowing students more freedom of choice, even permitting the better of them to finish in three years or proceed to a master's degree in four. Frieze, in reporting to the regents in June 1881, had suggested extending the principle of the new school to the entire faculty of literature, science, and the arts.[74]

Frieze and Adams now used the faculty committee as a vehicle to do just that. Its report recommended including the rest of the arts and sciences faculty in this "true University." A few modifications reassured the "old fogeys." Ultimately the faculty further insisted that the Ph.D. thesis "evince power of research and of independent investigation"—the standard adopted in 1879—and that doctoral candidates learn enough French and German "for purposes of study." But with these concessions (and with the support of Angell, who returned at midyear) Frieze and Adams at last pushed through the faculty in the spring of 1882 an idea of university education dramatically new for America.[75] Its name echoed Tappan: the University System.[76]

Conventional college and postgraduate programs remained in place alongside the University System. At the end of the sophomore year, having completed what Frieze thought of as gymnasium work, students elected either the ordinary credit system (itself a recent innovation) or the University System. The credit-system students took courses for two more years, accumulated credits, and earned a bachelor's degree, as American undergraduates still do. Students who opted to enter the "true University" attended lectures, took seminars, and pursued independent work, all focused in groups of studies. (An attempt by Frieze and Adams actually to divide the arts and sciences faculty into four subfaculties—professedly following German practice, though not in fact very closely—had failed of adoption.) At the end of two years, the students took examinations in one major field and two minors. Students who merely passed received a bachelor's degree. Students who passed with distinction and presented an acceptable thesis received a master's degree. At the end of the third year came another examination in the three fields and another thesis. Students awarded the bachelor's degree at the previous examination had a chance to present a thesis along with the examination and earn a master's. But for those students who had earned the master's a year previously, leaping this final hurdle brought a Ph.D.

This seemed very like Tappan's German program of advanced education. And both structure and inspiration were indeed similar. Yet much had transpired in the nearly two decades since Tappan's ouster. Graduate education had become a reality (if not exactly a numerically overwhelming one) at Michigan and elsewhere. The two or three "resident graduates" of the Tappan years had grown to a couple of dozen. Tappan's University Course took its rather airy form in a college populated by teenagers; Frieze and Adams could not help taking into account a critical mass of career-minded twenty-five-year-olds. Moreover Michigan faculty now had competing American programs of advanced education to measure their own against, not just foggily understood German ones. In the debate over the University System, professors drew comparisons to the Harvard Ph.D. as often as the German one.

And the example of Harvard, Yale, or Hopkins weighed on the side of greater specialization, heavier stress on research. Research and publication, and with them specialization, had by this time worked their way into the normative conception of the university professor (though not yet the college professor). Professors engaged in research expected their advanced students to work with them; students, for their part, began to expect training in research as part of normal preparation for the life of a professor.

Both professors and students began also to look upon the Ph.D. as certifying this sort of training. The degree was a foreign transplant brought in, repotted, watered, and beloved only by professors; it appealed, at first, to no other occupational group. Not surprisingly most of the candidates for it hoped to become professors. Thus the degree itself became linked to professorial training—especially training in the skill that distinguished the high-powered new-model professor from the tattered older version: research. This linkage was reinforced by the centrality of specialized research in the careers of German professors, even though the educational program of German universities did not focus on research. The Ph.D. was, in Germany, the ordinary arts degree. But as the professor's degree in America, it acquired the character of the German professor rather than of the program in which he lectured.

Adams's and Frieze's version of the German model had thus evolved some distance from Tappan's. As Tappan's disciples they kept alive a conception of German university education as culturally formative and broadly integrative. Yet with its focus on three limited fields and its specialized thesis, their University System was more cramped than Tappan's University Course—even if closer to the realities of German education. They had diluted Tappan's understanding of the German system, informed by the incipient liberal arts ideal, with a substantial admixture of utilitarian motives. The compromises forced on them by skeptical colleagues pushed them farther in this direction.

Thus research held a secure place in the University System. Both Frieze and Adams believed that university professors bore an obligation to expand knowledge. The flexible rubrics of the University System allowed students to train for a specialized academic research career; a few of them, particularly in the natural sciences, seem to have done so.[77] President Angell went overboard in claiming that "original research of real worth will be expected in every case." In fact the requirements mandated research only "so far as the resources of the University permit"— not a stiff standard for students writing theses in, for example, American colonial history. Adams and Frieze would probably not have gone even this far, for they did not regard the Ph.D. as quintessentially a research degree. But their colleagues did and insisted that every thesis demonstrate the *capacity* for research.[78]

Yet the University System did not chiefly mean to train researchers or specialists.[79] Lecture courses, independent reading, and the occasional seminar were expected to dominate workloads—as one might suppose when students began after the sophomore year. The typical thesis probably amounted to nothing more ambitious than today's undergraduate senior honors thesis. Nor did the curriculum focus effort on one discipline—in contrast to the graduate programs then developing at the Hopkins and elsewhere.[80] Whether the major and minor fields bore any relationship to each other depended on the inclinations of particular students and professors. The University System fostered more concentration than the credit system, but it aimed no more at specialization than at the production of scholars.

The real intention was to produce effectively educated citizens. Frieze hoped to give students "a large and thorough preparation for the duties that will devolve upon them as citizens and members of society," to "fit them for those public duties to which every citizen is liable to be called."[81] Adams shared this outlook.[82] And on this point both were in harmony with Angell—which provides another reason for his support of the University System. In stressing the usefulness of such training—"preparation for duties" as distinct from formation of character—all three were leaning toward the utilitarian paradigm of college reform.

Finally, though, the University System subordinated utility and special training to wider ideals. An advanced education was here not tightly focused but integrative. In the view of Frieze and Adams, even students training as specialists should learn to put their advanced training in the service of the commonweal. Even students intending a research career should learn to fit their research into broader advances in knowledge. And conversely even students seeking a general education should learn to handle some special field with technical sophistication. Advanced education was still to be liberal education, though less full-blooded than in Tappan's version. As a later advocate of the University System explained, "the argument for a certain degree of specialization does not rest upon the demand for specialists but upon the claim that some practice in specialization is necessary to complete a liberal education. An educated man ought to be able to pass just criticism on the intellectual products of his own time."[83] It was this sort of advanced but liberal education that Tappan believed German universities to supply. It was to provide this education that Frieze and Adams tried to reform the college—and simultaneously channel the emerging demand for graduate training—into the University System.

There is little point in rehearsing the actual deficiencies of the University System in supplying the article in question, which were considerable. There is even less reason to speculate on whether the University System could have realized this perhaps utopian vision. For the system sputtered and wheezed little past wishful thinking.[84] Few faculty or students seemed to know what to do with it. Frieze and Adams could persuade their colleagues to approve the institutional changes constituting the University System; they could not implant in their minds the larger vision of the German university that infused these arrangements with appealing meaning. Only a handful of students entered the program.[85] At first the majority proceeded directly to master's degrees; but by 1896 the old notion had decisively reasserted itself that the bachelor's was the proper undergraduate degree; and the University System became simply an alternative to the credit system as *preparation* for an advanced education. No undergraduate ever proceeded to a Ph.D. on the University System. When Adams left for Cornell in 1885, only Frieze remained to speak for Tappan's idea of advanced education. He died in 1890. In effect the University System had predeceased him.

Its demise in no way cramped the growth of other species of advanced education. What became the conventional form of graduate education flourished in impudent good health—and without, it seems, deliberate feeding. Graduates showed up to work for an advanced degree, and faculty dealt with them catch-as-catch-can. The number of graduate students quintupled in the decade after 1881; by its end Angell was handing out three or four doctorates annually.[86] The students finally grew so numerous, their training so confused, that in 1891 the college set up a graduate school to manage the operations.[87]

The infant graduate school was swaddled in repeated invocations, almost ritual incantations, of its German pedigree.[88] Professors and students alike seem to have looked to Germany as their intellectual homeland. But their Germany was not Tappan's, Frieze's, or Adams's. It was the land of the *German professor*, not of German *education*. The operative image now of the German university refracted the Berlin of the research ideal, not of the *Bildung* ideal. The Ph.D. became linked exclusively to specialized training in original research. Descriptions of graduate courses stressed their technical nature and highlighted the distinction between graduate and undergraduate work.[89] Beginning in 1894, Ph.D. candidates had to choose as their two minor studies "cognate[s] to the major"; one of them could be "a more thorough treatment" of the major. The language requirement insisted on French and German "sufficient for purposes of research," as opposed to the earlier "purposes of study." The Ph.D. thesis *had* to be "an original contribution to scholarship or scientific knowledge," "confined within narrow bounds," requiring at least "the greater part of one academic year" to prepare.[90]

The graduate student's virtue, one Michigan professor wrote in 1892, "is an independent scholarly grasp of one or two subjects." This man conceded that imparting a "general education" is "an honorable calling"—may even be good for the researcher in small doses—but "it is not the proper function of a university professor."[91] So much for Tappan. General education belonged in the preparatory years of the college. Advanced education meant specialized research training. Just when the liberal arts paradigm was finding a permanent home in the liberal arts college, the utilitarian paradigm was settling down for a long winter's nap in (among other places) the graduate school.

These sharp distinctions between undergraduate and graduate education did not force themselves on the university. To the contrary, the *inability* to find any real difference between the supposed two levels embarrassed Michigan professors time and again in the early years of graduate education.[92] They drew the line, not to map an existing divide, but to create one. An increasingly specialized and research-minded professoriat believed that mature knowledge should belong in specialized divisions, separate from general culture; and they acted so as to give life to their belief. By doing so they brought to birth the graduate school and killed the University System.

VI

Tappan's vision of the American college transformed into a true university starved in an environment that gave it no sustenance. For by the 1880s the American college had reconstructed itself in forms that left no place for any scheme like the University System. On the one hand, the liberal arts paradigm had defined the *college* as a place where students absorbed general culture before going on to advanced training. The turn-of-the-century college might voice the Mr. Chips ideal of the Amhersts and Williamses; it might fly the flag of maturity-through-independence, like the Harvards and Michigans with their elective systems. But general education, understood as the province of the college, was inevitably understood as preparatory.

On the other hand, the utilitarian paradigm increasingly expressed itself in specialized training, with knowledge cut up into segments related only instrumentally. To the traditional law schools, medical schools, and divinity schools were added engineering schools, business schools, education schools, and the like. The new graduate schools of arts and sciences resembled these, with the crucial difference that the graduate school defined its subject (its equivalent of engineering or divinity) not as any applied skill but as "pure knowledge." This knowledge meant, not the general culture of the college, but specialized disciplines only marginally related to the discourse of other specialized disciplines. And advanced education meant training in research in one of these specialized disciplines. A student who moved from the preparatory education of the college to the advanced education of the graduate school left general culture behind.

And this increasingly clear division of labor brought with it a change in the meaning of "the German model." If Michigan is typical, German influence neither increased nor diminished between the 1850s and the 1890s. (And the histories of other major universities do suggest, mutatis mutandis, a similar pattern.) But what German example was held to teach varied enormously from time to time and place to place. Broadly and very tentatively speaking, in the 1850s (and probably earlier), the university-gymnasium distinction, the lecture system, and perhaps the *Bildung* ideal suggested ways to upgrade college education—but probably nothing like the professional graduate school. Yet by the 1880s the German research ideal suggested, or at least legitimized, just the sort of undergraduate-graduate distinction institutionalized in the graduate school. To be sure, German universities had changed over these years; most to the point, by the 1880s seminars and laboratories had developed into highly visible institutions dedicated to research. But more important were changes in the American context, notably in the character of the professoriat, which encouraged American academics to read the German evidence differently.

Out of the cocoon of the old-fashioned American college, then, emerged that strange schizophrenic native to the New World, the American university. The graduate school and the new-model college evolved as distinct, largely unconnected entities. In them the same faculty often taught, students moved from one to the other; but in each, different educations and different conceptions of knowledge prevailed.

For a while in the 1850s and 1860s, it looked as if the Prussian road would lead Americans to something rather like a supercharged liberal arts college, drawing students from a souped-up high school. But around the 1870s most American academics began interpreting the highway markers differently; so the road veered sharply. More precisely Americans discarded the *educational* program of German universities.[93] They then took the German invention of highly specialized *professorial* research—not, properly speaking, a part of German university education at all—and built on it the advanced segment of American university education. Precisely because specialized research training made no sense for most university students, such advanced education had to be split off from the ordinary university course. This division compounded the irony of stealing the ordinary German degree for the use of the graduate school.

This transmogrification of German practice was the really substantial American contribution to the research university. The Germans invented the research ideal. The Americans invented an institution to house and perpetuate it. By throwing this distinction into sharper relief—and by clearing away the underbrush that has obscured some roads not taken—Michigan's story helps to clarify the knotty problem of German influence in American university history.

It also reminds us that the founding principles of the graduate school defined graduate training in self-conscious opposition to general education and common culture. The ever-narrowing gyre of specialization was no accidental spin-off from the modern fragmentation of knowledge, but the flight plan of the graduate school from its launching.

A "Curious Working of Cross Purposes" in the Founding of the University of Chicago

WILLARD J. PUGH

*T*n 1888 Frederick T. Gates, corresponding secretary of the American Baptist Education Society, completed a survey of Baptist higher education in the United States and presented his findings at a Baptist clergy conference in Chicago. From his study of the western frontier, he predicted that Michigan, Indiana, Illinois, Wisconsin, Iowa, Missouri, Nebraska, Kansas, Colorado, and the Dakotas would become the population center of the United States and the "ultimate base of American power." He discovered that Baptist colleges in this area were "unevenly distributed, feeble in resources, narrow in area of attractive influence, and obscurely located." Only 54 percent of the students in these colleges completed a four-year program, and only twenty-five male students graduated each year. The level of instruction was rudimentary, and the colleges were poorly endowed. Gates estimated that five thousand Baptist students were lost each year to state universities and rival sectarian colleges. He predicted that the West would soon contain the majority of northern Baptists, and argued that western education be a Baptist priority. He presented two alternatives: the Baptists might erect more frontier colleges such as Kalamazoo, Shurtleff, and William Jewell, or they could concentrate on major cities such as Denver, Minneapolis, and Chicago. Gates preferred the latter. He described Chicago as "the most commanding social, financial, literary, and religious eminence in the west," and exhorted its pastors to establish a Baptist college. Graduate education and faculty research did not appear in his report: for western Baptists these were not important issues.[1]

When Gates completed his survey, Baptists were already contemplating plans for a "first class college" in Chicago, a graduate research university with no college in New York, and a national university in Washington, D.C. John D. Rockefeller was expected to become the patron of these institutions. On a carriage ride in Central Park in 1887, Rockefeller invited Yale University professor William Rainey Harper to participate in the founding of the graduate research university in New York, conceived by Augustus H. Strong. Rockefeller finally rejected this idea, but Harper never forgot their conversation. When later offered the presidency of a Baptist college in Chicago, Harper held out for something higher. At a meeting in Poughkeepsie, New York, he concluded that Rockefeller was planning to establish the graduate research university in Chicago. He persuaded Rockefeller to provide an endowment for graduate studies at that college, which became the University of Chicago, and the founding of a graduate research university became the great prepossession of his life. Shortly before its opening in 1892, the University of Chicago was contrasted with Harvard, Yale, and Princeton, described as essentially colleges; and Harper announced that research would be primary at Chicago. Harper and his head professors envisioned a graduate research university, but Rockefeller and the Chicago Baptists had foreseen a college. This created a "curious working of cross purposes." Rockefeller's gifts provided generous salaries for Chicago's head professors, and several buildings; but they did not provide the "material requisites" for research, including a central library, laboratories, apparatus, or funds for specific research projects. When Chicago's other major donors failed to provide the required funds, Harper promoted the university's vast horizontal expansion. He emphasized teaching and undergraduate work, and colleges became more prominent in his organizational plan. These developments gradually shifted the university's "center of gravity."[2]

Laurence Veysey recognized the importance of graduate education and research at Chicago, but he sensed that research was "blended" and "reconciled" with the aims of "public service" and "liberal culture." In *The Emergence of the American University*, Veysey argued that although Harper "promoted research with undeniable zeal," his emphasis was "uneven," and his primary aim was empire building. Veysey concluded that "Chicago never clearly 'stood for' anything in the sense that Cornell had stood for democracy and Johns Hopkins had stood for research." This observation suggests that Veysey did not appreciate the "cross purposes" of the university's founding fathers.[3]

Chicago

When Gates completed his survey, major plans for higher education were being developed by Baptists in Chicago, New York, and Washington. The first University of Chicago expired in 1886, due to its failure to pay off debts incurred with the construction of its main building. Following its foreclosure, Thomas W.

Goodspeed of the Baptist Union Theological Seminary in Morgan Park conceived a plan to establish a college as an adjunct to the seminary. Prior to 1886 the seminary held its classes at the first University of Chicago, which was situated on the south side of the city. In 1887 Goodspeed issued a two-thousand-word statement outlining his rationale for organizing a new university in Chicago. Observing that Baptists had no superior educational institution in the West, he argued that a "first class college" would "aid in raising up an educated ministry." He described Chicago as "the commercial, political, social, religious, educational center of a wide empire," and remarked that the proposed institution would certainly become "the greatest in our denomination." He decided that the cost of establishing a college in the city was prohibitive, and he recommended the suburb of Morgan Park, where Baptists were offered a $24,000 building, twenty acres of land, and a $5,000 pledge for a new college building. Goodspeed added that he had already acquired the 7,000-volume library of the first University of Chicago, and that certain members of the seminary faculty were willing to assist the college in its opening years by volunteering to teach. With the provision of "ample grounds, two buildings, a library and $150,000 endowment," the Baptist brethren would rally, student enrollment would swell, new departments would be added, and the college would finally rank with such leading Baptist universities as Rochester and Hamilton. His proposal was endorsed by William Rainey Harper, a former instructor at the seminary, who had rejected an opportunity to be president of the first University of Chicago prior to its closing. Goodspeed estimated that this project would require a founder's pledge of at least $50,000, and in January 1887 he and Harper wrote to enlist the support of Standard Oil Company president John D. Rockefeller, a leading patron of the seminary.[4]

Rockefeller reviewed the Goodspeed and Harper communications, and referred them to Rochester Theological Seminary president Augustus Hopkins Strong, whom he had known in Cleveland's Baptist circles. Strong was an alumnus of Yale College and of the Rochester Theological Seminary who had also studied at the University of Berlin. Strong was "happy to commend Dr. Goodspeed's plan," but he qualified this by observing that the Morgan Park Seminary was "planted in the mud" in a "forlorn" setting twelve miles south of Chicago. He sensed that another feeble college would fail to attract Chicago students and Chicago philanthropy, arguing instead that the institution should be placed in the city with a much larger endowment.[5]

New York

Rockefeller's apparent interest in the Morgan Park proposal prompted Strong to reinstate an earlier plan of his for a Baptist university in New York City. In his correspondence with Rockefeller, beginning in January 1887, Strong had described the deficiencies of Baptist higher education and the need for a Baptist university at the nation's commercial capital. He reported that the Baptists were "unspeakably behindhand" in educational matters: instead of building for the future, they were allowing rival denominations to surpass them in educational planning. The denomination had no seminary equal to the Union Theological Seminary in New York, and no college as influential as the leading eastern colleges. The "best and brightest" Baptists were deserting the denomination to study at Harvard, Yale, and Princeton. He proposed a university, combined with a theological seminary, "where, as at Johns Hopkins, there shall be a large number of fellowships, where research shall be endowed, where the brightest men shall be attracted and helped through their studies, where the institution itself shall furnish a real society of people distinguished in science and art." In a later postscript he remarked that the institution would not compete with any Baptist college or seminary—that it would be "a University proper, an institution for advanced students only," and that his principal objective was the "endowment of higher education and research."[6]

During the summer of 1887, Strong vacationed with Rockefeller in Europe and presented "the whole story" of his plan for a graduate university in New York. He had developed and discussed his ideas with Rockefeller beginning in 1880, and later he outlined them in *A Detailed Argument and Plan,* which he distributed to leaders of the Baptist Church. In this pamphlet he defined the university as a graduate institution with no college. It would offer professional training and train original investigators. Strong was familiar with the writings of Daniel Coit Gilman and with the founding of Johns Hopkins University, and he felt that Hopkins had compromised its high standards by including a college in its plans. He urged the Baptists to institute "a true University of the highest sort" in emulation of the world-leading University of Berlin.[7]

Strong believed that a metropolis was the only suitable location for such a university. He reported that European students were trained in major cities, and he predicted a similar development for the United States. He detected two signs of this shift: graduates of Yale were leaving New Haven to study law, medicine, and theology in New York; and the Harvard Medical School had been moved to Boston. Strong suspected that Cambridge and New Haven were destined to decline as America became more urbanized. He also felt that the founder of Stanford may have imperiled its prospects by locating it on a farm in Palo Alto. He urged the Baptists to "capture New York" by creating "a true university." He imagined it "on the grounds of the present Bloomingdale Asylum," which was located between Broadway and Amsterdam Avenue just north of 116th Street.[8]

Strong estimated that his university would require an initial endowment of $4 million, and sixteen annual supplements of $1 million, for a total of $20 million. He envisioned a Department of Philosophy and Arts something like the philosophical faculty at Johns Hopkins, with professorships in "Philosophy, Political Economy, Rhetoric, Logic, Sanskrit, Greek, Latin, German, French, English, Romance Languages, Comparative Philology, History, Mathematics, [and] Pedagogics." He proposed "the endowment of medical research" and studies in "Astronomy, Physics, Chemistry, Biology, Morphology, Applied Mathematics, Geology, Mineralogy, Electricity, Zoology, Agriculture, Botany, Mechanical Engineering, Civil Engineering, [and] Optics." An endowment for the sciences would support "original research." On this subject he remarked that the investigations of professors at Johns Hopkins, such as physicist Henry A. Rowland, had earned Johns Hopkins "a name throughout the civilized world." Like Johns Hopkins, his university would promote the higher work, but it would exclude undergraduates and provide schools of law, medicine, and theology. Strong's emphasis on graduate education and scientific research added a new dimension to the Baptist discussions.[9]

Despite its progressive features, his plan contained several concessions to Baptist evangelicalism. The theology department would occupy "the centre of the whole." The science departments would be expected to supplement the "half-truth" of evolutionism by supporting "God's creatorship, governance and miraculous interposition." Infidels would be excluded from the faculty. The university president would be an ordained Baptist minister who had mastered the tenets of "moral science." Instead of mirroring the methods of the German seminar, the university would require "frequent recitation and examination." And it would propagate "distinctively Christian truth."[10]

On 24 September 1887 Strong met with William Rainey Harper to enlist his support for this plan. Following their brief encounter, Strong told Rockefeller that the Yale professor viewed it as a "practicable plan," which would "transform our whole denomination in ten years, both in New York and in the country." He remarked that Harper was willing to "give his whole life to such enterprise if he could further it." But he added that Yale president Timothy Dwight was trying to keep him in New Haven by offering him the headship of a department of linguistics, and by asking him "to organize at Yale somewhat the same scheme of general linguistic study by post-graduates which I want him to do in New York." Strong described Harper as a teacher, scholar, and editor of Old Testament studies. As an editor he was "trying to imitate the work of the Professors at Johns Hopkins, who spread abroad in periodicals printed with the sanction of the University, the results of the investigations made in their several departments." Strong argued that the loss of Harper would be "the greatest loss our denomination has sustained during this century." And four days after their meeting, he reported: "Professor Harper sees that there is no possibility of New Haven's competing with

New York in University instruction and therefore jumps at the chance of carrying out my plan." In urging Rockefeller to act immediately on the proposal, Strong's proddings apparently became excessive. On 30 November, Rockefeller decided to end all further discussion. His decision delivered a deathblow to Strong's project, but these aspirations were not forgotten.[11]

At the beginning of November, Rockefeller had arranged a private meeting with Harper. Harper later confided to one of his assistants that Rockefeller had taken him "riding in Central Park behind a span of very valuable horses, that they had talked for hours, that Mr. R. had put him through the greatest examination he had ever been subjected to, asking him all about his plans, his family, his studies, etc. etc. and had unfolded to him a plan he was considering of putting $8 [million] or $10,000,000 into the founding of a great University in New York City in which he wished Dr. Harper to have a leading place." The ride in Central Park marked a major turning point in the Baptist negotiations: Harper sensed that Rockefeller was planning a great graduate university, and he became a key negotiator in the events that followed.[12]

Washington

In addition to the Baptist plans for Morgan Park and New York, President James C. Welling was hoping to transform Columbian University in Washington, D.C., into a national university—the realization of the plans of George Washington, Thomas Jefferson, and James Madison to erect "A Great National University at the Seat of the Federal Government." Welling described Washington as the science capital of the United States, and as the annual gathering place of American learned societies. Under leaders such as Columbian University trustee Joseph Henry, the city had assembled a corps of some six hundred scientists. It was also the headquarters of several societies of science, including the Anthropological Society, the Biological Society, the Botanical Society, the Chemical Society, the Mathematical Section of the Philosophical Society, and the National Geographic Society. The city boasted America's largest libraries, and the National Museum collections of natural history, archeology, ethnology, orientalia, and Native American artifacts.[13]

Welling pointedly observed that Harvard, Yale, and Princeton had to fund their own libraries, laboratories, and museums; but Columbian could utilize the abundant resources of the federal government. He also noted that Andrew Dickson White, the former president of Cornell, had suggested that a "great university" in Washington might equal the University of Berlin in the achievements of its faculty. Welling reported that Columbian had already established a college, and schools of science, medicine, dentistry, and law. He planned to establish "a

School of Politics and of Public Economy," and studies in humanities, linguistics, pedagogy, philosophy, and theology. He expected to promote faculty research, and to encourage the publication of research findings in fields such as comparative philology, Egyptology, Assyriology, and "the new Psychology." He urged the Baptists to act quickly lest a "full-fledged" university such as Johns Hopkins be established in Washington by another group. Welling's ideas were remarkably similar to those of Augustus Strong. In fact he confided that his plan was "precisely Strong's," and that he hoped to abolish Columbian's college. In 1888 a committee appointed by the American Baptist Education Society reviewed the Columbian proposal. Prominent among its members was William Rainey Harper.[14]

Negotiating the University of Chicago

Proponents of the Chicago, New York, and Washington proposals shared one thing in common: they were waiting for John D. Rockefeller. On 13 October 1888 he appeared in Poughkeepsie and met with Vassar College president James M. Taylor and William Rainey Harper, who was teaching weekend Bible study classes. Harper reported to Goodspeed that during this visit Rockefeller "talked for hours in reference to the scheme of establishing the great University at Chicago instead of New York." Rockefeller had compiled "a list of reasons why it would be better to go to Chicago than to remain in New York," and Harper felt that the New York endowment might be "diverted to Chicago." Harper reported that Rockefeller was "practically committed to the thing," and that the "great plan" was for "(1) a college and university at Chicago; (2) a theological seminary of high grade in New York City; (3) the organization of colleges in the West." Harper felt that the plan was "absolutely certain," and that the scale of the institution was the only matter unresolved. He sensed that Rockefeller was prepared to endow a much larger project than the Morgan Park proposal, and he added: "I have every time claimed that nothing less than four millions would be satisfactory to begin with, and have expressed my desire for five."[15]

Two days after this meeting, Gates presented his findings on Baptist higher education at a conference in Chicago, and a copy of his report was sent to Harper and Rockefeller. The report reinforced the perception that a college in Chicago was a Baptist priority. During the summer of 1888, Gates had been pondering "the Baptist educational chess board" for a strategic move that would solve the denomination's problems. He opposed the further endowment of its "neglected, feeble, and ill-patronized colleges," which were "condemned to an early death by reason of impossible locations in remote country hamlets." After reviewing a manuscript of Strong's proposal, he concluded that the Baptists would be reluctant to adopt a "great supplemental University," even though the idea was supported by "some forty leading Baptist divines and influential laymen of the East." And Strong had indicated that Rockefeller was not prepared to launch a $20 million project. Gates was also skeptical about the Washington proposal. He characterized the nation's capital as a transient community, lacking in "permanent local wealth." He felt that federal libraries, laboratories, and museums could never replace the privately held resources of a university, and he concluded that a national university in Washington was "illusory." He perceived that the Baptists would be more receptive to a national network of academies and colleges that would address local community needs. And he felt that Strong's scheme might be trimmed at the top, and broadened at the base, into a symmetrical educational system, "graduated from the home upward," with a university in New York and colleges and academies strategically planted throughout the United States. Gates predicted that Rockefeller would be captivated by "a scheme so vast, so continental, so orderly, so comprehensive, so detailed." And Gates thought that Strong would be willing to revise his plan accordingly.[16]

On 9 November, Goodspeed proposed a $2 million college in Chicago and a Rockefeller pledge of $1.5 million. Sensing that the plan had been compromised, Harper recommended "a University of the highest character, having also a college." Goodspeed was concerned about Augustus Strong's reaction to the Chicago proposal, and he urged Harper to disavow the notion that the "great University" was being planned for Chicago. Goodspeed envisioned "a first class College with certain graduate departments, a western Yale." And he wrote to Gates: "In regard to Dr. Strong, he is really in favor of what we want here. We do not want the great University he has planned consisting of post graduate departments only, to cost $30,000,000 or $40,000,000. . . . But we do want an institution of the first rank among American institutions and I understand Dr. S. to favor this." Sensing that Strong's support was needed to consummate the plan, Goodspeed cautioned Gates to project a more modest image of the Chicago proposal: Strong "should be led to feel that this is not his University transferred to Chicago but something radically different."[17]

On 3 December 1888 Gates presented an edited version of his Chicago address to the Executive Board of the American Baptist Education Society in Washington. At the organizational meeting of the society in May 1888 some of its prominent members expected the Columbian University project to be a Baptist priority, and a majority of the Executive Board was selected accordingly. The meeting was held on the Columbian University campus, and Washington was expected to become the national headquarters of the society. James C. Welling referred to the Columbian proposal as "the first duty of Baptists." Harper countered by reporting that John D. Rockefeller had endorsed the Chicago plan. The board voted unanimously to establish a "thoroughly equipped Baptist institution of learning in Chicago," and this project became a Baptist priority. Strong and Welling sensed that these developments would not eclipse their plans, and they resumed their respective campaigns for the "great university."[18]

In January 1889 Gates recommended to Rockefeller that the question of a university at Chicago should be "held in abeyance," and that the founding of a college would "almost of necessity be the exclusive work of the earlier years." Gates felt that a college in Chicago was a denominational priority, but he opposed the endowment of a "great university" in Washington, New York, or Chicago. Rockefeller asked Gates to evaluate the viability of the Chicago proposal, and a nine-member Committee of Inquiry, headed by Harper, endorsed the basic points of a paper submitted by Goodspeed for a Baptist college in Chicago. On 18 May 1889 the American Baptist Education Society endorsed the Chicago proposal, and Gates announced that Rockefeller would contribute $600,000 for the college.[19]

Once the Chicago proposal was adopted, Harper became the leading candidate for the college presidency. Augustus Strong questioned his religious orthodoxy, and Yale president Timothy Dwight offered him the deanship of the faculty of philosophy and fine arts and the headship of the Semitics department. But Harper, as Gates recalled, was mainly concerned about continuing "his chosen life work of Old Testament research, criticism, and instruction." Goodspeed wrote that Harper was ultimately drawn to Chicago primarily because of his interest in creating a university, as opposed to a college. On 31 July 1890 Harper wrote to Goodspeed that "what ought to be done, what the denomination will expect, what the world will expect" could be achieved only with "an assurance of an additional million." And on 9 August 1890 Harper wrote to Rockefeller:

> The denomination and indeed the whole country, are expecting the University of Chicago to be from the very beginning an institution of the highest rank and character. Already it is talked of in connection with Yale, Harvard, Princeton, Johns Hopkins, the University of Michigan and Cornell. No one expects that it will be in any respect lower in grade and equipment than the average of the institutions to which I have referred, and yet with the money pledged I cannot understand how the expectations can be fulfilled. Naturally we ought to be willing to begin small and to grow, but in these days when things are done so rapidly and with the example of Johns Hopkins before our eyes, it seems a great pity to wait for growth when we might be born full-fledged.[20]

This letter, and Rockefeller's response to it, marked a major turning point in the negotiations. Harper was signaling to Rockefeller that a small Baptist college in

Chicago was unacceptable to him: that Baptists needed a great university similar to the one envisioned by Augustus Strong. Rockefeller responded with an additional pledge of $1 million, thus making possible a graduate institution. Harper, however, intensified his campaign for "the great university." In November 1890 he proposed the merger of Columbian University with the University of Chicago, and confided that his coming to Chicago was contingent on this. According to Gates, Harper sought this merger "tenaciously" until the end of his life.[21]

In his personal "Reminiscences," Goodspeed argued that "Dr. Strong's great graduate University in Chicago" was "almost precisely" what Harper wanted, "and what in case he became its President he was determined to have." Goodspeed elaborated:

> He wanted from the outset a great graduate University, with an undergraduate department as a temporary concession to the weakness of the founder and the Chicago brethren. He did not hesitate to say that it was his purpose to transfer the work of the Junior College to Morgan Park. His plan was a graduate University. Under the pressure of the opposing views of Mr. Rockefeller, Mr. Gates and myself & the impossibility of securing the necessary initial fund of four million dollars, he temporarily gave up, or seemed to give up. But he renounced at the same time any intention of accepting the Presidency, which Mr. Gates & I, from the first, insisted he must take. The presidency of a mere college had no attraction for him.

At this stage Harper became the key player in the negotiations. His recognition as the leading candidate for the college presidency, and his stature as a leading Baptist scholar, became his bargaining chips.[22]

William Rainey Harper

As he approached the prospect of creating "Dr. Strong's great graduate University in Chicago," Harper capitalized on his experience as a student, teacher, editor, and scholar. He began his meteoric career as an undergraduate at Muskingum College in New Concord, Ohio. In 1875, when he was eighteen years old, he completed his doctoral studies at Yale and received one of the first Ph.D.'s awarded at an American university.[23] He taught successively at Masonic College in Macon, Tennessee; at Denison University in Granville, Ohio; and at the Baptist Union Theological Seminary in Morgan Park, Illinois. He established the American Institute of Hebrew, served as principal of the Chautauqua College of Liberal Arts, and edited two journals: the *Hebrew Student,* which was later called the *Old Testament*

Student, and *Hebraica.* In 1886 he accepted a professorship in Semitic languages at Yale and an instructorship in Hebrew at the Yale Divinity School. Three years later he was appointed Woolsey Professor of Biblical Literature at Yale.[24]

In the decade prior to the opening of the University of Chicago, Harper's interest in higher education and research was reflected primarily in his journal articles and editorials. In the first issue of the *Hebrew Student,* he alerted his American readers to some of the heated controversies of German scholarship, including the publication of Julius Welhausen's *History of Israel* and the ensuing debate over the authorship of the first five books of the Bible. In his earliest journals he described the progress of Semitic and biblical studies in Germany and listed examples of courses offered at the German universities. These reports were prominent features of Harper's journals. In 1884 he founded *Hebraica,* a more specialized journal of Semitic philology intended to "encourage original investigation" and to serve as a medium of communication for Semitic scholars.[25]

In the second issue of the *Hebrew Student,* Harper wrote that Germany was the world leader in Old Testament and Semitic scholarship: "In no other country do men give themselves up so entirely, so unreservedly to research and investigation; in no other country do men go down so deep." Harper qualified this by suggesting that German "depth" sometimes bewildered the American scholar, who preferred less "depth" and greater clarity. He observed that German academics were excessive in research, while Americans emphasized teaching at the expense of investigation. In his later notes on progress at the German universities, he suggested that German scholars were superior to American scholars because the latter had not discovered "the secret of independent research and original investigation." Harper argued that American scholars used reference books and "second-hand" interpretations rather than primary authors and original sources.[26]

In American universities, reports on Old Testament and Semitic scholarship also appeared as regular features of his journals. In 1886 he contested the notion that an American student needed to "finish" his work at a European university. Sensing that the benefits of European study were overrated, he argued that American academics were generally better teachers. German research findings were accessible to American students in the numerous publications of the German presses, and an American student would profit most from European study when he could "stand alone," after mastering the rudiments of his subject. In 1890 he saw signs that "investigation, as distinguished from mere teaching," was beginning in the leading American universities.[27]

In the field of Semitic philology Harper outlined a research agenda for scholars. His long checklist of challenges included the discovery, interpretation, and publication of Arabic, Aramaic, Assyrian, Babylonian, Hittite, and Phoenician inscriptions; publication of a Semitic comparative grammar and Assyrian and Hebrew lexicons; the study of civilizations antecedent to the Semites; the study of Israel's tribal religions; the publication of a biblical theology; the preparation of a Hebrew dictionary and introductory texts for the study of Chaldee, Syriac, Ethiopic, Arabic, and Assyrian; studies in Semitic ethnology and biblical chronology; and a scholarly introduction to the Old Testament in English.[28]

Harper's Plans

Harper began his work as president of the University of Chicago on 1 July 1891, fifteen months before the opening day of classes. His organizational plans were outlined in six official bulletins, which described the work of the colleges, the academies, the graduate schools, the divinity school, and the extension division. Gates, Goodspeed, and Harper were concerned about Augustus Strong's reaction to Harper's organizational plan, and the official bulletins describe a university with broad educational aims, an institution "radically different" from Strong's graduate university. In his educational plans for undergraduates he proposed an academic college comprising the first two years of undergraduate work, and a university college comprising the third and fourth years. In marking the sharp division between the lower and the higher work, he stressed that the curriculum of the first two years of college was simply an extension of secondary education at a somewhat higher level. In his "First Annual Report," which was never published, he remarked that the aim of the last two years of college was to introduce students to the methods of research, and he predicted that the secondary schools would eventually absorb the lower work of the academic college. At this juncture graduate education was his primary aim.[29]

In his official bulletin on the graduate schools Harper outlined specific requirements for an LL.D. degree for scholars who had already earned their Ph.D. degrees. The bulletin stated that candidates for this degree were expected to pursue three more years of graduate work beyond the Ph.D., and to submit a thesis "scholarly in character, exhaustive in its subject matter." Harper felt that the investigator alone was qualified to teach the methods of research, and that students would never acquire this knowledge except by example. He remarked that the investigator needed a carefree environment, time, and "liberty of thought." Periodically teachers would be excused from lectures to permit them to "give their entire time to the work of investigation." Harper created a faculty comprised of head professors, professors, nonresident professors, associate professors, assistant professors, instructors, tutors, docents, readers, lecturers, fellows, and scholars. The appointment of docents and fellows was expected to promote research. A docent was "required to spend one-half his time in original investigation under the guidance of the Professor, the other half being devoted to the giving of instruction in his particular specialty." A fellow was "required to spend five-sixths of his time in original investigation under the guidance of the Professor, one-sixth being reserved for service in connection with the University." Each department was expected to publish "either a Journal or a series of separate studies," embodying the research of its faculty. Harper stated, "Promotion of younger men in the departments will depend more largely upon the results of their work as investigators than upon the efficiency of their teaching, although the latter will by no means be overlooked."[30]

In his "First Annual Report," Harper remarked that the university would promote the primacy of research and the subordination of teaching. He repeated this at the annual meeting of the American Baptist Education Society in 1892:

> To arouse in the mind of the student a desire for research, however low or high may be the grade of the student, is the greatest accomplishment of the teacher. To do this, the teacher must set the example, must himself be constantly searching for new truth. It is this which gives freshness and life to the work of the class room. Investigation, therefore, is the first thing, mere teaching is secondary.

At the same meeting, Gates announced that the University of Chicago would be primarily a research institution for college graduates, affording opportunities "not surpassed by the German universities." He contrasted Chicago with Harvard, Yale, and Princeton, which he characterized as colleges. And he recalled that the idea of founding "a costly graduate school" was first suggested by Strong.[31]

In his personal "Reminiscences," Goodspeed referred to "that curious working of cross purposes which came very near disastrous consequences in the history of the new University." He elaborated:

> When at the first meeting at Vassar Mr. Rockefeller suggested that Chicago rather than New York was the location for the University, Dr. Harper supposed he meant Dr. Strong's great graduate University, whereas Mr. Rockefeller had nothing of this sort in mind. He was thinking of University in the ordinary sense, as he knew American Universities, a high grade college out of which there should develop, in course of time, more or less rapidly, a great University with many graduate departments, including, perhaps in the end *every* department of learning.

Goodspeed argued that Harper had misinterpreted this meeting in Poughkeepsie: that Rockefeller did not wish to establish the great university in Chicago.

Goodspeed recalled that Harper was captivated by the thought of creating the great university—that it became the great prepossession of his life. Goodspeed, Gates, and Rockefeller were planning a college. Harper was planning a university. The university's opening years were profoundly affected by these "cross purposes."[32]

The Opening

Harper emphasized graduate education and faculty research at the first meeting of the senior faculty. He mentioned the possibility of moving first- and second-year college students to another campus in order to focus the university's resources on the higher work. At this stage he accepted the colleges as a compromise, as a temporary concession to Rockefeller, Gates, Goodspeed, and the Chicago Baptists; but he envisioned a graduate research institution. E. H. Moore recalled that during the first year, Harper "made us all feel his conception of a research institution of the highest grade as the goal of our efforts."[33]

Harper emphasized graduate work at the university's first convocation in January 1893. He viewed the opening convocation as an opportunity to "bind together into a unity the many complex and diverging forms of activity which constitute our university life and work." George E. Vincent, who joined the university as assistant in sociology, described the original faculty as an embodiment of "divers customs, habits, and ideals"—individuals from Harvard, Yale, Cornell, Michigan, Wisconsin, Johns Hopkins, Berlin, Freiburg, Leipzig, Oxford, and Cambridge—each embracing "a peculiar conception of a university." Vincent reported conflicts among the bearers of competing ideals: "The sons of Harvard praised the ways of Cambridge; the men from New Haven had much to say of the Yale spirit; the Hopkins doctors and the Germans were keen for research; the men of the Middle West were a bit impatient with what they deemed the conservatism of the East." Harper wrote that the greatest problem confronting the university was that of whether or not the faculty, comprised of individuals "representing many different types of educational thought, would work together harmoniously and with one common spirit." Sociologist Albion W. Small remarked that no president of a university "ever assumed a more formidable task of unifying unlike individuals in one faculty."[34]

Robert Herrick, an instructor in Chicago's English department, wondered what prototype the university would adopt: whether it would become "the American college with its group of professional schools, or the English Oxford with its care for the individual soul or the German university." Herrick hinted that the institution was conceived at the beginning of the "post-graduate" era. He contrasted the creation of specialists at Chicago, and its "serious, scholarly atmosphere," with the emphasis on character formation in the New England college. He reported that a growing graduate enrollment in the West was promoting a more general recognition of the Ph.D., and he predicted that the West would benefit from Chicago's doctors of philosophy.[35]

The "Dark Side"

Herrick was optimistic about the university's future, but there were obstacles to its lofty ambitions. In his early convocation statements Harper observed that the western colleges, which provided the lion's share of the university's graduate students, were not equipped to do the higher work. The endowment was also a "dark side of the picture." Millions of dollars had been pledged, but most of this income was restricted to instruction. Harper stated that in order to "meet the purposes of a university as distinguished from a college," the institution needed funds for books and apparatus. University libraries and laboratories, he said, had yet to receive one dollar where they should have received five. This lack of resources was perhaps a result of Goodspeed's suggestion to Rockefeller that the founder's gifts should be used for endowment, and not for buildings, books, or apparatus. Goodspeed felt that funds from other sources would provide these, but his remarks were made when the institution was conceived as a college.[36]

Rockefeller was also influenced by Augustus Strong. In 1887 Strong suggested that, like Johns Hopkins, the great Baptist university should begin without a large educational plant: "Bricks and mortar, the erection of buildings, should be the last thing. Temporary accommodations will answer, as at Johns Hopkins, until the thing gets a good start." Strong asserted that the university's permanence would depend on the "endowment of instruction." Like Johns Hopkins, it "might begin with rented quarters." Rockefeller undoubtedly pondered these remarks. Aware that the first University of Chicago had failed due to an indebtedness incurred with the construction of its main building, his initial gift of $600,000 was designated as an endowment for "current expenses," and "not for land, buildings, or repairs." His second gift of $1 million provided an endowment for graduate work, theological education, and a dormitory for the Divinity School. His third gift of $1 million provided an endowment for faculty salaries and fellowships, and $5,000 for books and apparatus. These gifts provided generous salaries for Chicago's head professors, but provisions for aiding faculty research, such as libraries and laboratories and funding for specific research projects, were not included in the early Rockefeller gifts.[37]

Throughout the Harper administration, the university's annual expenditures exceeded its income, and Rockefeller provided additional funds to cover these deficits. Goodspeed wrote that funds for the "highly developed graduate University" that Harper envisioned were "ludicrously inadequate." Its financial problems began in 1892, when $185,000 was budgeted for faculty salaries and $250,000 was actually spent. At the end of the first year the board of trustees discovered that the university was already $500,000 in debt. At the outset of the worsening economic conditions caused by the financial panic of 1893, board of trustees president Martin Ryerson recommended the elimination of all expenditures for books and apparatus, cuts in staff, and the elimination of the summer quarter. Harper threatened to resign if these measures were adopted. On 21 August 1893 the *New York Daily Tribune* reported: "While there are no debts pressing heavily on the university (to the knowledge of the journalist), the trustees find it impossible to carry out at present plans for the development of the great school as projected, and an unpleasant postponement of certain proposed improvements is unavoidable." In October the university received a Rockefeller pledge of $500,000, but its deficits amounted to $53,000 in 1894, $47,000 in 1895, and $97,000 in 1896. In October 1895 Rockefeller provided an additional $1 million for endowment, and pledged an additional $2 million to match other gifts. As a result the university received $5 million. Most of these gifts were used to cover earlier expenditures, and to provide new buildings and equipment, and the tradition of deficit spending continued.[38]

Another "dark side of the picture" was the university's provisions for science research. Some of Harper's head professors of science, and particularly those recruited from Clark University, envisioned science laboratories at Chicago comparable to those in Germany, and most of them expected to work at a graduate research institution. However, Rockefeller's early gifts to the university did not support this work. They provided a generous endowment for teaching, a dormitory for the Divinity School, a power plant, a dormitory for the Morgan Park Academy, a building for the University of Chicago Press, a building for the Law School, a temporary building for the junior college women, a temporary building for the School of Education, and a building for the secondary school. They did not provide the "material requisites" for science research, such as laboratories, observatories, and equipment. During the Harper administration, these "material requisites" were provided almost exclusively by Chicagoans. The university received major gifts for the advancement of science from Charles T. Yerkes, Helen Culver, Sidney A. Kent, and Martin Ryerson; and a major bequest from the estate of William H. Ogden; but even these funds failed to provide the facilities envisioned by Chicago's head professors.[39]

In 1903 the University of Chicago issued the Decennial Publications, summarizing the major achievements of its academic units during the first ten years. In the first volume of these publications, Rollin D. Salisbury, dean of the Ogden Graduate School of Science, described the state of teaching and research in each of the university's departments of science. He reported that some departments were adequately established, but others lacked "space, apparatus, and books," and all could utilize "a larger equipment and a larger instructional and investigative force." Some departments were occupying temporary quarters, some instructors were overburdened with teaching, and most departments needed larger laboratories, more equipment, more books and better library facilities, funds for specific research projects, and more time for investigation. Salisbury reported "epoch-making" investigations in some sectors, but he found that the university had generally failed to make adequate provisions for research, and many departments had reached the stage where a small appropriation might result in major returns. At the university's Decennial Celebration in 1901, Martin Ryerson acknowledged the university's failure to provide "the material requisites" for scientific and scholarly research, and remarked that the institution's rapid growth had made it impossible to promote this work.[40]

In 1901 the *Dial* reported that the University of Chicago had outlived its reputation as "the Baptist school on the Midway," that it was recognized for promoting the highest standard of scholarship, and that the proportion of "highly-distinguished scholars" on its faculty was probably equal to that of any American university. The article, written anonymously, explained that Chicago had "from the beginning encouraged original research," and that members of its faculty—in the departments of "physics, physiology, economics, sociology, anthropology, and classical philology"—had added considerably to knowledge. Reflecting on "the leading idea for which this University has stood," the writer suggested that "educational experimentation," rather than research, was its dominant feature.[41]

Teaching

At the beginning of his administration, Harper emphasized the primacy of research and graduate work. He expected to move the academic college to Morgan Park and focus the university's resources on the higher work. This plan was opposed by Rockefeller, Gates, and Goodspeed. When he realized that Rockefeller was not planning to create Strong's great graduate university in Chicago, or to support the level of research envisioned by Chicago's head professors, and when he realized that gifts and bequests from Chicago's other major donors would not adequately support this work, he promoted instead the university's vast horizontal expansion. He developed plans for a college of commerce and administration, a law school, a medical school, a school of education, and a school of technology. Teaching and the work of the colleges became increasingly prominent in his organizational plan.[42]

These developments gradually shifted the university's "center of gravity." Harper never explained why graduate education and faculty research were no longer primary, or why teaching and undergraduate work were no longer subordinate but equally important. Rather, this change was reflected chiefly in his quarterly statements, in one of his articles on higher education, and in a letter to mathematician E. H. Moore. In a quarterly statement presented in 1896, Harper referred to the University of Chicago as a teaching institution and observed that its junior instructors were neglecting their teaching responsibilities. He remarked that although the young instructor might prefer to spend all his time on research, the university could not endow this as a full-time activity, and all instructors were expected to teach. In 1899 he rejected the notion that graduate education was primary. Writing to E. H. Moore, he remarked that college and graduate work were of equal importance. Harper also criticized the higher learning in Europe. He observed that some Americans, after taking their Ph.D.'s abroad, were teaching research methods to college freshmen and sophomores, which he regarded as a total waste of time. He attacked "the German experience" and the tendency of some Americans "to Germanize everything," and asserted that studies at a German university had injured many Americans. In 1902 he reported that the work of the faculty consisted of teaching, research, and administration; and that all three functions were of equal importance. He applauded the well-rounded academic who divided his time among these three activities. Registration statistics suggest that Chicago did not emerge as the graduate institution envisioned by Harper. In 1905, for example, the university had 1,140 graduate students and 2,307 students in the various colleges; and a major portion of faculty time was spent on undergraduates.[43]

The gradual weakening of the research imperative was also reflected in Rollin D. Salisbury's report, which appeared in the Decennial Report in 1903. Salisbury suggested that teaching and research were the twin aims of the university's science departments—that their "first effort" was "to make provision for their students," and their second "to make themselves centers of investigative work." He observed that the American university had only recently recognized research as one of its central aims, and that it was expected to become a dominant feature in the future. But he argued that research "should not be allowed to overshadow or in any way dwarf the work of instruction." He criticized the tendency to belittle teaching, and asserted that "the two great phases of university work should be developed side by side."[44]

The recognition of teaching and undergraduate work, which were "secondary" when the university opened, represented a major change in the university's trajectory, and this change was also reflected in Harper's plans for horizontal expansion. In 1901 he estimated that an additional $26,635,000 was required to "round out" his plans for the university, including $9,910,000 for new buildings and land and $7,450,000 for Schools of Art, Medicine, Music, and Technology. Goodspeed reported that most of Harper's projects were launched without sufficient capitalization, because of inaccurate estimates of costs and means, and because of Harper's "well-founded" faith in the resources of the founder. In 1903 the budget committee of the board of trustees, led by Harper and Martin Ryerson, met with Gates and John D. Rockefeller Jr. to assess the university's mounting deficits. Following this conference, the founder denied any further endowment to the university, and Harper requested a six-month leave of absence. He retreated to the grounds of the Yerkes Observatory and resumed his work as a scholar.[45]

In 1904 Rockefeller appointed Starr J. Murphy, personal friend of Frederick T. Gates, to investigate the university's financial condition. For the 1904–1905 academic year, the university's deficit was expected to reach $245,761. Murphy reported a prevalent lack of budgetary restraint: the celebrated Decennial Publications, a multivolume collection of monographs representing the university's first efforts in scientific and scholarly research, were more costly than expected; the university's eleven journals might be published by learned societies. He opposed the policy of promoting younger instructors and argued that their departures would promote the work of other institutions, and cited a report indicating that faculty salaries at Harvard could be trimmed by $25,000 without compromising the interests of the undergraduates. Characterizing the university's financial state as "perilous in the extreme," he recommended a reconstitution of the board of trustees. He informed Rockefeller that an additional endowment of $7 million was required to cover deficits, and he advised him to withhold any further funding until firmer management was in sight. He urged the university to balance its budget, reduce the size of its faculty, and abandon any plans for further expansion.[46]

Responding to Murphy's findings, Goodspeed remarked that he had always opposed rapid institutional growth, and that the recommendations should be accepted. Goodspeed sensed, however, that Murphy was somewhat biased. As an alumnus of a small college, he had developed a "deep rooted distrust" of a large university: "Its multi-form life is an offence to him. Its function of research he cannot appreciate. The fact that a man, engaged in important and far reaching investigation teaches little is evidence that he is receiving money he has not earned." Dean Harry P. Judson felt that Murphy's findings challenged the university's founding principles, which included (1) graduate instruction and research, (2) freedom to pursue original investigation, and (3) a small student-faculty ratio. He agreed that the university might save money by changing its policy with regard to teaching, but not without sacrificing some of these principles. Their loss would shift the university's "center of gravity" from graduate education and faculty research to undergraduate teaching, and the University of Chicago would "thereby sink to the level of the many institutions which, while really colleges, are adding a small portion of advanced work in the hands of overburdened teachers under the name of a graduate school."[47]

The Colleges

During the course of his administration, Harper became a prominent figure in American higher education and a leading spokesman for higher learning. His discussions with university presidents Nicholas Murray Butler, Charles W. Eliot, Daniel Coit Gilman, and Benjamin Ide Wheeler resulted in the founding of the Association of American Universities, which promoted higher standards for the Ph.D. But Harper was also interested in the lower work. At the University of Chicago, he created a College of Commerce and Administration, a College of Education, a College of Religious and Social Science, and a College for Teachers. He envisioned a College of Practical Arts and a Railway College. He became a principal organizer of the North Central Association of Colleges and Secondary Schools, which promoted higher standards of college education. In the Decennial Report, and in a proposal to Andrew Carnegie, he envisioned a foundation to promote the work of the colleges, which included a national scholarship program and a plan for creating higher admission standards. He published several textbooks for college students, served as superintendent of Sunday schools at the Hyde Park Baptist Church, became an active member of the Chicago Board of Education, and lectured on college campuses throughout the United States. In his capacity as head professor of the Department of Semitic Languages and Literature, he taught courses for undergraduates. Titles of some of his writings on higher education reflect his interest in the college. These include "Alleged Luxury among College Students," "The College Officer and the College Student," "The College President," "Entrance Requirements—The Chicago System," "The Length of the College Course," "On Coeducation," "The Pay of American College Professors," "The Scientific Study of the Student," "Shall College Athletics Be Endowed?" and "The Situation of the Small College." In an article entitled "Higher Education in the West," he argued that the colleges of the West had reached a higher stage of evolution than the colleges of New England, and that the former were more practical, progressive, and serious.[48]

Shortly after the university opened, Harper created a system of university houses to promote "a college spirit." He recognized that a small college provided an environment that was lacking in a larger university. He promoted college athletics, gave "pep talks" to varsity football players, and marched in the band. In

1905 he established eight separate colleges for first- and second-year students, and the college meeting replaced the divisional lecture. Changes in the college curriculum during the Harper era reflected the university's vast horizontal expansion, and its founding of schools of law and education. The emphasis on research, appearing in his "First Annual Report," was supplanted by an emphasis on practical and professional training.[49]

One of Harper's lasting contributions to higher education was his plan to divide the four-year college program into two separate segments. He suggested that some American colleges, which were not equipped to do the higher work, should award an "Associate" degree at the end of the sophomore year. Physicist Robert A. Millikan recalled that Harper developed a German model for organizing American colleges into a university system. He imagined that students from other colleges would complete their first two years of undergraduate work and transfer to Chicago, where "real university work was to begin." Millikan added that Harper's plan was to elevate the standards of the American high school to those of the German *Gymnasium*. As a result of these reforms Harper was widely recognized as the founder of the junior college movement.[50]

Harper never rejected the idea of moving the first two years of college to another campus. This objective reappeared in his Decennial Report. His gradual acceptance of the standard model of a college with certain graduate departments and professional schools, and his gradual recognition of the equal importance of teaching and research, were perhaps a reflection of the sudden surge in college enrollment that occurred in the final decades of the nineteenth century. Harper was an avid player of the numbers game. Before the university opened, he predicted that within ten years Chicago's student body would be larger than that of Harvard or Yale. He achieved this by enrolling approximately two college students for every graduate student, and this ratio was maintained throughout his administration.[51]

Harper was also compromising with his fellow founding fathers. Gates felt that the Baptists should not have established another Johns Hopkins—that they should have focused on the founding of academies and "old-fashioned" colleges. In 1892 Goodspeed told Harper that Chicago could easily create "the greatest under-graduate school in the world." In 1897 he asserted, "If my views had prevailed, we should have had in Chicago an institution located on a single block of ground with three or four small buildings, and the character of the institution would have been simply that of a small but respectable college." Harper's acceptance of the colleges was also a matter of fiscal necessity. University of Chicago historian Barry Karl wrote that college work provided a firmer foundation than graduate work: "During the leaner years, undergraduate education with its steady assurances of tuition and conservative community support provided a more secure base for development than the ideals of graduate education, although the fact that the university had come into being on the strength of the latter revolution created a problem."[52]

Harper died before his fiftieth birthday, thirteen years after the university opened. At the end of the Harper administration, English professor John M. Manly reported that his colleagues had failed to do the research that was expected because they were working primarily with undergraduates. John U. Nef asserted that Chicago's growing enrollment of undergraduates had resulted in the subordination of graduate education and faculty research. Geologist Thomas C. Chamberlin recalled that Chicago was "dominantly collegiate" under Harper. And historian Francis W. Shepardson remarked that the opening chapter of the university's history was "largely the biography of President Harper."[53]

The Crisis of the Old Order
The Colleges in the 1890s

∼

ROGER L. GEIGER

he 1880s were the Indian summer for multipurpose colleges, an interlude of relative tranquillity although their season was nearly past. Perhaps it was coincidence that the number of colleges peaked in 1893, the year a financial panic touched off a severe economic downturn.[1] But hard times more likely aggravated conditions that were rooted in an increasingly anachronistic structure. The multipurpose colleges were denominationally based and locally focused in an age of diminishing sectarianism and expanding organizational scope. The years around 1890 were the fulcrum of impending change—the moment when the colleges slipped onto the defensive. At issue was the institutional division of labor in American education—where and for how long would preparatory, collegiate, professional, and advanced academic studies take place.[2]

Proponents of the new universities were most conspicuous in voicing doubts about the future viability of the existing collegiate system. President Eliot in some ways dropped the gauntlet when he urged that the college course be shortened to three years. Although a strong supporter of liberal education, he felt that a four-year course unduly delayed students planning professional studies and careers.[3] President Charles K. Adams of Cornell argued that the natural dividing line between college and university work occurred between the sophomore and junior years, where university students at this time made a de facto transition from required to elective courses. Daniel Coit Gilman of Johns Hopkins recognized the same breakpoint, but thought that colleges should incorporate the last two years of preparatory work, thus educating students from approximately ages sixteen to twenty.[4] Andrew D. White took a similar view, recommending that colleges become "intermediate institutions forming the connecting link between the public-school system and the university system," especially since competing with universities was "becoming more and more hopeless."[5]

Interestingly these "university men" took the traditional view of the college's essential role as a preparatory institution. This was the nub of the 1828 Yale Report, and it was the root as well of the college's own claim to four years of a student's life. As intermediate institutions, their true function was, according to the older view, "to create mental and moral power" through strenuous mental discipline; or in more modern terms, to convey "liberal culture" for its own sake.[6] This task required four years and provided the foundation for further practical, professional, or specialized studies. Around 1890, college defenders were condemning what they perceived to be encroachment from below by secondary schools,[7] while generally applauding the notion that universities ought to operate at a more rarefied, advanced level. In their minds the contemporary confusion over respective roles could be resolved if each grade of institution would confine itself to its own sphere. For the colleges, this meant explicit repudiation of university work.[8]

One expositor of this orderly tripartite division added a telling qualification to his scheme: "I do not include Normal schools, which are an anomaly in our system, as at present conducted, and which, like other professional and technical schools . . . should . . . *follow* and not *precede* a college course."[9] Much of advanced education in the United States, it would seem, did not square with this vision of the college's intermediate place. In fact the colleges had to come to terms with an expanding high school sector of as yet undefined scope, universities laying claim to the higher learning, and professional schools that had become uncoupled from collegiate education.

Secondary education was as amorphous as higher education before 1890. Bureau of Education figures did not even list public high schools as a separate category.[10] Overall, secondary education seems to have grown by about 75 percent during the 1880s, with enrollments in preparatory academies and collegiate preparatory departments, the principal feeders to the colleges, rising nearly as fast. After 1890, however, this picture changed. Private secondary and collegiate preparatory students increased only slightly in the 1890s, while public high school students jumped by 167 percent (table 11). Finding an accommodation with this mushrooming sector posed an acute problem for college admissions.

High schools were first established in the largest cities and gradually spread to other population centers. As terminal institutions for most students, they were only loosely articulated with other sectors, including the colleges. Just one in

TABLE 11

SECONDARY ENROLLMENTS AND GRADUATES, 1890–1900

	1890	1895	1900
Public Schools			
Enrollment	202,963	350,099	519,291
College Prep Students	29,289	48,146	56,202
College Prep Graduates	6,565	11,903	18,663
Private Schools			
Enrollment	94,981	118,347	110,797
College Prep Students	26,298	32,051	35,315
College Prep Graduates	4,923	5,733	5,673
Preparatory Departments in Colleges*			
Enrollment	47,911	54,012	56,285
"Graduates" [est. completers]	8,424	9,722	10,131

*Including women's colleges and scientific school. For purposes of estimation, the annual yield of students prepared for college is assumed to approximate that for private secondary schools—18% of enrollment.

three students reached the senior year in this era, and only about 30 percent of graduates had prepared for college. Still, given their massive expansion during the 1890s—and beyond—even this meager yield soon grew to constitute the principal source of potential college students (table 11). Public high school graduates were, ipso facto, nonaffluent, making them far more likely to attend local urban institutions or tuition-free state universities. Nevertheless the colleges could scarcely ignore this deepening pool of potential students.[11]

Relations between the high schools and the colleges varied greatly across regions. In the Northeast, the New England Association of Colleges and Preparatory Schools was formed in 1885 chiefly to deal with college admissions requirements that were growing more stringent and varied. The Association of Colleges and Preparatory Schools of the Southern States, on the other hand, represented an effort by the stronger institutions in that region to prevent colleges from luring students away from the schools before they graduated. In general the colleges sought more rigorous academic preparation of high school students, particularly in Greek, while the high schools, mindful of their varied clientele, resisted what they saw as domination by the colleges. By one count, there were twenty-three college and educational associations attempting to resolve the tangled strands of college admissions by the late 1890s.[12] Events in Ohio present one scenario for this basic predicament.

The Association of Ohio Colleges—a comparatively undiluted expression of the college interests—appointed a committee to work toward "closer and graduated relations" with the high schools in 1888. In a spirit of compromise it urged the colleges to accept all academic subjects for admission, including modern languages in lieu of Greek. From the high schools, it asked four years of "severe language training" in Latin, accompanied by offerings in the basic academic fields. Consensus was not easily reached, however. Some colleges refused to countenance lowering their standards by admitting students without Greek. High school teachers, who had generally not attended college, apparently gave little encouragement for their students to do so. They also seem to have resisted suggested visitations by representatives of the colleges to examine and rate their curriculum. Essentially rebuffed by the high schools, association members argued about language requirements for admission for the rest of the 1890s, eventually adopting a rather hollow formula.[13] By then, however, the rear-guard action in defense of the classical course was irretrievably lost.

The unwillingness of the high schools to teach Greek, in Ohio and elsewhere, contributed significantly to the demise of the classical course.[14] In 1890 the A.B. still signified completion of the classical course almost everywhere except Harvard; by 1900 most colleges had combined it with the B. Litt., B. Phil., and/or B. Letters in an undifferentiated Bachelor of Arts degree.[15] Powerful curricular trends, borne by the growth of the academic disciplines and the elective system, lay behind this development. For the colleges, however, the demise of the classical course undercut their pretense of a distinctive, intermediate role. Henceforth the colleges had little recourse but to teach a portion of university academic subjects, and at more than a rudimentary level.

An elective academic curriculum required greater scale and resources than did the several degree courses of multipurpose colleges. This point was illustrated inadvertently by Hiram College president E. B. Wakefield in 1900. Seeking to defend the middling position of colleges, he estimated that the educational needs of an average collegian could be met fully with a faculty of twenty-five.[16] As a benchmark, twenty-five faculty members were well above the ten thought adequate by the association two decades earlier. The evolution of the college curriculum in the 1890s, far from providing colleges with the protected niche they had traditionally occupied, drew them into implicit competition with universities.

The surge of high school graduates in the 1890s was clearly more beneficial to universities than to colleges. In Ohio, collegiate enrollments rose from 3,681 to 5,807 for the decade. However, 73 percent of the additional students swelled the classes of just three institutions—Ohio State (+801), Cincinnati (+466), and

Western Reserve (+292). Each represented a different type of modern university (state, municipal, and endowed), and all were located in cities. Elsewhere fluctuations appear to have an almost random character. Of the three largest denominational colleges, Ohio Wesleyan gained 55 students, Oberlin lost 201, and Wooster was virtually unchanged (-8). Denison became coeducational and gained enrollment (+106), but for Marietta coeducation brought a loss (-15). Kenyon, remaining conservative and male, grew from 38 to 96; Capital did the same and shrank from 71 to 39. The most eclectic of the colleges—Scio, Mount Union, and Baldwin—nevertheless all experienced substantial declines.[17] These results may be considered representative of the experience of multipurpose colleges across the country. Actual developments at each college were strongly affected by local circumstances, and thus are perhaps most indicative of pervasive instability. Nevertheless few colleges made significant progress toward long-term viability, and those offering numerous programs to irregular students may have faced the greatest difficulties.

The experience of Ohio's universities was duplicated on a national scale. The 14 institutions that Edwin Slosson dubbed the "Great American Universities" by themselves accounted for one-third (ca. 23,000) of 70,000 additional students in the 1890s (and they include only 5 state universities). Although these institutions were in the forefront of the academic revolution, most of their growth was due to the proliferation of professionally oriented schools. The University of California offered 9 undergraduate colleges and 6 professional schools, and the other state universities offered similar, if less numerous arrays. Among endowed universities, Harvard and Cornell offered 10 units of study; Columbia, Penn, and even staid Yale each had 9.[18] The universities in the 1890s raised the multipurpose paradigm to a new level. Their numerous schools were themselves specialized entities that underwent further academic development. Much of the additional student demand seemed to be for this type of study (table 12).

The 70,000 additional students in the 1890s (+71.5 percent) consisted of 40,000 undergraduates and 30,000 professional or graduate students. Since the universities claimed the lion's share of new undergraduates, the colleges' prospects for gaining enrollments were rather bleak. In 1900 the modal college still had only 83 students. The evident areas of growth—medicine and dentistry, graduate study in the arts and sciences, and a surge of students studying the law—were not those that colleges could exploit.

The swelling interest in graduate education that occurred in the 1880s was interpreted differently by some colleges than by contemporary devotees of *Wissenschaft*. College charters typically authorized the granting of all customary degrees, and master's degrees had long been awarded to their own graduates. Many colleges consequently interpreted doctoral education as yet another area of

TABLE 12

INSTITUTIONS AND ENROLLMENTS IN HIGHER EDUCATION, 1890 & 1900

Type	1889–1890 Students	1899–1900 Students
Colleges & Universities	46,131	82,264
Schools of Technology	7,577	11,954
Colleges for Women A	1,979	4,872
Colleges for Women B	10,013	11,006
SUBTOTAL	**65,700**	110,106
Men	44,926	72,336
Women	20,774	37,770
Undergraduate	63,983	104,027
Graduate	1,717	6,079
Schools of Theology	7,013	8,009
Schools of Law	4,518	12,516
Medicine	20,714	37,377
Regular	13,521	22,752
Eclectic	719	746
Homeopath	1,020	1,909
Dental	2,643	7,928
Pharmacy	2,811	4,042
TOTAL HI ED ENROLLMENTS	**97,945**	167,998
Normal Schools, Teaching Programs	34,814	69,593
Commercial Colleges	78,920	91,549
Population, 15–19	6,557,600	7,556,089
HI ED Enrollments	1.49%	2.22%

opportunity. Although an occasional diploma mill appeared, most colleges ingenuously sought to offer an additional service and perhaps to bolster their status by doing so. The Association of Ohio Colleges, always mindful of standards, established guidelines for the Ph.D. in 1881.[19]

In Ohio (the only state in which this has been analyzed) at least twelve colleges, or about a third of the total, listed doctoral programs by the early 1890s, but only the one at Ohio State proved lasting.[20] The "collegiate doctorates" of this era reflected a delusion on the part of multipurpose colleges that they might capitalize on the popularity of graduate studies. In their catalogues they detailed structured, residential programs: three years of study were generally the standard, capped by a thesis that, in the words used by Ohio University, would contribute "some new discovery, however slight."[21] In practice, students must have done most of this work on their own, whether on campus or more likely off. Thus these doctoral "programs" consisted largely of examinations for fees. Often the first recipients were members of the college's own faculty; subsequent graduates were typically nearby teachers or clergymen. The University of Wooster was far and away the state leader, granting 120 Ph.D.'s from 1880 to 1900. Mount Union, with no library, awarded 16 doctorates (1888–1898). Findlay College, which opened in 1886, awarded 2 Ph.D.'s in 1889—1 to a faculty member. Richmond College had only 4 undergraduates in 1899, but awarded 5 Ph.D.'s. Ohio State University, by way of comparison, granted only 3 doctorates before 1900.

Sentiment in the colleges was often ambivalent toward these doctoral programs. The Denison faculty voted against offering the doctorate in 1888, but a program was instituted by an ambitious new president four years later. Opposition to these practices smoldered in the emerging academic profession. The American Philological Association passed a resolution condemning the promiscuous granting of honorary doctorates in 1881, and it was seconded by the American Association for the Advancement of Science. By the 1890s the focus of concern had become the supposedly earned collegiate doctorates. The formation of the Association of American Universities (AAU) in 1900 was principally an effort by the country's leading universities to safeguard the value of the American Ph.D.[22] The awarding of collegiate doctorates withered soon afterward.[23] Whether or not this was due to the AAU is difficult to say. As one of the principal standardizing agencies, it certainly possessed the power to decry substandard programs. For the colleges, however, these misconceived Ph.D. programs were above all symptomatic of an identity crisis. After the turn of the century (if not earlier) their academic inadequacy apparently became a source of embarrassment. In short order one college after another renounced granting doctoral degrees. Across the country the colleges largely disappeared from the doctoral lists. In the matter of graduate education, at least, the colleges recognized one function that they did not wish to perform.

Professional education presented a situation altogether different from graduate education. Each of the noble professions of theology, medicine, and law had its own relationship with colleges, but all had evolved since 1850 into educational alternatives, more competitive than complementary. By the end of the century only a minority of students took a bachelor's degree before embarking on professional studies (table 13).

TABLE 13

PERCENTAGE OF COLLEGE GRADUATES IN PROFESSIONAL SCHOOLS
1880–1900

	1880	1890	1900
Theology	26.4	22.2	29.2
Law	24.2	21.8	17.5
Medicine (Regular)	7.9	9.0	10.2

Although the percentages in table 13 may be slightly understated,[24] they nevertheless reveal that the college's purported role of providing preprofessional education was largely a fiction in these decades.

The low proportion of future clergy who graduated from college is further corroboration of the differentiation of the multipurpose college from its classical predecessor. The proliferation of theological seminaries since early in the century had effectively consolidated the final college years of study with pastoral and theological training. Not incidentally these seminaries represented a higher priority for support from the churches than did their respective colleges. Regional and denominational differences were nevertheless pronounced. The oldest seminaries on the East Coast largely sought college graduates as students, but the evangelical denominations looked to the seminaries for their ministers with less regard for prior training. Since many seminaries were formally or informally associated with a college, aspiring ministers often became irregular students in the kind of Bible course first fashioned at Oberlin. Schools of theology, unlike their counterparts in law and medicine, desired at least some college study from their students. Except for some eastern schools, however, in 1900 they were still far from being graduate institutions.[25]

The dynamics of law and medicine differed in being governed by professional bodies and state laws. For both, the last decades of the century were a time of expansion and turmoil. Until the Civil War, schools of law and medicine existed under proprietary arrangements and may or may not have been connected with a college. Many of the larger colleges had such relationships at one time or another, but their very nature made them unstable. Conditions in the schools mirrored those in the professions, where the effects of Jacksonian democracy had vitiated most state controls over professional practice, thus separating licensing from formal education.[26] The subsequent evolution of legal and medical education, then, reflected efforts to reimpose standards for professional licensing and practice. Both fields faced the same fundamental challenges: instituting an academic curriculum of appropriate length, installing professional faculty to teach it, and raising requirements for admissions.

As of 1870, the year before Charles Eliot engineered the reform of the Harvard Medical School, medical education throughout the country conformed to the same debased pattern.[27] The schools, whether or not affiliated with universities, were proprietary in nature in that practitioner-teachers were compensated directly from student fees. The standard courses, taught by lectures (except for anatomy), ran four or five months and were repeated each year. Students who registered for two iterations, and paid additional graduation fees, were awarded M.D.'s. At this juncture, states began to reestablish licensing laws, which automatically granted such graduates the right to practice. Whatever slight augmentation of expertise this brought, it had the effect of encouraging the proliferation of even weaker proprietary schools, which in turn discouraged others from raising standards.[28] The next two decades nevertheless witnessed a transformation of medical education led by the most reputable university-affiliated schools.

Undergirding this transformation was an academic revolution in medicine that resulted from bringing advances in basic biological science to bear on problems of health and disease. As in other academic fields, the German universities showed the way: hundreds of Americans returned from studying there fired with the spirit of scientific medicine.[29] Eliot's 1871 reforms at Harvard created an organization that could encompass, cultivate, and teach such knowledge.

Harvard instituted a graded course that extended over three nine-month terms, thus roughly tripling the amount of instruction. Students were led progressively through the preclinical sciences, taught in laboratories instead of lecture halls, followed by clinical instruction. The Harvard medical school was also incorporated into the financial structure of the university, so that professors received salaries instead of student fees. The new pattern required a level of resources to which few universities could aspire, and was resisted as well by much of the medical profession. Only a handful of imitators emerged in the 1870s, notably Penn, Yale, and Michigan. Reform to this point stemmed chiefly from the initiatives of modernizing universities rather than the profession. During the

1880s, the three-year graded program became the desired standard, but only a third of medical schools had adopted it by 1890.[30]

The 1890s marked a second, decisive phase in the reform of medical education, a phase that culminated in 1910 when the Flexner Report administered the coup de grace to the proprietary schools.[31] The Association of American Medical Colleges (AAMC) was revived in 1889 and became a powerful standardizing force. It admitted only schools having the new curriculum, laboratory instruction, and entrance requirements. In 1891 the National Conference of State Medical Examining and Licensing Boards recommended that applicants for licenses be graduated from a three-year graded course. Harvard and the newly opened Johns Hopkins Medical School then lengthened their course to four years, which the AAMC and the licensing boards promptly endorsed.[32] Not only had the requirements for an M.D. been greatly expanded, but the advantage to future practitioners shifted decisively away from cheap degrees and in favor of rigorous preparation.

The reformation of medical education largely bypassed the multipurpose colleges. The unreformed medical schools had been essentially open to all comers, and in any case did not presuppose knowledge that might be taught in the colleges. Urban proprietary schools, in particular, catered to a clientele that could scarcely afford to prepare for college, let alone attend. When attention was directed to admission criteria around 1890, the immediate goal was to demand a high school degree. The Johns Hopkins Medical School was far ahead of the times when it

TABLE 14

BACHELOR'S DEGREES AND PROFESSIONAL DEGREES
1880–1900*

	1880	1890	1900
Bachelor's Degrees	4,450	6,324	13,477
A.B.	3,300	3,533	7,275
B.Sc. or Eng.	900	1,469	3,226
Others	250	1,322	2,946
Professional Degrees	5,049	7,701	10,233
Theology	719	1,372	1,773
Medicine	3,241	4,556	5,219
Law	1,089	1,424	3,241

* Reliable degree totals are surprisingly elusive: bachelor's degrees for 1880 are estimated; for 1890 are those of 1888; professional degrees from Reed, Training for the Law, 443.

required a bachelor's degree from its applicants. Harvard followed in 1900, with less than total success. A more realistic standard emerged after 1900 among the stronger schools, requiring college courses in biology, chemistry, and physics. Before this, however, studying medicine was largely an alternative to attending college, and a popular one as well considering the rising prestige of scientific medicine. Circa 1890, more M.D.'s were being conferred than A.B.'s (table 14).

The same drive to raise professional and educational standards was present in law, but the dynamics differed significantly from medicine.[33] At the time of the Civil War, requirements to practice law were minimal throughout the country, and lawyers chiefly prepared themselves in law offices whether they attended law school or not. As in medicine, attempts to raise standards in the following years greatly stimulated the formation of professional schools. Perhaps the law was perceived as somewhat more respectable than medicine because most actual or aspiring universities added law schools between the Civil War and the century's end. Multipurpose colleges seem to have followed the same impulse, but most of their efforts were later abandoned.[34] Insofar as law schools attracted less-prepared students, they could be more a rival than a complement to a college. (At larger universities law schools were self-contained.) After 1890 two distinct markets for legal education became apparent, and multipurpose colleges were ill suited to compete in either.

Eliot's Harvard was the fount of reform for legal education as it was for medical. The Harvard Law School pioneered an academic approach to the law by introducing the case method, and it instituted a two-year graded course. But the process of upgrading the content, length, and admission requirements for law schools proceeded more slowly than in medicine. Harvard attempted to impose a three-year course in 1899, and the law schools organized a standardizing association in 1900. The states nevertheless remained reluctant to require aspiring lawyers to attend law school. The law simply did not possess a scientific base equivalent to the preclinical sciences, and bar examinations, ignoring case-method pedagogy, remained a low hurdle for entering practice.

Large opportunities consequently existed for "unrespectable" law schools to offer students from diverse backgrounds courses designed essentially for passing the bar exam. Such schools offered evening classes to part-time students, particularly in the cities. This kind of legal education appeared in the 1890s and expanded rapidly after 1900, offered in some cases by university-affiliated law schools and in others by independent proprietary schools.[35] The other market for legal studies consisted of "respectable," university-based law schools for full-time day students. They followed the Harvard pattern, adopting the case method and valuing legal scholarship. They also favored higher standards and became the constituency of the Association of American Law Schools. As of 1890, full-time students greatly outnumbered those studying part-time, but over the next decade that balance began to shift. After 1900, part-time urban schools such as Georgetown University and Chicago Kent were among the largest in the country.[36] Multipurpose colleges had neither the wealth to operate a reformed law school nor the locus to serve urban evening students. Thus the law schools they actually founded from 1870 to 1900 for the most part soon closed.[37]

The evolution of training for the law and medicine from what were essentially trade schools to respected professional schools was almost exclusively the work of the universities. However, during the last two decades of the century, more-or-less reformed university units coexisted with more-or-less unreformed proprietary schools. During the 1880s, in particular, it appeared that professional education had become largely decoupled from higher learning in the arts and sciences. More students graduated from professional schools in these years than from colleges (table14), and only a minority did both (table 13).

This anomalous situation began to change in the 1890s as the number of college graduates more than doubled. The link was not forged until after 1900, however, when the better medical schools demanded college science from their students and the better law schools sought applicants having at least two years of collegiate study. Little wonder, though, that at the outset of the 1890s the educational role of the colleges was in doubt.

"Time was when the college was the top of the educational system in the United States," observed Columbia president Seth Low in 1892. "[I]t is so no longer, and it never can become so again."[38] Low was addressing the college's relations with those same institutions just discussed, and he accurately identified the current moment as a time of transition. Over the next quarter century, the American college did in fact adjust to an intermediate position in the hierarchy of knowledge and training, and one that before long became highly esteemed for its own peculiar merits. The revalidation of collegiate education involved more than establishing clear lines of demarcation with other sectors. The upper threshold of secondary education was defined after 1900 with assistance from the College Entrance Examination Board and the so-called Carnegie unit. The acceptance of the full undergraduate college as a component of the American university clarified the relation of college to graduate study. And the inexorable rise of professional schools—in stature and standards—eventually justified the preprofessional role that colleges had always coveted. Within this organizational space, however, the leading eastern colleges fashioned an alluring image comprised of liberal culture, based on selective borrowings from the academic disciplines, and an exuberant peer culture, incorporating a secular orientation toward worldly success and extracurricular student activities.[39] This vision of the place and purpose of college could be embraced by university presidents, alumni supporters, and collegians themselves. In the opening decades of the new century, it became the predominant image of American higher education.

This world, however, was far removed from that of the multipurpose colleges. Most of these institutions themselves persisted, but to survive in a new era they had to change their fundamental nature. The mixing of students from different age ranges and with different levels of preparation was antithetical to the emerging peer culture. Denominationalism fit uncomfortably with the lure of secular success. And only the largest and wealthiest among them could readily, or credibly, emulate the disciplinary curriculum. Between 1890 and World War I, the multipurpose college for all practical purposes ceased to exist. The liberal arts college, denominational or otherwise, would continue to constitute a distinctive sector of American higher education, and a century later would be found once again fulfilling multiple purposes for a varied clientele.[40] But the era had passed for the institution that had characterized American higher education from 1850 to 1890.

Notes

Preface

1. Peter Novick, *That Noble Dream: The "Objectivity Question" and the American Historical Profession* (New York: Cambridge University Press, 1988), 577–92; Thomas Bender, "The Need for Synthesis in American History," *Journal of American History* 73 (1986): 120–36.

2. I have attempted to provide a framework for a dynamic view of the history of American higher education, based on published work: Roger Geiger, "The Ten Generations of American Higher Education," in *American Higher Education in the Twenty-first Century,* ed. Philip G. Altbach, Robert O. Berdahl, and Patricia J. Gumport (Baltimore: Johns Hopkins University Press, 1999), 38–69.

Introduction

1. Beverly McAnear, "College Founding in the American Colonies, 1745–1775," *Mississippi Valley Historical Review* 42, 1 (1955): 24–44; Colin B. Burke, *American Collegiate Populations: A Test of the Traditional View* (New York: New York University Press, 1982), 54.

2. In 1800, the Harvard teaching faculty consisted of the president, 3 professors, and 6 tutors. Both Yale and Princeton had only 1 professor. In 1900, nine universities had more than 200 faculty, including Harvard, still well in the lead, with approximately 450.

3. The origins of the traditional interpretation ought to be explored. Most likely its central tenets were axiomatic before World War II. R. Freeman Butts's admirable study, for example, is structured around the triumph of the elective system; see *The College Charts Its Course* (New York: McGraw-Hill, 1939).

4. Walter P. Metzger, *Academic Freedom in the Age of the University* (New York: Columbia University Press, 1961), 4; originally published with Richard Hofstadter as *The Development of Academic Freedom in the United States* (1955).

5. Richard Hofstadter, *Academic Freedom in the Age of the College* (1955; reprint, New Brunswick, N.J.: Transaction Publishers, 1996); see introduction by Roger L. Geiger, xv–xxi.

6. Frederick Rudolph, *The American College and University: A History* (1962; reprint, Athens: University of Georgia Press, 1990); John S. Brubacher and Willis Rudy, *Higher Education in Transition: A History of American Colleges and Universities, 1636–1956* (New York: Harper, 1958).

7. The origin of revisionism bears some resemblance to a Kuhnian "scientific revolution." Independent scholarship by Colin Burke, James Axtell, David Potts, and David Allmendinger resulted in findings that contradicted the prevailing paradigm. Articles by the latter three appeared in the *History of Education Quarterly* (winter 1971). A group largely composed of revisionists has also been associated with the founding of the *History of Higher Education Annual* in 1981.

Bruce Kimball offers a highly inclusive view of the movement and not surprisingly finds it internally inconsistent; see "Writing the History of Universities: A New Approach?" *Minerva* (1986): 375–89. I employ a narrow definition here, considering as revisionists only those who frame their scholarship by employing the now stereotyped critique of the traditional view of the antebellum college. Solidarity among revisionists beyond this point is not implied.

8. James McLachlan, "The American College in the Nineteenth Century: Toward a Reappraisal," *Teachers College Record* 80, 2 (1978): 287–306.

9. Robert V. Bruce, "A Statistical Profile of American Scientists, 1846–1876," in *Nineteenth-Century Science: A Reappraisal,* ed. George H. Daniels (Evanston: Northwestern University Press, 1972), 63–94.

10. Peter Dobkin Hall, *The Organization of American Culture, 1700–1900: Private Institutions, Elites, and the Origins of American Nationality* (New York: New York University Press, 1982).

11. Ronald Story, *The Forging of an Aristocracy: Harvard and the Boston Upper Class, 1800–1870* (Middletown, Conn.: Wesleyan University Press, 1980).

12. David Allmendinger, *Paupers and Scholars: The Transformation of Student Life in Nineteenth-Century New England* (New York: St. Martin's, 1975).

13. Burke, *American Collegiate Populations,* chaps. 3, 4.

14. Stanley A. Guralnick, *Science and the Ante-bellum College* (Philadelphia: American Philosophical Society, 1975). Guralnick is a historian of science and has not identified with the revisionists.

15. Caroline Winterer, "The Humanist Revolution in America, 1820–1860: Classical Antiquity in the Colleges," *History of Higher Education Annual* 18 (1998): 111–30.

16. Guralnick and Hall have explicitly defended the Yale Report as a timely document, although without reference to the transformation under way in classical studies. See Guralnick, *Science,* 29–33; Hall, *Organization of American Culture.* See also Hall's chapter in this volume, "Noah Porter Writ Large?"

17. Union nevertheless had fairly strong offerings in science and in 1845 began offering a degree in civil engineering; see V. Ennis Pilcher, *Early Science and the First Century of Physics at Union College, 1795–1895* (Schenectady: Union College, 1994), 31–48.

18. Francis Wayland was author of *Elements of Political Economy* (1837), a distillation of classical free-market economics that was the most widely used text at midcentury, and his approach to reforming the colleges reflected these doctrines. See William J. Barber, ed., *Economists and Higher Learning in the Nineteenth Century* (1988; reprint, New Brunswick, N.J.: Transaction Press, 1993), 72–86; David B. Potts, *Baptist Colleges in the Development of American Society, 1812–1861* (1967; reprint, New York: Garland, 1988), 316–32.

19. Burke, *American Collegiate Populations*, 1–9. Any attempt at a definitive enumeration of colleges or students during this era is frustrated by the fact that colleges not only expired, but were also reborn, and their status was often uncertain from year to year. Enrollments at colleges, even if reported, varied considerably during the school year. The data utilized here—from Burke to 1860 and from annual *Reports of the Commissioner of Education* after 1870—are taken to be good approximations, certainly adequate to portray a general picture of college development.

20. Donald C. Tewksbury, *The Founding of American Colleges and Universities before the Civil War* (New York: Teachers College Press, 1932).

21. For the persistence of the idea of too many colleges, see Samuel Miller, *Brief Retrospect of the Eighteenth Century*, 2 vols. (1803), 2:272–75; Geiger and Bubolz's chapter in this volume, "College As It Was in the Mid–Nineteenth Century"; William Rainey Harper, *The Prospects of the Small College* (Chicago: University of Chicago Press, 1900).

22. Natalie A. Naylor, "The Ante-bellum College Movement: A Reappraisal of Tewksbury's 'Founding of American Colleges and Universities,'" *History of Education Quarterly* 13 (1973): 26–74.

23. Thomas J. Wertenbaker, *Princeton, 1746–1896* (1946; reprint, Princeton: Princeton University Press, 1996); Mark Noll, *Princeton and the Republic, 1768–1822: The Search for Christian Enlightenment in the Era of Samuel Stanhope Smith* (Princeton: Princeton University Press, 1989); Howard Miller, *The Revolutionary College: American Presbyterian Higher Education, 1707–1837* (New York: New York University Press, 1976). Miller endorses the great retrogression thesis while Noll rejects it; see also Geiger's introduction in *Academic Freedom*, xix–xxi.

24. Roger Geiger, "The Reformation of the Colleges in the Early Republic, 1800–1820" (paper presented to the History of Education Society Meeting, October 1998).

25. David B. Potts, "American Colleges in the Nineteenth Century: From Localism to Denominationalism," *History of Education Quarterly* 11 (1971): 363–80, and "'College Enthusiasm!' as Public Response, 1800–1860," *Harvard Educational Review* 47 (1977): 28–42.

26. Natalie A. Naylor, "Raising a Learned Ministry: The American Education Society, 1815–1860" (Ed.D. diss., Columbia University, 1971); Paul Moyer Limbert, *Denominational Policies in the Support and Supervision of Higher Education* (New York: Teachers College, 1929).

27. Laurence Veysey, *The Emergence of the American University* (Chicago: University of Chicago Press, 1965).

28. George E. Peterson, *The New England College in the Age of the University* (Amherst, Mass.: Amherst College Press, 1964); Marilyn Tobias, *Old Dartmouth on Trial: The Transformation of an Academic Community in Nineteenth-Century America* (New York: New York University Press, 1982).

29. W. Bruce Leslie, *Gentlemen and Scholars: Colleges and Community in the Age of the University, 1865–1917* (University Park: Pennsylvania State University Press, 1992); David B. Potts, *Wesleyan University, 1831–1910: Collegiate Enterprise in New England* (New Haven: Yale University Press, 1992).

30. Walter P. Metzger, "The Academic Profession in the United States," in *The Academic Profession: National, Disciplinary, and Institutional Settings,* ed. Burton R. Clark (Los Angeles: University of California Press, 1987), 123–207, quote on 180.

31. Leslie, *Gentlemen and Scholars,* 4–5; Burke, *American Collegiate Populations,* 8.

32. Nor, it should be added, has the traditional view offered anything like a restatement of its position in light of recent scholarship. Walter Metzger has conceded a good part of the revisionist findings, and he has suggested a chronological classification of colleges as a possible synthesis. The original colonial colleges, he argues, manifested curricular progress in the antebellum years, while the generation of colleges founded after 1830 largely justified the strictures of the traditionalists ("Academic Profession," 127–28). Superficially plausible, this typology breaks down as one ponders the exceptions like Oberlin (f. 1832) and the University of Michigan (f. 1837). Metzger's anticipated volume on the history of the academic profession may provide a richer and more nuanced exposition.

33. Brooks Mather Kelley, *Yale: A History* (New Haven: Yale University Press, 1974), 66–70. The literature on student disorders is cited in Jackson's chapter in this volume, "The Rights of Man and the Rites of Youth."

34. From the student strike to shorten the college course at Dickinson College in 1798 to the last major eruption at Harvard in 1834, at least twenty-seven disturbances of this type occurred; see Geiger, "Reformation of the Colleges," 8. Student defiance of college authorities remained virtually endemic in southern universities.

35. Steven J. Novak, *The Rights of Youth: American Colleges and Student Revolt, 1798–1815* (Cambridge: Harvard University Press, 1977).

36. Gordon S. Wood, *The Radicalism of the American Revolution* (New York: Vintage, 1991), part 3.

37. Burke, *American Collegiate Populations,* 115–18; Geiger, "Reformation of the Colleges," 11–16.

38. Charles E. Cuningham, *Timothy Dwight, 1752–1817* (New York: Macmillan, 1942). Historians often use the term *parental discipline* to mean the exact opposite of Dwight's empathetic approach, but his sense of the term seems to have been understood in the 1820s; see Geiger, "Reformation of the Colleges," 45–53.

39. Tutors, who had borne the brunt of enforcement, were replaced by instructors at most colleges; and colleges also employed more professors, more of whom were not ministers.

40. Allmendinger, *Paupers and Scholars,* 80–94.

41. Samuel Eliot Morison, "The Great Rebellion at Harvard College and the Resignation of President Kirkland," *Publications of the Colonial Society of Massachusetts* 27 (1928): 54–112. In the later riots at Harvard and Yale, factionalism among students was a significant factor, which suggests some ebbing of discipline without corresponding growth of student responsibility.

42. James McLachlan, "The *Choice of Hercules:* American Student Societies in the Early 19th Century," in *The University in Society,* ed. Lawrence Stone, 2 vols. (Princeton: Princeton University Press, 1974), 2:449–73. Also Thomas S. Harding, *College Literary*

Societies: Their Contribution to Higher Education in the United States, 1815–1876 (New York: Pageant Press, 1971).

43. Frederick Rudolph, *Mark Hopkins and the Log: Williams College, 1836–1872* (New Haven: Yale University Press, 1956), 59, 62.

44. Codman Hislop, *Eliphalet Nott* (Middletown, Conn.: Wesleyan University Press, 1971).

45. Bagg discusses crew regattas and the first "base ball" games, but he is always careful to distinguish contests between class teams and those of the "university club"—a distinction that soon disappeared. See Ronald Smith, *Sports and Freedom* (New York: Oxford University Press, 1988).

46. Cornelius Howard Patton and Walter Taylor Field, *Eight O'clock Chapel: A Study of New England College Life in the Eighties* (Boston: Houghton Mifflin, 1927); Henry Seidel Canby, *Alma Mater: The Gothic Age of the American College* (New York, 1936).

47. Peterson, *New England College*, 27–51; George W. Pierson, *Yale College: An Educational History, 1871–1921* (New Haven: Yale University Press, 1952), 3–43.

48. Leslie, *Gentlemen and Scholars*, 237–49.

49. Robin Lester, *Stagg's University: The Rise, Decline, and Fall of Big-Time Football at Chicago* (Urbana: University of Illinois Press, 1995), 7–12. Social mores are often seen most clearly from the perspective of outsiders; see Dan A. Oren, *Joining the Club: A History of Jews and Yale* (New Haven: Yale University Press, 1985), 17–37.

50. Potts, *Wesleyan University*, 213–20; Slosson, *The Great American Universities* (New York, 1910), 331–33; Charlotte Williams Conable, *Women at Cornell: The Myth of Equal Education* (Ithaca: Cornell University Press, 1977), 115–19.

51. Helen Lefkowitz Horowitz, *Alma Mater: Design and Experience in the Women's Colleges from Their Nineteenth-Century Beginnings to the 1930s* (New York: Knopf, 1984), 147–78.

52. Dan Oren finds evidence of growing social stratification at Yale in the 1890s, but after 1900 it was obvious enough to elicit explicit comment; see *Joining the Club*, 17–37. Social stratification at Princeton developed so rapidly that it was considered a "social crisis" by 1907; see Henry Wilkinson Bragdon, *Woodrow Wilson: The Academic Years* (Cambridge: Harvard University Press, 1967), 317–21.

53. Robert Polk Thomson, "The Reform of the College of William and Mary, 1763–1780," *Proceedings of the American Philosophical Society* 115, 3 (June 1971): 187–210; David Robson, "College Founding in the New Republic, 1776–1800," *History of Education Quarterly* 23 (fall 1983): 323–41. College demographics are presented by regions in Burke, *American Collegiate Populations*.

54. George W. Pierson, *Yale: A Book of Numbers* (New Haven: Yale University Press, 1977), 4. Until 1821, Yale college students were called "academical students" in the catalogue, but beginning in 1822 they were called "undergraduates."

55. [John Kirkland], "Literary Institutions—University," *North American Review* 7 (July 1818): 270–78, quote on 276; Geiger, "Reformation of the Colleges"; Robert A. McCaughey, "The Transformation of American Academic Life: Harvard University, 1821–1892," *Perspectives in American History* 8 (1974): 239–332, and *Josiah Quincy,*

1772–1864: The Last Federalist (Cambridge: Harvard University Press, 1974), 163–78; Richard Yanikoski, "Edward Everett and the Advancement of Higher Education and Adult Education in Ante-bellum Massachusetts" (Ph.D. diss., University of Chicago, 1987), 113–240.

56. Geiger, "Reformation of the Colleges"; Guralnick, *Science,* passim; Caroline Winterer, "Humanist Revolution in America."

57. *Quarterly Register* (August 1840): 110–16. "Eastern" colleges here comprise the states of New Hampshire, Massachusetts, Rhode Island, Connecticut, New Jersey, and eastern New York: 15 colleges. The remaining 7 colleges had 5 or 6 professors.

58. The development of the Harvard College faculty, which doubled from 1845 to 1869, can be followed in McCaughey, "Transformation of American Academic Life," 263–74.

59. Joseph F. Kett, *The Pursuit of Knowledge under Difficulties: From Self-improvement to Adult Education in America, 1750–1990* (Stanford: Stanford University Press, 1994), 89–97. The educational level of academies varied enormously, but here again the Northeast possessed the most rigorous academies as well as boarding schools; see James McLachlan, *American Boarding Schools* (New York: Scribner's, 1970).

60. Levi Hedge to William Harris, 20 March 1820, Columbia College Papers, Columbia University Special Collections.

61. Naylor, "Raising a Learned Ministry."

62. *Quarterly Register* (April 1829): 205–9; Naylor, "Raising a Learned Ministry," 127–41.

63. Rudolph, *Mark Hopkins,* 201–14; Laura Hadley Moseley, ed., *Diary, 1843–1852, of James Hadley* (New Haven: Yale University Press, 1951), 308.

64. Darryl L. Peterkin, "Lux, Libertas, and Learning: The First State University and the Transformation of North Carolina" (Ph.D. diss., Princeton University, 1995), 39–48, 97–119.

65. A similar ideology suffused the College of William and Mary; see Denise A. Riley, "Masters of the Blue Room: An Investigation of the Relationship between the Environment and the Ideology of the Faculty of the College of William and Mary, 1836–1846" (Ph.D. diss., Ohio State University, 1997).

66. This pattern of a state-supported university was repeated with some differences in Alabama and Mississippi. See Frank W. Blackmar, *A History of Federal and State Aid to Higher Education in the United States* (Washington, D.C., 1890).

67. *Quarterly Register* (1840): 189.

68. Kemp Plumer Battle, *Memories of an Old-Time Tar Heel* (Chapel Hill: University of North Carolina Press, 1945), 80.

69. Aldea Godbold, *The Church College of the Old South* (Durham, N.C., 1944); Joe L. Kincheloe, "The Antebellum Southern Evangelical and State-Supported Colleges: A Comparative Study" (D.Ed. diss., University of Tennessee, 1980). Manual labor received a strong endorsement from the American Education Society in 1829. See E. Cornelius, "The Union of Study with Useful Labor," *Quarterly Register* 2 (November 1829): 57–70; also see Kett, *Pursuit of Knowledge,* 128–33.

70. Jurgen Herbst, *From Crisis to Crisis: American College Government, 1636–1819* (Cambridge: Harvard University Press, 1982), 219–31; David Robson, *Educating Republicans: The College in the Era of the American Revolution, 1750–1800* (Westport, Conn.: Greenwood Press, 1985), 187–259.

71. Daniel T. Johnson, "Puritan Power in Illinois Higher Education prior to 1870" (Ph.D. diss., University of Wisconsin, 1974).

72. The conventional assumption that these colleges depended chiefly on tuition is so misleading that it is worth quoting a well-informed contemporary: "The receipts from tuition in the Collegiate Department cannot under the most favorable circumstances, be expected to meet more than one-third of the cost of instruction. Taking all the colleges in the United States into account, and it is estimated the cost of instruction for each collegian per annum is not less than from $125 to $150. The usual charges are from $25 to $50 per annum. In the Theological Department tuition is free" (*Report of the Board of Trustees of the University at Lewisburg* [27 July 1858], University Archives, Bucknell University).

73. This facet of midwestern denominational colleges has been elaborated by Doris Malkmus, "Small Towns, Small Sects, and Coeducation: The Origins of Midwestern Rural Gender" (paper presented to the History of Education Society annual meeting, Chicago, Ill., 31 October 1998). My thanks to the author.

74. The exception, noted by David Potts, occurred when denominations sought to move a college to a more central or suitable location; see "College Enthusiasm."

75. Potts, "From Localism to Denominationalism," 363–80. Formerly a popular subject, the growth in denominational control needs a fresh examination; see Limbert, *Denominational Policies.* In one of the few recent studies covering the second half of the century, the importance of intradenominational conflict among Lutherans clearly stimulated the founding of colleges; see Richard W. Solberg, *Lutheran Higher Education in North America* (Minneapolis: Augsburg, 1985). David Potts's important study, *Wesleyan University,* on the other hand, reveals the importance of denominational donors.

76. The data presented by Burke (*American Collegiate Populations,* 15–18, 54) cannot be compared directly with those reported in the *Reports of the Commissioner of Education* (RCE) beginning in 1875; see Geiger's chapter in this volume, "The Era of Multipurpose Colleges in American Higher Education, 1850–1890." Burke reports 16,600 students in 201 colleges in 1860. The 1875 RCE reports 26,353 college students in 355 colleges; however, there were also 5,504 collegiate students in schools of science, and 9,592 students in the collegiate course of women's colleges. These last two categories were not enumerated by Burke, but expanded greatly from 1860 to 1875.

77. Robert Wiebe, *The Search for Order, 1877–1920* (New York: Hill and Wang, 1967), 111–32. Burke's data on graduate mobility suggest that a college education was also a ticket off the island; see *American Collegiate Populations,* chap. 4.

78. Frederick T. Gates, "The Need of a Baptist University in Chicago, as Illustrated by a Study of Baptist Collegiate Education in the West," 3, 6, Correspondence of Frederick T. Gates, 1888–1906, box 1, folder 2, Joseph Regenstein Library, University of Chicago (my thanks to William Pugh for this document).

79. Kathryn M. Kerns, "Farmers' Daughters: The Education of Women at Alfred Academy and University before the Civil War," *History of Higher Education Annual* 6 (1986): 11–28.

80. Nancy Beadie, "From Academy to University in New York State: The Genesee Institutions and the Importance of Capital to the Success of an Idea, 1848–1871," *History of Higher Education Annual* 14 (1994): 13–38.

81. Roger Geiger, "The Colleges in the Three Ages of the University" (paper presented to the History of Education Society annual meeting, October 1997).

82. Veysey, *Emergence of the American University,* 60.

83. The absence of local engineers to build railroads was the stimulus for the University of North Carolina. See Kevin B. Cherry, "Bringing Science to the South: The School for the Application of Science to the Arts at the University of North Carolina," *History of Higher Education Annual* 14 (1994): 73–95. There is an extensive literature on developments in chemistry, including Guralnick, *Science.*

84. Kelley, *Yale,* 181, italics added. Within the Department of Philosophy and the Arts, the School of Applied Chemistry began in 1847 and was joined by the School of Engineering in 1852; those schools were combined into the Yale Scientific School in 1854, which in 1861 was renamed the Sheffield Scientific School in honor of its benefactor, Joseph E. Sheffield.

85. Yanikoski, "Edward Everett," 198–240.

86. The Lawrence School became part of the Harvard Graduate School of Arts and Sciences in 1890; Princeton's Green School of Science was absorbed gradually; and last to be fully integrated was the Sheffield School at Yale.

87. Christie Anne Farnham, *The Education of the Southern Belle: Higher Education and Student Socialization in the Antebellum South* (New York: New York University Press, 1994), 18, passim.

88. Robert S. Fletcher, *A History of Oberlin College, from Its Foundation through the Civil War* (Oberlin College, 1943), 375–85.

89. Horowitz, *Alma Mater,* 28–68; Patricia Ann Palmieri, *In Adamless Eden: The Community of Women Faculty at Wellesley* (New Haven: Yale University Press, 1995).

90. Linda R. Buchanan, "Not Harvard, Not Holyoke, Not Howard: A Study of the Life and Death of Three Small Colleges" (Ph.D. diss., Georgia State University, 1997), 157–75.

91. Richard L. Wing, "Requiem for a Pioneer of Women's Higher Education: The Ingham University of Le Roy, New York, 1857–1892," *History of Higher Education Annual* 11 (1991): 61–79.

92. For antebellum developments, see Richard Storr, *The Beginnings of Graduate Education in America* (Chicago: University of Chicago Press, 1953).

93. The classic presentation of this case is Joseph Ben David, *The Scientist's Role in Society* (Chicago: University of Chicago Press, 1970).

94. Hugh Hawkins, *Pioneer: A History of the Johns Hopkins University, 1874–1889* (Ithaca: Cornell University Press, 1960).

95. Hadley, *Diary, 1843–1852,* 308.

96. For an overview of Eliot's revolution, see Samuel Eliot Morison, *Three Centuries of Harvard* (Cambridge: Harvard University Press, 1936), 323–99; for a deeper analysis of

Eliot himself, see Hugh Hawkins, *Between Harvard and America: The Educational Leadership of Charles W. Eliot* (New York: Oxford University Press, 1972), passim.

97. Louise L. Stevenson, *Scholarly Means to Evangelical Ends: The New Haven Scholars and the Transformation of Higher Learning in America, 1830–1890* (Baltimore: Johns Hopkins University Press, 1986), 38. To appreciate how and why this form of scholarship became quickly outmoded, see Julie A. Reuben, *The Making of the Modern University: Intellectual Transformation and the Marginalization of Morality* (Chicago: University of Chicago Press, 1996), 69–73, 89, passim.

98. William L. Kingsley, *Yale College: A Sketch of Its History,* 2 vols. (New York, 1879), 1:161.

99. Roger L. Geiger, *To Advance Knowledge: The Growth of American Research Universities, 1900–1940* (New York: Oxford University Press, 1986), 48–52.

100. Peterson, *New England College;* Leslie, *Gentlemen and Scholars.*

101. In this respect, Hall adds a new perspective to the conclusions of Laurence Veysey (who also quotes Veblen extensively): "Stylized social ambition, more than a quest for academic excellence, captured the new American university; . . . [L]argely an agency for social control . . . the custodianship of popular values comprised the primary responsibility of the American university" (*Emergence of the American University,* 440).

102. Bragdon, *Woodrow Wilson,* 312–36.

103. Geiger, *To Advance Knowledge,* 18–19; Hugh Hawkins, *Banding Together: The Rise of National Associations in American Higher Education, 1887–1950* (Baltimore: Johns Hopkins University Press, 1992), 10–15; Audrey N. Slate, *AGS: A History* (Washington, D.C.: Association of Graduate Schools, 1992), 1–19. By 1909 the Association of American Universities (AAU) was asked to pronounce on the fitness of college degrees, and in 1913 it published a list of accredited colleges (ibid., 36–37).

104. In 1910 Kendric C. Babcock, higher education specialist at the Bureau of Education, prepared a classification (never published) of the colleges on the basis of the readiness of graduates for work toward a master's degree. Out of 344 institutions rated, only 59 colleges and universities achieved the highest rating (graduates could complete an M.A. in one year), and 44 qualified for their better students. Presumably the 250 unclassified institutions would have rated poorly. See David Webster, *Academic Quality Rankings of American Colleges and Universities* (Springfield, Ill.: C. C. Thomas, 1986), 33–39.

105. Edwin Slosson provides a candid assessment of these multifarious initiatives only slightly after Harper's demise, but he too emphasizes that "President Harper put the advancement of knowledge foremost among the functions of a university" (*Great American Universities,* 405–41, quote on 435).

106. Harper, *The Prospects of the Small College.*

107. Lester, *Stagg's University,* 15–19. In a characteristic statement, Harper in 1896 said, "The athletic work of students is a vital part of the student life . . . a real and essential part of college education" (19).

108. For additional evidence on this point, see Pugh's entire article in the *History of Higher Education Annual* 15 (1995): esp. 112–16; and his "Beginning of Research at the University of Chicago" (Ph.D. diss., University of Chicago, 1990).

109. These features are still evident in Patton and Field, *Eight O'clock Chapel,* even though the New England colleges described there were well ahead of those elsewhere in the country.

Curriculum and Enrollment

1. For a review of the early studies of college student populations, see David B. Potts, "Students and the Social History of American Higher Education," *History of Education Quarterly* 15 (fall 1975): 317–27.

2. See David B. Potts, "'College Enthusiasm!' as Public Response, 1800–1860," *Harvard Educational Review* 47 (1977): 28–42; and James McLachlan, "The American College in the Nineteenth Century: Toward a Reappraisal," *Teachers College Record* 80, 2 (December 1978): 287–306.

3. Commissioned by the Carnegie Council on Policy Studies, Rudolph's book was published in San Francisco by Jossey-Bass in 1977. For other statements of the established interpretation, see John S. Brubacher and Willis Rudy, *Higher Education in Transition,* 3d ed., rev. and enlarged (New York: Harper and Row, 1976), 35, 69–74; and Burton J. Bledstein, *The Culture of Professionalism: The Middle Class and the Development of Higher Education in America* (New York: Norton, 1976), 203.

4. Rudolph, *Curriculum,* 53, 52, 55–58, 60, 61, 77, 99, 102.

5. Frederick Rudolph, *The American College and University: A History* (New York: Knopf, 1962), chaps. 3–11; Richard Hofstadter and Walter Metzger, *The Development of Academic Freedom in the United States* (New York: Columbia University Press, 1955), chap. 5; Richard Hofstadter, "The Revolution in Higher Education," in *Paths of American Thought,* ed. Arthur M. Schlesinger Jr. and Morton White (Boston: Houghton Mifflin, 1963), 269–90; and Laurence Veysey, "Stability and Experiment in the American Undergraduate Curriculum," in *Content and Context: Essays on College Education,* ed. Carl Kaysen (New York: McGraw-Hill, 1973), 1–63.

6. Rudolph, *American College,* 134.

7. Rudolph, *Curriculum,* 71–72.

8. Ibid., 75, 74–75, 74, 73, 75.

9. Ibid., 68, 113, 209–10.

10. Walter B. Kolesnik, *Mental Discipline in Modern Education* (Madison: University of Wisconsin Press, 1958); Henry Ellis, *The Transfer of Learning* (New York: Macmillan, 1965), 64; and David G. Winter et al., "Grading the Effects of a Liberal Arts Education," *Psychology Today* 12 (September 1978): 69–74, 106.

11. See, for example, Rudolph's use on 73 of R. Freeman Butts, *The College Charts Its Course* (New York: McGraw-Hill, 1939), and his use on 75 of Veysey, "Stability and Experiment."

12. David Allmendinger, *Paupers and Scholars: The Transformation of Student Life in Nineteenth-Century New England* (New York: St. Martin's, 1975).

13. Yale College, annual catalogues, 1828–1860.

14. Rudolph, *Curriculum,* 79–84.

15. Ibid., 78–79.

16. Robert A. McCaughey, *Josiah Quincy, 1772–1864: The Last Federalist* (Cambridge: Harvard University Press, 1974), 147–48, 163–78.

17. Ibid., 249.

18. Richard Storr, *The Beginnings of Graduate Education in America* (Chicago: University of Chicago Press, 1953), chap. 4.

19. McCaughey, *Josiah Quincy,* 169.

20. Rudolph, *Curriculum,* 85–87.

21. Codman Hislop, *Eliphalet Nott* (Middletown, Conn.: Wesleyan University Press, 1971), 227.

22. Ibid., 232; and note from Hislop, 20 August 1978.

23. John S. Whitehead, *The Separation of College and State: Columbia, Dartmouth, Harvard, and Yale, 1776–1876* (New Haven: Yale University Press, 1973), 127.

24. Franklin B. Hugh, *Historical and Statistical Record of the University of the State of New York during the Century from 1784 to 1884* (Albany, N.Y.: Weed, Parsons and Company, 1885), 168.

25. Cornelius Van Santvoord, *Memoirs of Eliphalet Nott, D.D., LL,D. for Sixty-two Years President of Union College* (New York: Sheldon and Company, [ca. 1876]), 152–54.

26. Rudolph, *Curriculum,* 87–88, 109.

27. Ibid., 110; Walter C. Bronson, *The History of Brown University, 1764–1914* (Providence, R.I.: Brown University, 1914); and Butts, *The College Charts Its Course.*

28. Bronson, *History of Brown,* 282–90, 321–23.

29. Francis Wayland, *Report to the Corporation of Brown University on Changes in the System of Collegiate Education, Read 28 March 1850* (Providence, R.I.: George H. Whitney, 1850), 28–31.

30. Rudolph, *Curriculum,* 101; F. A. P. Barnard, *Analysis of Some Statistics of Collegiate Education; A Paper Read before the Trustees of Columbia College, New York, January 3rd, 1870, by the President of the College* (New York: Columbia University, 1870).

31. Rudolph, *Curriculum,* 101; Edward Hitchcock, *On the Decrease of the Relative Number of College-Educated Men in Massachusetts during the Present Century* (n.p., n.d., [ca. 1877]).

32. Rudolph, *Curriculum,* 84.

The Rights of Man and the Rites of Youth

1. Eliphalet Pearson, Journal of Disturbances, 2, Pearson Papers, Harvard University Archives.

2. Daniel Appleton White, "Reminiscences of College Life, 1793–1797," 85, Harvard University Archives. This incident is also mentioned in Pearson, Journal, 18.

3. Frank Otto Gatell, *John Gorham Palfrey and the New England Conscience* (Cambridge: Harvard University Press, 1963), 37. Palfrey used his guns as a proctor in 1817, but discharge of firearms by students is evident as early as 1788. See Pearson, Journal, 5; White, "Reminiscences," 91.

4. This idea was first brought to historical prominence by David F. Allmendinger, "The Dangers of Ante-bellum Student Life," *Journal of Social History* 7 (1973): 75–85. The most significant works on college rioting are listed in the following notes.

5. The notion that student disturbances were fomented by the scions of the wealthy was first suggested by Samuel Eliot Morison, *Three Centuries of Harvard* (Cambridge: Harvard University Press, 1936), 179–80. For a more empirically grounded study that reaches somewhat different conclusions, see Kathryn McDaniel Moore, "The War with the Tutors: Student-Faculty Conflict at Harvard and Yale, 1745–1771," *History of Education Quarterly* 18 (1978): 115–28. It should be noted, however, that Morison's impressions concerned the tumults of the early Republic, whereas Moore deals exclusively with the pre-Revolutionary period. Steven J. Novak argues that there is a qualitative difference between Harvard's colonial "disturbances" and its antebellum "riots," a view that seems to be based upon insufficient familiarity with the documents presented below and that also begs the question of how one might objectively quantify violence and disorder. See *The Rights of Youth: American Colleges and Student Revolt, 1798–1815* (Cambridge: Harvard University Press, 1977), 5–7.

6. On youth as a precipitating factor in the riots of the 1790s, see Novak, *Rights of Youth.* Disruptions caused by "mature" students are discussed by David Allmendinger, *Paupers and Scholars: The Transformation of Student Life in Nineteenth-Century New England* (New York: St. Martin's, 1975).

7. On the inherent (yet apolitical) radicalism of studenthood, see, for example, Lewis S. Fuer, *The Conflict of Generations: The Character and Significance of Student Movements* (New York: Basic Books, 1969); and Seymour Martin Lipset, "Students and Politics," in *The Berkeley Student Revolt: Facts and Interpretations,* ed. Seymour Martin Lipset and Sheldon S. Wolin (New York: Doubleday, 1965), 1–9. Studies that focus on specific grievances include William C. Lane, "The Rebellion of 1766 in Harvard College," *Publications of the Colonial Society of Massachusetts* 10 (1905): 33–59; Sheldon S. Cohen, "The Turkish Tyranny," *New England Quarterly* 48 (1974): 564–83; James R. McGovern, "The Student Rebellion in Harvard College, 1807–1808," *Harvard Library Bulletin* 19 (1971): 341–55; and Samuel Eliot Morison, "The Great Rebellion at Harvard College and the Resignation of President Kirkland," *Publications of the Colonial Society of Massachusetts* 27 (1928): 54–112.

8. The connections between student societies and social order were first adumbrated by James McLachlan, "The *Choice of Hercules:* American Student Societies in the Early 19th Century," in *The University in Society,* ed. Lawrence Stone, 2 vols. (Princeton: Princeton University Press, 1974), 2:449–94, esp. 474–75. The following analysis is greatly indebted to McLachlan's scholarship. My thinking in this account was also shaped by the experience of serving as freshman proctor at Harvard College between 1990 and 1993.

9. On the impoverished state of the college in 1780, see Sidney Willard, *Memories of Youth and Manhood* (Cambridge: John Bartlett, 1855), 1:100–103.

10. [Willard Phillips], "Anti-Don-Quixotism, or, A Vindication of the Students with respect to the late Occurrences in Harvard. By Bartholomew Bystander" [1807], unpaginated MS, Harvard University Archives.

11. Eliphalet Pearson to Edward Holyoke, 28 April 1798, quoted in McLachlan, "*Choice of Hercules*," 462, 463. Pearson, like most other eighteenth-century professors, believed that the patriarchal/domestic model of governance was the most appropriate for Harvard.

12. See Joseph F. Kett, *Rites of Passage: Adolescence in America, 1790 to the Present* (New York: Basic Books, 1977), esp. 11–37; and Ross W. Beales Jr., "In Search of the Historical Child: Miniature Adulthood and Youth in Colonial New England," *American Quarterly* 27 (1975): esp. 383–91.

13. Victor Turner, *The Ritual Process: Structure and Anti-structure* (Ithaca: Cornell University Press, 1977), 95.

14. Kett, *Rites of Passage*, 29–31; Beales, "In Search of the Historical Child," 391–97.

15. On the liminal status of college students, see Kett, *Rites of Passage*, 51–61; and McLachlan, "*Choice of Hercules*," 462–66. On the conceptual confusions that this liminality could engender, one might note the example of student John Frye, who was prosecuted in 1770 for criminal violence and described in court as "an Infant and Student at Harvard College." Quoted in Theodore Chase, "Harvard Student Disorders in 1770," *New England Quarterly* 61 (1988): 39.

16. An excellent discussion of faculty-sanctioned student politicization is offered by David W. Robson, *Educating Republicans: The College in the Era of the American Revolution, 1750–1800* (Westport, Conn.: Greenwood Press, 1985), 143–77. Novak goes so far as to suggest that student *radicalization* was considered acceptable. See *Rights of Youth*, 3–5.

17. Turner, *Ritual Process*, 94–95.

18. John Clarke, *Letters to a Student in the University of Cambridge, Massachusetts* (Boston: printed by Samuel Hall, 1796), 27.

19. Anon., *A True Description of a Number of Tyrannical Pedagogues, A Poem. Dedicated to the Sons of H******d* ([Boston], 1769), 8; [William Austin], *Strictures on Harvard College. By a Senior* (Boston: printed by John W. Folsom, 1798), 8; unidentified student, quoted in Sheldon S. Cohen, "Harvard College on the Eve of the American Revolution," in *Sibley's Heir: A Volume in Memory of Clifford Kenyon Shipton* (Boston: Colonial Society of Massachusetts, 1982), 182.

20. My understanding of the faculty ideal of college life and of student identity is based upon an analysis of the various laws in effect at Harvard between 1788 and 1793. Until 1790 the *Laws of Harvard College* existed only in manuscript form. They were recited orally at the beginning of each academic year, and a copy was available in the buttery at all times for students to consult. After 1790, no doubt in response to increasing tumultuousness in the college, the *Laws* were wholly reformulated and seven hundred copies printed for distribution to members of the student body—an action that further exacerbated hostility on the part of students. The manuscript *Laws* of 1767, which operated (with subsequent emendations) until 1790, were reproduced and edited by Samuel Eliot Morison, "College Laws and Customs," *Publications of the Colonial Society of Massachusetts* 31 (1935): 347–82. After this point one consults *The Laws of Harvard College* (Boston: printed by Samuel Hall, 1790). On the transition from manuscript to printed laws, see William C. Lane, "Manuscript Laws of Harvard College," *Publications of the Colonial Society of Massachusetts* 25 (1923): 244–53.

21. "The Philanthropist. No. VI," *Massachusetts Magazine* 1 (June 1789): 338. The philosophical exemplars of this position included Ralph Cudworth, Thomas Reid, Dugald Stewart, and Richard Price. On the American vogue for rational intuitionism, see Daniel Walker Howe, *The Unitarian Conscience: Harvard Moral Philosophy, 1805–1861* (Middletown, Conn.: Wesleyan University Press, 1988), 45–68.

22. "The Philanthropist. No. III. Addressed to Students at Colleges and Universities," *Massachusetts Magazine* 1 (March 1789): 140–41. Students' confessions of guilt, often penned by professors and merely assented to by the students themselves, refer often to the "exhilaration" or "distraction" of "the passions" as a leading cause of waywardness. See, for example, Faculty Records 6 (1788–1797): 5, 13, Harvard University Archives. For additional faculty discussion of unruly passions, see Eliphalet Pearson, "Address to Students," 21 May 1789, Addresses and Exhortations to Students, Administrative Records of College Disorders, 1789–1809, Harvard University Archives.

23. On the tensions between reason and passion in moderate educational theory, see Philip Greven, *The Protestant Temperament: Patterns of Child-Rearing, Religious Experience, and the Self in Early America* (New York: Meridian, 1977), 151–261.

24. The most detailed analysis of the early Harvard curriculum, although it stops short of the period under consideration, is Thomas Jay Seigel, "Governance and Curriculum at Harvard College in the 18th Century" (Ph.D. diss., Harvard University, 1990).

25. David Kendall, "An Inquiry 'Whether the time usually spent in the study of the dead languages be usefully occupied,'" 52, Bowdoin Prize Essay, 1796, Houghton Library, Harvard University.

26. [Austin], *Strictures on Harvard*, 29.

27. Joseph Dennie to Roger Vose, 1 June 1788, *The Letters of Joseph Dennie, 1768–1812*, ed. Laura Green Pedder, University of Maine Studies, 2d ser., 36 (Orono: University of Maine Press, 1936), 8.

28. Entry for 13 June 1786, *Diary of John Quincy Adams*, ed. David Grayson Allen et al. (Cambridge: Belknap Press of Harvard University Press, 1981), 2:49.

29. Entry for 3 May 1786, ibid., 2:25.

30. *Laws of Harvard College*, 42, 45–47.

31. *Catalogus Librorum in Bibliotheca Cantabrigiensi Selectus, frequentum in Usum Harvardinatum, qui Gradu Baccalauri in Artibus Nondum Sunt Donati* (Bostoniae: Typis Edes and Gill, 1773), [3]. My translation is drawn from Keyes D. Metcalf, "The Undergraduate and Harvard Library, 1765–1877," *Harvard Library Bulletin* 1 (1947): 30.

32. Herbert M. Morais, *Deism in the Eighteenth Century* (New York: Russell and Russell, 1960), 161 n. 5.

33. "College Laws and Customs," 362; *Laws of Harvard College*, 34–35.

34. Erving Goffman, *Asylums: Essays on the Social Situation of Mental Patients and Other Inmates* (Harmondsworth: Penguin Books, 1968), 11.

35. *Laws of Harvard College*, 28; "College Laws and Customs," 359, 358.

36. "The Harvard Diary of Pitt Clark, 1786–1791," in *Sibley's Heir*, 257 and n. 2 (entries for 8, 10 December 1787). For additional examples of (unsuccessful) student

petitions, see Cohen, "Harvard College on the Eve of the American Revolution," 182; and entry for 11 April 1787, *Diary of John Quincy Adams,* 2:205.

37. Joseph Story to William F. Channing, 23 September 1843, quoted in William W. Story, *Life and Letters of Joseph Story* (Boston: Charles C. Little and James Brown, 1851), 1:49. See "College Laws and Customs," 350; *Laws of Harvard College,* 35.

38. Quoted in George P. Schmidt, *The Old Time College President* (New York: Columbia University Press, 1930), 78.

39. Joseph Dennie to Roger Vose, 24 February 1790, *Letters of Joseph Dennie,* 15.

40. See Robert A. McCaughey, "The Transformation of American Academic Life: Harvard University, 1821–1892," *Perspectives in American History* 8 (1974): esp. 246–55; and Kett, *Rites of Passage,* 55.

41. White, "Reminiscences," 93. "The colloquy between Leonard and the President was much longer than appears from notice of it," White added (95). I have punctuated White's account to facilitate easier reading.

42. Pearson, Journal, 5; White, "Reminiscences," 89–91.

43. Joseph Dennie to Roger Vose, 24 February 1790, *Letters of Joseph Dennie,* 14. John Abbot was a tutor at the college.

44. B. C., "The Author's Advice," in Benjamin Church, Commonplace Book, Houghton Library, Harvard University. Boxing referred to the officially sanctioned punishment of boxing a student's ears. It was banned in 1755.

45. James C. Scott, *Domination and the Arts of Resistance: Hidden Transcripts* (New Haven: Yale University Press, 1990), 23. Scott's work has played an absolutely pivotal role in helping me form my understanding of student life at Harvard.

46. John Henry Tudor, "A Registry of College Adventures, 1799," 47, Harvard University Archives.

47. Goffman, *Asylums,* 170.

48. On alcohol as an alleged cause for riotous behavior, see Jonathan Fisher, "Sketches of the Life of Rev. Jonathan Fisher, 1812," 25–26, Harvard University Archives; White, "Reminiscences," 21; and Faculty Records 6: 4–5. On sinfulness as a motivation for disorder, see Novak, *Rights of Youth,* 3–4. For a good contemporary example of such thinking, see Phillis Wheatley, "To the University of Cambridge, in New-England," *Poems on Various Subjects, Religious and Moral* (London: printed for A. Bell, 1773), 15–16 (esp. ll. 24–30).

49. Scott, *Domination and the Arts of Resistance,* 150–52.

50. For instances of jostling or fighting when moving between buildings, see White, "Reminiscences," 34–36, 85, 87.

51. Ibid., 41; Pearson, Journal, 4. On hissing as a well-entrenched convention, see [Phillips], "Anti-Don-Quixotism"; and [Benjamin Homer Hall], *A Collection of College Words and Customs* (Cambridge: John Bartlett, 1851), 161–62. Hall's work is the nearest thing we have to an ethnography of student culture at eighteenth-century Harvard. I am currently working on a longer study of student culture at Harvard from 1707 to 1806.

52. White, "Reminiscences," 46–47.

53. Entry for 8 May 1786, *Diary of John Quincy Adams,* 2:29.

54. On bell sabotage, see White, "Reminiscences," 81, 89; Pearson, Journal, 12, 15. The tradition continued well into the next century. See Kirk Boott to Eliza Boott, 20 November 1807, Welch Family Papers, Lincoln, Massachusetts. I would like to thank Nathaniel Welch of Lincoln for allowing me to consult and cite these letters.

55. On candle snuffing, see White, "Reminiscences," 81, 85; Pearson, Journal, 2.

56. On Bible theft, see White, "Reminiscences," 81, 83; Pearson, Journal, 6, 8, 11.

57. In my discussion of theft, I do not consider acts such as bell and Bible stealing, which were motivated solely by a desire to sabotage the college schedule. The only other discussion of student theft of which I am aware is Kathryn McDaniel Moore, "Old Saints and Young Sinners: A Study of Discipline at Harvard College, 1636–1734" (Ph.D. diss., University of Wisconsin, 1972), 186–87.

58. Lane, "Rebellion of 1766," 44; McGovern, "Student Rebellion in Harvard College," 343; Joseph Thaxter quoted in Cohen, "Harvard College on the Eve of the American Revolution," 179 n. 6. See also the citations in n. 53. For a good discussion of commons, see [Hall], *Words and Customs,* 71–76.

59. *Laws of Harvard College,* 60–61.

60. This happened very often. On one notable evening (6 April 1792), no less than twenty-four students were caught surreptitiously supping at Bradish's and fined two shillings each. See Faculty Records 6: 144; *Laws of Harvard College,* 22.

61. Morison, *Three Centuries of Harvard,* 117; Pearson, Journal, 8; Corporation Records, 2:73; Pearson, Journal, 16. For earlier instances of food theft, see Moore, "Old Saints and Young Sinners," 171–72.

62. E. P. Thompson, "The Moral Economy of the English Crowd in the Eighteenth Century," in *Customs in Common: Studies in Traditional Popular Culture* (New York: New Press, 1993), esp. 238–44; and "The Moral Economy Reviewed," in ibid., esp. 336–51. Charles Tilly's gloss on Thompson is especially germane to the experience of the college appropriators: "The term 'moral economy' makes sense when claimants to a commodity can invoke non-monetary rights to that commodity, and third parties will act to support *these* claims" (338 n. 2).

63. The following narrative is based primarily on Pearson, Journal, 1–14.

64. Writing in his diary in 1789, Jonathan Fisher noted that noisy parties were "common" in the wake of exhibitions. See "Sketches of the Life of Rev. Jonathan Fisher," 25.

65. Pearson, Journal, 2.

66. Faculty Records 6: 10–11.

67. [Phillips], "Anti-Don-Quixotism."

68. *Laws of Harvard College,* 16, 17, 17.

69. [Phillips], "Anti-Don-Quixotism." On the notion of custom as a body of unwritten rights, see E. P. Thompson, "Introduction: Custom and Culture," in *Customs in Common,* esp. 1–15; and J. G. A. Pocock, *The Ancient Constitution and the Feudal Law* (Cambridge: Cambridge University Press, 1957). Students, wrote undergraduate Pickering Dodge, believed it to be "their duty and their privilege to support ancient customs" (quoted in Morison, "Great Rebellion at Harvard College," 67). For examples of student disorders being provoked by violation of such customs, see Lane, "Rebellion of 1766,"

50–51; and Cohen, "Turkish Tyranny," 567. Harvard's customs were kept alive and commemorated for the most part through word of mouth. Ralph Waldo Emerson, for example, wrote a drinking song to commemorate the rebellion of 1822. In other cases, however, accounts of disorders were penned with an eye to posterity, and manuscript copies handed down from class to class. See, for example, Lane, "Rebellion of 1766," 43 n. 2; Chase, "Harvard Student Disorders in 1770," 27 n. 2; *Diary of John Quincy Adams,* 2:182 n. 1; and "Editor's Preface," in *The Rebelliad; or Terrible Transactions at the Seat of the Muses; A Poem in Four Cantos* (Boston, 1842), 6. For a pioneering account of manuscript culture at Harvard, see Jeffrey Walker, "'The War of Words' in Harvard's Class of '54: Collegiate Literary Culture in Eighteenth Century America," in *Early American Literature and Culture: Essays Honoring Harrison T. Meserole,* ed. Kathryn Zabelie Derounian-Stodola (Newark: University of Delaware Press, 1992), 132–48. It is evident that accounts of college uprisings were kept alive, at least in part, to sustain an awareness of student customs and the battles that had been waged in order to protect them. These customs are not to be confused with the "college customs" concerning the fagging of freshmen, which were sanctioned by the faculty, and which were, in any case, on the wane by the 1780s.

70. Fisher, "Sketches of the Life of Rev. Jonathan Fisher," 42.

71. [Austin], *Strictures on Harvard,* 18. For criticisms of the student notion of genius, see Philo-Mathesis, "Strictures on the Literary Exhibitions of the Students in Harvard College," *Monthly Anthology and Magazine of Polite Literature* 1 (December 1803): 57–59; Studiosus, "On the Absurdity of Some Popular Opinions in Harvard College," *Monthly Anthology and Magazine of Polite Literature* (January 1804): 103–6; and Cantabrigiensis, "Remarks on the Erroneous Opinion of Students, respecting Genius and Application," *Monthly Anthology and Magazine of Polite Literature* (April 1804): 277–78.

72. Willard, *Memories of Youth and Manhood,* 1:301–3.

73. Josiah Quincy, *The History of Harvard University* (Boston: Crosby, Nichols, Lee and Co., 1860), 2:279–80.

74. Faculty Records 6:107; [Hall], *Words and Customs,* 114. The ruse may have been a cruel play on the custom of *non valui* (I was sick) that excused a student from reciting or answering a question. See [Hall], *Words and Customs,* 218.

75. Faculty Records 6:106–8; [Hall], *Words and Customs,* 114.

76. The problem flared up a year later, in April 1792. See Fisher, "Sketches of the Life of Rev. Jonathan Fisher," 59; Faculty Records 6:145.

77. Faculty Records 6:125–26.

78. Ibid., 127–28. Paine later changed his first name, becoming Robert Treat Paine Jr. Charles Angier was so well known among students for the amount of alcohol that he gathered up and dispersed in his room that for twenty years after his departure from the college in 1793, his former suite in Hollis Hall was known as The Tavern. See [Hall], *Words and Customs,* 297.

79. Pearson, Journal, 16.

80. On the Guy Fawkes Night tradition in America, see David D. Hall, *Worlds of Wonder, Days of Judgement: Popular Religious Belief in Early New England* (Cambridge: Harvard University Press, 1990), 210–11.

81. White, "Reminiscences," 81–83; Pearson, Journal, 17.

82. Morison, *Three Centuries of Harvard*, 183. Despite the wealth of documentary evidence to the contrary, Morison supposed that this society was a "cruel hoax" on the faculty.

83. Faculty Records 6: 194. The subscribers are named in Pearson, Journal, 17.

84. Faculty Records 6: 194; White, "Reminiscences," 85.

85. Edith Davenport Fuller, "Excerpts from the Diary of Timothy Fuller, Jr., an Undergraduate in Harvard College, 1798–1801," *Cambridge Historical Society Proceedings* 11 (1916): 38.

86. White, "Reminiscences," 85; Pearson, Journal, 18.

87. E. P. Thompson, "Rough Music," in *Customs in Common*, 467–531, quote on 480. Significantly Thompson notes that "Charivaris" flourished on Guy Fawkes Day (5 November), which was the event that possibly sparked the disorders in the first place (481 n. 2).

88. White, "Reminiscences," 87. Olds's attacker was one Shackleford. He did not appear to be punished, nor can I find any other information concerning him in the college records.

89. Faculty Records 6: 197–205; White, "Reminiscences," 89–97. The majority of these students did not return to Harvard.

90. [Austin], *Strictures on Harvard*, 8.

91. The following discussion is based upon Bernard Bailyn, *The Ideological Origins of the American Revolution* (Cambridge: Harvard University Press, 1967); Gordon S. Wood, *The Creation of the American Republic, 1776–1787* (New York: Norton, 1972); and J. G. A. Pocock, "Civic Humanism and Its Role in Anglo-American Thought," in *Politics, Language and Time: Essays on Political Thought and History* (New York: Athenaeum, 1973), 80–103.

92. On the masculine underpinnings of republican political ideology and Enlightenment philosophy, see Linda K. Kerber, *Women of the Republic: Intellect and Ideology in Revolutionary America* (New York: Norton, 1986), 15–32; and Ruth H. Bloch, "The Gendered Meanings of Virtue in Revolutionary America," *Signs: Journal of Women in Culture and Society* 13 (1987): 37–58. It should be noted that while in the late twentieth century the opposite of the word *man* is usually *child* or *woman*, in the minds of the eighteenth-century students a third term—*unmanly*—was often used. It referred to men (adult males) who either could not or did not act in a manly or civic fashion. Unmanliness and even effeminacy should not be, as they so often are, confused with acting like a woman. One could be a man and yet (be forced to) act in an unmanly fashion. This was the grievance of the students.

93. Classical republican authors taught at Harvard in the 1780s included Virgil and Cicero, and later Sallust, Livy, and Xenophon. See Robson, *Educating Republicans*, 166.

94. See Cohen, "Turkish Tyranny," 567; Anon., *A True Description;* [John Quincy Adams], "Lines upon the Late Proceedings of the College Government," quoted in *Diary of John Quincy Adams*, 2:179; Joseph Dennie to Roger Vose, 17 August 1790, *Letters of Joseph Dennie*, 61. On eighteenth-century perceptions of Turkey as an exemplary despotism, see Bailyn, *Ideological Origins of the American Revolution*, 63–64.

95. [Hall], *Words and Customs*, 185–87; Thomas Hutchinson, *The History of the Colony and Province of Massachusetts Bay*, ed. Lawrence Shaw Mayo (Cambridge: Harvard University Press, 1936), 3:135.

96. In what is otherwise one of the best discussions of Harvard in the late eighteenth century, Sheldon S. Cohen has argued that political ideals mattered little to the disorderly students. His extensive citation of student mobilizations seems to contradict his own thesis, however, to which one must add that Cohen utilizes a fairly rigid and academic conception of "politicization" in his argument. Clearly it would be "erroneous," as Cohen puts it, to compare the Harvard students to the "Students for a Democratic Society," but to dismiss the butter riots of 1766 as a matter "of the stomach, not of politics" seems to conflate *casus belli* and cause, especially in the light of work undertaken by E. P. Thompson and others on food riots in the eighteenth century. See Cohen, "Harvard College on the Eve of the American Revolution," passim, quotes on 188, 189. More surprising is the assent of Bernard Bailyn, who argues that the riots "had no ideological content, academic or otherwise. They were simply explosions of pent-up adolescent energies against the tightly paternalistic, and *increasingly* paternalistic system." From the utterances and behaviors of the students, however, it would seem evident that while they did see the struggle against the immediate government as a struggle against paternalism, they framed the struggle itself in ideological terms. See Bernard Bailyn, "Why Kirkland Failed," in *Glimpses of the Harvard Past* (Cambridge: Harvard University Press, 1986), 26–27. My thoughts with respect to the ideological underpinnings of student disorder are in accord with Kett, *Rites of Passage*, 59.

97. [Joseph Tufts], *Don Quixots at College; or, A History of the Gallant Adventures Lately Achieved by the Combined Students of Harvard University; Interspersed with Some Facetious Reasonings. By a Senior* (Boston: Etheridge and Bliss, 1807), 4–5.

98. Joseph Dennie to Roger Vose, 1 June 1788, *Letters of Joseph Dennie*, 9.

99. For examples of radical artisanal republicanism, see Eric Foner, *Tom Paine and Revolutionary America* (Oxford: Oxford University Press, 1976); Sean Wilentz, *Chants Democratic: New York City and the Rise of the American Working Class, 1788–1850* (Oxford: Oxford University Press, 1986); and Gary B. Nash, *The Urban Crucible: Social Change, Political Consciousness, and the Origins of the American Revolution* (Cambridge: Harvard University Press, 1979). I feel it is worth emphasizing the fact that students' use of republican language for their own ends in no way invalidates or makes disingenuous the role of republicanism in their thought. There existed no one monolithic republicanism that the students retroactively adopted to justify their ends. Rather, republicanism constituted a diffuse (and almost invisible) language that could shape and in turn be shaped by almost any event or series of events. The students' republicanism resembled that of the lower orders not because they shared a common *economic* identity, but because both shared a common experience of subjection.

100. See Willard, *Memories of Youth and Manhood*, 1:260–61; [Hall], *Words and Customs*, 314–16, 160–61.

101. On class formation at Harvard, see Henry D. Sheldon, *Student Life and Customs* (New York: D. Appleton, 1901), 84–87.

102. *Laws of Harvard College*, 36–37; Quincy, *History of Harvard University*, 2:276.

103. Each class, with the permission of the president, was allowed to convene up to four ad hoc meetings per year. See *Laws of Harvard College*, 35.

104. Willard, *Memories of Youth and Manhood*, 2:2.

105. [William Biglow], *Classology: An Anacreontic Ode, in Imitation of "Heathen Mythology"* (Boston: Thurston, Torry, and Emerson, 1843), 8.

106. E. Anthony Rotundo, *American Manhood: Transformations in Masculinity from the Revolution to the Modern Era* (New York: Basic Books, 1993), 31–55.

107. Tudor, "Registry of College Adventures," 15–19. Fishing is best described as a form of sycophantism. See [Hall], *Words and Customs,* 128–29.

108. Timothy Bigelow, *An Oration, Pronounced at Cambridge, before the {____}, at Their Annual Meeting on Thursday, July 21, 1796* (Boston: Manning and Loring, 1796), 8.

109. Quoted in Oscar M. Voorhees, *The History of Phi Beta Kappa* (New York: Crown, 1945), 9, 10.

110. Anthony Earl of Shaftesbury, *Characteristics of Men, Manners, Opinions, Times, with a Collection of Letters* (Basil: printed for J. L. Legrand, 1790), 1:62, 57, 64.

111. [Thadeus M. Harris], "On Literary and Benevolent Associations," *Literary Miscellany* 1 (1805): 8. This is an abridged version of an oration delivered to the Harvard Phi Beta Kappa in 1790.

112. Turner, *Ritual Process,* 95.

113. [John Pierce], "Advice to a Student of Harvard University in a Series of Letters. Letter I," *Literary Miscellany* 1 (1805): 51. Pierce's authorship is asserted by Willard, *Memories of Youth and Manhood,* 2:143.

114. Quincy, *History of Harvard University,* 2:398; ØßK Records 1 (1781–1803): unpaginated (entry for 8 September 1789), Phi Beta Kappa Papers, Harvard University Archives.

115. Entry for 5 September 1787, *Diary of John Quincy Adams,* 2:284.

116. Quincy, *History of Harvard University,* 2:397–98.

117. Socius, "For the Centinel," *Columbian Centinel,* 15 May 1793 (quotation); and Socius, "For the Centinel," *Columbian Centinel,* 5 June 1793. The first letter was replied to by Petros, "For the Centinel," *Columbian Centinel,* 22 May 1793.

118. Samuel Shapleigh to the president in Connecticut, 17 October 1796, quoted in the *Catalogue of the Harvard Chapter of Phi Beta Kappa Alpha of Massachusetts,* ed. William Coolidge Lane (Cambridge: Riverside Press, 1912), 136.

119. Tudor, "Registry of College Adventures," 71.

120. McLachlan, *"Choice of Hercules,"* 472. David S. Shields has pointed out that organizations such as Phi Beta Kappa resembled the coffee house debating societies known as "penny universities" (David S. Shields to Leon Jackson, private correspondence, 26 May 1994).

121. The following account is based on ØßK Records 1: undated pages, 9–13.

122. Turner, *Ritual Process,* 103.

123. Georg Simmel, "The Secret and the Secret Society," in *The Sociology of Georg Simmel,* ed. and trans. Kurt H. Wolff (New York: Free Press, 1950), esp. 345–48. See also Sissela Bok, *Secrets: On the Ethics of Concealment and Revelation* (New York: Vintage, 1984).

124. Turner, *Ritual Process,* 103. Although the members came increasingly to deny the fact, Phi Beta Kappa's use of arcana and ritual were drawn directly from the Freemasons. The connections have been usefully explored by William T. Hastings, *Phi Beta Kappa as a Secret Society* (Washington, D.C.: United Chapters of Phi Beta Kappa, 1965).

125. See David S. Shields, "Anglo-American Clubs: Their Wit, Their Heterodoxy, Their Sedition," *William and Mary Quarterly,* 3d ser., 51 (1994): 293–304.

126. The honor/dignity distinction was first formulated by Peter Berger, Brigette Berger, and Hansfried Kellner, *The Homeless Mind: Modernization and Consciousness* (New York: Vintage, 1974), 83–84, 88–89. For an exemplary historical application that has greatly directed my thinking, see Edward L. Ayers, *Vengeance and Justice: Crime and Punishment in the 19th-Century American South* (Oxford: Oxford University Press, 1984), esp. 13–33.

127. Robert A. McCaughey, "The Usable Past: A Study of the Harvard College Rebellion of 1834," *William and Mary Law Review* 11 (1970): 587–610.

128. The following observations are heavily indebted to Ronald Story, *The Forging of an Aristocracy: Harvard and the Boston Upper Class, 1800–1870* (Middletown, Conn.: Wesleyan University Press, 1980); David B. Tyack, *George Ticknor and the Boston Brahmins* (Cambridge: Harvard University Press, 1967); and Robert A. McCaughey, *Josiah Quincy, 1772–1864: The Last Federalist* (Cambridge: Harvard University Press, 1974).

College As It Was in the Mid–Nineteenth Century

1. David Allmendinger, *Paupers and Scholars: The Transformation of Student Life in Nineteenth-Century New England* (New York: St. Martin's, 1975), 3.

2. This chapter reviews a student memoir written in 1853 but only published in 1996: James Buchanan Henry and Christian Henry Scharff, *College as It Is, or, The Collegian's Manual in 1853,* with an introduction by ed. J. Jefferson Looney (Princeton: Princeton University Libraries, 1996). This volume provides the opportunity to interpret the meaning and significance of the entire genre of student writing about their colleges in the middle of the nineteenth century. The following titles, listed chronologically, are mentioned:

Ezekial Porter Belden, *Sketches of Yale College by a member of that Institution* (New York, 1843).

David A. Wells and Samuel H. Davis, *Sketches of Williams College* (Williamstown, Mass., 1847).

Benjamin H. Hall, *A Collection of College Words and Customs* (Cambridge, Mass., 1851; rev. ed., 1856).

Charles A. Bristed, *Five Years in an English University,* 2 vols. (New York, 1851).

The University Quarterly: Conducted by an Association of Collegiate and Professional Students in the United States and Europe, 4 vols. (New Haven, Conn., 1860–1861).

George R. Cutting, *Student Life at Amherst College: Its Organizations, Their Membership and History* (Amherst, Mass., 1871).

Lyman H. Bagg, *Four Years at Yale* (New Haven, Conn., 1871).

[Some additional material has been added to the original—Ed.]

3. College reminiscences began to appear in the 1880s, and became legion with the establishment of regular alumni publications early in the twentieth century. Two famous exemplars are Cornelius Howard Patton and Walter Taylor Field, *Eight O'clock Chapel: A*

Study of New England College Life in the Eighties (Boston: Houghton Mifflin, 1927); and Henry Seidel Canby, *Alma Mater: The Gothic Age of the American College* (New York, 1936).

4. *Fair Harvard* (New York, 1869) by William Tucker Washburn (Harvard '62) may have been the first widely read novel of college life. It depicts almost total preoccupation with extracurricular activities, including much mischief. Within a decade, novels portraying Harvard, Yale, and Princeton students in this light had become commonplace. See John E. Kramer Jr., *The American College Novel: An Annotated Bibliography* (New York: Garland, 1981), 6–15.

5. Not considered in this review are student diaries, since they were not written for the public. However, one informative diary that bears comparison with the Henry and Scharff memoir is William Gardiner Hammond, *Remembrance of Amherst: An Undergraduate's Diary, 1846–1848*, ed. George F. Wicher (New York: Columbia University Press, 1946). Unlike later memorialists, Hammond appears to have been an all-around collegian *and* a model student. Remarkably Hammond actually envisioned a grander account of student life: "I have a favorite conception, which in the hands of one whose genius should be adequate to the task might be carried out, I think, in a most grand work. It is the inward life of a student. Suppose him beginning young: describe the phases of his mind, the stages of development, the fluctuations of his opinions, the progress of his studies, the working of his passions. The whole work should be devoted wholly to this: the plot simple, and subordinate characters only instruments for the development of the principal. Such a work well written would be an era in literature" (63).

6. For student rebellions at Princeton, see Mark A. Noll, "Before the Storm: Life at Princeton College 1806–1807," *Princeton Library Chronicle* 42 (1981): 145–64; (and for 1823) Thomas Jefferson Wertenbaker, *Princeton, 1746–1896* (Princeton: Princeton University Press, 1946), 176–78. For general causes, see Leon Jackson, "The Rights of Man and the Rites of Youth: Fraternity and Riot at Eighteenth-Century Harvard," in this volume.

7. James Buchanan Henry was the orphaned son of a Presbyterian minister who was raised by his uncle James Buchanan, later the fifteenth president of the United States. He was seventeen when he entered Princeton. Christian Henry Scharff was born in the Netherlands, moved to Newark at age nine, and matriculated at sixteen. See "Introduction," xxv–xxxii.

8. *College As It Is,* 198.

9. "Dismission" was separation from the college for an indefinite time, but with the right to request reinstatement. Expulsion was permanent—the ultimate punishment the college could impose; see Hall, *College Words and Customs,* 102, 108.

10. In a rare gesture of moderation, the faculty, in 1828, recommended that students be allowed some time "to be absent from their rooms for the purpose of recreation and exercise" (Princeton Faculty Minutes, 15 September 1828). Our thanks to Ronald A. Smith for this reference as well as other suggestions.

11. *College as It Is,* 136.

12. *Sketches of Williams,* v.

13. *Sketches of Yale,* x. Belden graduated in 1844 and thus composed *Sketches* while still a student. Almost two hundred pages, much descriptive material was derived from

printed sources. His motivation beyond these remarks is obscure, but he was clearly devoted to Yale and as an alumnus became an assiduous secretary of his class.

14. *College Words and Customs,* iv.

15. *College as It Is,* 14.

16. Francis Wayland, *Report to the Corporation of Brown University on Changes in the System of Collegiate Education, Read 28 March 1850* (Providence, R.I.: George H. Whitney, 1850); Henry Tappan, *University Education* (New York, 1851), 68.

17. Published in New Haven, January 1860 through October 1861. The original issue was entitled *The Undergraduate,* but was identical in purpose. The participation of professional students and American students studying in Europe was complementary, since they could reflect upon their recent undergraduate experiences as well as describe postgraduate opportunities. Participating colleges spanned the East Coast from Penn to Bowdoin (but not Princeton!) and extended west as far as Beloit.

18. "Prospectus," *University Quarterly* (January 1860): 1–18, quote on 5. See also the description by Lyman Bagg, *Four Years at Yale,* 448–54.

19. *University Quarterly* (January 1861): quote on 169, 189–91.

20. *University Quarterly* (January 1860): 10.

21. Lyman Bagg was paid an average of $25 per week for 44 weeks by publisher Charles C. Chatfield to write *Four Years at Yale.* The contract (17 August 1870) stipulated that Bagg remain anonymous and that his compensation remain secret. He posed as an editor of Chatfield's paper, the *College Courant,* during this time. See Yale University Archives, Lyman H. Bagg Papers, box 3.

22. *Four Years at Yale,* 588. Maclean's successor at Princeton, James McCosh (1868–1888), resisted the kind of toleration described by Bagg, and instead persisted in the Sisyphean labor of attempting to enforce all college regulations. See J. David Hoevelar Jr., *James McCosh and the Scottish Intellectual Tradition: From Glasgow to Princeton* (Princeton: Princeton University Press, 1981), 260–61.

23. Bagg contributed the articles "Boating Clubs" and "The Bully Club" to William L. Kingsley's *Yale College: A Sketch of Its History* (New York, 1879).

24. John Maclean, "Inaugural Address," in *History of the College of New Jersey, 1746–1854,* vol. 2 (1877; reprint, New York: Arno Press, 1969), 411–36, quote on 427. Noah Porter's views were somewhat more nuanced while still considering the religious mission to be paramount; see *The American College and the American Public* (New Haven, Conn., 1870), chap. 11.

25. None of these works acknowledges the presence of older students, who were common earlier in the century (see n. 30, below) and who typically prepared for the ministry. During the presidency of James Carnahan (1824–1854), a fairly consistent 17 percent of Princeton graduates became ministers; see Maclean, *History of the College of New Jersey,* 2:344–45. Indigent students, likewise, receive no mention, although they continued to attend Princeton in the age of McCosh; see Hoevelar, *McCosh,* 259–60.

26. *College as It Is,* 177.

27. *Four Years at Yale,* 691. Bagg's emphasis on character was congruent with eastern colleges' own evolving interpretation of their mission, particularly educating the "whole

man." See George E. Peterson, *The New England College in the Age of the University* (Amherst, Mass.: Amherst College Press, 1964), 34–37.

28. *Four Years at Yale,* 178–79.

29. Ibid., 689; *College as It Is,* 107.

30. Allmendinger, *Paupers and Scholars,* 129–38; Joseph F. Kett, *Rites of Passage: Adolescence in America, 1790 to the Present* (New York: Basic Books, 1977).

31. The self-perpetuating upper-class eating clubs appeared in the 1880s; see Alexander Leitch, *A Princeton Companion* (Princeton: Princeton University Press, 1978), 146–49. In Henry and Scharff's day, temporary eating clubs were organized by less wealthy students, with the result that "the quality of their board" was determined by "the quantity of their funds" (*College as It Is,* 72).

32. Samuel Eliot Morison, *Three Centuries of Harvard* (Cambridge: Harvard University Press, 1936), 260.

33. William Hammond (see n. 5) was an exceptional student who cultivated a genuine love of classical literature and, like Bristed, attempted further study in Europe after graduation.

34. *Four Years at Yale,* 696–97. If a consensus can be inferred from these comments, it might be that students had little desire for more interesting classes, but sought more time to do interesting things outside the classroom. Such a view would underline the emerging centrality of the extracurriculum.

35. The important point, often overlooked, is that student writings show them to be quite concerned with class standing, and particularly that it measure intellectual attainments justly. Students at Hamilton College were indignant when marks for deportment were incorporated into class rankings: "[T]he students are very unwilling that sliding down hill, or singing songs upon the College grounds, should, in any way, help to measure their intellect" (*University Quarterly* [January 1861]: 169). William Hammond (see n. 5) was also concerned with the process of determining class standing.

"We Desired Our Future Rulers to Be Educated Men"

1. This chapter was made possible with the assistance of the Huntington Library, San Marino, California.

2. In 1803 Drayton wrote a defense of slavery, the first produced by a sitting governor in the U.S. See Larry Tise, *Proslavery* (University of Georgia Press, 1987), 38. See also Henry Adams, *History of the United States during the Administration of Jefferson and Madison* (New York: Library of America, 1986), 104.

3. John Drayton to the General Assembly, 23 November 1801, Governors Messages, Legislative System, 1800–1830, South Carolina Department of Archives and History, Columbia (hereafter cited as SCDAH).

4. John Belton O'Neall, *Biographical Sketches of the Bench and Bar of South Carolina,* vol. 1 (Charleston: S. G. Courtney and Co., 1859), 245.

5. "Phocion" [Henry William DeSaussure], *Letters on the Questions of the Justice and Expediency of Going into Alterations of Representation in the Legislature of South Carolina as Fixed by the Constitution* (Charleston, 1795), 8–9.

6. William Harper, *Memoir of the Life Character and Services of the Late Hon. Henry William DeSaussure* (Charleston: W. Riley, 1841), 23. Other contemporaries also noted the resistance of the up-country to the proposed college. See John Belton O'Neall, *An Oration Delivered to the Clariosophic Society Incorporate and the Inhabitants of Columbia, on the Anniversary of the Society, December 5, 1826* (Charleston: A. E. Miller, 1827), 12–13.

7. *Annals of Congress,* lst Congress, 2d session, February 1790, 1198.

8. Henry William DeSaussure to Ezekiel Pickens, 27 October 1805, Henry W. DeSaussure Papers, South Caroliniana Library (hereafter cited as SCL), Columbia.

9. The total number of matriculants is unknown. In the first years of the twentieth century, a professor at the University of South Carolina, Andrew C. Moore, gathered an extraordinary cache of evidence on all alumni of South Carolina College (later the University of South Carolina [USC]). Moore sent out detailed questionnaires to alumni and their children asking for details on alumni: parents, place and date of birth and death, marriage, wife, and children, pre- and postcollegiate schooling, debate society and whether a graduate, publications, military service, profession, political officeholding, etc. Although the information he got was often incomplete, Moore turned the questionnaires (which number in the thousands) into brief biographical sketches. He apparently intended to write a book but died before doing so. He published only a list of the alumni, which he admitted to be incomplete. See A. C. Moore, *Roll of Students of South Carolina College, 1805–1905* (n.p., 1908). The background data on individuals are fragmentary, so statistical analysis would entail excessively large margins of error, plus unquantifiable biases, while suggesting a degree of precision that is misleading. For the purpose of generalizing about the alumni, the original questionnaires, which are on file at McKissick Museum, USC, were supplemented with other archival and bibliographical sources. This will hereafter be cited as *Moore Records.*

10. *Charleston Mercury,* 5 January 1836. The term *alumnus/i* will be used in the extended sense to refer to all those who matriculated at the college, not just those who graduated. The number after the name of alumni indicates year of graduation/withdrawal from the college.

11. James Dellett to Joseph B. Earle, 29 May 1833, Dellett Papers, Alabama Department of Archives and History, Montgomery.

12. "Incognito," *Tallahassee Floridian and Journal,* 8 December 1860.

13. Henry L. Pinckney, *The Necessity of Popular Enlightenment to the Honor and Welfare of the State* (Columbia, 1845), 28.

14. Edwin L. Greene, *A History of the University of South Carolina* (Columbia: State Company, 1916), 68–78.

15. Hutson, "South Carolina College in the 1850s," *Sewannee Review* 18 (July 1910): 341.

16. Charles Woodward Hutson to "Dear Father," 17 February 1857, Charles W. Hutson Papers, SCL, Columbia.

17. Quoted in Hollis, *South Carolina College,* 230.

18. William H. Russell, *My Diary North and South: The Civil War* (1863; reprint, New York: Harper and Brothers, 1954), 62.

19. James Henly Thornwell, *Letter to His Excellency Governor Manning on Public Instruction in South Carolina* (n.p.: R. W. Gibbes and Co., 1853), 26.

20. John Creighton McMaster, Notebook 1834, SCL, Columbia.

21. William Paley, *Principles of Moral and Political Philosophy,* rev. ed. (Boston, 1845), was the required text that covered these issues.

22. McMaster, Notebook 1834, SCL, Columbia.

23. Chalmers Davidson, *The Last Foray, The South Carolina Planters of 1860* (Columbia: University of South Carolina Press, 1971), 21.

24. Senators and governors of Florida, Georgia, Mississippi, Alabama, and Virginia sent their sons to South Carolina College.

25. George Blackburn, *Narrative of the Transactions at South Carolina College during the Last Three Courses* (n.p., n.d., [ca. 1814]), 60.

26. There were of course prominent exceptions to this rule, but the exceptional abilities of the poor scholars who became college graduates made them seem more numerous than they really were. Joshua Hudson, who graduated first in the class of 1852, was one of the "poor scholars" who made good. See Joshua Hudson, *Sketches and Reminiscences* (Columbia: State Company, 1903), 19–23.

27. "Chester" letter, *Columbia Southern Chronicle,* 7 December 1842.

28. The *Moore Records* suggest that roughly the wealthiest one thousand families in the state formed an exceedingly complex reticulation of family connections. Many of those who lived long lives were widowed and remarried once or twice, which multiplied the connections.

29. William J. Grayson, "The Character of a Gentleman," *Southern Quarterly Review* (January 1853): 69.

30. Reminiscing about Maxcy, William Grayson stated that "he professed a control over the hearts and minds of his pupils that no one of his successors has equalled or approached. . . . His eloquence was irresistible. No youth however rough his training could withstand its power" (Robert D. Bass, "The Autobiography of William Grayson" [Ph.D. diss., George Peabody College for Teachers, 1931], 85 [hereafter cited as Grayson, "Autobiography"]).

31. The records for the students' misconduct, the *Minutes of the Trustees of the South Carolina College* (hereafter cited as *TM*) and the *Minutes of the Faculty of South Carolina College* (hereafter cited as *FM;* original volumes of both *TM* and *FM* in McKissick Museum, USC, Columbia), are not complete. At some earlier time these documents were tampered with. Sections of both were excised with a sharp, razorlike instrument. The missing pages do not comprise a substantial amount of the documents, but they probably contained some exceptional data. Some of the Record Books for the Clariosophic and Euphradian Societies are lost as well. See *TM,* 21 April 1813.

32. Grayson, "Autobiography," 86.

33. E. Merton Coulter, *College Life in the Old South* (New York: Macmillan, 1928), passim. See also John Hope Franklin, *The Militant South* (Cambridge: Harvard University Press, 1956), 134.

34. This was not the case at the University of Alabama, for example. Cheating was common, and the sense of honor was not as strict as at South Carolina College. See James

B. Sellers, *History of the University of Alabama* (Birmingham: University of Alabama Press, 1953), 215.

35. James H. Carlisle, "College Reminiscences," in *Centennial Celebration of the Granting of the Charter to the South Carolina College* (Columbia: Lucas Richardson Co., 1901), 33.

36. *Minutes of the Clariosophic Society of South Carolina College* (hereafter cited as *CM*), 20 May 1820; John Chambers was the thief. Original volumes in McKissick Museum, USC, Columbia.

37. George McDuffie was the best example of a young alumnus who fought a highly publicized duel in the process of beginning a political career, but there were dozens of similar examples. See Edwin L. Green, *George McDuffie* (Columbia: State Company, 1936), 34.

38. Maximilian LaBorde, *The History of the South Carolina College from its Incorporation, Dec. 19, 1801 to Dec. 19, 1865; Including Sketches of Its Presidents and Professors, with an Appendix* (Charleston: Walker, Evans and Cogswell Co., 1874), 174.

39. Paley, *Principles of Moral and Political Philosophy* (Boston, 1827), 108. The undergraduates who studied this text were deeply influenced by the standards contained in it. William J. Grayson, writing some forty years after his graduation, cited Paley's book in an essay he wrote, "The Character of the Gentleman," *SQR* (January 1853): 59.

40. William Ellet, secretary of the faculty, to Trustees, 27 November 1839, *Miscellaneous Trustees Records,* McKissick Museum, USC, Columbia.

41. Lieber diary, 14 February 1838, in Perry, *Francis Lieber* (Boston: James R. Osgood and Co., 1882), 26.

42. Quoted in C. W. Lord, "Young Louis Wigfall, South Carolina Politician and Duelist," *SCHM* 59, 1 (January1958): 106.

43. Alvy King, *Louis T. Wigfall; Southern Fire Eater* (Baton Rouge: Louisiana State University Press, 1970), chap. 1.

44. William Campbell Preston to Louis T. Wigfall, 19 January 1860, Wigfall Papers, Library of Congress.

45. Bruce D. Dickson, *Violence and Culture in the Antebellum South* (Austin: University of Texas Press, 1979), chap. 1, passim.

46. Joseph H. Dargan to William Harper and the Board of Trustees, 2 December 1834, Thomas Cooper Papers, SCL, Columbia.

47. Marion Sims, *The Story of My Life* (New York, 1884), 88–89.

48. Thomas Palmer to Harriet Palmer, 9 May 1822, Palmer Family Papers, SCL, Columbia.

49. Bertram Wyatt-Brown, *Southern Honor: Ethics and Behavior in the Old South* (New York: Oxford University Press, 1984), passim.

50. Kenneth S. Greenberg, *Masters and Statesmen: The Political Culture of American Slavery* (Baltimore: Johns Hopkins University Press, 1985), 23–41, and John Lyde Wilson, *The Code of Honor* (1838), passim.

51. Sims, *The Story of My Life,* 92.

52. Max Weber, *Economy and Society,* ed. Gunther Roth and Claus Wittlich, vol. 1 (New York: Free Press, 1961), 241–46.

53. William Campbell Preston to Col. Cunningham, 11 February 1833, William C. Preston Papers, SCL, Columbia.

54. Green, *George McDuffie,* 33–36.

55. *Charleston Mercury,* 23 July 1823.

56. William Freehling, *The Road to Disunion* (New York: Oxford University Press, 1990), chaps. 4 through 8 show in great detail the connection between Cooper, James Henry Hammond, and other alumni (such as Pinckney and Davis) in treating the Gag Rule as a catalyst for secession.

57. See the articles signed "T. C." in the *Philadelphia Democratic Press,* 19 December 1819; 6 January 1820.

58. LaBorde, *History of South Carolina College.*

59. Cooper, *Dr. Cooper's Defense before the Board of Trustees,* from the Columbia (S.C.) *Times and Gazette,* 14 December 1832, 7. Cooper liked to strike the pose of a consistent advocate of free speech and thought, but this was more a convenient ploy than disinterested principle. In 1837, when the international copyright bill came before Congress, Cooper wrote to Congressman Francis Elmore, "[T]ake care that no clause is insidiously introduced to compel the South under law to admit abolition books" (Cooper to Francis Elmore, 3 May 1837, Cooper Papers, SCL, Columbia). Freedom of expression was not for abolitionists; it was for nullifiers. The year after his acquittal, his supporters would demonstrate their regard for freedom of expression and thought by requiring the "Test Oath."

60. Thomas Cooper to David McCord, 16 July 1828, Cooper Papers, SCL, Columbia.

61. Thomas Cooper, *To Any Member of Congress from a Layman* (Columbia, 1831), 9.

62. *Camden Journal,* 17 December 1831.

63. William Brearly to Rev. John McLean, 22 November 1822, William Brearly Papers, SCL, Columbia.

64. Thomas Cooper, *Lectures on the Elements of Political Economy,* 2d ed. (Columbia, 1829), 118.

65. Dumas Malone, *The Public Life of Thomas Cooper* (New Haven: Yale University Press, 1926), 282–90, passim.

66. *Columbia Telescope,* 6 July 1827.

67. Thomas Cooper to Joseph Parker, 21 February 1829, Cooper Papers, SCL, Columbia.

68. Cited in William Freehling, *Prelude to Civil War* (New York: Harper and Row, 1965), 206. The speaker was James Henry Hammond.

69. Thomas Cooper, *Address to the Graduates of the South Carolina College of 1820* (Columbia, 1821), 2. Cooper said much the same thing in his *Address to the Graduates of the South Carolina College of 1830* (Columbia, 1831), 6.

70. Gage, McMaster, and Witherspoon Notebooks, SCL, Columbia.

71. McMaster Notebook, SCL, Columbia. Henry was absent from the faculty from 1834 to 1842. He taught other classes in addition to moral philosophy.

72. Ibid.

73. Cited in Daniel Hollis, *History of South Carolina College* (Columbia: University of South Carolina Press, 1951), 262. The speaker, James Thornwell, was referring to the noted

orator William Campbell Preston. Both were alumni and both became presidents of the college.

74. *Charleston Mercury,* 14 August 1832.

75. *Moore Records.*

76. G. W. Featherstonaugh, *Excursions through the Slave States* (London, 1844), 157.

77. Ibid., 156.

78. Ibid., 157–58.

79. Ibid., 158.

80. Ibid.

81. *CM,* 4 May 1809.

82. Ibid., 27 February 1813.

83. Ibid., 12 June 1819.

84. Ibid., 7 June 1806; 7 June 1807; 26 March 1808; 30 April 1808; 3 June 1809; 24 November 1810; 6 March 1813; 20 May 1815; 26 April 1816; 27 December 1817; 31 January 1818; 22 November 1818; 27 February 1819; 3 April 1819; 22, 29 January 1820; 18 March 1820. It must be remembered that this represents only one of the two debate societies. Slavery was probably debated just as often in the Euphradian Society, whose minutes are lost for the Maxcy years.

85. Ibid., 26 March 1808; 24 November 1810.

86. Ibid., 3 June 1809.

87. Ibid., 27 April 1816.

88. Ibid., 3 April 1819.

89. Ibid., 29 January 1820.

90. Ibid., 22 November 1818.

91. Ibid., 31 January 1818.

92. Ibid., 25 February 1809; 19 February 1820.

93. Ibid., 27 February 1819; 18 March 1820.

94. Ibid., 12 March 1812; 6 March 1813.

95. Ibid., 7 June 1806.

96. Ibid., 7 June 1807. See also 30 January 1808.

97. Ibid., 26 October 1816; 27 December 1817.

98. See, for example, William Johnson, *Nugae Georgae, An Essay Delivered to the Literary and Philosophical Society of Charleston, South Carolina, October 14, 1815* (Charleston: J. Hoff, 1815), 33–34.

99. *CM,* 13 January 1821.

100. Ibid., 2 March 1822.

101. Ibid., 18 March 1826. Similar sentiments were expressed 22 November 1828.

102. *Minutes of the Euphradian Society* (hereafter cited as *EM*), 8 May 1824; 16 April 1825; 25 March 1826; 20 October 1827; 29 December 1827; 26 January 1829; 20 February 1830; 20 March 1830; 22 October 1831; 28 April 1832; 16 May 1835. *CM,* 24 November 1821; 27 March 1824; 1 April 1826; 9 December 1826; 31 March 1827; 27 October 1827; 7 March 1828; 13 March 1830; 26 March 1831.

103. The hardening of opinion on slavery is clearly evident in the career of Basil Manly. In April of 1821, Manly wrote a speech for the Euphradian Society called "On the Emancipation of Slaves" (Basil Manly Papers, SCL, Columbia). In this speech Manly argued that slavery was a particularly dangerous issue because it contributed to the growth of antagonistic parties, and the only way to avoid bitter factional disputes on this issue was to abolish slavery and colonize the freedmen, who were assumed to be dangerous to whites. Manly graduated, moved to Alabama, and gave up his antislavery views. He became the first president of the University of Alabama and one of the most prominent proslavery apologists. He was instrumental in dividing the Southern Baptist Church from the Northern, due to a controversy in 1844 over the ethics of slaveholding. He said a prayer at the opening of the Alabama Secession Convention, and shortly after wrote his son, "Thus you see, I have had a great deal to do with the whole thing. It was I who took the steps and wrote the Alabama Resolutions in '44 which separated the Denomination. This was the *entering wedge, driven far in*" (Basil Manly Sr. to Basil Manly Jr., 10 February 1861, Basil Manly Papers, box 1, folder 13, University of Alabama, Tuscaloosa).

104. *EM,* 12 March 1825; 22 November 1828; 28 December 1828; 23 January 1830; 8 May 1830; 29 October 1831; 3 November 1831; 17 March 1832; 6 April 1833. *CM,* 4 November 1826; 27 October 1827; 22 January 1828; 1 November 1828; 6 November 1830.

105. *EM,* 8 May 1830.

106. Ibid., 17 March 1832.

107. *CM,* 13 March 1830.

108. *EM,* 12 March 1825; 30 January 1830; 5 February 1830; 5 March 1831; 26 January 1833; 22 November 1834. *CM,* 13 January 1821; 2 March 1822; 21 January 1826; 8 November 1828; 21 November 1829; 13 March 1830; 9 October 1830.

109. *EM,* 12 March 1825.

110. Notebook, SCL, Columbia, containing undated (ca. 1857) clippings from the newspaper controversy between "Viator" and J. Stobo Farrow (hereafter cited as Viator Notebook).

111. Colyer Meriwether, *The History of Higher Education in South Carolina with a Sketch of the Free School System,* Bureau of Education Circular of Information, no. 3 (Washington: GPO, 1960), 209–10.

112. This is a part of the solution to the problem of antebellum South Carolina's anomalous political thought and institutions. See James Banner, "The Problem of South Carolina," in *The Hofstadter Aegis: A Memorial,* ed. Stanley Elkins and Eric McKitrick (New York: Knopf, 1974), 60–93.

113. There are hundreds of such letters in the papers of James Henry Hammond, clustered around the years of his greatest political aspiration, particularly 1839–1840, when he ran for governor.

114. Viator Notebook, SCL, Columbia.

115. "Chester" letter, *Columbia Southern Chronicle.*

116. Quoted in the *Columbia Daily South Carolinian,* 8 September 1857.

117. One obscure alumnus, James Hibben, freed his slaves, possibly for religious reasons. One or two others may have done the same, but such behavior was rare for any reason.

118. Perry, *Reminiscences,* 63.

119. Leroy Youmans, "The Historical Significance of South Carolina College," *Proceedings of the Centennial Celebration of South Carolina College* (Columbia: State Company, 1905), 162. Cheves was in good company. Jefferson Davis acknowledged his debt to Cooper's writings in a speech given at Charleston in 1863.

120. Joseph Daniel Pope, *The State and the College* (Columbia: Presbyterian Publishing House, 1892), 18.

121. Grayson, "Autobiography," 86.

122. Youmans, "Historical Significance," 37.

123. Oscar Lieber-Francis and Matilda Lieber, n.d. 1851, Lieber Papers, Huntington Library, San Marino, California.

124. Tommy Rogers, "The Great Population Exodus from South Carolina, 1850–60," *South Carolina Historical Magazine* (January 1967): 14–22.

125. Youmans, "Historical Significance," 159.

126. Ibid., 161–62.

Agency, Denominations, and the Western Colleges, 1830–1860

1. The best historiographical overview is James McLachlan's "The American College in the Nineteenth Century: Toward a Reappraisal," *Teachers College Record* 80, 2 (1978): 287–306. Some of the historical works that serve as the basis of the revisionist interpretations include David Potts, "American Colleges in the Nineteenth Century: From Localism to Denominationalism," *History of Education Quarterly* 11 (1971): 363–79, and "'College Enthusiasm!' as Public Response, 1800–1860," *Harvard Educational Review* 47 (1977): 28–42; David Allmendinger, *Paupers and Scholars: The Transformation of Student Life in Nineteenth-Century New England* (New York: St. Martin's, 1975); and Colin B. Burke, "The Quiet Influence: American Colleges and Their Students, 1800–1860" (Ph.D. diss., Washington University, 1973).

2. Potts, "From Localism to Denominationalism," 368–69, 377. Two other revisionists, Douglas Sloan and James Axtell, rightfully emphasize the key role of religious beliefs. See Axtell, "Death of the Liberal Arts College," *History of Education Quarterly* 2 (winter 1971): 345; Sloan, "Harmony, Chaos, and Consensus: The American College Curriculum," *Teachers College Record* 23 (December 1971): 227–32. There are also brief but inconclusive comments about the crucial religious dimensions of the antebellum colleges in McLachlan, "The American College in the Nineteenth Century," 300, 301–3.

3. The essay entitled "Uncommon Schools: Christian Colleges and Social Idealism in Midwestern America, 1820–1950," is the first of two parts of a larger publication of the Indiana Historical Society, *Lectures, 1976–77: The History of Education in the Middle West* (Indianapolis, 1978).

4. Sweet is the exception. He wrote a centennial history of DePauw University, where he taught before going to the University of Chicago. See William Warren Sweet, *Indiana Asbury-DePauw University: A History* (New York, 1937).

5. Sweet's own work is perhaps best summed up in his four-volume documentary collection entitled *Religion on the American Frontier, 1783–1850*. Subtitles include *The Baptists, 1783–1850* (New York, 1931); *The Presbyterians, 1783–1840* (New York, 1936); *The Congregationalists, 1783–1850* (Chicago, 1939); and *The Methodists* (Chicago, 1946). The best work of Sweet's students is in Colon B. Goodykoontz, *Home Missions on the American Frontier with Particular Reference to the Home Missionary Society* (Caldwell, Idaho, 1939), and in the essays of Frederick L. Kuhns, in *A History of Illinois Congregational and Christian Churches*, ed. Matthew Spinka (Chicago, 1944).

6. Smith, "Uncommon Schools," 5–15, 17–18, 20. See also Travis Hedrick, "Julian Monsen Sturtevant and the Moral Machinery of Society: The New England Struggle against Pluralism in the Old Northwest, 1829–1877" (Ph.D. diss., Brown University, 1974).

7. Potts, "College Enthusiasm," 42. See also *Baptist Colleges in the Development of American Society, 1812–1861* (1967; reprint, New York: Garland, 1988).

8. In 1851, fourteen years after Indiana Asbury University was established, the annual Report on Education to the Indiana Conference began with the assertion that "the great center of our educational system is the Asbury University" ("Minutes of the Indiana Annual Conference, Methodist Episcopal Church, 1851," 14). Over the years the Methodist conferences in the Hoosier State came to support other institutions—secondary schools, academies, female institutes, colleges—yet Indiana Asbury always occupied the central place in the detailed reports on those enterprises submitted annually to the conferences, a clear reflection of the key position Asbury occupied among Indiana Methodists (ibid., 14–20; 1849, 11–14; 1850, 11–18; 1853, 11–14; 1854, 14–16; 1858, 18–21).

9. "Minutes of the Board of Trustees, DePauw University *[sic]*," 1 March, 18 October 1837; "Journal of the Indiana Conference, Methodist Episcopal Church," 19 October 1838.

10. "Journal of the Indiana Conference," 28 October 1840. The first year's campaign hoped to raise $20,000 to purchase "Library, Chemical, and philosophical apparatus." The bishop of the Indiana Conference, planning to visit Europe in 1842, was to buy much of the needed equipment and books with this money (ibid.). There is no record available now of how much money was actually collected in 1841, nor is there a clear indication that a grassroots financial campaign of this magnitude was mounted annually, as the conference minutes suggest.

11. The colleges included in this study stated in their charters or constitutions that they were open to students of all religious groups without discrimination. Statements emphasizing the broad purposes and appeal of the colleges abound in the literature published by the schools and their supporting religious bodies.

12. "Minutes of the Board of Trustees, McKendree College," 18 November 1828; 30 October 1830.

13. "Journal of the Illinois Conference," 21 September 1829; 6 October 1830; 7 October 1835. Leading supporters of McKendree, including Peter Cartwright, the famous backwoods preacher, and Peter Akers, president of McKendree, were involved in the establishment of a second college in central Illinois.

14. Ibid., 1 October 1833; 12 February 1834; "Minutes of the Board of Trustees, McKendree College," 8 April 1834; 16 October 1832; 11 June 1832.

15. "Journal of the Illinois Conference, Methodist Episcopal Church," 29 September 1832; 20 September 1841; "Minutes of the Board of Trustees, McKendree College," 26 June 1838; 16 August 1843; 1 April 1846.

16. *Lebanon (Ill.) Journal,* 6 January 1848, 1.

17. For descriptions of the disputes that affected the Plan of Union schools in Illinois, see Charles H. Rammelkamp, *Illinois College: A Centennial History, 1829–1929* (New Haven, Conn., 1928), chaps. 6, 8; and Hermann Muelder, *Church History in a Puritan Colony of the Middle West* (Galesburg, Ill., 1937).

18. "Minutes of the Board of Trustees, Wabash College," 16 April 1833; 24 September 1834.

19. Knox occupied a less important position largely because its founders embraced a radical-perfectionist stream of ideology and theology, emerging originally in western and central New York, which the mainstream Presbygationalists looked upon with considerable suspicion. George Gale, a principal founder of Knox, viewed the college and the town-colony that was to develop with it as a center of abolitionist agitation and activity in central Illinois and a proving ground for perfectionist religious sentiments. Gale and the Oneida Institute he founded in western New York served as common intellectual ground for the early history of both Knox and Oberlin Colleges. See Hermann Muelder, *Fighters for Freedom: The History of Anti-slavery Activities of Men and Women associated with Knox College* (New York, 1959); Robert S. Fletcher, *A History of Oberlin College, from Its Foundation through the Civil War,* 2 vols. (Oberlin College, 1943), 1: chaps. 1–5.

20. "Minutes of the Board of Trustees, Wabash College," 27 December 1833; 18 July 1835, "Ormes" folder, Wabash College Archives. The first president of Illinois College, Edward Beecher, was the son of Lyman Beecher, the famous spokesman for evangelicalism in the first half of the nineteenth century. Elihu Baldwin, the first president of Wabash, came from a successful ministry in the Seventh Presbyterian Church in New York City and was well known in the denomination before he moved west. See Robert Merideth, *The Politics of the Universe: Edward Beecher, Abolition and Orthodoxy* (Nashville, Tenn., 1968), chap. 5; Edmund O. Hovey to Israel Dewey, 28 February 1835 (and attached flyers); Samuel G. Lowrie to Hovey, 5 January 1835, Hovey Letters, Wabash College Archives.

21. The first director of the SPCTEW was Theron Baldwin, a member of the small group of Yale graduates that founded Illinois College, an early faculty member at the college, and a trustee until death in 1870. Even after moving to New York City, Baldwin remained the closest confidant of Julian Sturtevant, the second president of Illinois College. See Baldwin-Sturtevant Correspondence, Illinois College Archives, and the many letters between the two men in SPCTEW Collection, Congregational Library, Boston. Wabash people participated in the meetings that led to the organization of the society in 1843. After that date Baldwin maintained regular contact with Wabash officials, and fundraising in the East was supervised by the society. See Theron Baldwin to Charles White, 12 June 1848; to John M. Ellis, 18 November 1848; to E. O. Hovey, 9 November 1858, in SPCTEW Letterbooks, Congregational Library, Boston. The financial support given to both Illinois College and Wabash by the society can be traced in the Annual Reports, beginning in 1844 and continuing into the 1860s.

22. Theron Baldwin especially disliked the president of Knox, Jonathan Blanchard, in part because of his unorthodox social and theological views and in part because he was pushy and abrasive in personal relations and in the demands he made on the society. See, for example, Jonathan Blanchard to Theron Baldwin, 14 October 1845, box 1, SPCTEW Correspondence; Baldwin to H. Smith, 10 November 1845, Baldwin to Blanchard, 27 December 1848, Baldwin to C. Y. Hammond, 9 September 1865, all in SPCTEW Letterbooks.

23. A collection of addresses and sermons entitled *Permanent Documents,* SPCTEW (many editions), presented first as talks at the annual meetings of the SPCTEW and then published for promotional use by the society over the years, is full of such ideas concerning the missionary role of education in the West.

24. Smith, "Uncommon Schools," 20, 21.

25. L. B. Lawson to Washington Leverett, 3 November 1858, Illinois Baptist Educational Society Correspondence, box 1, Shurtleff College Collection, Illinois State Historical Library; "Minutes of the Board of Trustees, Franklin College," 18 July 1835; "Minutes of the Baptist Association of Illinois," 1839, 7–9; 1840, 12–13, 15; 1844, 12–13; 1845, 10; "Minutes of the Annual Meeting, Indianapolis Baptist Association," 1850, 3, 4; 1843, 5; 1846, 7.

26. Deep divisions existed within Baptist circles in both Indiana and Illinois over the propriety of founding colleges at all. Antimission elements in the denomination, migrating especially from southern states, were highly suspicious of the efforts of former New England Baptists and their western allies to advocate a learned ministry and the colleges necessary for such a development. The antimission Baptists attracted wide support in the frontier society of the 1830s and 1840s. See John F. Cady, *The Origin and Development of the Missionary Baptist Church in Indiana* (Berne, Ind., 1942).

27. The Baptist college at Alton, Illinois, became Shurtleff College in 1836 in honor of Benjamin Shurtleff, a wealthy Boston physician who gave the college $10,000 in 1835 and made other donations later. "Minutes of the Board of Trustees, Shurtleff College," 25 November 1835; 29 January 1836. Franklin's eastern connections are demonstrated in John M. Peck to Jesse Holman, July 1834, and Garah Markland to Jesse Holman, 16 September 1836, Holman Correspondence, Franklin College Archives; "Minutes of the Massachusetts Baptist Missionary Society," 13 February, 12 August, 12 November 1838; 11 February 1829, Archives, Andover Newton Seminary.

28. A major denominational source of support for both Shurtleff and Franklin was the statewide Baptist Education Societies. In each state these societies were organized to collect money to support at Shurtleff and Franklin indigent students intending to enter the ministry. Over time the educational societies also became a denominational means of informal policy control at the two schools because they worked closely with the respective boards of trustees. See "Minutes of the Board of Trustees, Shurtleff College," 30 October; 4, 5 December 1850; "Minutes of the Indiana Baptist Education Society," 5 July 1834; 30 January 1836; 10 December 1840; 7 October 1841; 24 October 1861, Archives, Franklin College.

29. E. O. Hovey to Mary Hovey, 23 May 1839, Hovey Letters, Indiana State Library, Indianapolis; John M. Peck to J. N. Tolman, 24 December 1852, J. M. Peck Papers, Illinois

State Historical Library, Springfield, Illinois. In 1856 the president of Wabash College netted about $11,500 on agency, even though expenses were reported as almost $3,000—an unusually successful venture. Agents for Franklin College are estimated to have raised $10,600 over seven years for that school. See "Minutes of the Board of Trustees, Wabash College," 22 July 1856; William T. Scott, *History of Franklin College: A Brief Sketch* (Indianapolis, 1874), 4. See also "Report of Agency for Knox College from July to December 1847," in a folder entitled "Trustees' Minutes," George W. Gale Correspondence, Knox College Archives.

30. Only rough guesses can be made about the proportion of annual college budgets that were supported by the efforts of the agents. The trustees of Shurtleff College published in 1849 a summary of receipts and expenditures for the previous four years, with no breakdown of figures on an annual basis. The agent of the college reported cash collections of $2,565 during this time, about one-third of the monies disbursed finally by the college. At Knox in 1847 the president of the college reported that from July to December of that year he collected $1,789.50 in "cash obligations [pledges] and property." There is no record of the relationship of this sum to the total costs of the school for that year, but even six years later Knox's total annual expenses were only $4,340. It seems fair to assume that agencies like Blanchard's were crucial in sustaining the college. At Illinois College in 1855 the college debits were $6,653. The SPCTEW provided an "appropriation" of $1,500, thus covering almost 25 percent of the annual operating expenses. Money from the SPCTEW aided Knox in a similar manner in 1851 and 1853. Detailed records of collections of agents at Indiana Asbury, similar in total annual amounts gathered to those mentioned above, are also available for 1839 and 1844. *Watchman of the Prairies*, 28 August 1849, 2; "Report of Agency for Knox College from July to December 1849," "Trustees' Minutes," 25 June 1851; 22 June 1853, Knox College; Account Book of Agent S. C. Cooper, 1834–1844, Indiana Asbury University; "Trustees' Minutes," Illinois College, 12 July 1855.

31. The documentation is not overwhelming, but we can develop a fairly clear idea of the nature of these agency networks. For example, Wabash College reported contributions through agency solicitations from twenty-seven localities in Indiana during 1847, including towns like Indianapolis, Lafayette, and Terre Haute and small villages like Putnamville, Sugar Creek, and Hickory. A similar pattern of giving appeared in reporting building fund collections in 1850. Money for Wabash was also solicited and received from twelve towns in Connecticut, Massachusetts, New York, and Vermont in 1834, the first year the college was fully in operation. See Subscription Books, Wabash College, 1834, 1852, Wabash College Archives. The files of the SPCTEW also reveal in considerable detail the working of the agency system of the organization throughout New England. See, for example, Theron Baldwin to John M. Ellis, 8 August 1849, SPCTEW Letterbooks; J. W. Wood to Baldwin, 28 November 1851, B. C. Webster to Baldwin, 30 June 1855, SPCTEW Correspondence, box 1, Congregational Library, Boston.

32. Subscription Books, Wabash College, 1834–1852; Account Book of Agent S. C. Cooper, 1838–1844; "Notes, Endowment Funds," of William DeMotte, 1837–1857, Indiana Asbury University, DePauw University Archives. Each annual report of the SPCTEW included a detailed breakdown of contributions to the society and to specific western col-

leges, which confirms decisively the fact that most donations were very small amounts of money given by hundreds of largely unknown churchgoers.

33. I have yet to come across a printed version of one of these talks or sermons that minister-agents of the colleges must have delivered by the hundreds over the years. The content of these addresses probably paralleled the ideas regarding the nature and purposes of the western colleges articulated in presidential inaugural addresses, in statements by college officials in denominational periodicals, in printed copies of orations before student literary societies, and the like. *Permanent Documents*, SPCTEW contains vintage material in this regard.

34. Continuities and discontinuities with fund-raising practices of colleges in the colonial and early national period also should be commented upon briefly. Long before the founding of the schools studied in this chapter, colonial colleges began to develop funding techniques that were often similar to the techniques used in the Jacksonian era. By the time of the Revolution, land grants, money from private donors, fund-raising among alumni, funding appeals to the general populace, and frequent approaches to the colonial legislatures for grants from public monies had all been attempted. Parallels with the practices of the colleges of the mid-nineteenth century are striking. Representatives of King's (later Columbia) College in New York and of Princeton in New Jersey visited the mother country of England in search of funds, just as Presbyterian and Congregational agents from the Midwest scoured home parishes in New England for support in the 1840s and 1850s.

The colonial colleges, however, assumed the characteristics of public institutions even more than was the case with the antebellum schools. The powerful denominational ties so evident in the nineteenth century developed mostly from the time of the Revolution, the result of the separation of church and state that came with independence, and the subsequent rise of a national system of voluntaristic, evangelical churches. This voluntary system was fully articulated by 1830, and the fund-raising practices of the colleges founded after that date accurately reflected these post-Revolutionary ecclesiastical arrangements. See David C. Humphrey, *From King's College to Columbia, 1746–1800* (New York, 1976), 96–97, 121–22, 131–34, and Howard Miller, *The Revolutionary College: American Presbyterian Higher Education, 1707–1837* (New York: New York University Press, 1976), 72–75, 149–59, 254–58.

The Era of Multipurpose Colleges in American Higher Education, 1850–1890

1. This chapter is a portion of a larger project, "Dynamics of Institutional Change in Higher Education: American Colleges and Universities in the Nineteenth Century," which has been aided by support from the Spencer Foundation. A longer draft entitled "The Transformation of the Colleges" was presented in a symposium at the 1995 meeting of the History of Education Society. I am grateful for the comments given there by Colin Burke, Wayne Durrill, Bruce Leslie, and James McLachlan, as well as for the helpful suggestions of Hugh Hawkins, David Jones, and Roger Williams.

2. Laurence Veysey, *The Emergence of the American University* (Chicago: University of Chicago Press, 1965), 264–68; Samuel Eliot Morison, *Three Centuries of Harvard* (Cambridge: Harvard University Press, 1936), 361.

3. In addition to Veysey, *Emergence of the American University,* see Roger L. Geiger, *To Advance Knowledge: The Development of the American Research University, 1900–1940* (New York: Oxford University Press, 1986); Sandra Oleson and John Voss, *The Organization of Knowledge in America, 1860–1920* (Baltimore: Johns Hopkins University Press, 1978).

4. Colin B. Burke has described the antebellum colleges as "multilevel, multipurpose institutions"; see *American Collegiate Populations* (New York: New York University Press, 1982), 38.

5. A large literature exists on the crisis of the colleges, but it is largely limited to the established and more traditional institutions of the Northeast. See George E. Peterson, *The New England College in the Age of the University* (Amherst, Mass.: Amherst College Press, 1965); Marilyn Tobias, *Old Dartmouth on Trial: The Transformation of an Academic Community in Nineteenth-Century America* (New York: New York University Press, 1982); and W. Bruce Leslie, *Gentlemen and Scholars: Colleges and Community in the Age of the University, 1865–1917* (University Park: Pennsylvania State University Press, 1992). Studies of this phenomenon in Ohio focus on the colleges most closely resembling those in the East; see John Barnard, *From Evangelicalism to Progressivism at Oberlin College, 1866–1917* (Columbus: Ohio State University Press, 1969); Nancy J. Cable, "The Search for Mission in Ohio Liberal Arts Colleges: Denison, Kenyon, Marietta, Oberlin, 1870–1914" (Ph.D. diss., University of Virginia, 1984).

6. United States Bureau of Education, *Report of the Commissioner of Education* (Washington, D.C.: GPO, 1868, 1870–1914), hereafter cited as RCE.

7. Ibid., 1870, 72.

8. Colleges for women were separately analyzed in the earlier draft, "Transformation of the Colleges" (see n. 1). See the chapter in this volume, "Superior Instruction of Women."

9. *Historical Statistics of the United States.* Unless indicated otherwise, data are from the RCE.

10. Enrollment by sex is incompletely reported for 1880 but estimated to be 4,800 in coeducational colleges; the RCE reports 8,075 for 1890.

11. The supposed unpopularity of colleges was widely discussed in the 1880s. The basis for this notion was the stagnation of all collegiate enrollments relative to total population from 1874 to 1889 (RCE, 1874, 1900). A rejoinder to this argument was compiled by tracing male enrollments in 282 selected colleges from 1850 to 1890, and it found a 53.6 percent growth from 1881 to 1891 (Arthur M. Comey, "The Growth of Colleges in the United States," *Educational Review* 3 [1892]: 120–31). Decile years account for some of the discrepancy. College enrollments seem to have exceeded population growth from the Civil War until the panic of 1873, then to have tracked population growth until 1888, rising sharply after that date.

12. The opening dates of colleges have been taken from proximate editions of the RCE, thus minimizing the count of ephemeral institutions, while possibly missing some

that claim earlier opening dates after the fact. This method produces a conservative record of foundings; only 15 more institutions are counted (357 + 131) than the 473 colleges listed for 1900. This estimation seems consistent with Colin Burke's careful enumeration of antebellum colleges. Thus it represents a rough continuation of the data on institutions in *American Collegiate Populations.*

13. The peak number of colleges of the traditional type was reached in 1893: *U.S. Bureau of Education, Biennial Survey of Education, 1916* (successor to the RCE), 5. For an estimation of all baccalaureate-granting institutions in the United States over time, see Gloria J. Marshall, "The Survival of Colleges in America: A Census of Four-Year Colleges in the United States, 1636–1973" (Ph.D. diss., Stanford University, 1995), 67. This census is too broad to be relevant to this study.

14. Derek de Solla Price, *Little Science, Big Science, and Beyond* (1963; reprint, New York: Columbia University Press, 1986), 129.

15. Table 2 does not reflect more than 10 scientific schools dating from 1845 to 1860. See the chapter in this volume, "The Rise and Fall of Useful Knowledge."

16. Large individual philanthropic initiatives constituted an exogenous factor affecting the founding and placement of colleges. They served chiefly to increase the density of institutions in settled regions, but are too few to distort the logistic pattern. Some consequences of philanthropy are discussed below.

17. Michael McGiffert, *The Higher Learning in Colorado: A Historical Study, 1860–1940* (Denver: Sage Books, 1964), 13.

18. D. W. Meinig, *The Shaping of America: A Geographical Perspective on 500 Years of History,* vol. 2, *Continental America, 1800–1867* (New Haven: Yale University Press, 1993), 262–63. See also David K. Brown, "The Rise of U.S. Undergraduate Education: A Sociology of College-Founding, System-Building, and Credentialism, 1800–1930" (Ph.D. diss., Northwestern University, 1993), 116–29.

19. C. Harve Geiger, *The Program of Higher Education of the Presbyterian Church in the United States of America* (Cedar Rapids, Iowa: Laurence Press, 1940), 55–59, 79. The earlier pattern was for individual founders (often ministers) to establish colleges in conjunction with communities . Cf. David B. Potts, *Baptist Colleges in the Development of American Society, 1812–1861* (1967; reprint, New York: Garland, 1988), 11–78.

20. David B. Potts, "American Colleges in the Nineteenth Century: From Localism to Denominationalism," *History of Education Quarterly* 11 (1971): 363–80. Most earlier colleges had self-perpetuating boards of trustees (sometimes with ex officio public members) and were thus not directly controlled by churches.

21. Contemporaries regarded elaboration as axiomatic. The Baptist educator Frederick T. Gates surveyed the extent of Baptist coverage in the Midwest in 1888 and observed that American colleges were "chiefly local in their patronage" and that they "create the demand for the higher culture which they supply." By measuring the "area of their attractive influence," he calculated that the eleven Baptist colleges served only one-fifth of midwestern Baptists. Gates was criticizing the results of elaboration, which had produced "feeble institutions in obscure towns" ("The Need of a Baptist University in Chicago, as Illustrated by a Study of Baptist Colleges in the West," Correspondence of Frederick T.

Gates, 1888–1906, box 1, folder 2, Joseph Regenstein Library, University of Chicago). I would like to thank Bill Pugh for providing this document.

22. The College of New Jersey chose to locate at Princeton in the 1750s after just such a process; however, the pattern of putting a college up for explicit bidding is characteristic of this era and unusual before 1850. Potts, for example, emphasizes the interactions of founders, church bodies, and communities. Perhaps two of his sixteen Baptist colleges (Hillsdale and possibly Furman) chose the most lucrative offer for homes; see *Baptist Colleges*, 11–78. Many of the Ohio colleges, discussed below, went to the highest bidder.

23. Edward J. Power, *A History of Catholic Higher Education in the United States* (Milwaukee: Bruce Publishing, 1958), 36–48.

24. The seven-year course was considered the desirable standard after 1835, but the course lengths continued to vary widely. Interestingly Catholic colleges were quite open to commercial studies around midcentury, but kept them separate from the A.B. course (ibid., 83–86).

25. E.g., Villanova College operated from 1843 to 1845, from 1846 to 1857, and continuously from 1865. See David R. Contosta, *Villanova University: American—Catholic—Augustinian* (University Park: Pennsylvania State University Press, 1995), 17–25.

26. Power, *Catholic Higher Education*, 333–39. Power also provides a brief description of each college (255–332). His list is far larger than those reported in the RCE. All were initially men's colleges. Catholic colleges for women first appear at the end of the century and were founded in great numbers in the first three decades of the twentieth century.

27. Academic development within the classical college is not considered here; see *infra*. Introduction to this volume.

28. Almost every institutional history of this period gives an account of the classical college curriculum; the later classical curriculum at Yale is described in minute detail by Lyman Bagg, *Four Years at Yale* (New Haven, 1871).

29. One of the best treatments of these reforms is R. Freeman Butts, *The College Charts Its Course: Historical Conceptions and Current Proposals* (New York: McGraw-Hill, 1939), 131–43.

30. The report was written by President Jeremiah Day and Professor James L. Kingsley and published in the *American Journal of Science and Arts* 15 (January 1829): 297–351. The bulk of the report is reproduced in Richard Hofstadter and Wilson Smith, eds., *American Higher Education*, 2 vols. (Chicago: University of Chicago Press, 1961), 275–91.

31. Joseph F. Kett, *Rites of Passage: Adolescence in America, 1790 to the Present* (New York: Basic Books, 1977), 31–61.

32. Both institutions were "reformed" by Stephen Olin, president of Randolph-Macon, 1834–1837, and Wesleyan, 1842–1851. See David B. Potts, *Wesleyan University, 1831–1910: Collegiate Enterprise in New England* (New Haven: Yale University Press, 1992), 24–27.

33. These colleges did not necessarily train only ministers/teachers for the faith, but generally expressed this aim as their principal purpose in their founding documents.

34. A virtual continuity existed between the more advanced academies and these fledgling colleges. See Joseph F. Kett, *The Pursuit of Knowledge under Difficulties: From Self-*

improvement to Adult Education in America, 1750–1990 (Stanford: Stanford University Press, 1994), 90–95. See also Nancy Beadie, "From Academy to University in New York State: The Genesee Institutions and the Importance of Capital to the Success of an Idea, 1848–1871," *History of Higher Education Annual* 14 (1994): 13–38.

35. The "market revolution" is generally associated with the Jacksonian period. See Charles Sellars, *The Market Revolution, 1815–1848* (New York: Oxford University Press, 1990); Sean Willentz, "Society, Politics, and the Market Revolution, 1815–1848," in *The New American History,* ed. Eric Foner (Philadelphia: Temple University Press, 1990), 51–72. However, collegiate education reflected the social patterns that emerged in the wake of the market/transportation revolution, and is thus a lagging social indicator. The differences between a frontier and a settled community can be traced in Don H. Doyle, *The Social Order of a Frontier Community: Jacksonville, Illinois, 1825–1870* (Urbana: University of Illinois Press, 1978); and Meinig, *Shaping of America.*

36. Christie Anne Farnham, *The Education of the Southern Belle: Higher Education and Student Socialization in the Antebellum South* (New York: New York University Press, 1994), 15–17, passim.

37. The following discussion of Ohio colleges draws principally upon George W. Knight and John R. Common, *The History of Higher Education in Ohio,* Bureau of Education, Circular of Information no. 5, 1891 (Washington, D.C.: GPO, 1891); Charles A. Dominick, "Ohio's Antebellum Colleges" (Ph.D. diss., University of Michigan, 1987); Steven R. Mark, "Ohio Colleges and Universities during the Gilded Age: Institutional Evolution, Elective Curriculum, Graduate Education, and Commercial Programs" (Ph.D. diss., Bowling Green State University, 1991).

38. An additional antebellum Methodist college, Wilberforce, was chartered for African Americans in 1855 and transferred to the African Methodist Episcopal Church in 1863.

39. Western New York, which was closely linked with Ohio, had three antebellum coeducational colleges—Genesee, New York Central, and Alfred University; see Kathryn M. Kerns, "Antebellum Higher Education for Women in Western New York State" (Ph.D. diss., University of Pennsylvania, 1993).

40. Dominick, "Ohio's Antebellum Colleges," 248.

41. Ibid., quote on 241. Mount Union has a discursive history, which includes an account of the even more unorthodox Scio College; see Newell Yost Osborne, *A Select School: The History of Mount Union College and an Account of a Unique Educational Experiment, Scio College* (Mount Union College, 1967).

42. A. B. Huston, *Historical Sketch of Farmer's College,* Ohio Historical Society Archives Library.

43. Knight and Common, *History of Higher Education in Ohio,* 121.

44. The obstacles facing a state university in Ohio are well described in William A. Kinnison, *Building Sullivant's Pyramid: An Administrative History of the Ohio State University* (Columbus: Ohio State University Press, 1970).

45. Cable, "Search for Mission"; Barnard, *Oberlin College;* RCE, 1879–1880.

46. John M. Ellis, "Historical Sketch of the Association of the Colleges of Ohio" [1889], reprinted in Knight and Common, *History of Higher Education in Ohio,* quote on 246.

47. The recommended chairs were Latin, Greek, modern languages, mathematics, geology and natural history, chemistry and mineralogy, rhetoric, English and history, psychology, ethics and political science (ibid., 250).

48. Ibid., 251.

49. This neglected topic is one theme in the final chapter of Burke, *American Collegiate Populations.*

50. Mount Union College's total enrollment topped 800 in 1872, yet the college was deeply in debt and badly in need of additional facilities. Student numbers then dropped below 400 in the mid-1880s. The ensuing financial crisis was finally resolved by the actions of several dedicated trustees; but at the end of the 1880s the college had no endowment and no library (Osborne, *Select School,* passim).

51. Francis A. Walker, "The Place of Schools of Technology in American Education," *Educational Review* 2 (October 1891): 209–19.

52. Kett, *Pursuit of Knowledge,* 90–95.

53. Burke, *American Collegiate Populations,* 70; Walter C. Bronson, *The History of Brown University, 1764–1914* (Providence, R.I.: Brown University, 1914), 321–23; Morris Bishop, *A History of Cornell* (Ithaca: Cornell University Press, 1962), 90, 201–2.

54. Allen Marquand, "College Students Who Are Not Candidates for a Degree," *Proceedings, College Association of the Middle States and Maryland* 3 (1889): 1824. Marquand identifies three kinds of nondegree students: (1) "general" students, often admitted on conditions but unable to maintain the regular course; (2) mature "special" students, who sought only career-related subjects; and (3) "short-course" students, intending to enroll in professional schools without taking the full college course.

55. Average professorial salary was $1,330 in Ohio in 1898. See D. B. Purinton, "A Comparative Study of Colleges," *Transactions, Association of Ohio Colleges* 30 (1898): 14–25. Frederick Gates reported average professorial salaries at Western Baptist colleges in 1888 as $1,015 (loc. cit., n. 21, p. 11). Salaries in the East were about double those of the Midwest.

56. RCE, 1900, 1882. Returns from invested funds appear to have been around 5 percent; Catholic colleges rarely reported financial data; 58 colleges reported some endowment short of $25,000; and 81 had $25,000 to $100,000.

57. Deficits figure haphazardly in institutional histories, but are never treated systematically. The chronicler of Shurtleff College observed, "[I]n no year of the history of the College, from 1827 to 1899, has the annual deficit failed to appear" (Austin K. de Blois, *The Pioneer School* [New York, 1900], 251). Eastern colleges were no different (Potts, *Wesleyan University,* 58, 91, 161–62); Princeton, despite its wealth, had an annual deficit that was covered by the trustees (John M. Mulder, *Woodrow Wilson: The Years of Preparation* [Princeton: Princeton University Press, 1976], 164–65). Excessive debt was often the single factor causing colleges to close.

58. See Beadie, "Academy to University," and Dominick, "Ohio's Antebellum Colleges," 206–7. Subscriptions were the bane of many antebellum colleges: they were sold far too cheaply—a typical rate being $25 for six years of tuition, $50 for eighteen, and $100 for tuition in perpetuity for any holder. Often sold by college agents, some of the funds never reached the colleges; other proceeds were spent instead of invested.

59. Paul M. Limbert, *Denominational Policies in the Support and Supervision of Higher Education* (New York: Teachers College, 1929).

60. Knight and Common, *History of Higher Education in Ohio,* 188; Osborne, *Select School,* 202.

61. Burke, *American Collegiate Populations,* 222–24, passim; Robert Wiebe, *The Search for Order, 1877–1920* (New York: Hill and Wang, 1967).

62. The distinction between the urban phenomenon of relatively long-term career employment and the rural/small-town pattern of finding a livelihood, often by trying several occupations, needs further clarification. A college education did not at this juncture offer credentials for the former, but may well have provided useful skills for the latter.

63. William D. Overman, "Universities, Colleges, and Normal Schools in Ohio" (Columbus: Ohio State Archaeological and Historical Society, 1940).

64. The crisis of the multipurpose college after 1890 is analyzed in the last chapter in this volume, "The Crisis of the Old Order."

The Rise and Fall of Useful Knowledge

1. My thanks to Hugh Hawkins and Bruce Leslie for helpful comments.

2. Roger L. Williams has described the principal historical accounts of the land-grant colleges as "deterministic" and "romantic" (*The Origins of Federal Support for Higher Education: George W. Atherton and the Land-Grant College Movement* [University Park: Pennsylvania State University Press, 1991], 2). Social scientists too have succumbed to this romanticism; see Mary Jean Bowman, "The Land-Grant Colleges and Universities in Human-Resource Development," *Journal of Economic History* 22 (1962): 523–46. Like Williams's volume, this study seeks to examine contingent and contextual forces that shaped this form of higher education in the third quarter of the nineteenth century. See also Eldon Johnson, "Misconceptions about the Early Land-Grant Colleges," *Journal of Higher Education* 52, 4 (1981).

3. Daniel Coit Gilman, "Our National Schools of Science," *North American Review* (October 1867): 495–520, quote on 504. Earle D. Ross, in the most complete exposition of Morrill's relation to his eponymous act, felt that Morrill's views changed over time. His original thinking was focused solely on agriculture, but he later embraced the combined liberal and practical universities the act spawned. See "The 'Father' of the Land-Grant College," *Agricultural History* 12 (1938): 151–86. Morrill himself did not attend college, but in his retirement (before entering politics) he became a gentleman farmer and book collector. According to Coy Cross, he was quite knowledgeable of developments in agriculture on both sides of the Atlantic (personal communication; See also Coy F. Cross II, *Justin Smith Morrill: Father of the Land-Grant College* (East Lansing: Michigan State University Press, 1999).

4. Laurence Veysey subsumed these types of education under the rubric of "utility"; see *The Emergence of the American University* (Chicago: University of Chicago Press, 1965), 57–120. However, he dismisses the antebellum antecedents of this development (60) and focuses on a later stage of this debate.

5. Joseph F. Kett, *The Pursuit of Knowledge under Difficulties: From Self-improvement to Adult Education in America, 1750–1990* (Stanford: Stanford University Press, 1994), 102–41.

6. William Barton Rogers, "A Plan for a Polytechnic School in Boston," in *The Life and Letters of William Barton Rogers* (1896), 1:426–27.

7. William Arba Ellis, *Norwich University, 1819–1911* (Montpelier, Vt., 1911), 69–82; Gary T. Lord, "Alden Partridge's Proposal for a National System of Education: A Model for the Land-Grant Act," *History of Higher Education Annual* 18 (1998) .

8. Terry S. Reynolds, "The Education of Engineers in America before the Morrill Act of 1862," *History of Education Quarterly* 32, 4 (1992): 459–82; Alfred Charles True, *A History of Agricultural Education in the United States, 1785–1925* (Washington, D.C, 1929); Bruce Sinclair, *Philadelphia's Philosopher Mechanics: A History of the Franklin Institute, 1824–1865* (Baltimore: Johns Hopkins University Press, 1974), 108–34.

9. Reynolds, "Education of Engineers"; Samuel Rezneck, *Education for a Technological Society* (Troy, N.Y., 1968), 38–60.

10. These schools are described in Charles W. Eliot, "The New Education: Its Organization," *Atlantic Monthly,* February-March 1869, 203–20, 358–67, discussed below.

11. The Yale/Sheffield Scientific School was officially part of the Department of Philosophy and the Arts, which was the locus of graduate study. One of the seven options offered after 1864 was the "Select Course," which was a general scientific and literary course similar to the B.S. offered elsewhere. Sheffield granted a Bachelor of Philosophy degree. See Russell H. Chittenden, *History of the Sheffield Scientific School of Yale University, 1846–1922,* 2 vols. (New Haven, 1928), 1:37–147, quote on 140.

12. Richard Yanikoski, "Edward Everett and the Advancement of Higher Education and Adult Learning in Ante-bellum Massachusetts" (Ph.D. diss., University of Chicago, 1987), 185–240. From 1847 to the reforms of 1871, 856 students enrolled, more than half for a year or less; 200 B.S. degrees were awarded by examination. See Hector James Hughes, "Engineering," in *The Development of the Harvard University since the Inauguration of President Eliot, 1869–1929,* ed. Samuel Eliot Morison (Cambridge: Harvard University Press, 1930), 413–42, esp. 416, 426.

13. Unlike the circumstances at Yale and Harvard, Abiel Chandler's gift to Dartmouth reflected the populist interpretation of the useful knowledge tradition. Chandler sought to teach "the practical or useful arts of life" to students having "no other or higher preparatory studies . . . than are pursued in the common schools of New England" (Leon Burr Richardson, *History of Dartmouth College* [Hanover, N.H., 1932], quote on 422–23).

14. Kevin B. Cherry, "Bringing Science to the South: The School for the Application of Science to the Arts at the University of North Carolina," *History of Higher Education Annual* 14 (1994): 73–95.

15. Western colleges, in particular, developed a "scientific course" largely for students who were unprepared to study Greek and/or Latin. Oberlin, for example, instituted such a four-year course from 1850 to 1858; see Robert S. Fletcher, *A History of Oberlin College, from Its Foundation through the Civil War* (Oberlin College, 1943), 722–23. Indiana Asbury instituted a four-year B.S. course in 1859 in which much of the first year consisted of

preparatory subjects, and the entire course had about two-thirds overlap with the A.B. course; see George B. Manhart, *Depauw through the Years*, 2 vols. (DePauw University, 1962), 59–60.

16. V. Ennis Pilcher, *Early Science and the First Century of Physics at Union College, 1795–1895* (Schenectady, N.Y.: Union College, 1994), 31–48; Philip A. Bruce, *History of the University of Virginia, 1819–1919*, 5 vol. (New York: Macmillan, 1921), III, 40–1.

17. Walter C. Bronson, *The History of Brown University, 1764–1914* (Providence: 1914), 274–97, 319–26. The dilution of the classical course to three years was perhaps the gravest miscalculation of the New Course. Attempts to impose greater college discipline and to pay professors directly through student fees both generated problems. Agriculture and didactics were apparently never offered.

18. Daniel W. Lang, "The People's College, the Mechanics Mutual Protection and the Agricultural College Act," *History of Education Quarterly* 18 (1978): 295–321.

19. Winton U. Solberg, *The University of Illinois, 1867–1894* (Urbana: University of Illinois Press, 1968), 40–56.

20. Julianna Chaszar, "Leading and Losing in the Agricultural Education Movement: Freeman G. Cary and Farmers' College, 1846–1884," *History of Higher Education Annual* 18 (1998): 25–46.

21. Alfred C. True, *A History of Agricultural Education in the United States, 1785–1925* (Washington, D.C.: 1929), 23–94. Charles E. Rosenberg underlines the role played by dedicated, European-trained agricultural scientists, especially Evan Pugh, who became the first president of Pennsylvania's agricultural college, and Samuel William Johnson, who was affiliated with the Sheffield School (*No Other Gods: On Science and American Social Thought* [Baltimore: Johns Hopkins University Press, 1976], 135–52).

22. Margaret Rossiter, *The Emergence of Agricultural Science* (New Haven: Yale University Press, 1975); Stanley Guralnick, *Science and the Ante-bellum American College* (Philadelphia: American Philosophical Society, 1975), 114–16.

23. Reynolds, "Education of Engineers"; Pilcher, *Early Science at Union College*, 48–49.

24. Samuel Reznick, *Education for a Technological Society: A Sesquicentennial History of Rensselaer Polytechnic Institute* (Troy, N.Y.: RPI, 1965); Saul Sack, *History of Higher Education in Pennsylvania*, 2 vols. (Harrisburg: Pennsylvania Historical and Museum Commission, 1963), 478–80, 487–88; George Bugliarello, *Towards the Technological University: The Story of Polytechnic Institute of New York* (New York: Newcomen Society, 1975); Bruce Sinclair, "The Promise of the Future: Technical Education," in *Nineteenth-Century American Science*, ed. George Daniels (Evanston, Ill.: Northwestern University Press, 1972), 249–72.

25. Silas W. Holman, "Massachusetts Institute of Technology," in *History of Higher Education in Massachusetts*, Bureau of Education Circular no. 6, 1891 (Washington, D.C., 1891), 280–319, quote on 292.

26. Veysey, *Emergence of the American University*, 60.

27. Gilman, "Our National Schools of Science," 495–520, quote on 519.

28. Ibid., 518, quote on 519; Eliot, "New Education," 203–20, 358–67, esp. 359–60.

29. Gilman, "Our National Schools of Science," 519–20. Some of Gilman's ideas were influenced by two years spent in Europe. See his "Scientific Schools in Europe," *American Journal of Education 1* (1856): 315–28. By its own account, the Sheffield School "was almost exactly such a college as was contemplated in the [Morrill Act] of July 2, 1862" (*American Journal of Education* 25 [1875]: 357).

30. Gilman, "Our National Schools of Science," 507, 520.

31. Daniel Coit Gilman, "Report on the National Schools of Science," *Reports of the Commissioner of Education, 1871* (Washington, D.C., 1872), 427–43, quotes on 435–36.

32. The list and names of land-grant institutions changed annually for the first three decades after the Land-Grant Act. This discussion uses the list from the 1875 Report of the Commissioner of Education [RCE] (Washington, D.C., 1876). See also Edward D. Eddy Jr., "The Development of the Land-Grant Colleges" (Ph.D. diss., Cornell University, 1956), 90–156.

33. In two states, Mississippi and South Carolina, agriculturalists succeeded in wresting the land-grant endowment away from the state university and establishing an A&M college.

34. In both these cases there were antecedent institutions, California College and a projected Minnesota Agricultural College.

35. Carl L. Becker, *Cornell University: Founders and the Founding* (Ithaca: Cornell University Press, 1944); Andrew D. White, *The Autobiography of Andrew Dickson White*, 2 vols. (New York: Century, 1905).

36. Gilman, "Report," 432–34; RCE, 1880, 160–66.

37. State schools of mines were established, beginning in 1874, in Colorado, Michigan, South Dakota, New Mexico, and Montana. Polytechnics or institutes of technology established in the last quarter of the century include Case, Rose, Georgia Tech, Throop, Armour, and Clarkson.

38. Besides the Columbia School of Mines and the Thayer School of Engineering at Dartmouth, separately named science schools or departments were added to Penn, Princeton, Columbian (George Washington), Lafayette, and Boston University. The Bussey Institution was Harvard's Ag School. Harvard also had an ephemeral School of Mining and Practical Geology from 1865 to 1875. The schools of science created at Brown and Rutgers were the state's land-grant recipients. The RCE for 1871 identified 27 "scientific schools not endowed by Congress" (655). Much of this nomenclature was ephemeral.

39. Lehigh University was chartered as a polytechnic college, but always provided a literary course; see W. Ross Yates, *Lehigh University* (Bethlehem, Pa.: Lehigh University Press, 1992), 32–34, 75–76.

40. Verne A. Stadtman, *The University of California, 1868–1968* (New York: McGraw-Hill, 1970), 61–87; Fabian Franklin, *The Life of Daniel Coit Gilman* (New York, 1910), 110–81.

41. Gilman seems to have become disillusioned with the prospects of uniting undergraduate technical or scientific education with serious research or scholarship. He left the University of California determined to establish a purely graduate university when he was named the founding president of Johns Hopkins University; see Hugh Hawkins, *Pioneer: A*

History of the Johns Hopkins University, 1874–1889 (Ithaca: Cornell University Press, 1960), 15–28.

42. Eliot had been involved with attempted reforms to the Lawrence School and the actual formulation of the course at MIT; see Hugh Hawkins, *Between Harvard and America: The Educational Leadership of Charles W. Eliot* (New York: Oxford University Press, 1972), 34–44.

43. This view reflected an ideal at Harvard and Yale that was never attained. Eliot was well aware that most professional students did not possess a B.A. He deplored this situation and worked consistently to change it as president of Harvard. "The New Education" contains a sarcastic note on the "learned professions " (215) as well as statistics of the number of professional students having the B.A.

44. An instructor at Rensselaer Polytechnic Institute (RPI) argued that a college B.S. course was the proper preparation for studying practical science in a polytechnic school or institute; see S. Edward Warren, *Notes on Polytechnic or Scientific Schools in the United States: Their Nature, Position, Aims, and Wants* (New York, 1866), 40. The principal schools (my designation) were Michigan, Harvard, Yale, Union, Columbia, and RPI. Warren's figures are for 1864 or 1865. The Yale Scientific School advertised itself as catering to two classes of students: those who had not pursued a collegiate course and those who "having already graduated are disposed to pursue still further their scientific studies" (Chittenden, Sheffield Scientific School, 67–68).

45. From 1864, the seven departments were chemistry and mineralogy, natural history and geology, engineering, mechanics, agriculture, mining, and the "select course" in science and literature; see "New Education," 209.

46. Yanikoski, "Edward Everett," 230.

47. Eliot, "New Education."

48. Gilman made this same point, that mental discipline can be acquired as well from scientific and modern subjects as from classical studies, in the 1868 and 1869 Annual Statements of the Sheffield School. He and the governing board were responding to what they perceived to be a lack of appreciation by college educators for the value of scientific education; see Chittenden, Sheffield Scientific School, 135–39.

49. Eliot, "New Education, " 220.

50. Hughes, "Engineering," 413–27; Hawkins, *Between Harvard and America*, 207–15.

51. On the other hand, Eliot was able in 1906 to create the Graduate School of Applied Science, which conformed to the pattern he favored for undergraduate and professional studies; see Hughes, "Engineering," 427–33.

52. Alan I. Marcus, *Agricultural Science and the Quest for Legitimacy: Farmers, Agricultural Colleges, and Experiment Stations, 1870–1890* (Ames: Iowa State University Press, 1985).

53. Holman, "Massachusetts Institute of Technology."

54. Ibid., 316–17; Yates, *Lehigh*, 42; Sidney Sherwood, *The University of the State of New York* (Washington, D.C.: GPO, 1900), 384–85.

55. Monte A. Calvert, *The Mechanical Engineer in America, 1830–1910* (Baltimore: Johns Hopkins University Press, 1967), 87–106.

56. In Europe, this belief remained predominant for another century: universities were reserved for theoretical, academic subjects, and advanced technical education was offered in separate institutions—Technologische Hochschulen, Grandes Ecoles, or (for business) schools of economics.

"A Salutary Rivalry"

Abbreviations used in notes:
WCA—Western College Archives
OFC—Oxford Female College
WFS—Western Female Seminary
OFI—Oxford Female Institute

1. Christie Anne Farnham, *The Education of the Southern Belle: Higher Education and Student Socialization in the Antebellum South* (New York: New York University Press, 1994), 28, 12; Kathryn M. Kerns, "Farmers' Daughters: The Education of Women at Alfred Academy and University before the Civil War," *History of Higher Education Annual* 6 (1986): 11; see Geiger's chapter in this volume, "Superior Instruction of Women."

Some women's institutions founded during this period called themselves colleges, even if the education offered was not college level. Increasingly in this ten-year time period, however, women's schools set entrance and graduation requirements on a par with men's schools. One of the first of these was Elmira Female College in New York. When it opened in 1855, the requirements were similar to those at Amherst, although Elmira did not include as much Latin and Greek. Ten years later, Vassar opened, and with it began the era of the endowed women's college. Smith and Wellesley opened in 1875, and Bryn Mawr opened in 1884. See Barbara Miller Solomon, *In the Company of Educated Women* (New Haven: Yale University Press, 1985), 47–48, and Thomas Woody, *A History of Women's Education*, 2 vols. (New York: Science Press, 1929), 2:147.

2. Geiger, "Superior Instruction of Women."

3. Christie Anne Farnham argues persuasively that college education for elite women was less controversial in the South during the antebellum era than it was in the Northeast. See Farnham, *Education of the Southern Belle.*

4. Although Western Female Seminary left extensive records, the other two schools did not. Even so, some conclusions can be drawn based on the extant catalogues and circulars.

5. Sarah D. Stow, *History of Mount Holyoke Seminary, South Hadley, Mass. during Its First Half Century, 1837–1887* (South Hadley: Mount Holyoke College, 1887), 327–46. For information on Cherokee Female Seminary, see Devon A. Mihesuah, *Cultivating the*

Rosebuds: The Education of Women at the Cherokee Female Seminary: 1851–1909 (Urbana: University of Illinois Press, 1993). For a history of Mills College, see Rosalind A. Keep, *Fourscore Years: A History of Mills College* (Oakland: Mills College, 1931).

6. See, for instance, Kathryn Kish Sklar, "The Founding of Mount Holyoke College," in *Women and Power in American History,* ed. Kathryn Kish Sklar and Thomas Dublin (Englewood Cliffs, N.J.: Prentice Hall, 1991); Ronald W. Hogeland, "Coeducation of the Sexes at Oberlin College: A Study of Social Ideas in Mid-nineteenth Century America," *Journal of Social History* 6 (1972–1973): 160–76; Anne Firor Scott, "The Ever Widening Circle: The Diffusion of Feminist Values from the Troy Female Seminary, 1822–1872," *History of Education Quarterly* 19 (spring 1979): 3–25; David F. Allmendinger, "Mount Holyoke Students Encounter the Need for Life Planning, 1837–1850," *History of Education Quarterly* 19 (spring 1979): 27–46. For exceptions, see Kathryn M. Kerns, "Farmers' Daughters"; Kathryn M. Kerns, "Antebellum Higher Education for Women in Western New York State" (Ph.D. diss., University of Pennsylvania, 1993); Farnham, *Education of the Southern Belle.*

7. William E. Smith, *History of Southwestern Ohio: The Miami Valleys* (New York and West Palm Beach: Lewis Historical Publishing Company, 1964), 391; Walter Havighurst, *The Miami Years* (New York: G. P. Putnam's Sons, 1984), 13–15, 37, 103.

8. Havighurst, *Miami Years,* 57–60.

9. Olive Flower, *A History of Oxford College for Women, 1830-1928* (Oxford: Miami University Alumni Association, 1948), 5.

10. It is not clear whether all of the faculty members were employed full-time. Ibid., 24; OFC, *Third Annual Catalogue and Circular* (May 1857), 3; WFS, *First Annual Catalogue* (1856), 3, 4; OFI, *Seventh Annual Catalogue* (1855–1856), 3.

11. Narka Nelson, *Western College for Women* (Oxford, Ohio: Western College, 1967), 20.

12. Thomas J. Porter, *History of the Presbyterian Church of Oxford* (Oxford, Ohio, 1902), 25.

13. Ibid., 24, 25.

14. Ibid., 24.

15. Daniel Tenney, Executive Committee Report, 1855, folder 1.1, WCA.

16. OFI, *Seventh Annual Catalogue* (1855–56), 15.

17. For information on Mount Holyoke, see Elizabeth A. Green, *Mary Lyon and Mount Holyoke: Opening the Gates* (Hanover, N.H.: University Press of New England, 1979); Sklar, "Founding of Mount Holyoke College"; Stow, *Mount Holyoke;* Louise Porter Thomas, *Seminary Militant: An Account of the Missionary Movement at Mount Holyoke Seminary and College* (South Hadley: Mount Holyoke College, 1937).

18. OFI, *Fifth Annual Catalogue* (1854), 2.

19. Tenney, Executive Committee Report, 1855.

20. Daniel Tenney, Journal, folder 1.4, WCA.

21. Tenney, Executive Committee Report, 1855.

22. Nelson, *Western College,* 4, 7, 10.

23. Tenney, Journal, 5 June 1853.

24. WFS, Journal, 9 October 1855. The tradition of journal writing began at Mount Holyoke in 1845 as a way to stay in touch with Fidelia Fisk, the first Holyoke graduate to become a foreign missionary. Later, copies of the journal-letter were sent to other missionaries. When Western opened, faculty there began a record of events—especially of revivals and conversions—to send to missionaries as well as to Holyoke. A faculty member at Western and one at Mount Holyoke were assigned the role of journal writer; the two schools exchanged journals at the end of each term. See Stow, *Mount Holyoke,* 171.

25. Samuel W. Fisher, "John Calvin and John Wesley. An Address Delivered July 17, 1856 on the First Anniversary of the Western Female Seminary, Oxford, Ohio" (Cincinnati: Moore, Wilstach, Keys and Co., 1856), 49.

26. Ibid., 49–51.

27. Ibid., 51.

28. WFS, Journal, 22 May 1862.

29. Tenney, Executive Committee Report, 1855.

30. McKeen, "The Holyoke System," 7–8.

31. In *Alma Mater,* Helen Lefkowitz Horowitz suggests that the architecture of an educational institution reflects how the school views its mission and its students. Seminaries tended to be one large building, with public rooms downstairs and private rooms upstairs. Women could enter their bedrooms only by coming through a main, central door, climbing a central stairway, and walking down a common corridor. The physical setting of higher education perpetuated and reinforced the ideology of separate spheres. Women attended school in a domestic setting headed by a parental authority figure. Men's schools allowed more independence and freedom of movement. See Helen Lefkowitz Horowitz, *Alma Mater: Design and Experience in the Women's Colleges from Their Nineteenth-Century Beginnings to the 1930s* (New York: Knopf, 1984).

A homelike environment, in which the faculty assumed parental responsibilities for students, had been the goal in men's colleges in the colonial period. Men's colleges then were small and residential, and therefore the faculty were able to monitor and regulate students. But this was no longer true in the antebellum era. Rapid increases in student population led to a loss of institutional control over student behavior. In 1828 the president of Amherst still referred to his students as "his children," and wanted them to think of him as their father. But to most students, the president's views were an anachronism. In 1842 Francis Wayland, the president of Brown, criticized the design of men's colleges, saying that they "are never constructed with a view to supervision," and that they are open day and night, near "the usual temptations of youth." *Thoughts on the Present Collegiate System in the United States* (Boston, 1842).

32. WFS, Journal, 7 November 1855.

33. Ibid., 1 January 1857.

34. WFS, *Circular* (1854), 7.

35. WFS, Journals; see, e.g., 9 January 1856; 22 May 1862; 25 November 1862; 12 March 1863; 2 July 1863; June 1865; September 1865; 26 October 1865; 23 May 1866.

36. Ibid., 9 October 1855.

37. For example, ibid., 1 January 1856.

38. Ibid., 11 October 1856; 19 July 1858.

39. Ibid., 29 January 1857.

40. Ibid.; see, for example, 9 October 1855; 15 November 1855.

41. Ibid., 15 November 1855; 8 December 1856.

42. Ibid., 5 September 1864.

43. Ibid., June 1865.

44. Ibid., 20 November 1857.

45. Ibid., January 1858.

46. Lynn D. Gordon, *Gender and Higher Education in the Progressive Era* (New Haven: Yale University Press, 1990), 30.

47. OFC, *Third Annual Catalogue and Circular* (May 1857), 16.

48. Flower, *Oxford College*, 14–24.

49. There are two different estimates for the cost of the original seminary building. Nelson suggests that the building itself, exclusive of furnishings and landscaping, cost $33,000. A circular from 1854 states that the building cost $60,000. See Nelson, *Western College*, 29, and WFS, *Circular* (1854), 7.

50. Western Female Seminary Catalogues, WCA; Oxford Female Institute and Oxford Female College Catalogues, Havighurst Special Collections, King Library, Miami University.

51. WFS, *Circular* (1854), 5, 6.

52. Ibid., 8.

53. WFS, *Seventh Annual Catalogue* (1862), 19.

54. WFS, *Circular* (1860).

55. OFI, *Fifth Annual Catalogue* (1853–1854), 13.

56. OFI, *Seventh Annual Catalogue* (1855–1856), 11.

57. OFI, *Fifteenth Annual Catalogue* (1863–1864), 10.

58. OFC, *Third Annual Catalogue and Circular* (May 1857), 10, 18.

59. WFS, *Second Annual Catalogue* (1857), 11.

60. WFS, *Circular* (1854), 10.

61. WFS, *Second Annual Catalogue* (1857), 12, 13.

62. OFC, *Third Annual Catalogue and Circular* (May 1857), 19.

63. OFI, *Ninth Annual Catalogue* (1857–1858), 19.

64. *Oxford Citizen*, 28 February 1857, 3.

65. Flower, *Oxford College*, 27–39, 88–100.

66. Nelson, *Western College*, 55, 71.

67. Ibid., 95, 108–9.

68. Woody, *Women's Education*, 362.

69. Havighurst, *Miami Years*, chap. 27.

70. Nelson, *Western College*, 75.

71. *Memorial of the Re-union of the Classes of '56, '57, '58, '59, '60, '61, at the Western Female Seminary, Oxford, Ohio. May 6, 1876* (Cincinnati: McDonald and Eick, Printers, 1876), 22.

72. *Memorial. Twenty-fifth Anniversary of the Western Female Seminary, Oxford, Ohio* (Oxford, Ohio: Western Female Seminary Alumnae Association, 1881), 106, 180.

The "Superior Instruction of Women," 1836–1890

1. Seminaries and colleges for women are treated extensively, but separately, in Thomas Woody, *A History of Women's Education in the United States*, 2 vols. (New York: Science Press, 1929), 1:329–456; 2:137–223; such precedents are also recognized by Mabel Newcomer, *A Century of Higher Education for American Women* (New York: Harper and Brothers, 1959). More recent work on this subject has examined antebellum institutions, even though there was greater continuity than change in the 1850–1890 era; see Christie Anne Farnham, *The Education of the Southern Belle: Higher Education and Student Socialization in the Antebellum South* (New York: New York University Press, 1994); Kathryn M. Kern, "Antebellum Higher Education for Women in Western New York State" (Ph.D. diss., University of Pennsylvania, 1993); and Shirley Ann Hickson, "The Development of Higher Education for Women in the Antebellum South" (Ph.D. diss., University of South Carolina, 1985).

2. See the chapter in this volume, "The Era of Multipurpose Colleges in American Higher Education." The present chapter is an expanded and revised version of an unpublished section of that original study. The focus here is on institutions for the higher education of women, and no attempt will be made to recount the rich history of arguments for and against this endeavor.

3. Carole B. Shmurak and Bonnie S. Handler, "'Castle of Science': Mount Holyoke College and the Preparation of Women in Chemistry, 1837–1941," *History of Education Quarterly* 32 (fall 1992): 315–42, quote on 316; Sarah D. Stow, "Mount Holyoke Seminary and College," in George G. Bush, *History of Higher Education in Massachusetts*, Bureau of Education, Circular of Information no. 6 (Washington, D.C.: GPO, 1891), 400–419.

4. Woody, *Women's Education*, 441–56; Farnham, *Education of the Southern Belle*, passim.

5. Woody, *Women's Education*, 353–55; Joan N. Burstyn, "Catherine Beecher and the Education of American Women," *New England Quarterly* 47 (1974): 386–403; Catherine E. Beecher, *The True Remedy for the Wrongs of Women with a History of an Enterprise Having That for Its Object* (Boston, 1851).

6. E.g., just one-quarter of Mount Holyoke students, who were known for their dedication, completed the course (1837–1850). See David F. Allmendinger, "Mount Holyoke Students Encounter the Need for Life Planning, 1837–1850," *History of Education Quarterly* 19 (1979): 27–46; Hickson reports that 900 students graduated from four of her five schools out of 8,000 enrollees ("Higher Education for Women," 259).

7. The five schools studied by Hickson, which taught at approximately the same level, were named Georgia (later Wesleyan) Female College, Judson Female Institute, Salem Boarding School, Hollins Institute, and Limestone Springs Female High School; see "Higher Education for Women," 259.

8. Discussed by Farnham, *Education of the Southern Belle*, 190–91 n. 3.

9. Ibid., 28; Hickson, "Higher Education for Women," 277–78; Kerns, "Antebellum Higher Education for Women," 150–51; Margaret A. Nash, "'A Salutary Rivalry': The Growth of Higher Education for Women in Oxford, Ohio, 1855–1867," *History of Higher Education Annual* 16 (1996): 21–38.

10. New York Central College and the Seventh Day Baptist institution, Alfred University, are treated in Kerns, "Antebellum Higher Education for Women."

11. Quoted in Linda Rose Buchanan, "Not Harvard, Not Holyoke, Not Howard: A Study of the Life and Death of Three Small Colleges" (Ph.D. diss., Georgia State University, 1997), 132. Mary Sharp was originally chartered as Tennessee and Alabama Female Institute (1851); and Elmira as Auburn Female University (1852).

12. Woody, *Women's Education*, 2:171–76.

13. There were great variety and confusion in the diplomas and degrees offered by women's colleges. Many thought it inappropriate to award a bachelor's degree to a woman, or an Artium Baccalaureata to someone who had not studied Latin. Hence each institution tended to contrive its own unique awards.

14. Woody takes great pains to compare women's curricula with regional men's colleges; however, he generally uses their initial offerings, thus discounting their incremental progress, and he compares them chiefly for Latin and Greek, where women's colleges were unavoidably weakest due to the lack of preparatory training for girls; see *Women's Education*, 2:160–84. Farnham notes the inadequacies of large numbers of the smaller men's colleges; see *Education of the Southern Belle*, 21–28.

15. Textbooks used in female seminaries and colleges are listed in Woody, *Women's Education*, 1:552–62; 2:474–80; detailed curricula are given in Kerns, "Antebellum Higher Education."

16. The level of study for the ancient languages varied greatly across American colleges, but the standards at even the best schools were woeful in comparison with good European secondary schools. The ancient language standard makes sense only within the terms of the mental discipline paradigm, where more study is equated with greater education/mental discipline.

17. One source gives the number of chartered colleges in the South as 32 (Farnham, *Education of the Southern Belle*, 18 n. 17), and Woody lists 10 in the North (*Women's Education*, II: 145–47); both figures probably understate the total.

18. Ibid., 147.

19. Saul Sack, *History of Higher Education in Pennsylvania*, 2 vols. (Harrisburg: Pennsylvania Historical and Museum Commission, 1963), 571–77; cf. William Earle Drake, *Higher Education in North Carolina before 1860* (New York: Carlton Press, 1964), 253.

20. Keith E. Melder, "Woman's Calling: The Teaching Profession in America, 1830–1860," *American Studies* (fall 1972): 19–32; Allmendinger, "Mount Holyoke Students."

21. Farnham emphasizes the stereotype of the Southern belle and asserts that educational institutions organized "all aspects of the educational experience around the goal of producing an exalted notion of womanhood" (*Education of the Southern Belle*, 120). However, Hickson found that educated Southern belles exhibited "a strong preference for husbands from the learned professions . . . men of sufficient education and intellectual stature to appreciate the companionship of a well-educated wife" ("Higher Education for Women," 263–64). Hence, even though nearly all college women married

rather than worked, it would be misleading to regard their education as merely ornamental.

22. Drake, *North Carolina,* 257.

23. Quoted in Sidney Sherwood, *The University of the State of New York* (Washington,
D.C.: GPO, 1900), 447.

24. The Seven Sisters at their foundings embodied distinctly different interpretations
of women's collegiate education; see Helen Lefkowitz Horowitz, *Alma Mater: Design and
Experience in the Women's Colleges from Their Nineteenth-Century Beginnings to the 1930s*
(New York: Knopf, 1984). The following discussion focuses on Vassar, Wellesley, and
Smith, the institutions that faced most acutely the challenge of emulating the best male
colleges. Bryn Mawr was founded late enough to embrace the new correlates of quality—
electives and graduate education; Radcliffe and Barnard, as coordinate colleges, had an
already defined relationship with leading men's colleges; and Mount Holyoke, the pioneer,
had to modernize substantially when it became a college in the 1880s to attain the standard set by the other Sisters.

25. The following discussion of curriculum and students draws eclectically from the
following: Bush, *History of Higher Education in Massachusetts,* 400–443; Horowitz, *Alma
Mater,* 28–94; Newcomer, *Century,* 75–88; Virginia Onderdonk, "The Curriculum," in
Wellesley College, 1875–1975: A Century of Women, ed. Jean Glasscock (Wellesley: Wellesley
College, 1975), 122–63; Patricia Ann Palmieri, *In Adamless Eden: The Community of
Women Faculty at Wellesley* (New Haven: Yale University Press, 1995), 354, 161–80; Sher-
wood, *New York,* 446–65.

26. Woody, *Women's Education,* 2:182; Elaine Kendall, *Peculiar Institutions: An Infor-
mal History of the Seven Sister Colleges* (New York: Putnam's Sons, 1976), 113–19; Sarah H.
Gordon, "Smith College Students: The First Ten Classes, 1879–1888," *History of Education
Quarterly* 15 (1975): 147–67.

27. Quoted in Newcomer, *Century,* 82.

28. Vassar's enrollments seem to have been adversely affected by the opening of Smith
and Wellesley and the acceptance of women at Cornell after 1871, and thus remained weak
until 1890.

29. Sherwood, *New York,* 447.

30. Report of the Commissioner of Education, 1890 (Washington, D.C., 1891), 746:
quoting W. Le Conte Stevens, *North American Review,* 136:28.

31. Geiger, "The Era of Multipurpose Colleges in American Higher Education."

32. Richard L. Wing, "Requiem for a Pioneer of Women's Higher Education: The Ingham University of Le Roy, New York, 1857–1892," *History of Higher Education Annual* 11
(1991): 61–79. Rutgers Female College in New York City was a similar case, included in
Division A in 1891 but deceased in 1897.

33. Other additions were Sophie Newcomb and Randolph-Macon Women's College
(both coordinates); Simmons; Rockford when it received a college charter; and Trinity
College (District of Columbia), a Roman Catholic institution founded in 1900.

34. RCE, 1888, 596.

35. Buchanan, "Not Harvard," 110–75.

Noah Porter Writ Large?

1. The research on which this chapter is based has been generously supported by the AAFRC Trust for Philanthropy, the Aspen Institute's Nonprofit Sector Research Fund, the Lilly Endowment, Inc., and the Program on Non-Profit Organizations, Yale University. The chapter draws on a larger study commissioned by the National Center on Nonprofit Boards that will appear under the title "Remedying the Incompleteness of Democracy: An Overview of Board Governance in America."

2. The discovery of modernization, professionalization, and bureaucracy as underlying themes of post–Civil War American history began in the 1960s and grew out of Richard Hofstadter's efforts to use sociological theory to explain American reform movements. Because Hofstadter's work focused attention on the educational and occupational backgrounds of political actors, it profoundly influenced thinking in both the historiographical mainstream and in the embryonic community of educational historians.

Certainly the most influential of the efforts to reconceptualize the past in these terms is Robert Wiebe, *The Search for Order, 1877–1920* (New York: Hill and Wang, 1967). Other scholars carried the concept into particular domains of activity. Among the more notable of these efforts are Laurence Veysey, *The Emergence of the American University* (Chicago: University of Chicago Press, 1970), and Alfred D. Chandler, *Visible Hand: The Managerial Revolution in American Business* (Cambridge: Harvard University Press, 1965). Two important articles by Louis Galambos summarize and assess the implications of this body of work: "The Emerging Organizational Synthesis in American History," *Business History Review* 44 (autumn 1970), and "Technology, Political Economy, and Professionalization," *Business History Review* 57 (1982). While the work of Wiebe, Veysey, and Chandler tended to celebrate modernization and its institutional correlates, later scholarship, while elaborating on the implications of these trends, also criticized historians' uncritical appropriation of social science grand theory. Martin J. Sklar's *Corporate Reconstruction of American Capitalism, 1890–1916: The Market, the Law, and Politics* (New York: Cambridge University Press, 1988) is both a brilliant elucidation of the culture of capitalism and a critique of its interpretation. Thomas Bender's *Community and Social Change in America* (New Brunswick: Rutgers University Press, 1978) is essential to understanding the virtues and vices of this type of theoretically informed (and often misinformed) historiography. For a critique of the problematic relationship between the historiographies of business and education within this framework, see Peter Dobkin Hall, "The Managerial Revolution, the Institutional Infrastructure, and the Problem of Human Capital," in "Review Symposium on the Comparative Historical Analysis of Nonprofit Sectors," *Voluntas* 7, 1 (1996).

3. The most notable expressions of this historiographic reflex are to be found in Richard Hofstadter and Walter Metzger, *The Development of Academic Freedom in the United States* (New York: Columbia University Press, 1955), and in Richard Hofstadter and Wilson Smith, *American Higher Education: A Documentary History* (Chicago: University of Chicago Press, 1961). To his credit, Frederick Rudolph admitted the possibility that the Yale Report was more than a reactionary effort to resist the forces of modernization—see

The American College and University—A History (New York: Vintage Books, 1962), 130–34—but his more nuanced perspective was largely bypassed in the rush to embrace more theoretically driven (and ideologized) interpretations. Of the historians of Yale, George W. Pierson offered a lukewarm defense of the "Old Time College" in *Yale College: An Educational History, 1871–1921* (New Haven: Yale University Press, 1952). Pierson's protégé, John S. Whitehead, provided the most dispassionate, detailed, and contextualized accounts of the national dimensions of the laicization of university governance; see *The Separation of College and State: Columbia, Dartmouth, Harvard, and Yale, 1776–1876* (New Haven: Yale University Press, 1973).

4. Peter Dobkin Hall, *The Organization of American Culture, 1700–1900: Private Institutions, Elites, and the Origins of American Nationality* (New York: New York University Press, 1982). My speculations are supported by the recent work of Robert Finke and Rodney Stark, whose *Churching of America, 1776–1990* (New Brunswick: Rutgers University Press, 1992) suggests that, contrary to conventional wisdom, perhaps no more than 20 percent of Americans in 1800 belonged to churches.

5. Brooks Adams, *The Emancipation of Massachusetts* (Boston: Houghton, Mifflin and Co., 1887).

6. For a good overview of this, see George W. Pierson, *The Education of American Leaders: The Comparative Contributions of U.S. Colleges and Universities* (New York: Praeger, 1969). See also Bailey Burritt's classic, *Professional Distribution of College and University Graduates* (Washington, D.C.: GPO, 1912).

7. Alexis de Tocqueville, *Democracy in America* (New York: Knopf, 1945), 1:303.

8. Ibid., 32.

9. Ibid.

10. Oliver Wendell Holmes, *Autocrat of the Breakfast Table* (New York: Sagamore Press, 1957), 21–23.

11. Ronald Story, *The Forging of an Aristocracy: Harvard and the Boston Upper Class, 1800–1870* (Middletown, Conn.: Wesleyan University Press, 1980), 89–134; Seymour Harris, *The Economics of Harvard* (New York: McGraw-Hill), xxiii.

12. On this, see George W. Pierson, *A Yale Book of Numbers: Historical Statistics of the College and University, 1701–1976* (New Haven: Yale University Press, 1983), and Hall, *Organization of American Culture*, 161–62, 310–11. The best raw sources on the nativity and residence of Yale graduates are Franklin Bowditch Dexter, *Yale Annals and Biographies* (New York: Henry Holt and Co., 1903), which covers graduates of the college for the years 1701 through 1815, and his *Biographical Notices of Graduates of Yale College: Including Those Graduated in Classes later than 1815, Who Are Not Commemorated in the Annual Obituary Records* (New Haven: Yale University, 1913); and the *Yale Obituary Record,* published between 1841 and 1951, which contains biographies of all degree recipients roughly between 1815 and 1950.

13. In recent years, a great deal of able work has been done on the "benevolent empire" created by the evangelicals. The best overviews include Timothy L. Smith, *Revivalism and Social Reform: American Protestantism on the Eve of the Civil War* (New York: Harper and Row, 1957); Clifford S. Griffen, *Their Brothers' Keepers: Moral Stewardship in*

the United States, 1800–1865 (New Brunswick: Rutgers University Press, 1960); and Charles I. Foster, *Errand of Mercy: The Evangelical United Front, 1792–1837* (Chapel Hill: University of North Carolina Press, 1961). For a more recent interpretation of the role of evangelical Protestants in originating voluntary associations, see Peter Dobkin Hall, "Religion and the Organizational Revolution in the United States," in *Sacred Companies: Organizational Aspects of Religion and Religious Aspects of Organizations,* ed. N. J. Demerath et al. (New York: Oxford University Press, 1998), and "Religion and the Origins of Voluntary Associations," PONPO Working Paper no. 213 (New Haven: Program on Non-Profit Organizations, Yale University, 1994).

14. Thus, for example, as Ezra Stiles makes quite clear in his diary, his 1777 "Plan of a University," proposing the establishment of professorships in law, medicine, history, and belles lettres, was intended to make Yale appear less sectarian and more public serving in the hope of persuading the legislature to renew its annual grants in support of the college. See Ezra Stiles, *Literary Diary* (New York: Charles Scribner's Sons, 1901), 2:207–8. By far the best source on the general issue of college-government relationships is John S. Whitehead, *The Separation of College and State: Columbia, Dartmouth, Harvard, and Yale, 1776–1876* (New Haven: Yale University Press, 1973).

15. On the intricacies of ecclesiastical politics in eighteenth-century Connecticut, see Sidney Ahlstrom, *A Religious History of the American People* (New Haven: Yale University Press, 1972), 403–28; Richard Bushman, *From Puritan to Yankee: Character and the Social Order in Connecticut, 1690–1765* (New York: Norton, 1967); Charles Roy Keller, *The Second Great Awakening in Connecticut* (New Haven: Yale University Press, 1942). Edmund S. Morgan, *The Gentle Puritan: A Life of Ezra Stiles, 1727–1795* (New York: Norton, 1962), gives a particularly good account of the politics of "New Divinity" faction in the 1780s and 1790s.

16. Richard Purcell, *Connecticut in Transition, 1775–1817* (Middletown, Conn.: Wesleyan University Press, 1963).

17. In the early eighteenth century, Connecticut Congregationalists had moved from loose alliances between autonomous congregations toward a more centralized presbyterian polity, in which authority shifted to "associations" and "consociations" of ministers and elders. This enabled the church to define and enforce orthodoxy and—except in the face of broad-based challenges such as the Great Awakening—prevented the kind of factionalization characteristic of Massachusetts's churches. The best source on the differences between Massachusetts and Connecticut Congregationalism is Henry Martyn Dexter, *The Congregationalism of the Last Three Hundred Years as Seen in Its Literature* (New York: Harper, 1860). The protracted struggle over ecclesiastical polities and authority structures significantly paralleled and at times converged with conflicts over university governance.

18. The best source on the proliferation of education institutions and their denominational ties is Colin B. Burke, *American Collegiate Populations: A Test of the Traditional View* (New York: New York University Press, 1982).

19. On developing merchant group influence at Harvard, see Story, *The Forging of an Aristocracy.*

20. Stiles, *Literary Diary,* 3:457.

21. Ibid., 3:457–58.

22. On corporations as part of the Federalist-Congregationalist machine, see Purcell, *Connecticut in Transition.* See also Peter Dobkin Hall, "Organizational Values and the Origins of the Corporation in Connecticut, 1769–1860," *Connecticut History* 29 (November 1988): 63–90.

23. Tocqueville, *Democracy in America,* 1:203.

24. The Jeffersonians, like their leader, favored education in principle—but were seldom willing to devote resources to its support. In 1779 Jefferson persuaded Virginia's General Assembly to vote in favor of establishing a system of common schools—but neither succeeded in persuading it to allocate funds for its support nor showed himself willing to make it a major political priority. In areas like the Old Northwest, where migrants from Federalist New England and the Jeffersonian South settled in relatively equal numbers, the contrasts in institutional orientation became especially evident—with the latter showing themselves especially parsimonious with regard to supporting education and other eleemosynary enterprises. On this, see Peter Dobkin Hall, "The Spirit of the Ordinance of 1787: Organizational Values, Voluntary Associations, and Higher Education in Ohio, 1803–1830," in *Schools and the Means of Education Shall Forever Be Encouraged: A History of Education in the Old Northwest,* ed. P. H. Mattingly and E. E. Stevens Jr. (Athens: Ohio University Libraries, 1987), 97–114, and Peter Dobkin Hall, "Cultures of Trusteeship in the United States," in *Inventing the Nonprofit Sector and Other Essays on Philanthropy, Voluntarism, and Nonprofit Organizations,* ed. Peter Dobkin Hall (Baltimore: Johns Hopkins University Press, 1992), 144–70.

25. On the debate over the Smithsonian, see William J. Rhees, ed., *The Smithsonian Institution: Documents Relative to Its Origin and History,* Smithsonian Miscellaneous Collections 17, pub. no. 328 (Washington: Smithsonian Institution, 1879), 1–2, 58–62, 135–46, 148–54, 763–801.

26. Franklin Pierce, "Veto Message, May 3, 1854," in *Compilation of the Messages and Papers of the Presidents, 1789–1897* (Washington, 1898), 5:201.

27. On the majoritarian constraint, see Mancur Olson, *The Logic of Collective Action: Public Goods and the Theory of Groups* (Cambridge: Harvard University Press, 1971). See also James Douglas, "Political Theories of Nonprofit Organization," in *The Nonprofit Sector: A Research Handbook,* ed. W. W. Powell (New Haven: Yale University Press, 1987), 43–54.

28. George M. Frederickson, *The Inner Civil War: Northern Intellectuals and the Crisis of the Union* (New York: Harper and Row, 1967).

29. Frederic H. Hedge, "University Reform: An Address to the Alumni of Harvard, at Their Triennial Festival, July 19, 1866," *Atlantic* (September 1866): 296–307.

30. On Josiah Quincy's distortions of Harvard's financial history, see Harris, *Economics of Harvard,* xvi, 240–43.

31. Theodore Dwight Woolsey, "Dr. Hedge's Address to the Alumni of Harvard," *New Englander* 25, 4 (October 1866): 695–711.

32. Ibid., 699.

33. Ibid., 700–701.

34. Ibid., 701.

35. "Yale Alumni Dinner—A Pleasant Gathering at Delmonico's—Speeches of Hon. Wm. M. Evarts and Others," *New York Tribune,* 30 January 1869. See also "Dinner of Yale Alumni," *New York Times,* 30 January 1869, and "Yale College—The Dinner of the New York Alumni of Yale College," editorial, *New York Times,* 1 February 1869.

36. Ibid.

37. "Meeting of the New York Alumni," *New Englander* (April 1869).

38. Noah Porter, "American Colleges and the American Public," *New Englander* 28, 2 (1869): 272–91. Porter's essay appeared in six successive issues of the *New Englander* and was subsequently published in book form in 1870.

39. Timothy Dwight, "Yale College—Some Thoughts Respecting Its Future," *New Englander* (July 1870–October 1871).

40. Porter, "American Colleges," 275.

41. Ibid., 283–84.

42. Ibid., 285–87.

43. Ibid., 232.

44. Ibid., 282.

45. Ibid., 283.

46. Ibid., 289–90.

47. On Phelps, see biographical material in the successive yearbooks of the class of 1860 and his obituary in the 1894 *Obituary Record.* After graduating from Yale, Phelps received a law degree from Columbia in 1863. He served as a member of the Yale Corporation (1872–1892) and on the governing board of Yale's Sheffield Scientific School (1871–1894). Active in public life, he served in the United States Congress (1872–1874, 1882–1888), as ambassador to Austria (1881–1882) and Germany (1889–1893), and as judge of the New Jersey Court of Errors (1893–1894).

48. "Speech of William Walter Phelps," *College Courant,* 23 July 1870, 71–72.

49. In addition to the articles cited in this chapter, the public debate over Yale governance included offerings from Daniel Coit Gilman (who had hoped to succeed Woolsey as president) and James Dwight Dana. See Gilman, "Proposed Change in the Corporation of Yale College," *Nation,* 25 May 1870, and Dana, "What Yale College Needs," *Nation,* 25 May 1871.

50. Harris E. Starr, *William Graham Sumner* (New York: Henry Holt and Company, 1925).

51. W. G. Sumner, "The Ways and Means of Our Colleges," *Nation,* 8 September 1870, 154.

52. Ibid.

53. Ibid. On the alumni fund, see Brooks Mather Kelley, *Yale: A History* (New Haven: Yale University Press, 1974), 277ff., and Pierson, *Yale College,* 62, 588.

54. Kelley, *Yale,* 271.

55. Harris, *Economics of Harvard,* 270.

56. On Hadley, see Morris Hadley, *Arthur Twining Hadley* (New Haven: Yale University Press, 1948), and Kelley, *Yale,* 315ff. Kelley, under the thrall of Hofstadter and Metzger,

titled his chapter on Hadley's reign "Revival" (in contrast to his chapter on Porter, which was titled "Stagnation").

57. Pierson, *Yale Book of Numbers*, 548. A measure of the impact of including the alumni is the fact that the university's permanent funds jumped from $181,700 in 1875 (four years into the Porter era), to $484,594 in 1885 (at the beginning of the younger Dwight's regime), to $1.8 million (at the beginning of the Hadley regime).

58. Thorstein Veblen, *The Higher Learning in America* (New York: B. W. Huebsch, 1918). Veblen graduated from Carlton College in Minnesota in 1877, began his graduate studies at Johns Hopkins (presided over by Daniel Coit Gilman, whom Porter had driven into exile), then transferred to Yale to study under Porter. Whether he left Hopkins by necessity or preference is not known, but his choice of an institution nationally prominent for its opposition to the emergent plutocratic university model and his decision to study under Porter rather than William Graham Sumner is suggestive. I have not been able to locate any primary material on Veblen's activities at Yale or the content of his interactions with Porter.

59. Abraham Flexner, *Medical Education in the United States and Canada*, Bulletin no. 4 (New York: Carnegie Foundation for the Advancement of Teaching, 1910); Ellen Condliffe Lagemann, *The Politics of Knowledge: The Carnegie Corporation, Philanthropy, and Public Policy* (Middletown, Conn.: Wesleyan University Press, 1989); Steven Wheatley, *The Politics of Philanthropy: Abraham Flexner and Medical Education* (Madison: University of Wisconsin Press, 1988).

60. On corporate social responsibility in the progressive era, see Morrill Heald, *The Social Responsibilities of Business: Corporation and Community, 1900–1960* (Cleveland: Case Western Reserve University Press, 1969), and Peter Dobkin Hall, "Business Giving and Social Investment in the United States," in *Philanthropic Giving: Studies in Varieties and Goals,* ed. Richard Magat (New York: Oxford University Press, 1989), 221–44. David F. Noble, *America by Design: Science, Technology, and the Rise of Corporate Capitalism* (New York: Oxford University Press, 1977), and Guy Alchon, *The Invisible Hand of Planning: Capitalism, Social Science, and the State in the 1920s* (Princeton: Princeton University Press, 1985), provide the most detailed accounts of the alliances between progressive intellectuals and business.

61. Veblen, *Higher Learning in America*, 46.

62. Ibid., 47.

63. Ibid., 48.

64. Ibid., 52.

65. Ibid., 54–55.

66. Ibid., 58.

67. Ibid., 59.

68. Ibid., 59–60.

69. Ibid., 61.

70. Quoted in Hugh Hawkins, *Between Harvard and America: The Educational Leadership of Charles W. Eliot* (New York: Oxford University Press, 1972), 216.

71. Henry Adams, *The Education of Henry Adams* (Boston: Massachusetts Historical Society, 1918), 305–6.

72. Christopher Lasch, *The New Radicalism in America: The Intellectual as a Social Type* (New York: Vintage Books, 1963), xiv.

73. On business leadership in education, see Edward Chase Kirkland, *Dream and Thought in the Business Community, 1860–1900* (Ithaca: Cornell University Press, 1956), and Earl J. McGrath, "The Control of Higher Education in America," *Educational Record* 17 (April 1936).

74. These figures on participation in Yale fund drives are based on an in-house study I conducted in 1973, commissioned by the Campaign for Yale—the unsuccessful capital campaign that closed Kingman Brewster's regime. Yale's archives contain complete records on donors since the mid-eighteenth century. On the 1926–1928 campaign, see *The Yale Roll Call* (New Haven: Yale University, 1928), which contains a remarkably complete breakdown of donors by class, state, city, and size of donation. I used these categories to do retrospective analyses of the 1870, 1854, and 1830 drives.

75. Besides Veblen, the critical literature on business control of eleemosynary governing boards includes Gustavus Myers, *History of the Great American Fortunes* (New York: Modern Library, 1910); Scott Nearing, "Who's Who among College Trustees," *School and Society* 6 (8 September 1916): 297–99; Upton Sinclair, *The Goose-Step: A Study of American Education* (Pasadena: published by the author, 1923); Harold J. Laski, *The Dangers of Obedience and Other Essays* (New York: Harper Collins, 1930); William H. Allen, *Rockefeller: Giant, Dwarf, Symbol* (New York: Institute for Public Service, 1930); Eduard Lindemann, *Wealth and Culture* (New York: Harcourt, Brace and Co., 1936); Ferdinand Lundberg, *America's 60 Families* (New York: Vanguard Press, 1937); Horace Coon, *Money to Burn: What the Great American Philanthropic Foundations Do with Their Money* (London: Longmans, Green and Co., 1938); Gustavus Myers, *The Ending of Hereditary American Fortunes* (New York: Julian Messner, 1939).

76. Charles W. Eliot, "The New Education: Its Organization," *Atlantic Monthly,* February-March 1869, 203.

77. Charles W. Eliot, "Inaugural Address as President of Harvard College, October 19, 1869," in *Educational Reform—Essays and Addresses* (New York: Century Company, 1905), 12.

78. Ibid., 12.

79. Herbert Croly, *The Promise of American Life* (New York: Macmillan, 1909), 439. This volume is generally considered to be the definitive ideological statement of the Progressive movement, and Croly himself epitomized many of the central biographical themes of the culture of progressivism. Matriculating at Harvard in 1886, he experienced Eliot's educational vision in full flower and, as both his ideas and his career suggest, absorbed its essence. After serving as editor of the *Architectural Record,* a trade journal noted for its advocacy of city planning and other causes that would become central to the Progressive agenda, he became a political journalist. With backing from Morgan partner Willard Straight, he established the *New Republic,* the movement's most influential political periodical, in 1914. Like his mentor, Charles W. Eliot, Croly actively sought alliances with "progressive" businessmen. His 1912 biography of Marcus Alonzo Hanna, the national Republican leader credited by some to be the inventor of modern political life,

eulogized the possibilities of alliances between big business and social reform. The best biography of Croly is David W. Levy's *Herbert Croly of the New Republic: The Life and Thought of an American Progressive* (Princeton: Princeton University Press, 1985).

The German Model and the Graduate School

1. This chapter has benefited from the comments of several colleagues—Bernard Bailyn, Hugh Hawkins, David Hollinger, Joel Howell, George Marsden, Jonathan Marwil, Nicholas Steneck, and Stephen Tonsor—and from the financial support of the Rackham School of Graduate Studies. A version with thicker documentation appeared in *Rackham Reports*, 1988–89, 6–52; scholars wishing fuller detail of the history of the University of Michigan should refer to it.

2. The most cogent summing up of the story is Laurence R. Veysey's justly influential *The Emergence of the American University* (Chicago: University of Chicago Press, 1965), esp. 10, 12–13, 125–33, 153–58.

3. Significant scholarly pilgrimages to Germany began immediately after the War of 1812, when men like George Ticknor and Edward Everett studied in Germany and then returned to apply their foreign learning (at least temporarily and often without much effect) in American colleges. Ultimately some nine or ten thousand Americans matriculated in German universities between the end of the Napoleonic Wars and the outbreak of the First World War—often, however, seemingly only for a term. The statistical data are not full enough to permit more than broad generalizations about patterns of American attendance at German universities. The University of Göttingen seems to have been at first the most popular destination; see, e.g., Ilse Costas, "Die Sozialstruktur der Studenten der Göttinger Universität im 18. Jahrhundert," in *Anfänge Göttingen Sozialwissenschaft* (Göttingen, 1987), 128–29. Long before midcentury, however, Berlin, Halle, and Leipzig had achieved parity with Göttingen in numbers of American students. Heidelberg also became popular after about 1850. By the 1860s Berlin had become preeminent in attracting Americans.

There is no thorough study of the whole phenomenon, despite its importance to the German model of American university history. But see Carl Diehl, *Americans and German Scholarship, 1770–1870* (New Haven: Yale University Press, 1978), esp. chap. 3, and Jurgen Herbst, *The German Historical School in American Scholarship: A Study in the Transfer of Culture* (Ithaca: Cornell University Press, 1965), esp. chap. 1.

4. Among these educational investigators were Charles W. Eliot, the creator of modern Harvard; Daniel Coit Gilman, founder of Johns Hopkins; and Michigan's founding president, Henry P. Tappan. Travelers with other purposes who nevertheless devoted considerable time to studying German universities while on their journeys included Andrew Dickson White, founding president of Cornell; and Charles Kendall Adams, White's successor at Cornell (1885–1892) and then president of Wisconsin (1892–1902).

5. The most helpful monographs on the episodes mentioned are David Tyack, *George Ticknor and the Boston Brahmins* (Cambridge: Harvard University Press, 1967), chap. 3; Hugh Hawkins, *Pioneer: A History of Johns Hopkins University, 1874–1889* (Ithaca:

Cornell University Press, 1960), and *Between Harvard and America: The Educational Leadership of Charles W. Eliot* (New York: Oxford University Press, 1972); and Robert A. McCaughey, "The Transformation of American Academic Life: Harvard University, 1821–1892," *Perspectives in American History* 8 (1974): 239–332.

6. Influential examples include Burton J. Bledstein, *The Culture of Professionalism: The Middle Class and the Development of Higher Education in America* (New York: Norton, 1976); Thomas L. Haskell, ed., *The Authority of Experts: Studies in History and Theory* (Bloomington: Indiana University Press, 1984), part 2; and Magali Sarfatti Larson, *The Rise of Professionalism* (Berkeley: University of California Press, 1977). Professionalization was certainly *one* of the things involved in the emergence of the modern professoriat and research university, with all of the specialization involved in both. Whether professionalization is *the* key to understanding these developments is, to say the least, debatable. In any case professionalization makes a poor organizing theme for university history: it is too blunt an instrument and misses too much of what was going on within colleges and universities.

7. A study sensitive to both the pull of the German example and the American deviation from it is Nathan Reingold, "Graduate School and Doctoral Degree: European Models and American Realities," in *Scientific Colonialism: A Cross-cultural Comparison,* ed. Reingold and Marc Rothenberg (Washington, D.C.: Smithsonian Institution Press, 1986), 129–49.

8. "Qualified" means that the student had studied at a *Gymnasium* and earned an *Abitur.* It has been argued that the elective system was the American equivalent of *Lernfreiheit,* but this seems a pretty faint shadow of the real thing.

9. Most German students never even took a university degree but used their university studies as preparation for a *Staatsexamen.*

10. Charles William Eliot, *A Turning Point in Higher Education: The Inaugural Address of Charles William Eliot as President of Harvard College, October 19, 1869* (1869; reprint, Cambridge: Harvard University Press, 1969), 7. This distance from the German model did not much lessen during the remainder of Eliot's career; see Hawkins, *Between Harvard and America,* passim.

11. See, e.g., Veysey, *Emergence of the American University,* 158–59. The best study of the first decades at the Hopkins is Hawkins, *Pioneer.*

12. Richard Hofstadter and Wilson Smith, eds., *American Higher Education: A Documentary History,* 2 vols. (Chicago: University of Chicago Press, 1961), 1:256, 262–63; Motley to his mother, 1 July 1832, in *The Correspondence of John Lothrop Motley,* ed. G. W. Curtis (New York, 1900), 1:19–23.

13. On the inherited traditions, see especially Samuel Eliot Morison, *The Founding of Harvard College* (Cambridge: Harvard University Press, 1935), chaps. 1–10, notably chap. 4. Two recent studies cast light on the Renaissance origins of this curriculum and thus make clearer why it began to seem obsolete in the nineteenth century, though not much earlier: Anthony Grafton and Lisa Jardine, *From Humanism to the Humanities: Education and the Liberal Arts in Fifteenth- and Sixteenth-Century Europe* (Cambridge: Harvard University Press, 1986), and Bruce A. Kimball, *Orators and Philosophers: A History of the Idea of Liberal Education* (New York: Columbia University, 1986).

14. The Yale Report was published (slightly abridged) as "Original Papers in Relation to a Course of Liberal Education," *American Journal of Science and Arts* 15 (1829): 297–351. Most of it is reprinted in Hofstadter and Smith, *American Higher Education*, 1:275–91, from which the quoted phrase is taken (278).

15. For the sake of necessary compactness, this statement grossly oversimplifies a very confused situation. Clear distinction of these two paradigms is possible only in retrospect, though contemporaries were certainly aware of tugs in these directions.

16. Veysey, *Emergence of the American University*, comes close to this model, identifying three paradigms ("Liberal Culture," "Utility," and "Research") as competing with the old "Mental Discipline" for the soul of the university. Veysey neglects the longer historical context and meaning of the old classical curriculum (which he identifies solely with its antebellum defense as "Mental Discipline"). His category of "Research," we suspect, had less to do with *educational* programs than with other faculty activities, at least until very near the end of the century. This was, at any rate, true at Michigan, as appears below.

To say, as we do, that "the liberal arts ideal" had taken shape by the 1880s is to ignore a host of difficulties as to what it was; see Kimball, *Orators and Philosophers*.

17. Charles Eliot Norton, "Harvard University," in *Four American Universities: Harvard, Yale, Princeton, Columbia* (New York, 1895), 32–35 (page references 33–34 are occupied by a photograph). The relation of this educational ideal to the broader Victorian ideal of "culture" goes without saying.

18. Quotation from Reingold, "Graduate School," 135. For White's reliance on Tappan's vision, see Glenn C. Altschuler, *Andrew D. White: Educator, Historian, Diplomat* (Ithaca: Cornell University Press, 1979), 42. White's student and successor as professor of history at Michigan, Charles Kendall Adams, followed him as president of Cornell and then went on to become one of the two presidents who transformed Wisconsin into a research university. The other was Thomas Chamberlin, who received graduate training at Michigan in the afterglow of the Tappan years. See Merle Curti and Vernon Carstensen, *The University of Wisconsin: A History, 1848–1925*, 2 vols. (Madison: University of Wisconsin Press, 1949), esp. 1:545–46, 561–79.

19. For the early history of the university, see Wilfred B. Shaw, *The University of Michigan: An Encyclopedic Survey* (Ann Arbor: University of Michigan Press, 1942), 1:10–38, and Burke A. Hinsdale, *History of the University of Michigan*, ed. Isaac N. Demmon (Ann Arbor, 1906), chaps. 2–6. See also John D. Pierce, "Origin and Progress of the Michigan School System," *Pioneer Collections: Report of the Pioneer Society of the State of Michigan* 1 (1877): 37–45, and Charles Kendall Adams, *Historical Sketch of the University of Michigan* (Ann Arbor, 1876), 12.

Adams disclaims any Prussian influence on the university's internal organization or curriculum before Tappan's arrival, a conclusion supported by the other available evidence (16).

20. Hinsdale, *History*, 76; *University of Michigan Catalogue of the Officers and Students in the Department of Arts and Sciences, 1843–44* (Ann Arbor, [1843?]).

21. George Bancroft, Henry Barnard, and a New York minister, Rev. William Adams, possibly others, turned down the job before the regents finally named Tappan. It was Ban-

croft who raised Tappan's name, having heard of him initially, it seems, from none other than Victor Cousin. See Shaw, *Encyclopedic Survey,* 1:39–40; Charles M. Perry, *Henry Philip Tappan: Philosopher and University President* (Ann Arbor, 1933), 169–71.

22. Hinsdale, *History,* 42–43; Perry, *Tappan,* 169–70; Adams, *Historical Sketch,* 15–16. The quotation is from the first catalogue issued under Tappan's direction (1852–1853), which proudly declared that Michigan had copied its educational system from the Prussian; see *Catalogue of the Corporation, Officers and Students in the Departments of Medicine, Arts and Sciences in the University of Michigan, 1852–53* (Detroit, 1853), 19.

23. Henry P. Tappan, *A Discourse . . . on the occasion of his Inauguration as Chancellor of the University of Michigan, December 21st, 1852* (Detroit, 1852), 37, 40. For the course of events during Tappan's administration, see Hinsdale, *History,* chap. 7, and Shaw, *Encyclopedic Survey,* 39–53.

24. Quoted in Hinsdale, *History,* 43–44. Tappan wrote that he wished to make the "correspondence" between college and *Gymnasium* "as complete as possible" (*Catalogue, 1852–53,* 20). In his long-term ideal of American gymnasium feeding real American universities, and in his shorter-term goal of making the university at least a respectable *Gymnasium,* Tappan closely resembled George Ticknor at Harvard in the 1820s. See Tyack, *Ticknor,* chap. 3. It appears that the "German ideal" before 1860 was invoked more to support general elevation of academic standards and relegation of rote learning to secondary schools than to advance any scheme resembling a research university. The identification by Americans of the German university with the *discovery* of knowledge seems *mostly* a postbellum development. Cf. Veysey, *Emergence of the American University,* 128–29.

25. *Catalogue, 1852–53,* 20.

26. Tappan, *Discourse on Inauguration,* 42–45. The state legislature had mandated some such instruction in the Reorganization Act of 1851 (Hinsdale, *History,* 44). Tappan was quite likely also influenced by the similar curricular reform set in place by Francis Wayland at Brown two years before Tappan reached Ann Arbor.

27. Adams, *Historical Sketch,* 17.

28. Tappan, *Discourse on Inauguration,* 21–22, 35. These were the traditional four faculties of the German university. Medicine, law, and philosophy (i.e., the arts and sciences faculty, called at Michigan literature, science, and the arts), Tappan pointed out, were already organized. Recognizing that in an American state university theology must "be left to the different denominations," Tappan urged them to set up theological schools in Ann Arbor. (They did not take up his invitation.) See Tappan, *Discourse on Inauguration,* 47–48; *Catalogue 1860–61,* 32.

29. *Catalogue, 1852–53,* 21.

30. Ibid.

31. Yale Report, in Hofstadter and Smith, *American Higher Education,* 1:278.

32. *Catalogue, 1852–53,* 21.

33. Ibid., 21, 26.

34. Ibid. A decade later, in 1863, Harvard's President Thomas Hill inaugurated a superficially similar innovation called "University Lectures." Although regarded by Charles

W. Eliot as ancestral to the graduate school, this program differed from the University Course both in its more occasional nature and in its intended audience: a melange of curious citizens and interested postgraduates, as distinguished from graduate and equivalently prepared students pursuing a regular course. Cf. Charles H. Haskins, "The Graduate School of Arts and Sciences, 1872–1929," in *The Development of Harvard University since the Inauguration of President Eliot, 1869–1929*, ed. Samuel Eliot Morison (Cambridge: Harvard University Press, 1930), 453.

35. *Catalogue, 1852–53,* 26.

36. Tappan probably could not read German at this period of his life (indeed was not at ease even in French). Most of his crucial notions about German education seem to have come from Cousin's report on the Prussian system, itself more a reflection of Humboldt's ambitions than Prussian realities.

37. *Catalogue, 1852–53,* 28. Cf. Henry P. Tappan, "Annual Report of the Chancellor [October 1854]," in *University of Michigan Regents' Proceedings . . . 1837–1864* (Ann Arbor, 1915), 599; Hinsdale, *History,* 88. It is unclear whether Tappan originally expected students in the University Course to be examined or to take a degree, though the master's became explicitly linked to it in 1858–1859 when the University Course took rather scrawny flesh as the "Programme of Studies for the Degrees of A.M. and M.S."

38. Tappan seems especially to have encouraged research in the natural sciences. See Alan Creutz, "From College Teacher to University Scholar: The Evolution and Professionalization of Academics at the University of Michigan, 1841–1900" (Ph.D. diss., University of Michigan, 1981), 2:232, 243–48. This appearance may, however, owe more to accidents of personnel and to the American context (where academic research in the humanities developed later than in the natural sciences) than to any special proclivities of Tappan.

39. Tappan expected University Course students to pursue "free and independent study" as well as to attend lectures. See Tappan, "Annual Report [1854]," 599.

40. The use of the phrase "the University proper" to refer to the University System occurs in *Catalogue of the Officers and Students of the University of Michigan, 1854–55* (Ann Arbor, 1855), 33.

41. Henry P. Tappan, *University Education* (New York, 1851), 11, and "Report of the President [October 1856]," in *Regents' Proceedings . . . 1837–1864,* 664–66. In the latter document, Tappan made a distinction between teaching undergraduates and *lecturing to* graduates.

42. Tappan had a strong sense of the interconnectedness of all knowledge, utterly remote from caricatured notions of German professors, but fairly close to the German *Bildung* ideal associated with Humboldt's name. See, e.g., Tappan, *The University; Its Constitution: A Discourse Delivered June 22, 1858* [to the Christian Library Association of the University of Michigan] (Ann Arbor, 1858), 17–18.

43. The catalogues list specific courses beginning in 1858–1859, when the rubric of "Programme of Studies for the Degrees of A.M. and M.S." replaced the old "University Course" section, with its hopeful listing of twenty broad subjects under which instruction was eventually anticipated. Cf. *Catalogue, 1858–59,* 47. Names of students, including "resident graduates," were printed in the catalogues.

44. Cf. E. O. Haven, *Universities in America: An Inaugural Address Delivered in Ann Arbor, Michigan, October 1st, 1863* (Ann Arbor, 1863), esp. 3–5. Haven (mostly) tells his own story in the posthumous *Autobiography of Erastus O. Haven, D.D., LL.D.,* ed. C. C. Stratton (New York, 1883); see esp. chaps. 5, 7, 8.

45. *Catalogue, 1863–64,* 18; *1867–68,* 12; *1868–69,* 11; and *1870–71,* 11. The catalogues from 1864–1865 through 1866–1867 do not list graduate students; this does not prove that there were none.

46. Frieze's most lasting contribution to the university, not directly relevant here, was the admission of women on a basis of near equality with male students. There is no biography; see the accounts in the general university histories and James B. Angell, *A Memorial Discourse on the Life and Services of Henry Simmons Frieze, LL.D.* (Ann Arbor, 1890), quote on 16.

47. The *Abitur* not only certified successful completion of the gymnasium course but ipso facto qualified a student for university admission.

48. Hinsdale, *History,* 60; Creutz, *College Teacher,* 1:96–99, 156–57; and correspondence from school principals in the James B. Angell Papers, Michigan Historical Collections, Bentley Library, University of Michigan. Cf. University of Michigan *President's Reports.*

49. The only substantial biography is Shirley W. Smith, *James Burrill Angell: An American Influence* (Ann Arbor: University of Michigan Press, 1954); see also James B. Angell, *Reminiscences* (New York, 1912).

50. Angell did see some good things in the German university; and at least in his earlier years, he showed sympathy for research. His increasingly cautious attitude in his later career toward research is evident in, e.g., his *New Era in Higher Education* (Ann Arbor, 1902).

51. Angell, *Frieze,* 14, 21–22.

52. Adams to Herbert Baxter Adams, 9 February 1886, in *Historical Scholarship in the United States, 1876–1901: As Revealed in the Correspondence of Herbert B. Adams,* ed. W. Stull Holt (Baltimore, 1938), 79. On White at Michigan, see Ruth Bordin, *Andrew Dickson White: Teacher of History,* Michigan Historical Collections Bulletin no. 8 (Ann Arbor, 1958).

53. *Catalogue, 1858–59,* 40. Cf. *Catalogue, 1859–60,* 49. It is important to stress how great the change in college education was when its basis shifted from recitations to lectures—and how closely identified this method was with the German universities. See, e.g., the comments on a similar innovation at Harvard thirteen years later, in Chauncey Wright to Grace Norton, 13 January 1870, in Norton Family Papers, Houghton Library, Harvard University.

54. Adams taught both history and Latin from 1863 to 1867. The only biography is Charles Forster Smith, *Charles Kendall Adams: A Life Sketch* (Madison, 1924), about as full an account as the subtitle suggests. Adams's twenty-four years at Michigan get thirteen pages, the bulk of which, fortunately for present purposes, concern the method and character of his teaching, including the famous seminar. Adams's career is likely to remain obscure, for Smith (who based his own account largely on recollections of Adams's col-

leagues) noted that all personal papers were destroyed in a fire at Wisconsin. Information on Adams as president of Cornell (where he pretty clearly tried to transplant a version of the University System that he and Frieze had developed at Michigan) is in Morris Bishop, A *History of Cornell* (Ithaca: Cornell University Press, 1962), esp. chaps. 15–17; and on Adams as president of Wisconsin in Curti and Carstensen, *Wisconsin*, esp. 1:561–79.

55. *President's Report to the Board of Regents, for the Year Ending June 30, 1872* (Ann Arbor, 1872), 32–33. Adams later described the purpose of the course as "to direct the student in the work of original historical investigation" rather than to "impart actual instruction"; but he apparently meant that students were set to work in standard collections of printed sources to find data for their class essays, not that they were expected to come up with new ideas or information (*President's Report, 1874,* 27–28).

Henry Adams (who had himself approached, though never quite embraced, study at Berlin) was apparently teaching his students at Harvard by similar methods in 1870–1871, though the class seems not to have been called a seminar and never to have adopted training in original research as an explicit goal. Adams did introduce a postgraduate seminar, as such, in 1875. See Ernest Samuels, *The Young Henry Adams* (Cambridge: Harvard University Press, 1948), esp. 211–12, 215; Adams's own inimitable account is in *The Education of Henry Adams* (Boston, 1918), 299–304. On the introduction of the seminar more generally, see Veysey, *Emergence of the American University,* 153–58.

56. *President's Report, 1874,* 27–28.

57. E.g., the reference to *Quellen* in Moses Coit Tyler to George H. Putnam, 9 August 1875, quoted in Howard Mumford Jones, *The Life of Moses Coit Tyler* (Ann Arbor, 1933), 176. Tyler was Adams's first imitator.

58. We take "original research" in this sense to mean the effort to discover information, or implications of information, not previously recognized. Put differently, original research is the effort to advance knowledge.

59. A. D. White to J. B. Angell, 30 September 1874, Angell Papers; James B. Angell, *President's Report, 1883,* 9–10.

60. Jones, *Tyler,* 161, 164.

61. See, e.g., R. Steven Turner, "The Growth of Professorial Research in Prussia, 1818 to 1848—Causes and Context," *Historical Studies in the Physical Sciences* 3 (1971): 146.

62. This was, of course, not "teacher training" as in later education faculties. Cf. Wilhelm Erben, "Die Entstehung der Universitäts-Seminare," *Internationale Monatsschrift für Wissenschaft, Kunst, und Technik* 7 (1913): 1248–60. Erben's two-part article is the only substantial history of the German seminar, though hardly a satisfactory one. Less full but more easily available is the account in Friedrich Paulsen, *Geschichte des gelehrten Unterrichts,* ed. Rudolf Lehmann, 3d ed. (Berlin and Leipzig, 1921), which sketches the history of the seminar in 2:258–59, 270–75, passim.

63. The final abolition of the "in course" master's and the awarding of the first Ph.D. occurred in 1874; see *Catalogue, 1874–75,* 18. The twenty-one candidates are mentioned in Frieze to Angell, 9 October 1880, Angell Papers.

64. *Catalogue, 1874–75,* 18; *Catalogue, 1879–80,* 65. But note the absence of any such express requirement before 1879. The most explicit statement of faculty expectations in

the first years is a report of a faculty committee "to consider what steps should be taken in regard to examination of candidates for the degree of Doctor of Philosophy," 29 May 1876, Records of the Registrar, University of Michigan, Michigan Historical Collections. This report contains no mention of original research and no indication that the thesis was required to show such. Frieze and Adams were two of the three members of the committee.

65. See, e.g., George B. Groff to Angell, 8, 24 September, 15 November 1876; and C. K. Adams to ?, 15 June 1878, Angell Papers. The reports on examinations of candidates for advanced degrees, in Records of the Registrar, provide helpful instances of what sort of work was done. It does seem that natural scientists typically regarded the Ph.D. as a research degree from the outset.

66. Angell, *Frieze*, 26–27; Smith, *Adams*, 19.

67. Henry S. Frieze, *The President's Report to the Board of Regents, for the Year Ending June 30, 1880* (Ann Arbor, 1880), 10.

68. Angell, *Frieze*, 29; Frieze, *President's Report, 1880*, 10–11.

69. Frieze to Angell, 9 July 1881, Angell Papers.

70. *Calendar of the University of Michigan for 1881–82* (Ann Arbor, 1882), 74–82; Frieze, *President's Report, 1881*, 2–4; C. K. Adams to Angell, 6 July 1881, Angell Papers.

71. Alexis Angell to J. B. Angell, 10 October 1881; cf. M. L. D'Ooge to Angell, 29 November 1881, and W. H. Pettee to Angell, 28 November 1881; all in Angell Papers. Curiously the opposition was initially led by Martin L. D'Ooge, the only Michigan professor at the time who held a German Ph.D. (Leipzig, 1872). D'Ooge came around to the support of Frieze's proposed University System later in the fall, indeed served on the committee that devised it.

72. Frieze to Angell, 25 October, 26 November 1881, Angell Papers.

73. See packet marked "Relations of the School of Political Science to the Literary Department," Reports and Resolutions, 2nd Semester, 1881–1882, Records of the Registrar.

74. Adams to Angell, 6 March 1881, Angell Papers; Frieze, *President's Report, 1881*, 4–18. (These pages comprise the fullest statement of Frieze's idea of a university and are essential to understanding what happened in 1880–1882.)

75. Frieze to Angell, 26 November 1881; "Relations of the School to the Literary Department." For the language requirement, see Reports and Resolutions, 2nd Semester, 1881–1882, Records of the Registrar. Although the language requirement appears separately from the resolutions enacting the University System in the faculty records, the timing of its adoption—1 May 1882, the same date the University System was approved—leaves little doubt that it was part of the same package. To assuage faculty concerns that students would fritter away their time, each student had a three-member faculty committee to supervise her or his program: the putative ancestor of the dissertation committee.

76. For the development of the University System, see Frieze, *President's Report, 1881*, 4–18; Frieze to Angell, 26 November 1881; and "Relations of the School to the Literary

Department." For its final form, see *Calendar, 1882–83,* 63–65, subsequent *Calendars,* and Angell to Helen Magill, 3 May 1882, Angell Papers.

77. At every stage of the development of advanced degrees at Michigan, training in the natural sciences seems to have been more research-oriented than in other fields.

78. For the faculty's insistence on research, see Angell to Magill, 3 May 1882; *Calendar, 1882–83,* 63–65.

79. Along with the correspondence, faculty debates, and programmatic statements surrounding the origin of the University System, the records of student programs in Records of the Registrar give some sense of the aims of the system.

80. The Hopkins requirements for the Ph.D. in history and political science, for example, retained the German idea of a major field and two minors but insisted that a student's minors both be "akin to his major course." Requirements reprinted in Holt, *Historical Scholarship,* 14–15.

81. Frieze, *President's Report, 1881,* 2–3.

82. See, e.g., Adams to J. T. Moore, 2 February 1882, and Moore to Adams, 7 February 1882, Charles Kendall Adams Papers, Michigan Historical Collections. Bert James Loewenberg notes how this attitude distinguished Adams from the "scientific historians" like Herbert Baxter Adams; see *American History in American Thought: Christopher Columbus to Henry Adams* (New York: Cornell University Press, 1972), 468.

83. *University [of Michigan] Record* 2 (1892): 58–59.

84. In a cryptic note in the University System records, in Records of the Registrar, Adams complained that the School of Political Science "entered the Dark Ages June 24, 1883. The Renaissance has not yet come." What this means remains obscure, but an important part of the story may never come to light.

85. No more than thirteen undergraduates ever took degrees on the University System in any one year; by the end of the 1880s the number had dwindled to three or four annually. Most of the few students came, in fact, from Adams's School of Political Science. When Adams departed for Cornell in 1885, that trickle soon dried up. These data are compiled from the *President's Reports* and the (incomplete) records of examinations under the University System in Records of the Registrar.

86. See Angell, *President's Reports.* For numbers of graduate students, see *University Record* 2 (1892): 78.

87. Angell, *President's Report, 1892,* 13–15.

88. See, e.g., *University Record* 1 (1891), and 2 (1892): passim.

89. See *Announcement of the Graduate School, 1892–93* (Ann Arbor, 1892), 14–38, and subsequent years.

90. *Calendar, 1893–94,* 119–20.

91. Likewise, "the most important work of the university professor, ideally considered, is the advancement of science. His calling is to work on the frontier and his best work will necessarily be done with a few students who are themselves preparing to be investigators" (*University Record* 2 [1892]: 79).

92. See, e.g., *University Record* 2 (1892): 2–3; *Announcement of the Graduate School, 1892–93,* 13.

93. Rejection was not necessarily deliberate. How well Americans, even those who studied in Germany, understood the German system is still very much an open question.

A "Curious Working of Cross Purposes" in the Founding of the University of Chicago

1. "The Need of a Baptist University in Chicago, as Illustrated by a Study of Baptist Collegiate Education in the West," [15 October 1888], Correspondence of John D. Rockefeller (Founder) and His Associates (hereafter cited as JDR). All papers cited in this chapter are published with permission from the Department of Special Collections, University of Chicago Library.

2. Thomas W. Goodspeed to John D. Rockefeller, 7 January 1887, JDR; Goodspeed, "Reminiscences of Thomas Wakefield Goodspeed," 260, Thomas Wakefield Goodspeed Papers (hereafter cited as TWG); Harper to Goodspeed, 5 November 1888, JDR; Goodspeed, "Reminiscences," 297; *University Record* 6 (1901): 105; Harry P. Judson, "Copy of statement to Mr. Murphy," n.d., Presidents' Papers, 1889–1925 (hereafter cited as PP).

3. Laurence R. Veysey, *The Emergence of the American University* (Chicago: University of Chicago Press, 1965), 375–76.

4. Thomas W. Goodspeed, *A History of the University of Chicago* (Chicago: University of Chicago Press, 1916), 19–33; Goodspeed to Rockefeller, 7 January 1887, JDR.

5. *Dictionary of American Biography*, s.v. "Augustus Hopkins Strong"; Strong to Rockefeller, 15, 17 February 1887, JDR.

6. Goodspeed, *History*, 36, 34; Strong to Rockefeller, 4 January 1887, JDR; Strong to Rockefeller, 22 February 1887 and undated "Postscript," JDR.

7. *Autobiography of Augustus Hopkins Strong*, ed. Crerar Douglas (Valley Forge, Pa.: Judson, 1981), 248–49; Augustus Hopkins Strong, *The Church and the University: A Sermon Preached before the Ohio Baptist Education Society at Its Annual Meeting in Cleveland, Ohio, October 23, 1888,—To Which Is Appended a Detailed Argument and Plan for the Establishment of a University in the City of New York, under the Control of Baptists* (Rochester: E. R. Andrews, 1889), 43–44; Strong, "A University—What It Is, and Why We Need One," n.d., JDR; Strong to Rockefeller, 22 February 1887, JDR.

8. Strong, *Detailed Argument and Plan*, 44–48.

9. Ibid., 58–72.

10. Ibid., 60, 67, 59, 87, 61, 43.

11. Strong to Rockefeller, 24 September 1887, JDR; Strong to Rockefeller, 8 October 1887, JDR; Strong to Rockefeller, 28 September 1887, JDR; Rockefeller to Strong, 30 November 1887, JDR.

12. Goodspeed, "Reminiscences," 260.

13. James C. Welling, *The Columbian University: Notes on Its Relations to the City of Washington, Considered as the Seat of a National University* (Washington, D.C.: Gibson Bros., 1889), 6–11.

14. Ibid., 16–23, 26–27; James C. Welling, *Brief Chronicles of the Columbian College from 1821 to 1873, and of the Columbian University from 1873 to 1889* (Washington, D.C.: Rufus H. Darby, 1889), 25.

15. Harper to Goodspeed, 15 November 1888, JDR.

16. Frederick T. Gates, *Chapters in My Life* (New York: Free Press, Macmillan, 1977), 95, 103–4; Gates to Henry L. Morehouse, 9 October 1888, JDR.

17. Harper to Goodspeed, 5 November 1888, JDR; Goodspeed, *History,* 47, 49; Goodspeed to Harper, 24 November 1888, JDR; Goodspeed to Harper, 7 December 1888, JDR; Goodspeed to Harper, 30 November 1888, JDR; Goodspeed to Gates, 29 November 1888, JDR.

18. Goodspeed, *History,* 5–7; Gates, *Chapters,* 102–3.

19. Gates to Rockefeller, 13 January 1889, JDR; Goodspeed, *History,* 62, 58, 67.

20. Gates, "Editor's Note" attached to Harper to Gates, 26 July 1890, JDR; Strong to Harper, 25 December 1888, JDR; Harper to Goodspeed, 4 June 1890, JDR; Goodspeed to Gates, 2 September 1891, JDR; Gates, "Editor's Note" attached to Harper to Gates, 5 August 1890, JDR; Goodspeed, *History,* 131–32; Harper to Goodspeed, 31 July 1890, JDR; Idem to Rockefeller, 9 August 1890, JDR.

21. Gates to Rockefeller, 21 January 1889, JDR; Gates, "Editor's Note" attached to Harper to Gates, 5 August 1890, JDR; Harper to Henry L. Morehouse, 11 November 1890, JDR.

22. Goodspeed, "Reminiscences," 297.

23. In his doctoral studies in comparative philology, Harper worked under the tutelage of William Dwight Whitney, who was widely regarded as the leading American philologist. Whitney studied Sanskrit at Yale under Edward E. Salisbury, and both had studied at the University of Berlin. In 1854 Whitney was appointed professor of Sanskrit at Yale, a position that he held for forty years. During this period he published more than 350 books and articles on Sanskrit, comparative philology, linguistics, modern languages, and lexicography. Whitney was Harper's mentor. In 1882 Harper reported that Whitney had done more to further Oriental research than any American scholar. *The National Cyclopaedia of American Biography,* s.v. "William Dwight Whitney"; *Dictionary of American Biography,* s.v. "William Dwight Whitney"; William R. Harper, "Editorial Notes," *Hebrew Student* 1 (April 1882): 11.

24. Goodspeed, *History,* 98–104.

25. Harper, "Editorial Notes," *Old Testament Student* 3 (1883–1884): 25; Harper, "The Purpose of Hebraica," *Hebraica* 1 (1884): 1–2.

26. Harper, "Editorial Notes," *Hebrew Student* 2 (1882–1883): 216–17; Harper, "Editorial Notes," *Old Testament Student* 4 (1883–1884): 379; Harper, "Old Testament Notes and Notices," *Old Testament Student* 7 (1887–1888): 103.

27. Harper, "Editorial," *Old Testament Student* 6 (1886–1887): 3; Harper, "Editorials," *Old Testament Student* 10 (1890): 197.

28. Harper, "Editorial," *Old and New Testament Student* 10 (1890): 195–96; Harper, "The Purpose of Hebraica," *Hebraica* 1 (1884): 1–2.

29. William R. Harper, "The University of Chicago, The First Annual Report, President Harper, 1892," 145–49, undated typescript.

30. University of Chicago, *Official Bulletin, No. 4. Graduate Schools of the University* (Chicago, April 1892), 2, 5, 8; Harper, "First Annual Report," 148–49.

31. Harper, "First Annual Report," 149; Harper, "Some Features of an Ideal University," *Third Annual Meeting of the American Baptist Education Society, Held with the Southern Baptist Convention, Birmingham, Ala., May 8th and 9th, 1891* (Chicago: James Guilbert, [1891]), 58, 57; Harper, "Address of President W. R. Harper, Ph.D., of the University of Chicago," *Fourth Annual Meeting of the American Baptist Education Society, Held at Philadelphia, Pa., May 28, 1892* (New York: Wynkoop and Hallenbeck, [1892]), 36–37, 16–18.

32. Goodspeed, "Reminiscences," 297.

33. Goodspeed, *History,* 247; Moore to Alonso K. Parker, 25 October 1914, TWG.

34. Hermann E. von Holst, "The Need of Universities in the United States," *Quarterly Calendar* 2 (May 1893): 7; "The Quarterly Statement of the President of the University. For the Quarter Ending January 1, 1893," ibid., 9; George E. Vincent, "The University of Chicago," *Outlook* 71 (1902): 842; William R. Harper, "President's Letter of Transmission," *President's Report, July, 1897–July, 1898,* viii; Albion W. Small, "William Rainey Harper, the Man," *University Record* 10 (1906): 66.

35. Robert Herrick, "The University of Chicago," *Scribner's Magazine* 18 (1895): 397–417.

36. "The Statement by the President of the University for the Quarter Ending July 1, 1893," *Quarterly Calendar* 2 (August 1893): 9; "Quarterly Statement of the President of the University, January 1, 1893," 12; Goodspeed to Rockefeller, 22 November 1888, JDR.

37. Letter from Strong to Rockefeller, titled "A Postscript to My Letter of Three or Four Weeks Ago—Demanding No Answer," n.d., JDR; Strong, *Detailed Argument and Plan,* 62; Goodspeed, *History,* 15–18, 66, 163, 182.

38. Goodspeed, "Reminiscences," 299; Goodspeed, *History,* 188; Storr, *Harper's University,* 244–57; Goodspeed, *History,* 276–83.

39. Ibid., 497–98.

40. Rollin D. Salisbury, "The Ogden Graduate School of Science," *President's Report, 1892–1902,* 53–58; *University Record* 6 (1901): 105.

41. "The University of Chicago," *Dial* 30 (1901): 390.

42. Goodspeed, "Reminiscences," 297.

43. "The Sixteenth Quarterly Statement of the President of the University, October 1, 1896," *University Record* 1 (1896): 383–84; Harper to Moore, 1 March 1899, WRH; Harper, *The Trend in Higher Education in America* (Chicago: University of Chicago Press, 1905), 78 n. 1, 97–98; "The President's Forty-first Quarterly Statement. The Spring Convocation," *University Record* 6 (1902): 386–88; "The President's Statement," *University Record* 7 (1902): 249–50; "Summary of Attendance by Quarters and for the Year 1904–5," *Annual Register, 1904–5,* 504–5.

44. Salisbury, "Ogden Graduate School," 53–54.

45. Goodspeed, *History,* 288–96, 315; Storr, *Harper's University,* 369–70.

46. Copy of Starr J. Murphy typescript, and Starr J. Murphy to the Trustees of the University of Chicago, 9 February 1905, Richard J. Storr Papers.

47. Goodspeed to Harper, 28 March 1905, PP; Goodspeed to Harper, 29 March 1905, WRH; H. P. Judson, "Copy of statement to Mr. Murphy," n.d., PP.

48. William R. Harper, "Higher Education in the West," *North American Review* 179 (1904): 584–90.

49. "The Statement of the President of the University for the Quarter Ending December 31, 1893," *Quarterly Calendar* 2 (February 1894): 10; "Quarterly Statement," *University Record* 10 (October 1905): 69.

50. "The President's Report," *President's Report, July, 1898–July, 1899*, 20–21; *The Autobiography of Robert A. Millikan* (New York: Prentice-Hall, 1950), 37–43.

51. *President's Report, 1892–1902*, 128; Goodspeed, *History*, 189.

52. Editor's note attached to J. G. Schurman to Gates, 5 February 1889, JDR; Goodspeed to Harper, 7 December 1892, JDR; Storr, *Harper's University*, 263; Barry D. Karl, *Charles E. Merriam and the Study of Politics* (Chicago: University of Chicago Press, 1974), 156.

53. John M. Manly, "The Department of the English Language and Literature," in *The President's Report: July, 1905–July, 1906* (Chicago: University of Chicago Press, 1907), 121; handwritten statement by Nef dated December 1906; Thomas Chrowder Chamberlin, "On Behalf of the Faculties of the University," in *The Quarter-Centennial Celebration of the University of Chicago*, ed. David Allan Robertson (Chicago: University of Chicago Press, 1918), 197, 199; Francis Wayland Shepardson, "William Rainey Harper, Biographical," *University Record* 10 (March 1906): 78.

The Crisis of the Old Order

1. See the chapter in this volume "The Era of Multipurpose Colleges in American Higher Education, 1850–1890," figure 1. This chapter was originally published as the concluding section of that study.

2. Commissioner of Education W. T. Harris noted in 1891 that since the Civil War there had been a "General elevation of the standard of admission to college by about one and one-half to two years. . . . [As a result,] the numerous smaller colleges having given up a year or more of their work to the preparatory schools feel very keenly the loss of students. Inasmuch as the larger colleges have developed into universities, there is evident the beginning of a crusade against the small college that will force it to step down into the work of secondary education and renounce the work of higher instruction" (*Report of the Commission of Education* [Washington, D.C., 1891], lvi; hereafter cited as RCE). Harris felt that the colleges could avoid this fate by de-emphasizing ancient languages in admissions and leaving "the fourth stage of education" to universities; however, the status of the colleges remained uncertain in this sympathetic commentary.

3. Hugh Hawkins, *Between Harvard and America: The Educational Leadership of Charles W. Eliot* (New York: Oxford University Press, 1972), 116–19; Hawkins presents Eliot's position on all of the educational sectors discussed below.

4. Charles K. Adams, "The Coordination of Colleges and Universities," and Daniel Coit Gilman, "The Shortening of the College Curriculum," *Proceedings, the College Association of the Middle States and Maryland* 2 (1890): 4–16, 16–20.

5. Andrew D. White, "The Future of American Universities," *North American Review* 151 (August 1890): 443–52, quotes on 446, 452.

6. These views appear in *Transactions, Association of Ohio Colleges:* C. L. Ehrenfeld, "The Aim of the College," 19 (1887): 619; T. J. Sanders, "The Place and Purpose of the College," 30 (1898): 514.

7. Fears of encroachment on the college course were raised by (1) academies that allegedly overprepared students; (2) Harvard's practice of raising admissions requirements, which were estimated to effectively add a year to secondary studies; and (3) Central High School of Philadelphia, which was chartered to offer the B.A. in these years and appeared on the college lists of the RCE.

8. William DeWitt Hyde [Pres. Bowdoin], "The Future of the Country College," *Atlantic Monthly,* December 1888, 721–26.

9. Edward H. Magill [Pres. Swarthmore], "The Relations of the College to the University," *Proceedings, the College Association of Pennsylvania* 2 (1888): 17–20.

10. High schools were enumerated under "school Statistics of cities and towns." In 1886 these high schools accounted for 70,000 of 277,000 students receiving secondary education; see RCE, 1886, 362.

11. Central High School of Philadelphia, one of the country's oldest high schools, initiated a controversial transition to college preparatory studies around 1890; see David F. Labaree, *The Making of an American High School: The Credential Market and the Central High School of Philadelphia, 1838–1939* (New Haven: Yale University Press, 1988).

12. Edward A. Krug, *The Shaping of the American High School, 1880–1920* (Madison: University of Wisconsin Press, 1964), 123–45, passim; Edwin C. Broome, *A Historical and Critical Discussion of College Admission Requirements* (New York: Macmillan, 1903); RCE, 1897, 467.

13. *Transactions, Association of Ohio Colleges* 20 (1888): 20–30; 21 (1889): 70f.; 23 (1891): 85–87; 31 (1899): 53; 32 (1900): 37.

14. Greek requirements had been the bottleneck of college access throughout the nineteenth century and a cause for alternative degree courses after 1850. The refusal of public schools to accept this task (except perhaps in Massachusetts) guaranteed that this portal was too constricted for American higher education in a new era. Just 2 percent of public high school students in Ohio were enrolled in Greek in 1890, and that proportion fell during the decade. Latin, in contrast, flourished for a time; enrollments rose above 50 percent of high school students in Ohio and nationwide by 1900. This date probably represents the apogee of college influence over public schools.

15. Broome, *College Admission Requirements.*

16. E. B. Wakefield, "The Mission of the Endowed Colleges," *Transactions, Association of Ohio Colleges* 32 (1900).

17. Enrollments from RCE, 1900, and table 5, in "The Era of Multipurpose Colleges," in this volume; see also Nancy Jane Cable, "The Search for Mission in Ohio Liberal Arts Colleges: Denison, Kenyon, Marietta, Oberlin, 1870–1914" (Ph.D. diss., University of Virginia, 1984).

18. Edwin Slosson, *The Great American Universities* (New York, 1910); Roger L. Geiger, *To Advance Knowledge: The Growth of American Research Universities, 1900–1940* (New York: Oxford University Press, 1986).

19. Ellis, "Association of Ohio Colleges." Among diploma mills, Taylor University of Upland, Indiana, stands out for conferring 96 Ph.D.'s in 1900 and 1901; Gale College in Galesville, Wisconsin, granted 15 doctorates in 1899. Such remarkable bursts of doctorates were short-lived, indicating a stigma associated with the practice.

20. Steven R. Mark, "Ohio Colleges and Universities during the Gilded Age" (Ph.D. diss., Bowling Green University, 1991), 384–412. Mark lists the following programs— Denison, Findlay, Heidelberg, Mount Union, Ohio State, Ohio University, Ohio Wesleyan, Otterbein, St. Xavier, Cincinnati, Wittenberg, and Wooster; however, Ph.D.'s were conferred by Richmond and Oxford as well in the 1890s.

21. Ibid., 616.

22. RCE, 1890, 758–59; Hugh Hawkins, *Banding Together: The Rise of National Associations in American Higher Education, 1887–1950* (Baltimore: Johns Hopkins University Press, 1992); Geiger, *To Advance Knowledge,* 18–19.

23. Robert Kohler concludes that "collegiate doctorates" largely ceased by 1903; see "The Ph.D. Machine: Building on the Collegiate Base," *Isis* 81 (1990): 638–62 [643]. The RCE list of doctorates for 1905 (p. 542) shows at least 21 dubious degrees out of 361 awarded.

24. The percentages of college graduates among reporting schools for 1890 (when the data are available) may be estimated as follows: theology, 28.7 percent; law, 34.5 percent; medicine, 14 percent. Since it is unlikely that nonreporting schools equaled these levels, the true figure probably lies between these percentages and those given in table 13.

25. W. Bruce Leslie, *Gentlemen and Scholars: Colleges and Community in the Age of the University, 1865–1917* (University Park: Pennsylvania State University Press, 1992), 227. The Harvard Divinity School traced a pattern of development similar to medicine and law (described below): admissions were open to high school graduates when Eliot became president; only in 1882 was a college degree or its equivalent required of *degree* candidates. See Samuel Eliot Morison, ed., *The Development of Harvard University since the Inauguration of President Eliot, 1869–1929* (Cambridge: Harvard University Press, 1930), 463–68.

26. Joseph F. Kett, *The Formation of the American Medical Profession: The Role of Institutions, 1780–1860* (New Haven: Yale University Press, 1968), 14–30; John S. Haller Jr., *American Medicine in Transition, 1840–1910* (Urbana: University of Illinois Press, 1981), 200–201; Alfred Z. Reed, *Training for the Public Profession of the Law* (New York: Scribner's, 1921), 67–73; Robert Stevens, *Law School: Legal Education in America from the 1850s to the 1980s* (Chapel Hill: University of North Carolina Press, 1983), 69.

27. The following account draws on Haller, *American Medicine;* Martin Kaufman, *American Medical Education: The Formative Years, 1765–1910* (Westport, Conn.: Greenwood Press, 1976); William G. Rothstein, *American Physicians in the Nineteenth Century: From Sects to Science* (Baltimore: Johns Hopkins University Press, 1985); and Kenneth M. Ludmerer, *Learning to Heal: The Development of American Medical Education* (New York: Basic Books, 1985). For conditions in 1870, see Charles Warren, "Medical Education in the United States," RCE, 1870, 384–96.

28. Warren wrote: "[T]he medical colleges of this country are mostly joint-stock corporations, who furnish as little medical education as they can sell at the highest rate they

can obtain. Their number is excessive, and the competition between them very keen. They are consequently disinclined to introduce any new features which may scare students of low acquirement away, or which may add seriously to the expenses of the institution" ("Medical Education in the United States," 395).

29. Thomas Bonner estimated that 15,000 American physicians studied at German or German-language universities from 1870 to 1914; see *American Doctors and German Universities: A Chapter in International Intellectual Relations, 1870–1914* (Lincoln: University of Nebraska Press, 1963), 23.

30. For an account of the meager progress of reform, see RCE, 1883, clxv–clxxix; Rothstein, *American Physicians,* 285.

31. Abraham Flexner, *Medical Education in the United States and Canada* (New York: Carnegie Foundation for the Advancement of Teaching, 1910); Ludmerer, *Learning to Heal,* 93–101, 168–90.

32. Rothstein, *American Physicians,* 285–88. An American Medical College Association had existed from 1876 to 1882, but it expired from an inability of its membership to accede to the new reforms.

33. On legal education in this era, see Stevens, *Law School;* and Reed, *Training for the Law.*

34. Cf. the chronological list of law schools in Reed, *Training for the Law,* 423–30.

35. This account oversimplifies a complex picture. Earlier legal education was often designed to be part-time because students were assumed to be spending the remainder of their time in law offices. Some universities (Minnesota, New York University) developed parallel day and night programs. See ibid., 394–402.

36. Joseph F. Kett, *The Pursuit of Knowledge under Difficulties: From Self-improvement to Adult Education in America, 1750–1990* (Stanford: Stanford University Press, 1994), 261–69.

37. A rough count (given definitional ambiguities) shows 37 such schools failing versus 6 enduring to 1920 at Illinois Wesleyan (f. 1874), Drake (f. 1875), Valparaiso (f. 1879), Willamette (f. 1884), Ohio Northern (f. 1885), and Wake Forest (f. 1895).

38. Seth Low, "Higher Education in the United States," *Proceedings, the College Association of the Middle States and Maryland* 4 (1892): 50–60, quote on 58.

39. Leslie, *Gentlemen and Scholars,* 189f.

40. "Liberal Arts II Colleges" (as defined in the pre-1994 Carnegie Foundation for the Advancement of Teaching, *Classification of Institutions of Higher Education*) granted a majority of degrees in vocational subjects and offered both short courses and master's degrees to students of all ages. Often the lineal descendants of multipurpose colleges, they had apparently rediscovered their spirit as well.

Select Bibliography

General and Miscellaneous

Bailyn, Bernard. *Education in the Forming of American Society.* Chapel Hill: University of North Carolina Press, 1960.

Bender, Thomas. *Intellect and Public Life: Essays on the Social History of Academic Intellectuals in the United States.* Baltimore: Johns Hopkins University Press, 1993.

Blackmar, Frank W. *A History of Federal and State Aid to Higher Education in the United States.* Washington, D.C., 1890.

Bledstein, Burton J. *The Culture of Professionalism: The Middle Class and the Development of Higher Education in America.* New York: Norton, 1976.

Brown, David K. *Degrees of Control: A Sociology of Educational Expansion and Occupational Credentialism.* New York: Teachers College Press, 1995.

Cremin, Lawrence A. *American Education: The National Experience, 1783–1876.* New York: Harper and Row, 1980.

Finkelstein, Martin. "From Tutor to Specialized Scholar: Academic Professionalization in Eighteenth and Nineteenth Century America." *History of Higher Education Annual* 3 (1983): 99–122.

Geiger, Roger. "The Ten Generations of American Higher Education." In *American Higher Education in the Twenty-first Century*, edited by Philip G. Altbach, Robert O. Berdahl, and Patricia J. Gumport, 38–69. Baltimore: Johns Hopkins University Press, 1999.

Goodchild, Lester F., and Harold S. Wechsler, eds. *ASHE Reader: The History of Higher Education.* 2d ed. New York: Simon and Schuster, 1997.

Hall, Peter Dobkin. *The Organization of American Culture, 1700–1900: Private Institutions, Elites, and the Origins of American Nationality.* New York: New York University Press, 1982.

Herbst, Jurgen. *From Crisis to Crisis: American College Government, 1636–1819.* Cambridge: Harvard University Press, 1982.

———. *And Sadly Teach: Teacher Education and Professionalization in American Culture.* Madison: University of Wisconsin Press, 1989.

Hofstadter, Richard, and Wilson Smith, eds. *American Higher Education: A Documentary History.* 2 vols. Chicago: University of Chicago Press, 1961.

Horowitz, Helen Lefkowitz. *Alma Mater: Design and Experience in the Women's Colleges from Their Nineteenth-Century Beginnings to the 1930s.* New York: Knopf, 1984.

Kett, Joseph F. *The Pursuit of Knowledge under Difficulties: From Self-improvement to Adult Education in America, 1750–1990.* Stanford: Stanford University Press, 1994.

Marsden, George M. *The Soul of the American University: From Protestant Establishment to Established Nonbelief.* New York: Oxford University Press, 1994.

Palmieri, Patricia A. "From Republican Motherhood to Race Suicide: Arguments on the Higher Education of Women in the United States, 1820–1920." In *Educating Men and Women Together: Coeducation in a Changing World*, edited by Carol Lasser. Urbana: University of Illinois Press, 1987.

Power, Edward J. *Catholic Higher Education in America*. New York: Appleton-Century-Crofts, 1972.

Rothblatt, Sheldon. *The Modern University and Its Discontents: The Fate of Newman's Legacy in Britain and America*. Cambridge: Cambridge University Press, 1997.

Rudolph, Frederick. *The American College and University: A History*. Introductory essay by John Thelin. 1962. Reprint, Athens: University of Georgia Press, 1990.

Sack, Saul. *History of Higher Education in Pennsylvania*. 2 vols. Harrisburg: Pennsylvania Historical and Museum Commission, 1963.

Solberg, Richard W. *Lutheran Higher Education in North America*. Minneapolis: Augsburg, 1985.

Solomon, Barbara Miller. *In the Company of Educated Women: A History of Women and Higher Education in America*. New Haven: Yale University Press, 1985.

Storr, Richard. *The Beginnings of Graduate Education in America*. Chicago: University of Chicago Press, 1953.

Whitehead, John S. *The Separation of College and State: Columbia, Dartmouth, Harvard, and Yale, 1776–1876*. New Haven: Yale University Press, 1973.

Woody, Thomas. *A History of Women's Education in the United States*. 1929. Reprint, New York: Octagon Books, 1966.

To 1850

Burke, Colin. *American Collegiate Populations: A Test of the Traditional View*. New York: New York University Press, 1982.

Findlay, James. "Western Colleges, 1830–1870: Educational Institutions in Transition." *History of Higher Education Annual* 2 (1982): 35–64.

Hofstadter, Richard. *Academic Freedom in the Age of the College*. With a new introduction by Roger L. Geiger. 1955. Reprint, New Brunswick, N.J.: Transaction Publishers, 1996.

Lord, Gary Thomas. "Alden Partridge's Proposal for a National System of Education: A Model for the Morrill Land-Grant Act." *History of Higher Education Annual* 18 (1998): 11–24.

McLachlan, James. "The American College in the Nineteenth Century: Toward a Reappraisal." *Teachers College Record* 80, 2 (1978): 286–306.

Mattingly, Paul H. "The Political Culture of America's Antebellum Colleges." *History of Higher Education Annual* 17 (1997): 73–96.

Miller, Howard. *The Revolutionary College: American Presbyterian Higher Education, 1707–1837*. New York: New York University Press, 1976.

Naylor, Natalie. "Raising a Learned Ministry: The American Education Society, 1815–1860." *History of Education Quarterly* 24 (1984): 479–97.

————. "The Theological Seminary in the Configuration of American Higher Education: The Ante-bellum Years." *History of Education Quarterly* 17 (1977): 17–30.

Potts, David B. "American Colleges in the Nineteenth Century: From Localism to Denominationalism." *History of Education Quarterly* 11 (1971): 363–80.

————. *Baptist Colleges in the Development of American Society, 1812–1861.* 1967. Reprint, New York: Garland, 1988.

————. "'College Enthusiasm!' as Public Response, 1800–1860." *Harvard Educational Review* 47 (1977): 28–42.

Reynolds, Terry S. "The Education of Engineers in America before the Morrill Act of 1862." *Higher Education Quarterly* 32 (1992): 459–82.

Whitehead, John S., and Jurgen Herbst. "How to Think about the Dartmouth College Case." *Higher Education Quarterly* 26 (1986): 333–50.

After 1850

Anderson, James D. *The Education of Blacks in the South, 1860–1935.* Chapel Hill: University of North Carolina Press, 1988.

Clifford, Geraldine Joncich. "No Shade in the Golden State: School and University in Nineteenth-Century California." *History of Higher Education Annual* 12 (1992): 35–68.

Johnson, Eldon. "Misconceptions about the Early Land-Grant Colleges." *Journal of Higher Education* 52 (1981): 333–51.

Kohler, Robert E. "The Ph.D. Machine: Building on a Collegiate Base." *Isis* 81 (1990): 638–62.

Leslie, W. Bruce. *Gentlemen and Scholars: Colleges and Community in the Age of the University, 1865–1917.* University Park: Pennsylvania State University Press, 1992.

Marcus, Alan I. *Agricultural Sciences and the Quest for Legitimacy: Farmers, Agricultural Colleges, and Experiment Stations, 1870–1890.* Ames: Iowa State University Press, 1985.

Metzger, Walter. *Academic Freedom in the Age of the University.* 1955. Reprint, New York: Columbia University Press, 1961.

Peterson, George E. *The New England College in the Age of the University.* Amherst, Mass.: Amherst College Press, 1965.

Ross, Earle D. *Democracy's College: The Land-Grant Movement in the Formative Stages.* Ames: Iowa State College Press, 1942.

————. "The 'Father' of the Land-Grant Colleges." *Agricultural History* 12 (1938): 151–86.

Stetar, Joseph M. "In Search of Direction: Southern Higher Education after the Civil War." *History of Education Quarterly* 25 (1985): 341–67.

Veysey, Laurence. *The Emergence of the American University.* Chicago: University of Chicago Press, 1965.

Williams, Roger L. *The Origins of Federal Support for Higher Education: George W. Atherton and the Land-Grant College Movement.* University Park: Pennsylvania State University Press, 1991.

Ideas

Barber, William J., ed. *Economists and Higher Learning in the Nineteenth Century.* 1988. Reprint, New Brunswick, N.J.: Transaction Publisher, 1993.

Graff, Gerald. *Professing Literature: An Institutional History.* Chicago: University of Chicago Press, 1987.

Guralnick, Stanley A. *Science and the Ante-bellum College.* Philadelphia: American Philosophical Society, 1975.

May, Henry. *The Enlightenment in America.* New York: Oxford University Press, 1976.

Oleson, Alexandra, and Sanford Brown, eds. *The Pursuit of Knowledge in the Early Republic: American Scientific and Learned Societies from Colonial Times to the Civil War.* Baltimore: Johns Hopkins University Press, 1976.

Oleson, Alexandra, and John Voss, eds. *The Organization of Knowledge in Modern America, 1860–1920.* Baltimore: Johns Hopkins University Press, 1979.

Reuben, Julie A. *The Making of the Modern University: Intellectual Transformation and the Marginalization of Morality.* Chicago: University of Chicago Press, 1996.

Sloan, Douglas. *The Scottish Enlightenment and the American College Ideal.* New York: Teachers College Press, 1971.

Stevenson, Louise L. *Scholarly Means to Evangelical Ends: The New Haven Scholars and the Transformation of Higher Learning in America, 1830–1890.* Baltimore: Johns Hopkins University Press, 1986.

Winterer, Caroline. "The Humanist Revolution in America, 1820–1860: Classical Antiquity in the Colleges." *History of Higher Education Annual* 18 (1998): 111–30.

Institutional and Biographical Studies

Beadie, Nancy. "From Academy to University in New York State: The Genesee Institutions and the Importance of Capital to the Success of an Idea, 1848–1871." *History of Higher Education Annual* 14 (1994): 13–38.

Curran, Robert Emmett, S.J. *The Bicentennial History of Georgetown University.* Vol. 1, *From Academy to University, 1789–1889.* Washington, D.C.: Georgetown University Press, 1993.

Hawkins, Hugh. *Between Harvard and America: The Educational Leadership of Charles W. Eliot.* New York: Oxford University Press, 1972.

———. *Pioneer: A History of the Johns Hopkins University, 1874–1889.* Ithaca: Cornell University Press, 1960.

Hislop, Codman. *Eliphalet Nott.* Middletown, Conn.: Wesleyan University Press, 1971.

Hoevelar, J. David, Jr. *James McCosh and the Scottish Intellectual Tradition: From Glasgow to Princeton.* Princeton: Princeton University Press, 1981.

Horowitz, Helen L. *The Power and Passion of M. Carey Thomas.* New York: Knopf, 1994.

Kerns, Kathryn M. "Farmers' Daughters: The Education of Women at Alfred Academy and University before the Civil War." *History of Higher Education Annual* 6 (1986): 11–28.

Kinnison, William A. *Building Sullivant's Pyramid: An Administrative History of the Ohio State University, 1870–1907.* Columbus: Ohio State University Press, 1970.

McCaughey, Robert A. "The Transformation of American Academic Life: Harvard University, 1821–1892." *Perspectives in American History* 8 (1974): 239–332.

Morison, Samuel Eliot, ed. *The Development of Harvard University since the Inauguration of President Eliot, 1869–1929.* Cambridge: Harvard University Press, 1930.

Noll, Mark. *Princeton and the Republic, 1768–1822: The Search for Christian Enlightenment in the Era of Samuel Stanhope Smith.* Princeton: Princeton University Press, 1989.

Palmieri, Patricia Ann. *In Adamless Eden: The Community of Women Faculty at Wellesley.* New Haven: Yale University Press, 1995.

Pierson, George W. *Yale College: An Educational History, 1871–1921.* New Haven: Yale University Press, 1952.

Potts, David B. *Wesleyan University, 1831–1910: Collegiate Enterprise in New England.* New Haven: Yale University Press, 1992.

Rudolph, Frederick. *Mark Hopkins and the Log: Williams College, 1836–1872.* New Haven: Yale University Press, 1956.

Solberg, Winton U. *The University of Illinois, 1867–1894: An Intellectual and Cultural History.* Urbana: University of Illinois Press, 1968.

Stameshkin, David M. *The Town's College: Middlebury College, 1800–1915.* Middlebury, Vt.: Middlebury College Press, 1985.

Storr, Richard. *Harper's University.* Chicago: University of Chicago Press, 1966.

Story, Ronald. *The Forging of an Aristocracy: Harvard and the Boston Upper Class, 1800–1870.* Middletown, Conn.: Wesleyan University Press, 1980.

Tobias, Marilyn. *Old Dartmouth on Trial: The Transformation of an Academic Community in Nineteenth-Century America.* New York: New York University Press, 1982.

Tyack, David. *George Ticknor and the Boston Brahmins.* Cambridge: Harvard University Press, 1967.

Students

Allmendinger, David. "Mount Holyoke Students Encounter the Need for Life Planning, 1837–1850." *History of Education Quarterly* 19 (1979): 27–46.

———. *Paupers and Scholars: The Transformation of Student Life in Nineteenth-Century New England.* New York: St. Martin's, 1975.

Farnham, Christie Anne. *The Education of the Southern Belle: Higher Education and Socialization in the Antebellum South.* New York: New York University Press, 1994.

Gordon, Lynn D. *Gender and Higher Education in the Progressive Era.* New Haven: Yale University Press, 1990.

Harding, Thomas S. *College Literary Societies: Their Contribution to Higher Education in the United States, 1815–1876.* New York: Pageant Press, 1971.

Kett, Joseph F. *Rites of Passage: Adolescence in America, 1790 to the Present.* New York: Basic Books, 1977.

Horowitz, Helen Lefkowitz. *Campus Life: Undergraduate Culture from the End of the Eighteenth Century to the Present.* New York: Knopf, 1987.

McLachlan, James. "The *Choice of Hercules:* American Student Societies in the Early 19th Century." In *The University in Society*, edited by Lawrence Stone, 2:449–94. 2 vols. Princeton: Princeton University Press, 1974.

Morison, Samuel Eliot. "The Great Rebellion at Harvard College and the Resignation of President Kirkland." *Publications of the Colonial Society of Massachusetts* 27 (1928): 54–112.

Novak, Steven J. *The Rights of Youth: American Colleges and Student Revolt, 1798–1815.* Cambridge: Harvard University Press, 1977.

Rury, John, and Glenn Harper. "The Trouble with Coeducation: Mann and Woman at Antioch, 1853–1860." *History of Education Quarterly* 26 (1986): 481–502.

Smith, Ronald. *Sports and Freedom.* New York: Oxford University Press, 1988.

Stevenson, Louise L. "Preparing for Public Life: The Collegiate Students at New York University, 1832–1881." In *The University and the City: From Medieval Origins to the Present*, edited by Thomas Bender, 150–77. New York: Oxford University Press, 1988.

Wagoner, Jennings L. "Honor and Dishonor at Mr. Jefferson's University: The Antebellum Years." *Higher Education Quarterly* 26 (1986): 155–80.

Wechsler, Harold S. *The Qualified Student: A History of Selective College Admission in America.* New York: Wiley-Interscience, 1977.

Zschoche, Sue. "Dr. Clark Revisited: Science, True Womanhood, and Female Collegiate Education." *History of Education Quarterly* 29 (1989): 545–70.

Index